FAILURE OF CHARISMA

FAILURE OF CHARISMA

THE CULTURAL REVOLUTION IN WUHAN

Wang Shaoguang

HONG KONG
OXFORD UNIVERSITY PRESS
OXFORD   NEW YORK
1995

Oxford University Press

Oxford New York
Athens Auckland Bangkok Bombay
Calcutta Cape Town Dar es Salaam Delhi
Florence Hong Kong Istanbul Karachi
Kuala Lumpur Madras Madrid Melbourne
Mexico City Nairobi Paris Singapore
Taipei Tokyo Toronto

and associated companies in
Berlin Ibadan

Oxford is a trade mark of Oxford University Press

First published 1995

Published in the United States
by Oxford University Press, New York

© Oxford University Press 1995

British Library Cataloguing in Publication Data
available

Library of Congress Cataloging-in-Publication Data
Wang, Shaoguang, 1954–
Failure of charisma : the Cultural Revolution in Wuhan / Shaoguang
Wang.
p. cm.
Includes bibliographical references and index.
ISBN 0–19–585950–2
1. Wu-han shih (China)—Politics and government. 2. China—
History—Cultural Revolution, 1966–1969. I. Title.
DS796.W8W36 1995
951.05′6—dc20   94–34568
CIP

Printed in Hong Kong
Published by Oxford University Press (China) Ltd
18/F Warwick House, Taikoo Place, 979 King's Road, Quarry Bay, Hong Kong

For my father and my mother

Preface

I HAVE been working on this book for several years. During that time, I received generous assistance from many individuals and institutions. Without their help, the book would not have been completed.

I thank my teachers at Cornell University. To the chairperson of my dissertation committee, Vivienne Shue, I extend my thanks for her confidence in the project and the sustained and tactful guidance she provided during the preparation of the manuscript. I am also indebted to the other two members of my committee, Martin Bernal and Benjamin Ginsberg, for their encouragement and suggestions. During my years at Cornell, many other scholars and friends also gave assistance. I am particularly grateful to Sherman Cochran, Michael Goldfield, Theodors Lowi, and Victor Nee for their unfailing support and invaluable comments and criticisms.

I also thank my colleagues at Yale University for providing me with an extremely hospitable environment in which to complete the book. I would like to thank particularly David Apter, Yitzak Brudny, Deborah Davis, William Foltz, David Mayhew, Bruce Russet, James Scott, Ian Shapiro, and Helen Siu.

I owe special thanks to the eighty-five interviewees who gave generously of their time in answering my questions and who trusted me with confidential information. Without their co-operation, this project would never have been possible. Because anonymity was promised to all of the interviewees, it is not possible to thank them individually.

While doing my field work in Wuhan, I spent many hours at the Wuhan Municipal Library, the Hubei Provincial Library, and the Wuhan Municipal Archives. My research was made easier by the help of the staff of the three institutions. They deserve thanks for their patience and willingness to accommodate themselves to my seemingly endless requests.

My research over the years has been supported by grants from a number of institutions. The Liu Memorial Award of Cornell University enabled me to visit Wuhan to gather data for this study. The Mellon Dissertation Fellowship and the MacArthur Foundation Fellowship in International Peace and Security provided tuition and stipend respectively for 1987–8 and for 1989. The Graduate School at Cornell University assisted with summer fellowships during the same period. The A. Whitney

Griswold Faculty Award of Yale University provided a grant in the late stages of writing and revision.

Stanley Rosen read the entire manuscript and offered constructive criticisms, for which I thank him.

I greatly appreciate the care with which Oxford University Press and its editors have supported this project.

Finally, my thanks, admiration, and love go to my wife, Liqun Zhao, who not only bore the brunt of typing the manuscript but also shared all the joys and sorrows with me; and to my daughter, Xiaoxi Wang, who grew up without me until her eighth birthday.

SHAOGUANG WANG
New Haven, Connecticut

Contents

Tables and Figures

Tables

Figure

Abbreviations

General

CCP   Chinese Communist Party
CPPCC   Chinese People's Political Consultative Conference
CRSG   Cultural Revolution Small Group
CYL   Communist Youth League
HPPC   Hubei Provincial Party Committee
HPRC   Hubei Provincial Revolutionary Committee
MAC   Military Affairs Commission
PLA   People's Liberation Army
PRC   People's Republic of China
WMPC   Wuhan Municipal Party Committee
WMR   Wuhan Military Region
WMRC   Wuhan Municipal Revolutionary Committee

Publications

CJRB   *Changjiang Ribao* [Yangtze Daily]
DFDS   *Zhonggong Wuhan Difang Dangshi* [The Local Party History of Wuhan]
HBRB   *Hubei Ribao* [Hubei Daily]
HYJL   *Hubei Shengwei Shujichu Changwei Huiyi Jilu* [The Minutes of Meetings of the Hubei Provincial Party Committee Secretariat]
JFJB   *Jiefang Junbao* [PLA Daily]
JHCL   *Zhongyang Fuzhe Tongzhi Jianghua Chaolu* [Selected Speeches of Central Leaders]
LSN   *Zhongguo Gongchandang Liushinian* [The Sixty Years of the Chinese Communist Party]
RGP   *Red Guard Publications*
RGPS   *Red Guard Publications, Supplement I*
RMRB   *Renmin Ribao* [People's Daily]
WGSL   *Wenge Yundong Licheng Shulue* [A Concise History of the Cultural Revolution]
WJHB   *Wuchan Jieji Wenhua Dageming Wenjian Huibian* [Selected Documents of the Great Proletarian Cultural Revolution]
WWDJ   *Wuhan Dichu Wuchan Jieji Wenhua Dageming Dashiji* [Chronicle of the Great Proletarian Cultural Revolution in Wuhan]
XHYK   *Xinhua Yuekan* [New China Monthly]

1

Introduction

DURING the ten years between 1966 and 1976, the Chinese people were repeatedly told the Cultural Revolution, under the invincible leadership of Mao Zedong, was advancing from one victory to another. However, this study of the Cultural Revolution in a Chinese city, Wuhan, presents a very different picture. The movement in retrospect seems to have lurched from crisis to crisis. For the first two years or so of the events described here (1966–8), China was in a state of anarchy. Mao, the man who had launched the movement, was unable to control it. Even after this chaotic period, the political process under Mao continued to deviate from the path he desired. Finally, in 1976, when Mao's corpse was barely cold, the radical leaders at the centre of the movement were rounded up at one fell swoop. In the years following the Cultural Revolution, Mao's political line has been grossly betrayed. It is no exaggeration to say that, by any measure, the Cultural Revolution was a colossal failure.

Most of the contemporary studies of the movement focused on élite politics, dealing with such issues as political intrigues, power struggles, policy conflicts, and the ups and downs of certain key figures. Mao's motivation in launching the upheaval drew the most attention.[1] Mao was, explicitly or implicitly, portrayed as a charismatic leader, and the Chinese people as his blind followers, or what Eric Hoffer calls 'true believers'.[2] No one denies that Mao was a close approximation of a charismatic leader. That characterization, however, gives rise to a puzzle. According to Max Weber, where charisma is genuine, the leader can generate in his followers such emotions as devotion, awe, reverence, and, above all, blind faith. In other words, in the eyes of true believers of a charismatic leader, the leader's saying a given thing is right makes it right. The leader sets the goals and selects the means. He can change them at will, even into their opposites, without necessarily losing support.[3] The question then is why the political process under Mao—a universally recognized 'charismatic' leader—always moved in directions other than what he intended, creating unexpected crises, stagnation, frustration, and social changes?[4]

The late 1970s and early 1980s saw the emergence of a different kind of study on the Cultural Revolution, works that approached the unprecedented upheaval 'from below'.[5] Based on painstaking interviews with Chinese refugees in Hong Kong, who were most likely of middle school students of 'middle' or 'bad' class backgrounds from the city of Guangzhou, those works strove to penetrate below the surface of political events in order to come to grips with the social factors that explained them. They all concluded that the participants in the events, far from being the undifferentiated crowd that many earlier writers had assumed, were actually split by political interests and social aspirations into numerous disparate groups, each with its own objectives. Those studies imply an answer to the question raised above: the participants in the Cultural Revolution were rational actors, whose pursuit of their own interests and independent agendas thwarted Mao's strategic plan.

While enriching our understanding of the social forces lying behind the apparent confusion and flux of the period from 1966 to 1976, however, these studies generally have four drawbacks. First, most of them centre on Guangzhou, a city close to Hong Kong, which may represent the exception rather than the rule. Second, most of them are based on the experiences of middle school students, who played at best a marginal role in politics. Third, most of those studies focus on the three years between 1966 and 1968, thus leaving the period from 1969 to 1976 virtually untouched. These geographical, sectoral, and time limitations condition the generalizations about the politics of the period drawn by those studies.[6]

If the first three drawbacks are due to the limits of information, the fourth drawback stems from a failure to appreciate the significance of models of collective action in the analysis of such a mass movement. They all agree that the participants were 'rational', but make no effort to explore the implications of that rationality. On the one hand, while asserting that the participants were rational actors, they fail to reconcile this observation with the fact that most Chinese were true believers in the true sense of the word: they submitted themselves to Mao willingly and without question. How could a charismatic leader's true believers be rational? This is a question that students of the Cultural Revolution should confront rather than avoid. On the other hand, they fail to engage Mancur Olson's challenge in a compelling manner. According to Olson, the individual members of a group of people who share some interests may have no interest in contributing to the common cause.[7] Those studies, however, generally start with identifying the backgrounds of the 'rebels' and the 'conservatives', and then jump to conclusions about the collective behaviours of the two factions. They seem to assume that a group of people with a common interest would act collectively in order to further it. Russell Hardin calls such an unarticulated inference 'the fallacy of composition'.[8] We do not intend to suggest that rational people would never act together or contribute together to further their common interests. They may; and in many cases, including during the Cultural Revolution, they did. But this must be explained, not merely assumed.[9]

This study also approaches the subject 'from below', but attempts to provide a new explanation for the behaviour of the masses during the Cultural Revolution—the ultimate cause of Mao's failure. It intends to remedy the four drawbacks identified above by widening the scope of investigation and sharpening our analytical tools. The scope of investigation is expanded in three ways. First, Wuhan, a large city in central China, has been chosen to be the focus of study. The revolutionary movement in this city has never before been systematically examined.[10] Second, it is concerned not only with micro-politics in middle schools, and for that matter in colleges, factories, hospitals, government agencies, cultural and scientific research institutions, and so on, but also with macro-politics in the city at large, and with the relations between micro-politics and macro-politics. Third, it discusses not only factionalism in the period of 1966–8, but also factionalism in the period from 1969 to 1976, which is a hiatus in the literature.[11] Whether this wider study is more representative than previous studies of politics in urban China during the Cultural Revolution is a decision I leave to others.

What is more important is to explore the implications of the assumption about the rationality of the participants. The main task here is to cast aside the fallacy of composition. Obviously, if we were not able to give a rationalistic account of the rise and fall of collective action, we might have to question the assumption that the participants acted rationally. For this reason, we will devote this introduction and the following ten chapters to explaining why millions of Chinese took part in collective actions during the period under review. The puzzle of Mao's failure of charisma can be readily solved, once we establish that the participants in the upheaval, despite their apparent irrationality, were indeed rational actors, whose involvement in collective action was guided by rational calculation. As for the question of how true believers could act rationally, the last chapter will attempt a theoretical explanation.

Framework of Analysis

Even today, some observers believe that the masses who participated in

the Cultural Revolution were not rational. In their view, for a time the
society was aberrant and everyone within it went mad. According to one
author,

> [During the movement], the people of China took their leader and
> elevated him beyond emperor to a god, exhibiting before Mao near-
> slavish subservience, blind obedience, unquestioning faith, offering to
> him the willing, even eager, sacrifice of their own freedom and inde-
> pendence of judgment.... So much did they love Mao, so greatly did
> they admire the Party, so timorous were they before authority, that faced
> with conflicts between their own individual perceptions and what the
> Party and Mao said was happening, many of them doubted not the Party
> or Mao but themselves. The capacity for independent human judgment,
> in these circumstances, was grotesquely, pathetically, tragically,
> maimed.[12]

Most of the people involved also insist now that they were 'blinded',
'hoodwinked', 'cheated', or 'used' by Mao.

It is undeniable that Mao was a charismatic leader and that the
Chinese people accepted his unchallenged supremacy. But it doesn't
follow that the masses had no worthwhile aspirations of their own. If we
assume, as Weber does, that Mao's followers were characterized by a
lack of self-interest and a blind obedience to him,[13] many of the
phenomena discussed in the following chapters would appear enigmatic.
The only behaviour that might be construed as irrational is random
behaviour. As we will show in this book, the actors did not act randomly
and their acts were not without a pattern; rather, they acted purposefully
in order to better their lives. It is therefore more realistic to assume that
those involved were rational than otherwise.

Once we assume this rationality, we have to face squarely Olson's
challenge. The enthusiastic involvement of millions of Chinese in the
events of the period should no longer be viewed as an inevitable process,
but as something inexplicable that needs to be analysed. We have to
explore the relationship between the behavioural characteristics of individual Chinese and the characteristics of group politics during the ten
years, or, to use Thomas Schelling's phrase, the relationship between
'micromotives and macrobehavior'.[14] Specifically, there are four key
questions that need to be addressed: In what sense were the participants
rational? Under what circumstances would rational individuals participate in collective action? Under what circumstances would rational
participants withdraw from collective action? How do we explain collective irrationality?

In What Sense Were the Participants Rational?

To act rationally means, in general terms, to choose better alternatives over worse ones. This simple definition implies the existence of four elements: (1) There are a set of *actors* (including both human actors and institutional actors) who are presumably purposive. (2) They confront a given set of *alternatives*. (3) They are endowed with *preferences* that are ordinal. (4) They select their preferred alternatives in an *environment* beyond their control. The environment defines the opportunities available through which those actors may pursue their interests, and imposes constraints on their choices.

Depending on the strength of the rationality postulates employed, we may distinguish between two definitions of rationality: the narrow definition of rationality and the broad definition of rationality.[15]

The narrow definition is based on four assumptions: (1) The actors seek to maximize expected utility. (2) They have only egoistic preferences. (3) They are self-conscious about their choices. (4) Only objective constraints are the direct determinants of action. The advantage of the narrow definition of rationality is that if we restrict the explanatory variables to specific kinds of preferences and constraints, the theory would have predictive power. The problem with the narrow definition is that it is too restrictive to apply to many real political issues, including the Cultural Revolution.[16]

In order to obtain a definition of rationality that appropriately explains politics in the real world, we have to take into account factors that issue from reality as people see it. In other words, the assumptions on which the narrow definition rests need to be modified to make them more realistic.

(1) The actors are more often than not what Herbert Simon calls 'satisficers' rather than utility-maximizers. Utility maximization serves better as a heuristic than a true representation of the human decision-making process. According to Herbert Simon, people seldom attempt to achieve a calculable optimization. Instead, they usually stop the search for better alternatives as soon as they have found one that gives an acceptable result. Since searching is costly, it is not surprising that rational actors tend to settle for what is adequate. In conditions of great uncertainty, such as the Cultural Revolution, actors are inclined either to minimize the risk of suffering the maximal harm (the minimax strategy) or to maximize the minimum payoff they could get (the maxmin strategy). Since in such circumstances, people's knowledge of the consequences of their decisions is likely to be extremely limited and partial, and many

unpredictable developments and repercussions are possible, it would be wiser to hedge one's bets, or, at the very least, to prevent major setbacks, than to strike out daringly in what might turn out to be foolhardy ventures.[17]

(2) The actors may have any preference ordering over various states of affairs. Two expansions are necessary here. First, people may be motivated primarily by more than just economic factors.[18] For many people caught up in the Cultural Revolution, power, status, prestige, psychic income, ego expansion, emotional gratification, and the like were much more meaningful than pecuniary gains. Second, their preferences could be ordered not only by a selfish principle, but also by an altruistic one, an ideal-regarding one, or any other.[19]

(3) The actors are not always conscious of their goals. People often act from unrecognized motives.[20] In fact, most of our seemingly rational actions are not fully consciously justifiable.[21] Therefore, we have no reason to expect that all political actions and political decisions emanate from deliberate calculations. In other words, it is possible for people sometimes to think and talk irrationally at the conscious level while acting rationally at the subconscious level. As Chapter 12 will illustrate, this is exactly what happened to most of the participants in the Cultural Revolution.

(4) All kinds of constraints and opportunities could be explanatory variables. The range of one's choices may be severely circumscribed or greatly facilitated by the external situation as well as by the capacities of the decision maker. Lack of information, for example, may significantly impede the ability of actors to make strategic calculations. 'Not only may information be imperfect, political actors may also be constrained by limited resources, poor communication, inadequate knowledge, inability to perceive the objective conditions and make complex calculations, and a host of other real-life mitigating factors.'[22] More important, political, economic, and social institutions could constrain or motivate individual choice.[23] In the name of the new institutionalism, it is now widely appreciated that institutions help to explain how the same set of preferences produces different outcomes when aggregated in different social settings. Normative systems, too, are likely to profoundly interfere with the individual's pursuit of private interests. The greatest influence which norms can have is to demand forms of conduct for their own sake and to limit the options open to the actors to pursue certain goals or to choose the means to pursue those goals. During the Cultural Revolution, people paid close attention to normative constraints (for example, 'fight self, champion the public') not only because they

wished to avoid negative external sanctions, but also because they had internalized such norms. Given those constraints, the actors could seldom choose the behavioural alternative that is objectively the best, from the viewpoint of an omniscient observer. 'To choose' is thus reduced to 'doing the best one can'.

(5) Human beings do not always act as cold calculators. Even writers like Anthony Downs, Mancur Olson, and Gordon Tullock, who claim that one gets much further with a narrow definition of rationality, allow some political behaviour being non-rational or irrational.[24] The uncritical acceptance of norms, for instance, is non-rational, for a rejection or modification of the norms would permit one to broaden the range of one's options.[25] Non-rationality could also occur through impulsive action. For instance, in addition to instrumental benefits, people sometimes seek expressive benefits.[26] Participating in political events may not be seen as a 'cost' by some participants; it may, on the contrary, bring them what Tibor Scitovsky calls 'pleasure',[27] especially when what is required is only 'acting together' rather than 'contributing together'.[28] Due to their possession of more disposable time than adults and their relative lack of political sophistication, youth in general and students in particular are most likely to be motivated by expressive benefits to engage in political activism.[29] This was part of the reason why, during the Cultural Revolution, students threw themselves into the movement without hesitation. The existence of non-rational and irrational elements in largely rational people's behaviours, however, does not make them irrational, just as their rationality could not prevent them from behaving, in some contexts, in non-rational and irrational ways. Once this is understood, we should be surprised neither by the observation that Mao's zealous followers could also act as rational calculators in the factionalist fighting of their units and their localities, nor by the fact that those rational actors did many things that non-participants might consider as absurd and ludicrous.

Whereas the narrow definition of rationality treats both maximization and rational calculation as postulates, the broad definition adopted in this study takes them as variables. In other words, motivations, preferences, mental conditions, and constraints (opportunities) are not 'given' but are context specific. The broader conception of rationality enables us 'to organize theoretical formulation and research inquiry around the question of the contextual conditions', and to determine 'under which [conditions] maximization and rational calculation manifest themselves in "pure" form, under which they assume different forms, and under which they break down'.[30]

While the broad definition of rationality allows a wider analytical range, it retains the basic assumption of the narrow definition of rationality, that is, human behaviour in general is goal-oriented and guided by roughly rational calculations. In other words, political actors are, to borrow a phrase from Jon Elster, 'strategically rational',[31] even though they may sometimes behave non-rationally and irrationally. Local irrationality can be imputed only against a broad background of rationality.[32]

Under What Circumstances Would Rational Individuals Participate in Collective Action?

Rational individuals would not participate in a social movement unless two barriers—concern about the risks involved and calculation of the costs—are cleared. By 'risks' I refer to the extrinsic costs of action in opposition, which are normally imposed by government reaction and suppression. By 'costs' I refer to the intrinsic costs of acting as a group, such as the costs of organization and communication. The worry about risks is a barrier to *action* and the concern about costs a barrier to *collective action*.

Political actors normally have to behave according to the prevailing rules of the game, which define the set of players, the set of permissible moves, and the sequence of those moves.[33] Known to each player, the rules are enforced by the state. By using or threatening to use coercive measures, the state can make the non-compliant action substantially less attractive than the compliant action, thus bringing about compliance. The rules of the game therefore, in effect, reduce the set of abstractly possible courses of action to the vastly smaller subset of feasible actions. Such institutional constraints are given and are not within the control of the agents. Acting in defiance of the rules of the game is a very risky business. When potential insurgents face a great likelihood of quick suppression, they tend to lie low so as to avoid the prohibitive costs. If the risks are clearly low, however, many may act.

In other words, political actors would have no incentive to act, collectively or otherwise, when action is widely regarded as futile, or as an ineffective symbolic protest at best, especially if the protest is likely to beget spiteful retribution from a repressive government.[34] One of the most important determinants of the emergence of a social movement is thus the political opportunity structure. Whether there is such an opportunity depends on the will and capacity of the regime to repress.[35] It has been established that social movements tend to gather momentum when a regime's repressive capacity has been weakened by international conflict or disunity within the governing élite, or when the rulers, for one reason or another, ease somewhat their grip on the political arena and tolerate, or even encourage, some previously forbidden behaviours.[36] In the case of the Cultural Revolution, it was Mao who opened the floodgates of social control. If he had not done so, the latent tensions in Chinese society might have persisted for decades without finding expression in open conflict. Furthermore, as Chapters 3 to 11 will show, the Cultural Revolution consisted of many radicalization–deradicalization cycles, the rhythm of which coincided with Mao's decisions to either deactivate or reactivate the apparatus of social control.

New opportunities can help to overcome the *action problem*, allowing any underlying anti-establishment impulses to enter politics. However, a movement does not automatically emerge out of favourable circumstances. It first requires the *collective action problem* to be overcome.

The collective action problem arises when a group of rational individuals share a common interest in the provision of a public good. A public good is a good which, roughly speaking, benefits all the members of the group regardless of whether they contribute in any way to its provision. The goals of revolutions and social movements (for instance, a new social order, consumer protection, or civil rights) are examples of public goods. The central relationship between the analysis of public good and the problem of collective action is that the *de facto* unfeasibility of exclusion from consumption of a public good allows people to be free riders, that is, to benefit from whatever amount of the good others provide without contributing themselves. If many people attempt to be free riders, little or none of the public good will be provided.

Since rational individuals will prefer to be free riders rather than to participate in collective efforts to obtain a public good, the key analytical problem becomes one of explaining why collective action occurs at all. The participation of millions of Chinese in collective action during the Cultural Revolution obviously contradicts the familiar logic of collective action. How could this happen? In the collective action literature, there have been numerous attempts to argue that under certain conditions rational individuals might find co-operation to be in their interest. Collective action occurs more widely than Olson's initial conjecture allows, because his prediction—that people tend to deflect or pass the costs of public goods provision on to others—can be modified by five important considerations: the nature of the goal, the type of actor, selective incentives, group size, and political entrepreneurs.

The Nature of the Goal

We might draw up a typology of the goals of collective action on two dimensions: public good versus public bad, and the binary provision versus continuous levels of provision.[37] The goal in opposing a public bad (for example, an effort to remove a chemical plant from a community, or a protest against China's class label system, which discriminated against certain social groups) is more likely to bring about collective action (if the action problem has been solved) than the goal of supporting a gain (for example, a call for voluntary recycling, or maintaining social order on a voluntary basis), for three reasons. First, the way costs are exacted in controlling a public bad differs from the way they are more commonly exacted in providing a good. Since the bad already exists, both action and inaction involve costs. Even if one chooses not to participate in a collective effort to end the harm, one suffers anyway. In such situations, people are likely to be less reluctant to co-operate. Second, losses are often felt more acutely than gains of a comparable magnitude. In other words, the gain from the elimination of a bad is often perceived to be much larger than the possible cost of participation, even when the benefits are discounted by the probability of failure. Third, if the public bad from which a group suffers comes from an external source, group members are likely to develop a sense of inequity. The moral reaction to this inequity could heighten the prospects for collective action.[38]

Similarly, binary goods or bads—goods or bads that one can either have or not (for example, good or bad political labels)—are more likely to elicit participation in collective action, because individual contributions to the provision of such goods or to the elimination of such bads have a pivotal impact on whether or not they are produced. Some goods or bads in this category (for example, the right to participate in political activities or the lack of such a right) have a crucial further property. Their provision or elimination is deemed so essential to the attainment of many, or even all, other aims that risk-averse individuals would decide to help pay for the collective action.

Combining the two arguments, we may conclude that people are much more likely to participate in collective action when they are interested in eliminating a binary bad than when they are pursuing other types of goals. As we will see, what motivated the rebels at the beginning of the Cultural Revolution was a desire for self-liberation from oppression— in other words, a desire to eliminate binary bads.

The Type of Actor

Some rational choice theorists assume that groups are symmetrical. That is, all members of a group have identical interests in the provision of a certain collective good, all place the same value on a given unit of the collective good supplied, and all place the same value on a unit of cost. The assumption that the actors are homogeneous and interchangeable, while useful for expositional purposes, is clearly unrealistic. People in fact are very different and thereby have varying thresholds for participation in collective action.[39] Because of the uncertain prospects of collective action, most potential activists are likely to be risk-averse. Even though they have a conditional willingness to participate, they will adopt a wait-and-see attitude to determine if collective action is likely to be viable before tossing their own hats into the ring. Some people, however, have extremely low or no thresholds for participation. They may view participation in collective action as a benefit rather than a cost to themselves. They may join collective actions to achieve self-realization, consciousness raising, self-respect, and the like. In any case, some individuals may 'value the collective good more and derive more psychological satisfaction from pursuing the collective good than others'.[40] The concept of thresholds helps us to account for the way in which political activism typically unfolds. Since people have different thresholds, the order of participation in collective action is bound to be staggered rather than simultaneous. Those having the lowest thresholds tend to play the role of initiators. What follows is a gradual accretion in membership or participation in a cause. Once the number of participants makes up a critical mass, there is likely to be a bandwagon effect.[41]

Other things being comparable, one should expect better prospects for successful collective action in the asymmetrical than in the symmetrical group. In China the rebels constituted an asymmetrical group, with students and backward workers having relatively low thresholds for participation. As we will see, the critical mass of a rebel movement was built up only gradually.

Selective Incentives

An individual with a high threshold would need some selective incentives or added inducement for participation over and above the benefits he or she would receive from the public good itself. Because this person would receive the public good regardless of the degree of contribution, selective incentives are necessary to elicit his or her share of the cost.

Unlike the public good that is available to everyone if it is provided at
all, selective incentives are contingent upon the behaviour of individual
agents. Selective incentives can be either positive or negative. Negative
incentives or punishments are linked to non-cooperative behaviour,
whereas positive incentives or rewards are linked to co-operative
choices. Selective incentives can also be material and social in nature.
Because material rewards are the most easily identified and the most
accurately measured, they are usually the first incentive we look for
when trying to find the motivation behind political participation. The
social incentives essentially derive from the desire for approbation and
the dislike of disapprobation, and work through mechanisms such as criticism and shaming by friends and associates. A number of studies have
shown how important social incentives are in mobilizing people to
contribute to collective action. Often individuals contribute to, or participate in, collective action because they are asked and tacitly pressured
to do so by friends, colleagues, work-mates, or co-members of the association's local branch or cell. They cannot say 'no' to them, since this
would result in a loss of approval, respect, or co-operation. Social incentives thus reduce the temptation to free ride and increase the attraction
of co-operation in collective action.[42]

As will be shown in the following chapters, selective incentives were
indeed indispensable to activism during the Cultural Revolution, especially among the adult participants.

Group Size

Small groups are more likely to have the ability to overcome the collective action problem than large ones. Unlike large groups in which individual contributions are trivial, having no discernible effect, small
groups have five advantages. First, a small group is more likely to be
privileged, that is, it contains at least one member who derives so much
benefit from the increased supply of the collective good that he or she
is willing to bear its entire cost unilaterally. Second, even if the group
is not privileged, individual members are likely to have a pivotal impact
on whether or not the public good is produced. Third, mobilized around
pressing, highly local problems, its members have a strong incentive to
bring about immediate, tangible benefits. Fourth, since the group
members already know each other, it is easier for them to monitor each
other's behaviour. A free rider can be readily detected and pressured to
do his or her part by the rest. Social pressure for co-operation is thus
generally much stronger in small groups than in large ones. Finally, the

organizational costs are lower in small groups than in large groups. Decision making in small groups is easier to co-ordinate and more likely to be interdependent. Group members can more readily convey their intentions to each other and arrive at a mutually beneficial co-operative agreement. Social sanctions can also be administered at relatively low costs.[43]

A large group might succeed in providing a public good if it has a federated structure that mobilizes support through numerous smaller, local branches.[44] Almost all the mass organizations in China during the Cultural Revoluation had such a federated structure.

Political Entrepreneurs

Selective incentives and a federated structure cannot, by themselves, be solutions to the collective action problem for a mass movement like the Cultural Revolution, unless some people are willing to provide and operate the two mechanisms. These political entrepreneurs are willing to pay the costs of soliciting and co-ordinating contributions in exchange for individual benefits such as power, prestige, or a share of the profits derived from the collective action.[45] The task of political entrepreneurs is to get others to do something they would not otherwise have done. The goal can be accomplished in two ways.

Movement initiators can use their organizational skills to goad their organizations into existence. By providing negative or positive selective incentives, for instance, they can induce or force others to participate in collective action. They can also expand the movement membership by breaking up a large goal into many steps with critical thresholds. A city-wide or nation-wide movement can be built upon the success of its solving local or smaller-scale collective action problems and bringing tangible benefits quickly.[46]

Political entrepreneurs may also be able to get others to contribute without the use of threats or offers. This would typically be done by what Michael Taylor calls 'persuasion', namely, providing information and arguments about the nature of the alternatives, about the costs and benefits attached to them, about the possible consequences of adopting different courses of action, about others' attitudes and beliefs, and so on.[47] Movement leaders can ignite large collective actions if they can convince people that their contribution will make a big enough difference, that everyone else is joining in, or that others' efforts are contingent on theirs.[48] By changing people's expectations and beliefs and injecting resources into the group, political entrepreneurs may make group efforts more productive, and thereby help to solve or remove collective action problems in a latent group.

Why are some people willing to take the high risks of initiating a movement and to underwrite the substantial start-up costs of organizations? One answer is that political entrepreneurs are self-interested: they found and expand organizations and seek to provide collective benefits to relevant groups, because their own careers will be enhanced by the size and prosperity of their organizations. For them, organizing the provision of collective benefits is an investment, which, like other types of investment, though running some risk, is expected to be profitable. Their pay-off for doing this is the reward to their own political careers. Alternatively, political entrepreneurs may be altruists who enjoy serving others.

The personal career incentive seems more suited to explaining ongoing rather than newly emerging organizations,[49] whereas altruism and a low participation threshold seem more plausible in accounting for the rise of movement initiators. Obviously, altruism and varying participation thresholds are not consistent with the assumption of narrow self-interest. In the real world, however, extra-rational considerations do spur people to take part in collective actions. Examples include religion, internal sanctions (such as guilt, loss of self-respect, and so on, which may result from failure to conform to a norm, to live up to one's own ideals, or to perform one's duties), moral motivations, altruistic motivations, expressive motivations, the desire for self-development through participation, and ignorance and misunderstanding. For co-operation to occur, such extra-rational elements are probably required, 'minimally as a sort of yeast to stir into the wild brew of exclusively rationalistic action'.[50]

Elster advises us: '[W]hen trying to explain individual participation in collective action, one should begin with the logically most simple type of motivation: rational, selfish, outcome-oriented behavior. If this proves insufficient to explain the phenomena we observe, we must introduce more complex types, single or in combination.'[51] The following chapters will follow this line of thinking.

In addition to political entrepreneurs, as we will see in the case of the Cultural Revolution in Wuhan, there may also be political forerunners. Political forerunners take part in collective action before others do because they have lower thresholds for participation. Their contribution to a non-excludable good may very well cause others to contribute. We know that most collective actions involve some form of conditional co-operation, for individuals tend not to co-operate unless others do as well.

The emergence of political forerunners provides a 'starter' around which conditional co-operation by others can develop. Some political forerunners may later turn themselves into political entrepreneurs, but most would not or could not do so. After all, political entrepreneurs need to be ambitious, articulate, and venturesome. They also need communication and organizational skills to provide potential activists with the signals and incentives that are necessary to collective action and organization building. Not all forerunners possess such qualities of leadership. However, by definition, all political entrepreneurs are political forerunners.

Under What Circumstances Would Rational Participants Withdraw from Collective Actions?

People engaging in a social movement normally have some goals in mind. In addition to group goals, those at the forefront of the movement are likely to seek attractive political positions. Such pay-offs to successful leaders, however, are typically beyond the reach of the rank and file, and the leadership usually has no way to provide alternative compensation to them.

If the movement succeeds, the leaders may win full-time institutional positions (such as becoming members of revolutionary committees) as a reward for their efforts; but in the eyes of the rank and file the usefulness of political activism is diminished. There is little more to be individually gained by many committed members from continued collective action. Since the ordinary members feel they have gained much of what they expected, the residual demands take on less importance. In other words, the marginal utility of further collective action is reduced. Many would believe that most of their work has been done and that others can provide the finishing touches. The result is that many activists will withdraw from the movement.[52] Chapter 8 will show that this is what occurred in Wuhan after the rebel forces won a triumph over their conservative opponents in the summer of 1967.

Conversely, if the movement fails to bring about what it is supposed to bring about, or more precisely, if the group goals appear to be unattainable or attainable only at a prohibitively high price, the rank and filers are likely to become disappointed. When the fruits of their labour do not live up to their expectations, they may stop trying and leave the movement. There is likely to be a bandwagon effect during the evacuation process just as during the mobilization process. The movement leaders also may be frustrated, but their greater investment in the cause makes it harder for them to quit.

During the Cultural Revolution, the rebel forces in Wuhan experienced many high and low points. When they were at a low ebb, many former activists became disheartened and disengaged themselves from further collective action. Some of these deserters rejoined the ranks when the rebels seemed to be regaining their feet. But, as Chapters 7 to 11 will show, most of them kept themselves out of the factional fighting, though their sympathies lay with their former comrades. In either case, individual calculations of the value of collective action were the determinant. By 1976, the rebel forces in Wuhan had shrunk to skeleton size, consisting mainly of movement leaders of various levels. Thus, both satisfaction and disappointment may lead to the demise of a movement. Activists tended to leave the rebel ranks when their factions were either on the ebb or on the flow. The federated structure of the movement was most able to motivate action when the factional fighting appeared to be a close match.

How Do We Explain Collective Irrationality?

The general consensus is that the Chinese were crazy during the years of the Cultural Revolution. How do we explain the apparent madness in people's behaviour? One explanation of irrational collective phenomena is that the aggregate of behaviours reflects the properties of individual behaviours. In other words, 'they are crazy' because 'he is crazy, she is crazy, everybody is crazy'.[53] But the aggregate of behaviours need not be an average of individual actions. Rather, it may acquire some of the emergent properties of a collective. It is not uncommon when the preferences or actions of rational individuals are brought together for the outcome to be collectively irrational. Anthony Downs argues that the aggregation of consistent individual preferences may give rise to an inconsistent collective preference ordering.[54] Olson shows that the pursuit of individual self-interest may be collectively self-defeating. Furthermore, we often find that otherwise reasonable people succumb to behaviour in groups that they would never initiate on their own. Interactions among people thus often lead to aggregate results that the individual neither intends nor needs to be aware of, results that sometimes have no recognizable counterpart at the level of the individual. In other words, rational people do not always produce rational results. To put this statement another way, we may conclude that collective irrationality can be accounted for in terms of a model of rational actors. You don't have to be crazy to act crazy. Perfectly rational actors may do something foolish when they act together. The rational actor model thus can be of great use in explaining why everything can go wrong, for the social outcomes may not be the result of the actors' intentions but of their actions.[55] The model offers a better explanation of the mass behaviour that occurred during the Cultural Revolution than one based on madness in individuals generating madness in crowds.

The Merits and Limits of the Rational Choice Model

This study attempts to use a rational choice approach to explain the mass behaviour exhibited in Wuhan from 1966 to 1976. However, this claim needs two qualifications.

First, analytical simplicity takes second place to realism in this study.[56] Many analysts have demonstrated that a model based upon a few stringent rationalistic assumptions can generate sophisticated hypotheses and offer a single parsimonious explanation of behaviour. Indeed, the most widely recognized advantage of the rational choice approach is its great elegance and simplicity of theoretical formulation. The highly touted virtues of elegance and simplicity, however, are attractive only in the abstract. When narrowly based rational choice models are applied to the rough-and-tumble world of real political conflict, they are often found to be lacking in concreteness and accuracy. Thus, one has to decide whether it is desirable to achieve parsimony at the price of implausibility.[57] Since history can never be deduced from theory, realism should take precedence over parsimony in studying political phenomena.

In this book, the rational choice approach is used in purely heuristic terms, as merely an efficient way of accounting for mass behaviour during the Cultural Revolution. This chapter started with a narrow conception of rationality, and gradually introduced certain realistic elements in order to increase its explanatory power. The analytical rigour of purely rationalistic approaches such as Olson's may be jeopardized by relaxing the most stringent rationalistic assumptions, but such modifications enable us to arrive at a more meaningful explanation of the Cultural Revolution.

Second, this study rejects the notion that the rational choice approach can explain every phenomenon. In fact, no abstract model can be comprehensive. Thus, when we use the rational choice approach, or any approach for that matter, we should appreciate its limitations and employ it in combination with other models.

There are many holes in the purely rationalistic models. For instance, preference and constraint are two of the most important independent

variables in any rational choice model. But the question of how preferences arise and where constraints come from cannot be answered within
the framework of rational choice.[58] Rational choice theories generally
treat people's preferences as exogenous to what has to be explained. As
Debra Friedman and Michael Hechter observe, 'Rational choice theory
is mute about what [people's] preferences might be and where they come
from'.[59] Similarly, rational choice theories also view constraints (opportunities) as external events.

If we are to account for the formation and alternation of preferences
and the presentation (or absence) of constraints (or opportunities), we
may need to resort to structuralist analyses. Structuralist theories insist
that structural conditions matter, for only such conditions can help us to
understand how particular arrays of choices come to be available to
particular categories of people at particular points. Structural conditions
have their own dynamics, independent of calculation of interest by those
who must live under them. Rational choice thinking cannot help in this
regard.[60] Obviously, structuralist and individualist political theories are
not necessarily incompatible. Structuralist theories may be better used
to explain certain results, and rational choice theories to account for
others.[61] In other words, a rational model is best used in conjunction with
other approaches. It is only when the rational choice approach is used
in conjunction with concepts and theories drawn from other approaches
that it acquires genuine explanatory power.

Instead of modifying the world to fit a single general model, this study
uses the rational choice approach as well as analytical tools borrowed
from other approaches. The deliberate eclecticism is a matter of necessity if we are to achieve an informed understanding of such a complicated historical phenomenon as the Cultural Revolution.[62] Chapter 2 will
show that a structuralist account of Chinese society in the years leading
up to the Cultural Revolution is complementary to a rationalistic analysis of the behaviour of the masses during the decade of upheaval.

The Cultural Revolution constitutes an excellent opportunity for
studying collective action. To understand collective action requires not
only abstract theorizing but also, as Hardin put it, 'such intensive observation as would try the patience of an anthropologist, and such attention
to nuance as would frustrate a philologist'.[63] Rational choice theorists
often adopt the economists' charming notion of stylized facts. While
such oversimplified accounts of real events are essential for building up
abstract models, they are more often than not highly distorted. Of course,
'facts' never speak for themselves, but there is no substitute for the careful and detailed study of how actors behave in actual situations. The

method of observed regularity, or what Clifford Geertz calls 'thick description',[64] is at least as important for advancing our understanding of political activity in rational terms as the method of postulated regularity.

For this reason, this book will not parade before the reader a series of abstract models and their applications. Rather, it will show through actual events the merits and limits of an overall conception of politics that takes as a starting point that political choices are made by thoughtful decision makers who want to realize certain ends. The ideas and theories put forward in this chapter will be consciously applied to the discussion of the behaviour of the masses during the Cultural Revolution, but the jargon of the discipline will be reduced to a minimum.

Methodology

In order to put the various issues under discussion in perspective, this book adopts a framework of chronological narration. By integrating socio-political analysis with historical narrative, the book attempts to present an actual history of the Cultural Revolution in Wuhan and the career patterns of various political groups formed in the city in the course of the movement. Obviously, a single unit can never adequately reflect the whole. This work therefore makes no claim to perfect representativeness. Yet the Cultural Revolution as played out in Wuhan does show some representative characteristics: in the rhythms of the movement, in the ubiquitous factionalism, in the dividing lines between the conservatives and the rebels, in the factionalist violence, in the political apathy of the later stages of the movement, and perhaps in many other ways.

Moreover, in some respects, the Cultural Revolution in Wuhan was probably more typical of factionalism during this period than that which erupted in Beijing, Shanghai, or Guangzhou, which have been the focus of previous studies. Strong central intervention distorted the pattern of factionalism in Beijing and Shanghai, in that whereas the workers' movement was underdeveloped in Beijing and the students' movement was overwhelmed by workers in Shanghai, the two movements as a rule were deeply intertwined in the provinces. Events in Guangzhou deviated from the general pattern in that after the Wuhan Incident of July 1967 (see Chapter 8), the so-called conservative forces were dispersed almost everywhere except in Guangzhou, where they survived because their patron, Huang Yongsheng—the local military chief—happened to have the firm backing of Lin Biao, then the designated successor to Mao. For these reasons, even though Wuhan does not provide a true microcosm, a case-study of the city nevertheless can be instructive about some general properties of factionalism during the Cultural Revolution which may not be observable in the cases of Beijing, Shanghai, and Guangzhou.

Although the book is arranged chronologically, each chapter, in addition to covering events in a given period, pays special attention to some theoretical issues of collective action, be it the importance of opportunity structure, the weight of selective incentives, the forms of conflicting groups, the role of political entrepreneurs, the formation of coalitions, the timing and reasons for activists to exit, the relationship between anarchy and violence, or some other matter. In order to understand the roots of the era's factionalism, Chapter 2 examines various cleavages that existed in Chinese society. Chapter 3 considers the importance of political opportunity. Existing patterns of behaviour largely persisted in the first few months of the Cultural Revolution, because the rules of the game had not yet changed much. Moreover, the high risks attached to insubordinate action deterred potential rebels from coming to the fore. Chapter 4 assesses the importance of political opportunity from the opposite angle. As Mao gradually incapacitated the existing structure of authority in the autumn of 1966, the risks associated with participation decisively lessened. Some political forerunners soon became political entrepreneurs. Due to their efforts, rebel forces were slowly mobilized. Chapter 5 analyses the composition of mass organizations during the movement and shows that factional divergence was a direct outgrowth of the preceding structure of social conflict. It also provides an explanation of why so many Chinese had incentives to participate in collective action.

Chapters 6 and 7 examine the patterns of conflict between the conservative and rebel factions, and Chapters 8 and 9 the patterns of conflict among the rebel organizations. Those chapters discuss such issues as the implications of anarchy, the formation of coalitions, violence between rival organizations, and the ebb and flow of factionalist activism.

Chapters 10 and 11 deal with factionalism in the later years, namely from 1969 to 1976, which has so far been almost a lacuna in the literature relating to the Cultural Revolution. The two chapters examine those aspects in which factionalism in the late stage was similar to, and different from, that in the earlier stage. The key issue here is why while the majority of former factionalist warriors became phlegmatic, a small number of people were still actively engaged in factional fighting.

In Chapters 2 to 11, I attempt to make three observations explicit:

(1) Mao was a charismatic leader, but the political process under him always deviated from the 'right path', the path he chose, during the decade of the Cultural Revolution.

(2) Participants in the movement were true believers of Mao, but their participation in, or withdrawal from, collective action was principally based upon their rational calculations of personal pay-offs. The reckoning of costs and benefits thus conditioned, to a large extent, the degree and manner of those true believers' involvement in the movement.

(3) It was the participants' pursuit of their own interests in both individual and collective actions that forced Mao to divert his energy into emergency salvage at each turn of the movement. When the genie of the Cultural Revolution grew much too large, Mao found himself impotent either to command it or to stuff it back into its bottle. The Cultural Revolution, a drama directed by a universally recognized charismatic leader, thus ended in a colossal failure.

Whereas the first eleven chapters demonstrate that the participants in the decade's events did act rationally, Chapter 12 sets out to explain how it was possible for sincere true believers of Mao to be rational actors at one and the same time. The explanation can only be found through theoretical deliberation, not empirical questioning. The final chapter of the book refutes Weber's assumption that charisma is intimately keyed to irrationality. It argues that the fatal deficiency of Weber's theory of charisma lies in its neglect of the cognitive dimension in the charismatic relationship. Once we recognize the existence of the cognitive aspect, there is nothing mysterious about the actors in the drama, despite their deep affective attachment to Mao, acting primarily out of self-interest and according to their own agendas. The failure of Mao's charisma thus ceases to be an enigmatic fact. The insights derived from this case-study may help us to better understand the phenomenon of charisma in general. Weber's conception of charisma as an extraordinary personal attribute has left the concept in a mire of confusion and impeded empirical research. More recent studies try to resolve such problems by redefining charisma as a relation rather than as a thing. Nevertheless, the charismatic relationship is still seen as one in which 'any directive on the part of the leader would be carried out by the follower without considering the merits of the directive'.[65] Not recognizing the followers' rationality, this new definition does not allow charisma to fail, which contradicts the case of the Cultural Revolution. Again, the neglect of the cognitive dimension in the charismatic relationship is where the definition goes wrong. This study shows that a truly charismatic leader could fail disastrously, because true believers could act rationally.

The materials presented in this study derive from six main sources: my own recollection of those years; my diary and personal correspondence with friends during the decade; national and local official publications; national and local newspapers run by mass organizations between 1966 and 1969; local archives; and, finally and most important, interview data. In 1986 I conducted field research in Wuhan. Due to the liberal atmosphere of that year, I was able to have access to the files of the Wuhan Municipal Education Bureau at the Wuhan Archives, and to local tabloids published during the Cultural Revolution at Wuhan Municipal Library and Hubei Provincial Library. I also interviewed eighty-five persons from all walks of life. What I learned from the interviews provided insights into the participants' motivations, the degree of their involvement in collective action, their behavioural patterns, and the timing of entrances and exits. A number of my interviewees were well-known factional leaders in the city during the movement. Their testimony was especially valuable in enabling me to establish linkages between politics at the grassroots and politics at the city level and beyond. Those sources complement one another. The interviewees' recollections and impressions were checked against contemporary documents and newspaper accounts.

2
The Roots of Discontent, 1949 to 1966

THE CULTURAL REVOLUTION did not emerge in China without a period of gestation. What happened in the decade between 1966 and 1976 derived from social, political, and economic tensions in China's recent past. More specifically, the factional fighting witnessed during the decade of turmoil was rooted in the social cleavages that had existed in Chinese society since the founding of the People's Republic of China (PRC) in 1949. Without a knowledge of these social conflicts, the factional wars of the Cultural Revolution would appear to be meaningless and incomprehensible. Why did millions of Chinese throw themselves into the movement? What forces turned a seemingly homogeneous nation into a battlefield? Why did some people become rebels attacking the establishment while others fought against the rebels to preserve the *status quo*? Why did some people prefer to stay away from politics during the fanatical decade? Those questions cannot be answered by merely investigating what political actors did, and did not, do during the period under review. Answers have to be sought by examining the power structure of society before the mid-1960s and the position of various social groups in such a structure. A structuralist analysis of Chinese society before the Cultural Revolution is thus the necessary prelude to an understanding of the sources of the preferred actions of the participants in the ensuing upheaval.

Before we begin to examine these pre-existing social cleavages, a few words about the city of Wuhan are in order.

Wuhan is the largest metropolis in central China. The Yangtze River (Chang Jiang), China's greatest arterial waterway, is joined at Wuhan by another river, the Hanshui. The Beijing–Guangzhou Railroad, the principal thoroughfare of communication between north and south China, passes through the city. The name of the city is a composite of those of its component parts, the former cities of Hankou, Hanyang, and Wuchang. Hankou lies on the north bank of the Yangtze at the mouth of the Hanshui; immediately opposite, in the angle of junction, is Hanyang; and a little below the confluence, on the south side of the

Yangtze, is Wuchang. The three cities were merged into a single city in 1950.

Given its unrivalled geographical centrality, Wuhan has been a major commercial and industrial centre since the middle of the nineteenth century. After 1949 the city continued to grow. Several dozen industrial complexes and hundreds of medium-sized and small factories were built in Wuhan during the first seventeen years of the PRC. By 1966, the population of Wuhan had grown to 2.5 million.[1]

Wuhan has also been a political centre. The 1911 Revolution broke out in Wuchang, and the Nationalists at one time located their national government in Hankou. From 1949 to 1954, Wuhan was the site of the Central South Military-Administrative Commission. In 1954 Wuhan became the capital of Hubei Province. Both provincial and municipal authorities have since been located in the city, with the former in Wuchang and the latter in Hankou. Prior to the mid-1980s, Wuhan was also the headquarters of the Wuhan Military Region (WMR), which supervised military units stationed in Hubei and Henan provinces. For the first seventeen years of the PRC, the local leadership was relatively stable. A group of local chiefs who had taken office in the mid-1950s still ruled Wuhan in 1966.

In 1966 the tripartite city was divided into six administrative districts, each with its distinct characteristics. Jianghan District, the centre of Hankou, was basically a commercial district with some small-scale, traditional industries. Hankou's industries were concentrated either on the outskirts of Jiang'an District or in Qiaokou District. Hanyang was a newly developed industrial area with few commercial establishments and almost no cultural or higher learning institutions. Colleges, universities, scientific research institutions, and literature and arts organizations were mostly located in Wuchang, as were large-scale modern industries. Qingshan District, also on the south bank of the Yangtze and about 20 kilometres east of Wuchang District, essentially comprised two giant companies: Wuhan and Iron Steel, and First Metallurgical Corporation.

Residential patterns of the city varied from one district to another, with Qiaokou, Hanyang, and Qingshan occupied mainly by industrial workers; Jianghan by non-proletarian labourers, the non-intellectual 'middle class', and former capitalists; Wuchang by intellectuals, and civilian and military functionaries serving the provincial government and the WMR; and Jiang'an by all kinds of people.

Like other Chinese cities, Wuhan was torn by three social divisions in the period leading up to the Cultural Revolution.

Cleavages between the Cadre Class and the Working Class

Although private ownership had been abolished in China by the mid-1950s, state ownership did not give all citizens equal rights to enjoy and dispose of property. The hierarchical structure of the division of labour remained intact. The economic division of labour gave some people the creative tasks of planning and ordering the work of others, while the majority had to do intellectually less demanding and more routine jobs.

In 1957, the same year that Milovan Djilas published his *The New Class*,[2] a young assistant professor at Beijing Aeronautical Engineering Institute, Zhou Dajue, independently developed a theory of a new class. Zhou argued that in China, national ownership of the means of production existed only in name. In reality, the means of production were controlled by a minority of individuals, who were not directly engaged in production but held leading positions in a network of productive organizations and acted as managers of the means of production. As a result of their control over the production process, they obtained economic advantages. Zhou concluded that those people formed a class of leaders (*lindaozhe jieji*) separated from the mass of the people and that the contradiction between the leaders and the masses was a class struggle.[3]

To the extent that those with directing power occupied positions very different from ordinary workers in social production and reproduction, there were indeed two basic classes in China's state socialist system: the cadre class and the working class. Since they were placed in different positions in the social production process, contradictions between the two classes were inevitable. In pre-Cultural Revolution China, however, this antagonism was largely obscured by internal conflicts within both the cadre class and the working class.

Cleavages within the Cadre Class

The cadre class was made up of three distinct groups of cadres: the political bureaucracy (*dangzheng ganbu*), the administrative and managerial personnel (*xingzheng guanli ganbu*), and technocrats and other specialists (*jishu ganbu*). The political bureaucracy included officials of the Chinese Communist Party (CCP), the Communist Youth League (CYL), the Trade Union, and the Women's Association; and staff of the political work, propaganda, personnel management, and security sections of each unit. They performed vital ideological, political, organizational, and coercive functions. Administrative and managerial personnel were those engaged in the management of production and reproduction, such as general management officials at various levels, and the chief staff in charge of accounting, bookkeeping, supply and distribution, and welfare. Technical-professionals who possessed knowledge and expertise were deemed important to the efficient achievement of government objectives. By virtue of their knowledge, they were able to influence, and even veto, decisions made by the other two groups. Included in this category were engineers and technicians in enterprises, teachers and scientists at educational and scientific research institutions, doctors, journalists, artists, and the like.[4]

There were sharp internal divisions among these different cadres. The political cadres, especially those at middle and lower levels, generally came from working-class or poor peasant backgrounds with little formal education, whereas most of the specialized personnel were from non-proletarian backgrounds and had received fairly good training. Administrative and managerial personnel tended to consist of people from both high and low origins. The different social origins and experiences inevitably created tensions.

Élite dualism is a special feature of the Communist system in its early years.[5] If China had had a large number of cadres who were not only politically reliable but also functionally competent, such conflict might never have arisen. But the sad fact was that when the CCP came to power, it faced a dilemma: while most of the revolutionary cadres lacked the basic training for managing socio-economic development, those who were competent tended to come from middle- or upper-class family backgrounds. The latter were considered not to be fully committed to the goals, values, and programmes of the new regime. Since there were few who were both politically reliable and technically proficient, China had to recruit some cadres for their reliability and others for their competence.

The People's Republic made serious attempts to promote people from subordinate social positions to ruling ones. After Wuhan was liberated by the Communists in May 1949, about 6,000 to 8,000 People's Liberation Army (PLA) officers, soldiers, and other revolutionary activists were assigned to take control of the city and given the title 'military representatives'.[6] Military representatives were sent to virtually every enterprise and government agency, and played the leadership role in each unit. Later, when the political situation stabilized, most of the military representatives were formally appointed as Party secretaries or directors in their respective units. Until the Cultural Revolution broke out, the leading cadres in many units were still former military representatives.

Veteran Communist cadres alone were apparently not sufficient in number to fill all the positions of power. A great number of workers and peasants were therefore placed in state and economic positions. Especially after a large-scale industrial construction programme was initiated in 1952, the shift of manual workers to managerial positions was accelerated.[7] By 1957, veteran cadres who had joined the Party before 1949 accounted for only 11 per cent of the cadre body in Wuhan; 89 per cent were new cadres.[8] The massive promotion produced a high degree of long-range mobility for persons of humble origins to obtain dominant political positions in society.

In order to prepare people of humble origins for positions of authority, the new regime attempted to create a new proletarian intelligentsia. In the early 1950s, 223 special cadre training schools were established throughout the nation. Students in those schools were mostly young, promising low-level cadres. Training was a stepping-stone for them to be promoted to more important positions. In 1956 alone, 15,958 students graduated from such schools. In addition, eighty-seven worker–peasant accelerated high schools were formed, most of which were attached to existing higher educational institutions, and graduates from which were to be accepted as regular or special college students. It was estimated that between 1950 and 1957, about 100,000 men and women enrolled in such training programmes.[9]

Despite those efforts, the general educational level of cadres remained low. In 1958, 50 per cent of China's middle- and upper-level cadres lacked education beyond the elementary level. The education level of low-level cadres was even poorer, with only 11 per cent of them having attended high school or above.[10] Since the Party desired rapid economic development and technological modernization, the skills of the specialists thus became indispensable. The Party had to reach a compromise with the well-educated and well-trained.[11]

Immediately after 1949 the urgent need to stabilize society and to maintain basic services forced the new regime to rely on former administrative and technical personnel of the Nationalist government to a considerable degree.[12] One year after liberation, a survey found that more than 50 per cent of cadres in Wuhan were retained Nationalist officials.[13]

The management skills of former capitalists were also greatly appreciated by the new government. When private industrial and commercial enterprises were being transformed into joint state–private ones in 1956, the government promised that all former capitalists would be assigned jobs suited to their abilities.[14] There were then 13,388 former private shareholders in Wuhan, among whom 6,480 were classified as active capitalists. All active capitalists were given jobs, and many of them became administrative, managerial, and technical cadres in new joint state–private enterprises (see Table 2.1). In some industries, former capitalists occupied more managerial positions than revolutionary cadres. In four of Wuhan's major industries—the machine-building, textile, light, and handicraft industries—for instance, among the 638 managers and deputy managers of 374 enterprises, 444 were former capitalists, accounting for 69.6 per cent of the total. The other 194 managerial posts were occupied by veteran Communist cadres and recently promoted workers, but they accounted for only 30.4 per cent of the total.[15]

The percentage of managerial positions held by former capitalists later declined as more workers were promoted to such positions. Nevertheless, most of the former capitalists who had been assigned to managerial positions in 1956 still held those positions in 1966.

Another important source of skilled cadres was intellectuals. The intellectuals constituted only a tiny group in China before the mid-1960s. In 1956 there were only 42,000 college teachers, 31,000 engineers, and 63,600 technicians in the whole country. Out of a total population of 650 million, there were only 3.84 million who could be defined as intellectuals by Chinese standards. Most of the intellectuals were from the formerly privileged classes. Up to 1966, only 24.8 per cent of Party secretaries and principals and 19.4 per cent of teachers in Wuhan's high schools were from worker or peasant family backgrounds; the rest were from non-proletarian backgrounds. In elementary schools the distribution was even more skewed. Only 19.8 per cent of all faculty members (including Party secretaries, principals, and teachers) were from good family backgrounds.[16] No matter how unreliable the Party thought those intellectuals were, they occupied most of the technical, professional, and academic positions throughout the period preceding the Cultural Revolution, because there were no other groups of people who possessed the knowledge and skills they had. The indispensability of intellectuals made their relations with the regime far more problematic than the relations between the new regime and retained Nationalist officials and former capitalists. At some points (1956 and early 1962), the CCP openly declared that intellectuals had become a part of the working class,[17] whereas at other times (1958 and late 1962), the Party denounced 'bourgeois intellectuals' as the main enemies of the proletariat.[18] In 1965, when discussing the fate of revolutions with the visiting French Minister of Culture, André Malraux, Mao asserted that intellectuals

Table 2.1 The Placement of Former Capitalists, 1956

Former Status	New Position	No.
	Deputy Provincial Governor	1
	Deputy Mayor	1
	Deputy Director of Provincial Bureau	3
Upper Bourgeoisie	Deputy Chairperson of Municipal	
	CPPCC	1
	Deputy Director of Municipal Bureau	5
	Adviser of Provincial or Municipal	
	Bureau	6
	Deputy District Magistrate	4
	Subtotal	*21*
	Member of Board of Directors	12
	Manager or Deputy Manager of	
	Large Company	14
	Head of Division in Large Company	9
Industrial Capitalists	Manager or Deputy Manager of	
	Factory	532
	Head of Division in Factory	282
	Technician	40
	Ordinary Personnel	1,839
	Subtotal	*2,728*
	Deputy Director of District	
	Commercial Bureau	6
	Manager or Deputy Manager of	
	Large Comapny	17
	Head of Division in Large Company	14
	Director or Deputy Director of	
	District Shop	42
Commercial Capitalists	Manager or Deputy Manager of	
	Shop	1,274
	Head of Division in Shop	84
	Adviser to Company	10
	Member of Board of Directors	24
	Technician	2
	Ordinary Personnel	2,258
	Subtotal	*3,731*

Source: Wuhan Party History Office, *DFDS*, pp. 272–3.

constituted a good part of the new revisionists in China, and therefore they were the most dangerous group for the Chinese revolution.[19]

Nevertheless, seventeen years (1949–66) was too short a period of time for the regime to train a new generation of specialists who were both technically proficient and politically reliable. The government thus had occasionally to permit full use of the existing pool of specialists.

The above discussion should have made it clear that the cadre class in the China before the mid-1960s consisted of two types of élite: the new political élite and the old professional élite. The two groups differed in social pedigree and formal education, as well as in function. Since they were recruited from such a wide variety of backgrounds and experienced daily competition over the allocation of power, status, and income, tensions and conflict were inevitable.

In the literature on state socialist societies, the importance of a Weberian notion of social closure has often been emphasized.[20] Social closure refers to the process by which social collectivities seek to maximize their own rewards by excluding competitors from access to rewards and opportunities. This entails singling out certain identifiable social or physical attributes as the basis for exclusion. For Weber, virtually any group attribute may be seized upon, provided it can be used for 'the monopolization of specific, usually economic opportunities'.[21] And naturally every group tends to adopt criteria that will enable it to claim a special and intrinsic quality of its own.[22]

Social closure was a strategy used by both the new and old élites to legitimize their claim to power and privilege. The professional cadres believed that, by virtue of their skills or education, they were the best qualified for all positions of strategic importance. They therefore longed to seize political authority from those they considered lacking in the technical and moral qualities needed to lead the nation.

This desire found dramatic expression during the Hundred Flowers Movement of 1957. Contemptuous of the low cultural level of political cadres, the retained Nationalist officials, former capitalists, and intellectuals had long resented Party veterans' receiving superior positions in the government and economy. For them, it made no sense to let nonprofessionals (*waihang*) lead specialists (*neihang*). The Hundred Flowers Movement provided them an opportunity to express their frustration. Former capitalists requested that the state withdraw its representatives from joint state–private enterprises because they held that revolutionary cadres and recently promoted workers had insufficient training or experience to manage the economy.[23] Even if the state would not give in, they hoped at least that the state cadres would limit themselves to political roles, leaving daily business to the old owners of enterprises.

The intellectuals ridiculed the veteran revolutionary cadres and cadres of worker–peasant origins as 'experts in class struggle'. According to them, what China really needed was 'experts in economic construction'. Therefore, the existing cadre composition and recruitment policy needed to be changed.[24] The main criterion for recruitment should be ability (*cai*) rather than political integrity (*de*). Since many political cadres didn't have much ability, a 'rightist' in Wuhan suggested:

> At least 10 to 30 per cent of Party members should be expelled from the Party. All veteran cadres of worker–peasant origins should resign from their posts while being allowed to keep their salaries. And all new Party members (and new cadres) should be forced to take part in retraining programmes.[25]

It was also proposed that a system of civil service examinations should be introduced and that people should be given an equal right to be cadre candidates regardless of their family backgrounds.

Former Nationalist military and administrative officials also took the opportunity to vent their resentment, complaining that some senior officials who had surrendered themselves to the PLA in 1949 were still unemployed in Wuhan. They believed it not only unfair but also unwise to leave those highly qualified persons out of productive work.[26] All these criticisms amounted to an implicit demand for the reallocation of power in society and for the closure of social and economic opportunities to nonprofessional cadres.

The old élite's attack provoked a strong reaction on the part of those against whom it was directed. The political cadres responded to the professional cadres' social closure challenge with their own social closure strategy. It was true that political cadres lacked knowledge and skills. However, they possessed an asset the professional cadres didn't have, that is, their humble but 'revolutionary' origins. Class labels thus could be used as a weapon for eliminating the competitive power of professional cadres.

After 1949, all Chinese citizens were classified. In the rural areas, class labels based on economic status before the land reform were used as the basis for the redistribution of property. There was no urban equivalent of the land reform. The class labelling in cities was a by-product of a series of political campaigns, including the Labour Insurance Registration Campaign (1951–4),[27] the Elimination of Counter-revolutionaries Campaign (1955–6),[28] the Socialist Transformation Campaign (1956),[29] and the Anti-Rightist Campaign (1957–8).[30] By 1958, city dwellers in all walks of life had been given such specific labels as capitalist, worker, urban poor, independent labourer (including hawker, small handicraftsman, and other petty proprietor), and clerk (including professionals and other intellectuals). Added to these economic labels were the political designations assigned to selected people: revolutionary soldier, revolutionary martyr, and revolutionary cadre on the one hand; and the negatives counter-revolutionary, rightist, and bad element on the other.[31]

At first, the government did not expect that class labelling would play a crucial role in daily life. According to 'The Decision on Class Labels in Rural Areas' issued by the Government Administration Council in 1950, landlords might change their class labels five years after the land reform if they took part in production activities and abided by the law. A similar principle was applied to rich peasants, who might change their class labels after three years. By 1956, when the Socialist Transformation was carried out, many landlords and rich peasants had already had their labels removed.[32] It was understood that private owners would be labelled as capitalists only for seven years, during which time they would receive dividends. In 1956 the Party even played down the significance of class labels by modifying the procedure for Party recruitment. According to the old constitution passed by the Party's Seventh Congress in 1945, non-proletarian applicants had to be recommended by four Party members, their sponsors must have long standing in the Party, and their probationary period would be longer than that of their proletarian counterparts. The Party constitution passed by the Eighth Congress standardized the recruitment procedure for all applicants, as the class label was considered to be losing its significance in Chinese society.[33]

The old élite's challenge during the Hundred Flowers Movement alarmed the Party. On the one hand, the class label was one of the main targets of the rightist's vigorous attack;[34] on the other hand, it was evident that a large number of rightists were of bad class origins.[35] The Party thus came to believe that one's family background and/or personal class status had a significant influence on one's political views and behaviours. Therefore, class status needed to be further emphasized rather than de-emphasized.[36]

Political cadres of various levels found that the emphasis on class status fitted in exactly with their group interest. Former Nationalist military and administrative officials, capitalists, and intellectuals were no doubt the best educated, best trained, and thereby best qualified for managing China's social, economic, and cultural affairs. Revolutionary cadres could not compete with them in terms of ability. Only under a different set of rules was it possible for the new élites to compete successfully with the old élites. Thus, they had every reason to give wholehearted support to policies that gave first priority to political integrity and that used class status as the prime measure of political integrity. The ranking of people according to class designations created a distributive structure of rewards and opportunities in which the dominant position of revolutionary cadres in society was secured.While the old élites' skills might still be used by the new élites who lacked such abilities themselves, it was not legitimate for the old élites to claim a leadership position in society on the basis of their professional abilities. Thus, they were politically castrated. As a result of ranking people in accordance with their family backgrounds, the professional cadres were compelled to live with their political inferiority, whatever else they might obtain.

In studying social closure, Frank Parkin points out that one of the most commonly used strategies for a given social group to maintain or enhance its privileges is to create another group or stratum beneath it.[37] Thus, class labelling should be understood as an application of such a strategy by political cadres to deter their potential challengers, rather than merely as a result of a mistaken policy.

Cleavages within the Working Class

The working class was not homogeneous either. The work-force, whether in the state sector or in the collective sector, was largely divided into three categories: activist, backward element, and middle-of-the-road.

The division was a by-product of the mass mobilization method of political and economic development, which, in turn, was a by-product of scarcity. In a poor country like China, one way to increase productivity was to mobilize underused labour power. But because it was poor, there were only limited resources to be used as rewards. The government thus had to supplement expensive material rewards with cheap moral rewards as much as it could.

The secret of mass mobilization lay in differentiating the masses and mobilizing the activists first, because it was impossible for a handful of organizers to mobilize all workers at once.[38] Workers thus were always encouraged to become activists by outdoing each other.[39] The activists were then used as task forces on which the leadership could rely, and as models for their fellow workers to follow.

To be an activist, one must be a rate buster in production as well as an enthusiastic fighter in major political campaigns and routine political activities.[40] However, those who met these qualifications didn't automatically become activists. Whether a person was qualified to be an activist was also subject to evaluation by his or her fellow workers and leaders. To be recognized as an activist, one thus had to be nominated by one's peers and endorsed by one's superiors.

Activists nominated by workers and those favoured by leaders often included the same group of people, but they were not necessarily identical. Leaders often kept a secret list of activists, including only those whom they trusted most and planned to recruit into the CCP and the CYL.[41] Even though such lists were kept secret, workers usually had a fairly clear idea about who were 'sweethearts' of the leaders, because the 'sweethearts' were treated differently. The Party and Youth League branches often initiated special activities such as study sessions, 'voluntary labour', and visits to places of interest, to which only activists were invited. More important, whenever there was a new central task, especially a political campaign, activists were often briefed in advance on what the task was and what they were expected to do.[42]

Leaders and workers usually knew who fell into the category of backward element in their units as well. In the seventeen years between 1949 and 1966, the general conception of 'backward' took three major turns. Before 1956, 'backward element' referred primarily to those who did not fulfil their production target, who did not make an effort to improve their skills, who did not use their abilities to the full, and who did not observe labour discipline.[43] After 1957, when politics was said to be in command, one's political performance carried more weight. Since it was intrinsically difficult to devise a clear and objective test of political activism, one's performance in political study sessions became the most commonly used measure of political consciousness.[44] Those who failed to attend such meetings regularly were often characterized by unit leaders and activists as 'not concerning themselves with politics'. Even passive attendants were thought to be 'indifferent to politics', because they rarely expressed themselves at those meetings.[45]

As a result of the severe economic situation in the early 1960s, the Party attempted to restrict mass consumption, which gave rise to a strong ascetic tendency. Frugality then began to be associated with 'proletarian virtue' and extravagance with 'bourgeois evil'.[46] Now one might be considered backward if any aspect of one's life-style was out of the ordinary, such as wearing brightly coloured clothes, applying hair oil, going to a restaurant, cultivating flowers, raising goldfish, or playing chess.[47]

As a result of the politicization of social life, the concept of backward was greatly broadened. Even those who worked hard and fulfilled their duties fairly well might be labelled 'backward elements'.

While activists were favoured by their leaders, backward workers were often discriminated against and isolated by their superiors and active colleagues. In extreme cases, some unit leaders even went so far as to hold public accusation meetings to struggle against backward workers or to humiliate them by posting their names on a wall.[48]

Neither activists nor backward elements accounted for the majority of employees in each unit. In between were 'middle-of-the road' workers, who acted like what some would call 'deferential' workers.[49] They viewed their superiors with respect and perceived themselves to be in a legitimately inferior position. They participated adequately in political and production activities, but without much enthusiasm. For them, politics meant merely shouting the prevailing slogans along with other workers, and production was nothing more than a way to earn one's living by honest work.

The politicization of social life in the early 1960s put a growing pressure upon the middle elements. It had been perfectly acceptable to stay middling in the previous period. Now, however, a person was likened to a boat sailing against the current: it would be driven back unless it forged ahead. In other words, everybody was left with only two options: to be an activist or a backward element. There was no longer an intermediate zone. This development further polarized workers. A survey of Chinese newspapers of the years between 1962 and 1966 suggests that the overt and covert conflicts between activists and backward elements were becoming more widespread and more serious than ever before.

Even in the early 1950s, such conflicts were considered to 'have damaged the unity of the working class'.[50] During the Hundred Flowers Movement of 1957, some repressed backward elements even launched an open attack against the activists,[51] but the Anti-Rightist Campaign soon silenced protesters.[52] In the years that followed, open criticism of activists subsided, but the contradiction between activists and backward elements persisted. The following extract from a *Worker's Daily* report of 1964 is typical of such conflict:

> [In this workshop], there were several backward workers. They did not observe labour discipline and never worked hard. They accepted only those job assignments that they thought were to their personal advantage. While others were working, they often strolled around the workshop visiting friends. The only thing they paid attention to was their personal material interests. One of them publicly professed, 'The only

incentive for me to work is money.' Whenever the discussion turned to who should receive bonuses, they insisted they were the best candidates. Other workers frowned on their deeds. However, whenever others criticized them, they would make unfounded counter charges against their critics. A senior worker often arrived early and left late and was always diligent and conscientious in doing his job, but he was often derided by those backward workers.

Since those backward workers lagged behind others both in their political consciousness and in their production skills, the leaders of the workshop lost confidence in them and rarely paid attention to them. When assigning jobs, the leaders gave the backward workers only unimportant, unskilled, easy-to-check assignments. If they did not do their work well, the leaders would criticize them. The leaders placed their hopes of reaching production targets on those who were more skilled and more willing to work hard. The leaders' relations with the advanced workers were usually very close and warm, but they always gave a cold shoulder to the backward workers. As a result, the backward workers had no chance to improve their skills, and their drive to work tended to become even lower. Due to their poor performance, they usually received a much lower bonus than the other workers and sometimes no bonus at all. Thus an antagonism developed between them and their superiors. They ganged up with one another and confronted the leaders by intentionally absenting themselves from meetings, by disobeying labour discipline, or by quarrelling with the leaders and activists. Faced with this situation, the leaders and activists designed three new rules for distributing bonuses: first, if one did not meet one's production target, one would get no bonus at all; second, if one was absent from meetings on three occasions without a good reason, one's bonus would be reduced; and third, if one disobeyed labour discipline, one's bonus would be either taken away or reduced. These rules, which were expected to deter the backward workers, resulted in more serious conflicts within the workshop. On the one hand, those who did not comply with the rules thought that those rules were not legitimate and insisted that they had the right to get a bonus just like everybody else. On the other hand, those who did comply with the rules hoped to stick to them and refused to share their bonuses with others. The antagonism was such that one backward worker threatened the head of the workshop with violence if he did not get his bonus.[53]

The leaders of both the Party and the government naturally wanted as many activists as possible amongst the ranks. Thus, leaders and activists at the grassroots level were always encouraged to help backward elements become advanced elements. But from the perspective of the activists, things were not that simple. Since the rewards were limited, expanding the ranks of activists could dilute the advantages that they as a minority enjoyed. Hence, at the same time as conscientious activists were sincerely concerned about helping their fellow workers, they viewed those colleagues as potential competitors. Having a vested interest in keeping the ranks of activists as selective as possible, they were often reluctant to throw open the doors to embrace everyone.[54] This strategy of social closure perpetuated the distinction between activists and the backward elements.

Workers who were considered backward were isolated from their peers. People usually tried to keep backward colleagues at a distance, because if they were too close to backward friends, they might also be considered backward.[55] However, the isolation had an undesired consequence: it bound the backward elements to each other for personal and moral support, which deepened the gulf between the backward workers on the one hand and leaders and activists on the other. In a sense, the backward workers possessed an important political capital. The fact that they were labelled as backward elements rather than as counter-revolutionaries or bad elements indicated that they were from good family backgrounds and had made no political mistakes. In other words, 'backward element' was the worst label they might receive. Once classified into this category, they had nothing more to lose. Unlike people in the middle, backward workers no longer had to be careful in order to avoid being classified as backward. And unlike those with political problems who were deprived of their political rights, backward workers did not have to be afraid of offending their superiors and active peers. Although leaders of Chinese enterprises had considerable discretion in the distribution of rewards and the application of punishments, they lacked the power to dismiss workers. Thus, backward workers often became the boldest critics of, and the strongest challengers to, the establishment within their units. Essentially, the backward workers strove to achieve a position equal to that of the activists. For this reason, they tended to de-emphasize the importance of political performance and called for increased personal freedom.[56] Ironically, in a politicized society, apolitical actors could not win the game unless they politicized themselves and made themselves into a strong political force. This is what happened to many former backward elements during the Cultural Revolution.

Asymmetrical Inequality

In the preceding sections, I have shown that the People's Republic was not a homogeneous society. The distribution of political power, economic rewards, and social privilege was anything but equal. This section measures the inequality between the main social groups along two dimensions: current life chance and possibility of career advancement. Inequality in life chance is always a potential source of political and social instability. The political implications of social mobility are also apparent. Upward mobility could provide the most able and ambitious members of the underprivileged class with an escape route, thereby easing some of the tensions generated by inequality. By contrast, downward mobility tends to make people frustrated, even though their current life chance is still higher than others'.

Some commentators have argued that economic inequality between the cadre class and the masses was one of the causes of the Cultural Revolution.[57] In fact, the economic inequality was not as great as many have believed it to be. After the Communist Revolution of 1949, the new regime followed a radical egalitarian income policy. In general, income distribution in China was highly egalitarian compared with the West and other socialist countries.[58]

In 1956 China adopted a Soviet-style wage system, in which administrative personnel were ranked into thirty salary grades. The official wage ratio between the highest and lowest grades was 28:1.[59] However, Mao Zedong, an enthusiastic champion of egalitarianism, disliked the system and over the next ten years the Party adopted a series of measures to narrow the differential between earnings.[60] By 1966 the differential had fallen to 17.5:1 (see Table 2.2). In 1964, when it was suggested that the highest salary for government officials should be reduced to 200 yuan a month,[61] even Mao felt it unnecessary.[62]

Very few provincial officials were ranked above the fifth grade. Ranked at the sixth grade, Wang Renzhong, the First Party Secretary of the Hubei Provincial Party Committee (HPPC), earned 308.3 yuan a month.[63] Song Kanfu, the First Secretary of the Wuhan Municipal Party Committee (WMPC), was a seventh-grade cadre, with a monthly salary of 275 yuan.[64] In Wuhan, a city with a population over of 2.5 million, there were no more than a dozen officials ranked above the seventh

Table 2.2 Cadres' Monthly Salary Scale in Wuhan, 1960–1976 (yuan)

Grade	5	6	7	8	9	10	11	12	13
Wage	*324.8*	*308.3*	*275.0*	*250.9*	*230.2*	*199.0*	*183.6*	*161.9*	*145.5*
Grade	14	15	16	17	18	19	20	21	22
Wage	*129.7*	*116.3*	*103.5*	*92.6*	*83.0*	*74.0*	*66.5*	*59.0*	*53.0*
Grade	23	24	25	26	27	28	29	30	
Wage	*47.0*	*41.0*	*35.5*	*31.0*	*28.5*	*26.0*	*24.0*	*22.0*	

Source: Hubei Provincial Labour Bureau, *Gongzi Biaozhun Xuanbian* [Selected Documents Concerning Wage Policy], Wuhan, 1973.

grade, and fewer than 100 were above the tenth grade. The total of so-called high-ranking cadres, those ranked at the thirteenth grade and above, was in the neighbourhood of 1,000. Most of the heads of administrative bureaux at the municipal level were ranked between the thirteenth and tenth grades, earning 140 to 200 yuan a month.[65] With few exceptions, Party secretaries and directors of most factories, schools, hospitals, research institutes, and government agencies were low-level or middle-level cadres (below the thirteenth grade). They made 50 to 130 yuan a month, higher than the average wage in their units but usually not the highest.[66] Overall distribution of the basic necessities of life was largely equal. There was no visible accumulation of wealth.

Per capita household income was distributed more equally than personal income. In 1965 the average per capita monthly income was 18.86 in Wuhan (see Table 2.3). The per capita income of Wang Renzhong's and Song Kanfu's families was 72.47 yuan and 60.07 yuan respectively, or 3.84 and 3.19 times the average.[67] In Wuhan there were probably few, if any, high-level Party cadres whose families' per capita incomes were higher than those of the Wangs and the Songs. This fact illustrates that the possibility of enjoying a very large income and wealth was circumscribed in socialist China.[68]

In addition to money income, high-ranking cadres received some non-monetary perks and privileges, such as a large apartment, a car, and special medical services. Middle- and low-level cadres usually didn't have such benefits. Their living space might be slightly larger than that allocated to their subordinates. However, this was not so much due to their being cadres as to their having been around in the 1950s when more space was available.[69]

If there were some rich people in Chinese society before the Cultural Revolution, they were to be found among the old élites. The Socialist Transformation Campaign of 1956 guaranteed that the capitalists' living standard would not be lowered. Whether their investments were

Table 2.3 Monthly Family Income in Wuhan, 1956–1965 (yuan)

Year	1956	1958	1959	1962	1963	1964	1965
Average Family Income	53.3	56.7	49.0	61.9	64.9	65.1	63.0
Average Income per Capita	15.6	16.0	18.1	18.9	19.2	19.3	18.9

Source: Wuhan Municipal Statistics Bureau, *Wuhan: 1949–1984*, p. 94.

profitable or not, they all received dividends of at least 5 per cent on their shareholdings (see Table 2.4). By September 1966, when this dividend was abolished, a total of 1.2 billion yuan had gone into the wallets of former capitalists.[70]

In addition to dividends, the former capitalists' salary levels were left unchanged, however high their salaries might have been before 1956. The bigger the capitalist they were, the higher the salary they usually received. A survey of seventy-three capitalists whose capital had been over 500,000 yuan showed that their average salary was about 500 yuan, higher than Chairman Mao's.[71] In many factories the salary of the former owner was higher than that of the Party secretary.[72] In 1964 a survey conducted in five cities, including Wuhan, found that 24,000 former capitalists in these cities received more than 100 yuan a month, among whom 1,240 earned over 300 yuan. One factory manager earned as much as 1,676 yuan a month.[73]

Some former capitalists had yet another source of extra income: room rental. In 1956, private owners in Wuhan let out a total of 3.64 million square metres of living space.[74] Even after the private room rental business was reformed in 1956 and again in 1958, they still received significant rental incomes, although the amounts were smaller than before.[75] Thus, relatively high salaries, dividend income, and rental income enabled former capitalists to enjoy a higher standard of living than most workers and revolutionary cadres. 'Before the Cultural Revolution,' a daughter of a former capitalist claimed, 'my family was quite well-off. We had never had to learn the real value of money.'[76]

Table 2.4 Shareholders' Dividends in Wuhan, 1956

Trade	No. of Shareholders	Capital (yuan)	Dividend (yuan)
Industry	5,915	33,084,483	1,761,042
Commerce	4,906	6,511,854	313,612
Restaurant	446	205,900	10,294
Construction	107	52,542	2,628
Transportation	474	892,964	44,618
Service	960	1,013,573	50,760
Agriculture	52	85,317	4,266
Minsheng Co.	72	420,000	33,600
Jianye Co.	456	1,553,100	66,860
Total	*13,388*	*43,819,733*	*2,287,680*

Source: Wuhan Party History Office, *DFDS*, p. 271.

Intellectuals often earned more than the Party bosses of their units.[77] It was almost a rule that engineers, professors, teachers, and doctors, rather than political cadres, earned the highest salaries in factories, colleges, schools, hospitals, and research institutes. Party secretaries attached to universities in Wuhan, for instance, were rarely ranked above the seventh grade (275 yuan), while first-grade professors earned 327 yuan. Party secretaries at polytechnic schools were rarely ranked above the twelfth grade (161.9 yuan), while first-grade teachers at polytechnics earned 207 yuan. Party secretaries at middle schools were rarely ranked above the fifteenth grade (116.3 yuan), while first-grade teachers earned 141.5 yuan. Party secretaries at hospitals were rarely ranked above the tenth grade (199 yuan), while first-grade physicians earned 316 yuan.[78]

Cultural élites could earn even higher incomes.[79] Chen Bohua, a famous Han opera actress in Wuhan, made 360 yuan a month before 1963 and 570 yuan after 1963,[80] which was twice as much as Song Kanfu earned. During the Three Difficult Years Period (1959–61), governments at all levels were instructed to prepare lists of top intellectuals and cultural élites in their regions. All those whose names were listed were entitled to receive extra food, meat, fish, and cooking oil, which was not available to Party cadres and ordinary citizens. Several thousand intellectuals (including doctors, teachers, artists, and scientists) were included on the list in Wuhan.[81] When Liu Shaoqi, then the head of the state, pointed out in 1966 that 'so-called bourgeois authorities usually lived better than us [top Party leaders]',[82] he was not exaggerating.

Of course, the income gap between ordinary intellectuals and workers was fairly small. Nevertheless, intellectuals in general earned more than workers.

Chinese workers were ranked into eight grades (see Table 2.5). An

Table 2.5 Workers' Monthly Wage Scale in Wuhan (yuan)

Category of Factory	Workers' Grades								
	1	2	3	4	5	6	7	8	Ratio
1	32.5	38.4	45.3	53.5	63.2	74.7	88.2	104.0	3.2
2	33.0	38.9	45.8	54.0	63.6	74.9	88.2	103.9	3.15
3	32.6	38.7	46.0	54.6	64.8	77.0	91.4	n.a.	2.8
4	32.5	38.3	45.1	53.1	62.6	73.7	86.9	102.4	2.8
5	30.5	38.6	41.8	48.9	57.2	66.9	78.3	91.5	3.15

Source: Hubei Provincial Labour Bureau, *Gongzi Biaozhun Xuanbian* [Selected Documents Concerning Wage Policy], Wuhan, 1973.

n.a. = not available

eighth-grade worker could make as much as a sixteenth-grade cadre earned. However, in the early 1960s, about 50 per cent of workers were below the fourth grade, and another 35 per cent were below the sixth.[83] Most workers thus earned from 40 to 60 yuan a month. As a result, income differentials between workers were very small. Even if we take overall income span into consideration, wage differentials were not great. At Zhongyuan Machine Factory, one of the largest enterprises in Wuhan, the Party secretary was an eleventh-grade cadre, earning 183.6 yuan a month, which was 5.6 times the lowest salary at the factory.[84] In terms of life-style, the difference was even narrower. The Party secretary had a slightly larger apartment in the living quarters provided by the factory for its staff and workers. But with a family of eight, he often found it difficult to make ends meet. Like other families in the living quarters, his family had to economize on food and clothing. The workers at the factory knew that their Party secretary lived frugally.[85] This case was by no means unique. Most political and administrative cadres lived quite modestly before the Cultural Revolution. None of them could afford the luxury life-style that some of the old élites were still enjoying. Economic difference, therefore, was not a big issue in Chinese society before 1966.

What may we conclude from the above observations? First, there was no property-owning class. Although some people's incomes were higher than the average, their incomes were fixed and could not be expanded. Second, the overall differentials in economic rewards were small. Third, only in the political sense could the political cadres be called the most privileged social group in Chinese society. In terms of material life, the old élites tended to fare much better than the new élites.

In modern times, educational attainment is a major determinant of future occupation placement. The socialist system is no exception.[86] The composition of students in educational institutions at different levels can therefore be used as a good indicator of the opportunity for upward mobility among various social groups.

In 1949, educated people were very much in short supply: the illiteracy rate was about 90 per cent.[87] In urban areas the rate was relatively lower, but the majority of students were from non-proletarian families. In Wuhan only 44.2 per cent of new elementary school students and 6.8 per cent of new middle school students were children of workers and peasants in 1950.[88]

The new regime was committed to changing the social composition of educational institutions at all levels to the advantage of workers and peasants. It was reasonably easy to achieve this goal at the lower levels.

By 1956 the proportion of students of worker–peasant origins had already reached 82 per cent in elementary schools, 66 per cent in junior high schools, and 64 per cent in polytechnic schools.[89] But in the same year, only 34 per cent of college students came from good family backgrounds, and these students were concentrated in small local normal and agricultural colleges. In prestigious universities, they accounted for only 10–20 per cent of the student body.[90] The state might be able to socialize private ownership of the means of production, but it could not socialize the human capital possessed by the old élites. Prosperous families could still better afford to support their children through higher education (both direct costs such as fees, supplies, and clothing, and indirect costs such as the income which students could otherwise have earned). Moreover, those with scarce skills and specialist training were able, within their family sphere, to perpetuate the advantages these skills and training had given them. The new regime thus faced a dilemma: while those who were academically most competent tended to come from nonproletarian origins, those who were from proletarian origins were in general academically less competent. Which group should be admitted to higher education? What principle should be adopted for admission? If a purely merit principle were to be taken as the sole criterion, universities and colleges would continue to be largely the exclusive domain of the old élites. Conversely, if affirmative action were pushed too far, the quality of education would be lowered.

This dilemma was not an acute problem before 1956, however, because for seven years there were more openings at the college level than there were senior high graduates. In 1957, however, the number of senior high graduates exceeded the projected number of college places available. This meant that new college students had to be selected. In the same year, facing challenges from the old élites, the government realized that it was dangerous to consider only academic performance in college admission.[91] As a result, the number of students from proletarian and peasant social backgrounds increased sharply over the next few years.[92]

Despite attempts to implement some affirmative action policies, students from proletarian backgrounds were still the minority in senior high schools and colleges. Table 2.6 shows the political backgrounds of college applicants in Wuhan in 1962. The better schools had fewer students from good backgrounds. The key schools tended to have fewer students with CCP and CYL membership than did ordinary schools. Overall, only about one-third of college applicants were from good family backgrounds. Even if applicants from good backgrounds were

Failure of Charisma

given priority for admission, a large percentage of new college students would still be from non-proletarian families.[93] Table 2.7 reveals that no college had more than 50 per cent of its students from good family backgrounds in 1962–3.

Economic difficulties during the period from 1960 to 1962 led to the closure of half of China's universities and colleges. As the competition for admission into higher educational institutions became fiercer, the government realized that merely compensatory policies favouring the children of workers and peasants in admission were not sufficient in

Table 2.6 The Political Background of College Applicants in Wuhan, 1962 (percentage)

School	Good Origin	Bad Origin	Others	CCP and CYL
Ordinary School	35.6	20.8	43.6	32.0
Municipal Key School	28.1	22.0	49.9	26.6
Provincial Key School	23.4	27.2	49.4	25.6
Average	30.4	22.9	46.7	28.5

Source: Archives of Wuhan Education Bureau.

Table 2.7 The Family Background of Students in Four Wuhan Colleges and in Three Other Colleges, 1962–1963 (percentage)

School	'Good'	'Bad'	'Middle'
Wuhan Normal College[a]	44.57	23.61	31.82
Wuhan Medical School[a]	34.06	27.29	38.65
Wuhan Nurses' School[a]	46.99	12.05	40.96
Wuhan Engineering School[a]	43.18	24.24	32.58
Zhongshan University[b]	40.00	30.00	30.00
Geographical Department of Beijing University[c]	40.00	23.00	37.00
Zhongshan Medical College[d]	23.4	n.a.	n.a.

Sources: (a) Archives of Wuhan Education Bureau.
(b) Elsie Collier, *China's Socialist Revolution*, New York: Monthly Review Press, 1973, p.130.
(c) *QNB*, 16 August 1966.
(d) *RGP*, 11: 3384.
n.a. = not available

helping them to win their fair share of higher education. At the Beidaihe Conference held in the autumn of 1962, Mao Zedong criticized the lenient policies aimed at bourgeois intellectuals and their children.[94] Thereafter, new negative affirmative action policies (strictly limiting the chances of young people from bad class backgrounds being admitted to college) were introduced on top of the positive affirmative action policies adopted previously (giving students with good class backgrounds extra points in college entrance examinations).

In late 1962 the Central Party Committee revised the political standards for enrolling college students. Fields of study in higher educational institutions had long been classified into three categories: open, restrictive, and highly restrictive, each of which had specified political criteria for admission.[95] The new document prohibited the children of capitalists and rightists from being admitted to highly restrictive fields; the children of landlords, rich peasants, counter-revolutionaries, and bad elements from entering restrictive fields; and those whose parents had been sentenced to death, to imprisonment, or to public surveillance for counter-revolutionary crimes from enrolling in any field.[96] Two years later the Party again revised the standards. This time, even applicants whose grandparents or siblings had been sentenced to the various punishments were subject to restrictions on admission. Overseas connections were also considered suspicious.[97] Before taking their entrance examinations, applicants were secretly screened and categorized by school authorities and police substations.[98] If an applicant was classified as 'not suitable for admission', then no matter how well he or she scored in examinations, admission would not be considered. Although students knew that investigation of their family background was a necessary step in the admission procedure, they were not aware of the existence of a list that contained the names of those who had absolutely no chance of admission. In 1964 such a list was leaked by accident in a high school in Wuhan, causing great disturbance among the students. After the incident, all schools were instructed to take extra precautions to keep the list out of the reach of students.[99]

Similar policies were introduced in middle schools. In the past, it had not been necessary to conduct family background investigations for senior high and polytechnic school admissions. In 1964, however, such investigation was institutionalized.[100] Meanwhile, measures were adopted to enhance the admission chances of good-origin students. Students from good class backgrounds who passed the entrance examination had the privilege of being admitted first. Even some students who failed the examination were admitted. Moreover, a small percentage of good-origin students (especially from families of workers, poor and low–middle-class peasants, and revolutionary martyrs) was exempt from the examinations.[101] As a result of those favourable affirmative action policies, the proportion of good-origin students in middle schools and colleges increased. Table 2.8 shows the changing composition of the student body in Wuhan's secondary schools from 1962 to 1965.

At the level of higher education, more than 70 per cent of college students admitted in 1964 and 1965 were from good class backgrounds in Wuhan, as well as in China as a whole.[102]

Despite all those efforts, the good-origin youth representation in senior high schools and colleges did not mirror the proportion of good-origin people in society at large. And the proportion of good-origin students potentially available for higher education became progressively smaller as each educational hurdle was crossed. In 1965, as Tables 2.8 and 2.9 show, proletarian youth still accounted for less than 50 per cent of senior high and college students, whereas 85.73 per cent of primary school students in Wuhan were from this group.[103]

Table 2.8 The Family Background of Students in Wuhan's Secondary Schools, 1962–1965 (percentage)

	Junior High			Senior High		
Year	'Good'	'Middle'	'Bad'	'Good'	'Middle'	'Bad'
1962	62.71	33.08	4.21	40.19	49.37	n.a.
1964	63.05	33.13	3.82	43.43	46.97	9.60
1965	61.82	35.60	2.58	46.67	47.59	5.74

Source: Archives of Wuhan Education Bureau.
n.a. = not available

Table 2.9 The Percentage of College Students with Good Family Backgrounds in China, 1951–1965

Year	1951[a]	1952[b]	1953[c]	1954[d]	1955[e]	1956[f]	1958[f]	1962[f]	1965[f]
Percentage	19.0	20.5	27.4	36.7	29.0	34.1	36.4	42.3	49.7

Sources: (a) *XHYK*, 1 (1958): 139.
          (b) *RMJY*, 10 (1957): 6.
          (c) *JYNJ*, p. 338.
          (d) *XHYK*, 9 (1955): 7.
          (e) *XHYK*, 7 (1957): 228.
          (f) K. S. Karol, *China: The Other Communism*, New York: Hill & Wang, 1968, p. 333.

It has been suggested that there were special boarding schools reserved exclusively for the children of the new élites in China in the years leading up to the Cultural Revolution.[104] In fact, special schools for cadres' children were not as common as many have believed. While there were a number of such schools in Beijing, most of the special schools in the provinces had been abolished in 1957.[105] Also, most special schools were at the elementary level and were designed to admit the orphaned children of revolutionary martyrs and small children of diplomatic personnel and high-level cadres (especially army officials) whose parents did not have time to care for them. Before 1957 there had been three special schools in Wuhan: two were closed in 1957 and the remaining school, the 1 August Elementary School, accepted only the children of army officials.[106] There was no special secondary school for cadres' children. Although the percentage of cadres' children in middle schools increased between 1962 and 1965, they were not over-represented as compared with the middle-origin group (see Table 2.10). This should not be surprising. Coming from peasant or worker origins, most cadres had little formal education themselves, and so could offer little help in their children's education. Moreover, because the new élites were relatively young, mostly in their thirties and early forties, their children were still too young for high school in the 1960s.[107]

In sum, the efforts of the Chinese Communists to proletarianize the nation's educational system and thereby to change the pattern of social status distribution were only partially successful. Despite class favouritist policies, China was falling short of the goal of inverting the old class order. The existence of greater opportunities for non-proletarian groups, as shown above, was inconsistent with the prevailing egalitarian ideology and political propaganda. However, positive and negative affirmative action policies vigorously implemented after 1962 threatened students from bad and even middle-class origins. The slogan of equality was generally accepted in China by the mid-1960s. The problem was

Table 2.10 The Percentage of Cadres' Children in Wuhan's Secondary Schools, 1962–1965

Year	Junior High	Senior High
1962	2.66	3.37
1964	3.43	5.25
1965	5.01	n.a.

Source: Archives of Wuhan Education Bureau.
n.a. = not available

that while the old élites and their children took it as the equality of opportunity, people of humble origins understood it as the equality of result.
Everyone thus felt victimized by discrimination in one way or another.[108]
As a result, tensions developed. The class line pushed students into
increasingly self-aware groupings.

The Gravity of Discontent

Exactly why the Chinese behaved in the ways they did during the
Cultural Revolution cannot be understood through study of the actual
events; the answer lies in the history and social structure of China in the
period leading up to those events. The first four sections of this chapter
suggest that three main lines of cleavage existed in urban China before
the Cultural Revolution: the structural cleavage between the cadre class
and the working class, the residual cleavage between the old élites and
people of humble origins, and the behavioural cleavage between
activists and the backward elements. Structurally, of the three social
cleavages the first was the most fundamental. From a long-term point of
view, the latter two were merely interim phenomena, whose importance
would fade as the system became consolidated. Nevertheless, the presence of the other two cleavages before the Cultural Revolution obscured
the contradiction between the élite and the masses and complicated the
power relations in Chinese society (see Figure 2.1).

In 1965 Mao Zedong pronounced, 'The bureaucratic class is a class
sharply opposed to the working class and the poor and the lower–middle
peasants. These people have become or are in the process of becoming
bourgeois elements sucking the blood of workers.'[109] It was a bold but
wrong assertion. Because of the two above-mentioned interferential
cleavages, the élite– mass distinction had not yet become the most politically relevant cleavage in Chinese society. Rather, in day-to-day politics, conflicts between the political élites and activists on the one side
and the functional élites and backward elements on the other were more
conspicuous.

The Alliance between Political Cadres and Activists

The revolutionary cadres were the dominant group in Chinese political
life. However, while their large quantum of power was undeniable, their
salaries were sometimes modest compared to the incomes of some
former capitalists, creative artists, and intellectuals. This was a long-
standing source of widespread discontent among veteran cadres.[110]

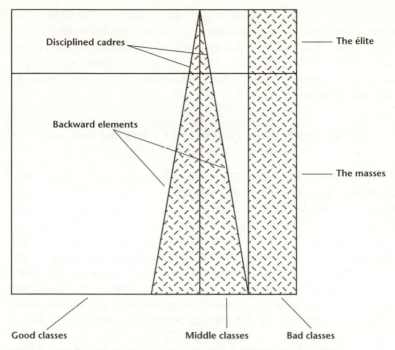

Figure 2.1 Social Cleavages in Pre-Cultural Revolution China

To be an industrial worker in China before the Cultural Revolution was to have a social standing of some dignity. Glorifying the workers' class designations was an important strategy used by political cadres to win allies in their effort to keep the old élites in a vulnerable position while utilizing their talents and skills. The high social standing attributed to workers, however, was not matched by their material position. They thus shared the political cadres' strong aversion to the relatively higher living standard of the old élites.[111] Before the Cultural Revolution, there had already been a widespread popular demand for reducing the high incomes of the old élites.[112] Small wonder that when the Cultural Revolution began, the old élites became the first victims of the movement. On the other hand, the workers' well-being had been significantly improved, compared to their own past before 1949. They therefore were generally happy with the changes brought about by the new regime, and were inclined to believe that further progress could be attained without departing from the fundamental principles of the system. In particular, worker activists tended to co-operate with political cadres to defend the *status quo*, as they did not feel that the expansion of the latter's power presented an immediate threat to their own interests. The chances for activists to advance encouraged their moral commitment to the existing social order. This was why the most spontaneous workers' movement during the Cultural Revolution, as we will see in the following chapters, turned out to be among the die-hard conservatives, who joined forces to confront the rebels.

The Alliance between Professional Cadres and Backward Elements

By virtue of their human capital, professional cadres were indispensable for managing the production and reproduction of goods and values. For this reason, the new regime allowed the old élites to receive relatively higher incomes than the general public. Fairly well-paid professional cadres, however, did not like to subordinate themselves to a socially and culturally inferior political leadership. The Hundred Flowers Movement manifested their desire for the reallocation of power in society. After 1957 the old élites' resentment over their political subordination did not vanish. Instead, as political pressures grew, this latent resentment, which would find outlets during the Cultural Revolution, became even more intense.

Like their active counterparts, the backward workers did not like the old élites, but they were preoccupied with their immediate concern over the discrimination exercised against them by political cadres and activists. Since both the backward elements and the old élites had been frequently victimized during various political campaigns by political cadres and activists, they had a common interest in joining forces to challenge the establishment. Such a coalition emerged during the Hundred Flowers Movement when the backward elements and the old élites fought side by side against the political cadres and activists, though it was soon crushed by their adversaries.[113]

The two 'alliances' had often confronted with each other in the past. At issue were power, status, and other scarce resources. Each strove not only to gain desired values but also to neutralize or eliminate rivals, although the confrontation was conducted mostly in a covert form before the outbreak of the Cultural Revolution.

The collisions between the two coalitions in some ways reflected the collisions between the cadre class and the working class. What the worker activists hated was the economic and cultural privileges of the old élites, whereas the backward workers were averse to the political privileges of the political cadres. Although the targets were different, their efforts revealed the opposing interests of the two classes. Like any coalition, the two coalitions under discussion were temporary alliances of distinct groups, which would take shape only when it was tactically necessary and situationally possible. Before 1966 the confrontation between the two coalitions was not normally noticeable. The tacit alliances came out into the open only when the Cultural Revolution broke out.

In the above analysis, the power relations that existed in Chinese society before 1966 have been intentionally simplified. For instance, the three lines of social cleavage discussed do not attempt to capture the complications of real life. Other cleavages existed between the employees of state and collective enterprises, between temporary and permanent workers within the state sector, between people living in different parts of the same city, between generations, and so on. Moreover, the three cleavages were not always as clear-cut as the above paragraphs seem to suggest. For instance, not every professional cadre came from a previously privileged family. And some members of the old élite might have been reduced to the status of manual labourers, thus losing their professional jobs. Similarly, not every political cadre had humble origins. Moreover, as will be discussed below, some political cadres might have as many grievances against the existing order as the old élites and backward elements. It also needs to be noted that the cleavage between the activists and the backward elements existed not only in factories but also in schools, hospitals, research institutes, cultural troupes, and government agencies. Nevertheless, as the following chapters will show, the distinction between the three cleavages provides a clear framework for analysing the seemingly tangled fighting between the various factions during the Cultural Revolution.

Finally, let us make a rough estimation of how large a proportion of the population in Wuhan fell in the grey area shown in Figure 2.1. Although Mao always insisted that class enemies made up no more than 5 per cent of the population, the actual proportion was much higher. As a 'peacefully liberated' city, Wuhan had more politically problematical persons than many other places. It was estimated that 22,000 Nationalist army officers and soldiers, 32,000 Nationalist militia men and women, 6,200 Nationalist policemen, and about 10,000 Nationalist government functionaries remained in the city after Wuhan was taken over by Communist forces in May 1949. There were a dozen large 'reactionary' secret societies. One of them, *Yiguandao*, for instance, spread its 17 sections and more than 200 branches all over the city and exerted tremendous influence on the social and economic life of tens of thousands of local residents. In some factories, over half of the workers had been members of the Nationalist Party or 'reactionary' secret societies. In the process of democratic reform of industrial enterprises (1951–4), 3 per cent of the workers (about 8,000 to 10,000) were formally labelled or struggled against as elements of 'reactionary feudal remaining forces'.[114] In addition, there were 40,000 capitalists in 1949.[115] In 1949 Wuhan had a population of one million. The above figures, though incomplete, show that much more than 5 per cent of the residents in the city were so-called elements of antagonistic classes.

In later political campaigns, more people became targets. During the Suppress the Counter-revolutionaries Movement (1950–3), several thousand people were convicted.[116] The Loyalty and Honesty Campaign (1951) found that 2,464 cadres had politically problematical personal histories.[117] The Elimination of Counter-revolutionaries Campaign (1955–6) identified 6,652 cadres as 'counter-revolutionaries' and 'bad elements'.[118] The Anti-Rightist Campaign formally imposed the label 'rightist' on 6,261 individuals and the label 'bad element' on 945 workers, clerks, and policemen. Meanwhile, 1,928 people were secretly categorized as 'central-rightists'.[119] During the Anti Right-Deviationists Campaign of 1959–60, 1,784 cadres (including 11.9 per cent of the high-ranking cadres of the city) were reduced to lower ranks or expelled from the Party, and another 1,139 were criticized.[120] In 1963 the WMPC reckoned that 10–15 per cent of the Party members in the city were problematical. Accordingly, during the Socialist Education Movement (1963–6), tens of thousands of Party cadres were purged and 6.35 per cent of the members were expelled from the CCP.[121] In addition, in the seventeen years between 1949 and 1965, 8,437 'counter-revolutionaries' were sentenced to imprisonment.[122] There might be some overlaps in the figures cited above, for some people were targets of more than one political campaign. However, one thing is clear: far more than 5 per cent of the population in Wuhan had been persecuted for one reason or another before the Cultural Revolution. Moreover, if a person was found to have a 'problem', not only his or her immediate family members but also relatives could be stigmatized. If those people were to be included, the total number of victims could exceed 20 per cent of the city's population.

Despite their grievances, such people were not in a position to challenge the establishment. In the spring of 1966 the Chinese political system seemed as stable as ever. No one expected any major disturbance. Previous events, the nature of power relations, states of mind, and moral conditions might have framed people's preferences, but there were political constraints over the range of their behavioural choices, which did not allow them to act in accordance with their own preferences. If nothing had happened to those constraints, the latent hostilities in Chinese society could have persisted for decades without surfacing in expressions of violence. As always, a catalyst was necessary to upset the political equilibrium. It was at this point that Mao decided to attack the establishment, even though he had helped to set it in place. In his view, socialist China was facing a great danger of capitalist restoration. In an attempt to purge China of revisionism, he launched the Cultural Revolution which was to astonish and frighten the world.

3

An Old Game with New Victims,
June and July 1966

THE CULTURAL REVOLUTION did not come about as an inevitable historical development. Rather, it was masterminded by Mao Zedong. On the night of 1 June 1966, by the order of Mao, the contents of a poster written by Nie Yuanzi and six other teachers and graduate students of Beijing University were broadcast over the nation's central radio network.[1] The poster criticized some 'representatives of the bourgeoisie within the Party' for trying to 'shelter the bourgeois authorities'. By broadcasting the poster, Mao hoped to convey an important message to millions of Chinese: it was not necessarily illegitimate to attack local Party authorities.[2] The signal was enhanced by a decision to dismiss Peng Zhen, the mayor of Beijing, and to reorganize the Beijing Municipal Party Committee, which was made public a few days later. The episode of 1 June has since been regarded as the beginning of the Cultural Revolution.

However, Mao's message did not get through to most Chinese. In the Chinese political system, the hierarchy of CCP organizations had monopolized both top-down and bottom-up communication. Bureaucrats at various levels served as what Kurt Lewin calls 'gatekeepers' to regulate information flow on behalf of the topmost leader—Mao.[3] They provided the masses with authoritative interpretations of Mao's messages, translated them into specific behavioural guidelines, and used rewards and punishments to enforce those guidelines. It was due to the existence of such a mighty mechanism that Mao had been able to produce united actions. However, the mechanism worked effectively and efficiently for Mao only when his directives largely fitted the interests of its operators. Otherwise, Mao's messages were likely to be distorted. This was the case, not because bureaucrats dared deliberately to act contrary to Mao's directives, but because they tended to interpret Mao's words in ways that coincided with their own interests. This was exactly what happened in June and July 1966: Party leaders from the centre in Beijing to the grassroots all perceived the new movement merely as yet another anti-rightist campaign.[4] In their understanding, any unauthorized attacks on Party branches or high-level Party officials amounted to an assault on the Party as such, which was an unpardonable crime. Only well-meaning criticisms of individual Party officials at the grassroots level were acceptable.

It never occurred to the bureaucrats that Mao was trying to put the whole system on trial. The rules of the game therefore changed little, and people were still supposed to play the same roles they had played before. As a result, power relations were left largely intact, the political opportunity structure remained unchanged, and the risks for potential insurgents were just as high as in the past. Furthermore, to discourage activities that might disturb the power equilibrium, the local authorities and social forces who had vested interests in preserving the *status quo* imposed heavy penalties on audacious behaviours by harshly punishing those who acted in ways that did not fully conform with the old rules of the game. In such a political environment, people were deterred from challenging the authorities, even if they had grievances against the establishment. Thus, although the first two months of the Cultural Revolution appeared to be seething with activity in certain sectors of Chinese society (particularly in the schools), Mao found the overall situation to be stagnant, because politics was conducted essentially in the old top-down way. Later, Mao asserted that a bourgeois reactionary line prevailed during this period of 'fifty days of white terror'.

New Anti-Rightist Campaign

In Wuhan, the Cultural Revolution began in April 1966. On his return to Wuhan from a conference held by Mao in Hangzhou in March, Wang Renzhong, the First Secretary of the Hubei Provincial Party Committee (HPPC), declared that cultural celebrities, or bourgeois authorities, were to be the target social group of the Cultural Revolution.[5] At a meeting held by the HPPC on 25 April, Wang asserted that a cultural revolution was necessary, because cultural and educational circles had been dominated by bourgeois intellectuals. He predicted that such a cultural revolution would ferret out 5 to 10 per cent of intellectuals as new rightists.[6]

It was in the local power élites' interest to attack their rivals, the bourgeois intellectuals. Once they learned that intellectuals would be the targets of the new movement, they plunged into the battle with immense zeal.

The masses of ordinary people and low-level cadres at first paid little attention to the Cultural Revolution. The use of the term 'Cultural Revolution' surprised no one, for the term had been popular since 1958.[7] What they did was merely to show due revolutionary enthusiasm. Superficially, the masses were active in the movement, writing posters and essays attacking the 'three-family village' and other 'anti-Party and anti-socialism black gangs'. But the distant targets in fact aroused little real interest. In the minds of most people, the targets of the current movement were those who had attacked the establishment rather than the establishment itself. In other words, they too considered the movement as another anti-rightist campaign.[8]

However, a small number of middle school and college students caught the message in Nie's poster, albeit only at face value. They had no intention of challenging the system, but they decided to model themselves on Nie's group, which had challenged the Party Committee of Beijing University. Being in their teens, and politically naive, those students had a low threshold for action. Without any personal experience of the Anti-Rightist Campaign of 1957–8, they had not learned how to assess potential risks in taking political action. Furthermore, they expected that criticizing individual Party cadres or Party branches would involve little risk, because Nie's action appeared to have been endorsed by Mao. A third reason for their readiness to act was that they were mostly from good class backgrounds which cushioned the risks.[9]

Immediately after the publication of Nie's poster, a number of students in Wuhan began to put up posters accusing their school Party committees of lacking zeal in their support of the campaign to criticize 'anti-Party and anti-socialism black gangs'. On 2 June, posters first appeared at Wuhan Institute of Topography.[10]

Local leaders were shocked by such a challenge. Since 1949, Party cadres had gone through many political movements. In almost all cases, they had played a leading role in the various campaigns. Only in early 1957 had political cadres been briefly challenged by others, but this had turned out to be a false alarm. Those who had dared to affront Party cadres paid a price. Now they found themselves facing open challenges from below for the first time in nearly ten years.[11] Their first reaction was to try to nip the dissension in the bud.

On 3 June the HPPC instructed Party organizations at all colleges and universities in Wuhan to seek 'unity of students' thinking'. Accordingly, in the following days, rallies were held on all the campuses. The Party secretary of Wuhan Institute of Topography admonished students at a rally, saying: 'Some of you are perplexed. It is true that the Beijing Municipal Party Committee and the Party Committee of Beijing University have been reorganized. But you should not conclude from these two isolated instances that all Party organizations should be regarded with scepticism, suspicion, or even outright hostility.'[12]

Before the local authorities were able to put down trouble-makers in the colleges, however, some middle school students jumped in. On 5 June a senior student at the No. 14 Middle School put up a poster entitled 'Questions for the Party Branch'. The school Party branch had required senior students to devote their energies to preparing for their college entrance examinations, while allowing the rest of the students to cut classes and take part in the movement. The poster considered this decision to have been wrong. 'It is a time to throw ourselves into the great battle of class struggle rather than a time to pursue peaceful bookish study', asserted the poster. This was the first instance of a high school student openly questioning the correctness of decisions made by a Party branch in Wuhan, and it immediately gained the attention of the HPPC and the Wuhan Municipal Party Committee (WMPC).[13]

On 9 June a big-character poster appeared on the No. 2 Middle School campus, the title of which, 'Bombard the Party Branch [of the school]', was so shocking that both the HPPC and the WMPC held emergency meetings to discuss the incident. Within twenty-four hours, the first work teams of 600 members were sent to a number of selected high schools.[14]

On 11 June, two seemingly more dangerous incidents occurred. At one school, a group of students put up a big-character poster attacking Song Kanfu, the First Secretary of the WMPC, by name; and at another school, it was found that some students had set up a secret organization called the Small Group of Revolutionary Action. When local Party leaders were informed of the two incidents, they were stunned that such 'counter-revolutionary activities' could happen in middle schools. On the same day, Song Kanfu indignantly went to the school in which the poster attacking him had appeared, to deploy a counterattack on 'monsters and ghosts'. And the HPPC dispatched an unusually large work team of 160 members to the school where a 'counter-revolutionary group' had been found.[15]

Such incidents, of course, did not happen in every school, and students who voiced their doubts about local Party bosses were few and far between. Those students quickly came under attack from all sides even without the instigation of school Party branches.

By mid-June the HPPC and the WMPC had completed their disposition of work teams into educational institutions. Virtually every school had a team assigned to it, and altogether more than 10,000 team members were involved. The work teams were warmly welcomed as 'representatives sent by Chairman Mao and the centre.' Unfortunately, however, 'Mao's representatives' had been assembled in such a hurry that they had no idea of what they were supposed to do.[16]

Nevertheless, local officials felt somehow reassured by the work teams garrisoned on campuses. The chaotic situation in the first few days of June reminded them of the spring of 1957 when a handful of right-ists openly attacked the CCP. Once again, some people had tried to seize the Cultural Revolution as an opportunity to make trouble. They must be rightists in the guise of revolutionaries.[17] The purpose of the current movement thus was to 'ferret out' hidden rightists.[18]

Since the Cultural Revolution was perceived as another anti-rightist campaign, local leaders felt that their experiences during past political campaigns, especially those in 1957, were still relevant in guiding the current movement. The criteria for judging rightists and extreme right-ists formulated in 1957 were once again brought out for reference.[19] Even a quota of rightists was set. At a meeting of the HPPC, Wang Renzhong reckoned: 'In 1957, a total of 550,000 rightists was ferreted out. This movement would uncover even more rightists. The percentage [of rightists in each unit] would be no less than three percentage points and it could reach five points.' More specifically, he declared that about 1 per cent of college students and senior high graduates would be labelled as rightists.[20] With all the preparations for another anti-rightist campaign ready, local leaders became eager to play a game with 'monsters and ghosts' just as Mao had played with the rightists in 1957: first letting them feel free to come out and then rounding up the whole gang at one fell swoop. They simply needed to be patient, waiting for the right moment to counterattack.

On 23 June, Xu Daoqi, the head of the Cultural Revolution Leading Group under the HPPC, cautioned the participants at an important meet-ing against impatience: 'A rash counterattack may alert crafty enemies. We therefore still need to be patient.'[21] A week later, at an enlarged meeting of the standing committee of the WMPC, Song Kanfu devel-oped the following theme:

> In general, we must create a political atmosphere in which people will relax their vigilance and behave according to their true colours, even if it means that some Party organizations may be put under fire for a moment.... We should not be afraid of disorder. Short-term chaos may be inevitable in such a movement. However, as long as we are well prepared, sooner or later it will be our turn.[22]

The long-cherished moment of counterattack finally came in July. In a letter to the HPPC dated 3 July, Wang Renzhong, who had been recently appointed a deputy head of the powerful central Cultural Revolution Small Group (CRSG), asserted that through the free airing of views in the previous month, almost all the 'monsters and ghosts' had revealed themselves. Using Mao's words, he called this a strategy of 'luring a snake out of its hole and then beating it'. He instructed that a counterattack against those 'monsters and ghosts' should be staged in the next ten to twenty days. As for how to select targets, he suggested two principles: 'to catch bandits, first catch the ringleader' and 'shoot the birds in the limelight'. As a prudent politician, Wang presented the letter to Mao, who had arrived in Wuhan on 28 June, asking for advice. Mao did not show any objection.[23] Wang therefore thought he had been given Mao's consent.

Wang Renzhong's counterattack by and large hit only student rightists. Unlike the politically immature students, adult Chinese were afraid of getting caught by a repeat of the tactics of the Anti-Rightist Campaign of 1957–8. Political movements had taught them to be clever, more cautious, and more deceitful. It was very difficult, therefore, to lure them out of their holes.[24]

In all, 254 college students from thirteen institutions were labelled 'sham leftists, real rightists' in Wuhan.[25] Compared to over 10,000 student rightists in Beijing, this number seemed unimpressive. In Wuhan, indeed, incidents of open confrontation with Party committees or with work teams were rare. Throughout June and July the HPPC and the WMPC were largely able to keep the situation under their firm control. The labelling of the students served as a warning sign to deter other potential challengers.

Tangled Fighting

In addition to the 254 students, however, there were other victims during the first two months of the Cultural Revolution. They were victimized not so much because they had challenged the authority of local Party leaders but because local Party leaders, as always, needed sacrificial objects for ritualistic purposes in political movements. The most convenient targets were those individuals who had problematical personal histories. Wang Renzhong made the point very clear: 'In this movement, you should look for targets in all directions. From great personages to ciphers, everybody can be exposed and denounced. The initiative of the masses must never be hurt.'[26] What he meant by 'everybody' of course excluded persons like himself.

Middle Schools

Wang's son, a junior high student, was among the first to put his father's instructions into practice. On 6 June he put up a big-character poster attacking a number of teachers at his school, hinting that his father had checked the draft of the poster. The younger Wang's action was thus considered extraordinarily significant and drew a great deal of attention. An organ of the WMPC, *Life in Party Branches*, even published the young student's articles on how to carry out the struggle against 'monsters and ghosts.'[27]

It may be an exaggeration to say that the poster by Wang's son alone triggered off a wave of high school students' insults against their teachers in Wuhan. In fact, it was a nation-wide phenomenon that teachers were humiliated in the early period of the Cultural Revolution. Liu Shao-qi's remark that the main task of the movement in middle schools was to purify the faculty ranks was probably responsible for the uprising.[28]

The most conspicuous targets were the so-called bourgeois authorities.[29] This was an extremely vague concept. In the political climate of the Cultural Revolution, anyone who had shown academic excellence was considered an academic authority and all academic authorities were regarded as bourgeois authorities. This label thus could be used against a large number of school teachers. A twenty-six-year-old temporary teacher, for instance, was condemned as a bourgeois authority simply because, despite his age, he had been generally acknowledged to be one of the most capable teachers in the school.[30] It was much harder for senior teachers to avoid being criticized as bourgeois authorities.

However loosely defined, the label of 'bourgeois authority' could not be applied to all teachers. But political labels were never in short supply. 'Worthy progeny of exploitative classes' was one widely used in Wuhan. At that time, about 40 per cent of the high school faculty in Wuhan were from bad class backgrounds. And among Party secretaries and principals of high schools, the percentage was even higher, reaching 48 per cent.[31] Anyone from the exploitative classes was now vulnerable to being called a 'worthy progeny'. A middle school teacher recalled:

> In my school, the first one who was inveigled against as a 'worthy prog-
> eny' was a teacher in his early thirties. He had collected many gramo-
> phone records of Chinese and Western classical music and often invited
> young colleagues to listen to them. This was revealed at the beginning
> of the Cultural Revolution, and he was charged with 'spreading decadent
> music'. As a capitalist's son, his action was interpreted as a sign of
> having never made a clean break with his bourgeois family.
>   Soon, I found that I myself was also in trouble. I was a Chinese

language teacher. Once, in a class, I misread the slogan 'The American imperialists are bound to lose, and the Vietnamese people are bound to win' the other way around. After the class, a student approached me to point out my negligence. I thought that he was making a fuss over a trifling matter. Now the old case was brought up again. Students also accused me of 'vilifying central Party leaders' because I had once used the term 'carnival' to describe the celebration activities held in Tiananmen Square on National Day. They asserted that 'proletarian revolutionary leaders' would never involve themselves in a 'carnival'. Relating the two cases to my bad class background (capitalist), the students condemned me as a 'counter-revolutionary'.

We were by no means the only two who suffered in this period. In one way or other, almost every teacher was charged with some sort of problem. Of course, those from bad backgrounds were the main targets.[32]

What happened in this school epitomized what was taking place in Wuhan's high schools at large.[33]

A few months later, school Party committees and work teams were criticized for having 'turned the spearhead of attack downward against the masses' in order to protect themselves. But many characterized this period as one of 'tangled fighting'.[34] In most cases, targets were not chosen by Party organizations and work teams. People were attacking each other because they felt great pressure to act. If they did not criticize someone else, they could be accused of resisting the movement. Although action would not neccessarily bring about rewards, however, inaction would almost definitely incur risks. In such a charged atmosphere, it was rational for people to try to demonstrate their revolutionary zeal by picking holes in others' words and deeds. Party organizations and work teams did not intervene because they had nothing to lose as long as the spearhead of struggle was directed downwards.

The 'tangled fighting', however, did not mean that students were blind in selecting their targets. Indeed, almost every student tried to find faults in the words and deeds of some teachers. But they rarely engaged in indiscriminate attacks. The specific targets the students focused on were usually teachers towards whom they bore malice for one reason or another. It was rare for students to attack teachers for whom they had had great respect unless they were forced to do so by tremendous external pressure.[35]

Among the teachers, the existing social and personal cleavages played an important role in deciding who attacked whom. Activists from good and middle-class backgrounds were usually most enthusiastic in attacking bourgeois authorities, in publishing others' records of past mistakes, and in ferreting out 'worthy progeny of the exploitative classes'. In the fanatical political atmosphere, those from bad class backgrounds felt even greater pressure to expose each other. Most people seemed to follow an unspoken rule: 'If I have to attack someone, I will attack those I don't like.' A middle school teacher described what happened at his school:

> At that time, it was impossible for anyone to stand by with folded arms. Especially for people like me who came from exploitative families, there were great pressures. You might be considered to bear resentment against the movement if you didn't appear to have wholeheartedly thrown yourself into it. Therefore everyone tended to rack his brain trying to dig up others' 'crimes'. Of course, no one was willing to hurt his or her friends. The spearhead of attack thus was usually directed at those for whom one had felt a repugnance before. In my school, there were two senior English teachers, Zhen and Zhou, both of whom had historical problems. Zhen put up a big-character poster against Zhou with a title 'Expose Zhou's Ugly Reactionary Features'; in response, Zhou wrote a poster entitled 'Look at Crimes Zhen has Committed'. Each of them wanted nothing less than the other's destruction because they had never gotten along. In my case, I did not like Sun [a fellow teacher]. I therefore chose Sun as my prime target.[36]

In most cases, high school students were not subjected to criticism at this stage.[37] Nevertheless, some students became victims of the 'tangled fighting'. A former middle school student recalled:

> At the very beginning of June, a 'minor three-family village' was uncovered in my school, the three members of which were students who had been fans of Deng Tuo's *Evening Chats at Yanshan* and Qin Mu's *Glean Cowries from the Sea of Arts*, two books that were condemned as 'poisonous weeds'. Soon after, a campaign to ferret out 'monsters and ghosts' was carried out in my school. Who were student 'monsters and ghosts'? Those who had often grumbled; those who had worn pretty dresses; those who had had love affairs; and the like. In my class alone, eighteen out of fifty students were denounced as 'monsters and ghosts'. Two of them were my best friends. Therefore I rose to defend them. Later, the three members of the 'minor three-family village' and the eighteen 'monsters and ghosts' and I all joined rebel organizations.[38]

Wherever such things occurred, it was again usually the enthusiastic student activists rather than the Party organizations or work teams who initiated the attacks. But there was a category of middle school students—hooligans—whose suppression was initiated by the local authorities. As classes were suspended and the prestige of teachers had been destroyed, hooligan students who had been stifled under normal conditions began to run rampant in some schools, which was considered a threat to the ongoing movement. Under orders from the HPPC and the

WMPC, 159 students from 39 middle schools were arrested between 16 June and 24 July.[39]

Educational reform was another issue that divided the student community. In mid June, Beijing issued two directives concerning senior high school admission and college recruitment. The existing admission system was condemned for having favoured the offspring of the non-proletariat classes rather than the children of good origins.[40] The two directives caused a stir among high school students, especially those who were to graduate that year. Students from good backgrounds were of course delighted with the new policy.[41] But students from bad and even middle backgrounds generally felt depressed. For the former, academic advancement had been their last opportunity for upward mobility. If this door to success was to be closed, there would be no other means available to them. The future for students from middle backgrounds also seemed bleak, because the policy which favoured students from good backgrounds naturally meant fewer opportunities for others. A speech delivered at a gathering of high school students by Deng Ken, Deng Xiaoping's younger brother and a deputy mayor of Wuhan, made them even more depressed. Deng said:

> If the children of workers and peasants don't have a better chance for higher education, how can we claim that our society is a socialist society? ... We must carry out the CCP's class line in high school and college admission, giving students from five good categories more chances.... As far as those from the exploitative classes are concerned...the only way for them to overcome the influence of bourgeois ideology and to thoroughly remould themselves is to become ordinary labourers and, best of all, to go to the countryside. It is wrong for them to demand an equal opportunity.[42]

Thirty-six thousand junior high graduates and 6,000 senior high graduates listened to the speech, which was broadcast through a wired broadcasting network. Twenty years later, a former high school student still remembered his ambivalent feelings while listening to the speech: 'By instinct I hated such a policy, but in reason I could not doubt it.'[43]

In July the municipal government reformed the senior high admission procedure. The entrance examination was abandoned and admission was based on students' class background and political performance. Students from bad family backgrounds were the losers. Among 36,000 junior high graduates, 89.43 per cent of students from good and middle backgrounds were accepted by senior high schools, while only 14.62 per cent of students with bad family backgrounds were granted the opportunity for future education.

One survey found strong resentment among those who had been excluded. Complaints ranged from 'With the possibility of going to college gone, we have no hope left' and 'The recommendation cannot discern merit. It is not fair' to 'The class line does us an injustice. We resolutely oppose it.' Students from intellectual and other middle families also encountered problems, particularly in the key schools. Good-origin students who had long felt uncomfortable with the dominance of children of intellectuals felt that it was time to use their superior class origins to overshadow the academic advantage of their classmates with intellectual backgrounds.[44]

The reform of high school and college admission made every student keenly aware of his or her social status and sensitive to changes in the political climate. The previous small rift between students from different backgrounds was becoming a huge gulf. Although overt conflicts were still rare, the latent tension was growing.

Colleges

The situation in colleges was not very different from that in middle schools, except in two aspects. First, the Party committees of five colleges were considered to have 'rotted', in the sense that they had been infiltrated by 'alien class elements'. While Party committees and work teams generally co-operated with each other in directing the movement in other colleges, the work teams took over the control of power in those five colleges. The Central China Institute of Technology was one such 'rotted' unit. Immediately after the work team arrived, it began to mobilize students to attack the political establishment of the institute. The work team hoped to focus criticism upon the leaders of the institute, but the victims were mostly the students' political instructors and Party branch secretaries. This was not surprising, for the latter were well known to the students and the students often had grudges against them for one reason or another. Sanctioned by the work team, impugnments against the power holders entailed no risk whatsoever. As a result, a large number of political cadres were labelled as 'black gang elements'. A similar situation was observed in the other four colleges where the Party committees were also put aside by the work teams. This explains why many Party cadres attached to those colleges later became supporters of the rebel organizations.[45]

Second, unlike their counterparts in the middle schools, college students were old enough to be legitimate objects of attack. In high schools, only teachers might be ferreted out as 'worthy progeny of the exploitative classes'. This label, however, could be applied to college students.[46] Even students from good family backgrounds could be targets. One of the prevailing slogans at that time was 'everyone, no matter what background he comes from, can be criticized in the form of a big-character poster if there are some elements in his words and deeds that run counter to Mao's Thought'. Accordingly, a campaign against 'unhealthy trends and evil practices' was conducted, along with one aimed at 'ferreting out the worthy progeny of the exploitative classes'. As a result, some students from good family backgrounds (mostly back-ward elements) came under attack. In the Central China Normal College, for example, by the end of July, more than 300 students had been denounced in the form of big-character posters, which accounted for 10 per cent of the student body. The situation in other colleges was much the same.[47]

In colleges, again, the selection of targets was largely decided by the students themselves rather than by Party organizations or work teams.[48] Largely because there was no clear guideline for selecting the objects of attack, the targets in colleges were diverse. Teachers or students, Party cadres or rank-and-filers, and those from bad or good class backgrounds all might fall victim to the 'tangled fighting'. This feature of the move-ment in higher educational institutions in the early stages of the Cultural Revolution probably contributed to the relatively blurred distinction, in terms of membership composition, which occurred later between rebel and conservative organizations in the colleges.[49]

Although the Party organizations and work teams did not pinpoint the targets, this does not mean that they were free of responsibility for what was happening in their jurisdictions. Party organizations and work teams encouraged students and teachers to attack each other because they hoped that 'true monsters and ghosts' would be revealed in the process. For them, the fact that some innocent people might be falsely accused was just a price any political movement had to pay.[50] The victims, however, could forgive neither the classmates or colleagues who had attacked them nor the work teams and Party organizations that watched while they were suffering.

Other Sectors

At the beginning of the Cultural Revolution, the Socialist Education Movement (1963–6), which had not yet finished in Wuhan, still had work teams in the city.[51] The work team and the Party committee gener-ally had a division of labour: the former was supposed to direct the political campaign, while the latter was responsible for everything else. The relationship between the two varied from unit to unit. In most cases, they co-operated with each other very well; but in some units, they were antagonistic to each other.[52]

In such units as hospitals, scientific research institutes, and cultural institutions where a large proportion of the employees were intellectuals, 'bourgeois authorities' and 'worthy progenies' were the main targets, just as they were in schools. In those units, usually a large percentage of staff members were denounced.[53]

In factories, where there were few who could be labelled as 'bourgeois authorities', the spearhead of struggle was directed at those with bad records and towards backward elements. However, the workers and low-level cadres in factories were generally neither as enthusiastic as the young students nor as politically sophisticated as the intellectuals. In their minds, the Cultural Revolution was mainly a movement designed to attack bourgeois intellectuals, which was not really relevant to their lives.[54] Only a few political activists with relatively good educations were prompt in responding to the work teams' call. They mostly either attacked those who had been denounced in previous political campaigns or criticized the trivial misdeeds of the backward elements. It was not uncommon for 10 to 20 per cent of the employees of a unit to be criticized in the form of big-character posters.[55] Wuhan Telecommunications Bureau was an extreme case, with about 80 per cent of the employees being criticized in this form. An unwritten rule of the game was, 'When you are accused of having committed some "crime", don't try to clear yourself of the accusation by arguing with your critics.' Arguing with one's critics was considered an action that could sabotage the movement. The best self-defence strategy, therefore, was to attack others. Attacking others not only demonstrated that you were willing to take an active part in the movement but also was a way to take revenge on those who had initiated attacks on you. 'Tangled fighting' was the inevitable result of such a rule.

When such fighting started to evolve within a unit, the work team was instructed by the HPPC and the WMPC to prepare a secret list dividing the people of the unit into five categories: leftist, middle leftist, middle element, middle rightist, and rightist.[56] When the list was ready, the work team would inform some activists of the names of those who should be targets in the next stage of the movement and those who should be won over. The targets picked by the work teams would then be formally denounced. At the Wuhan Heavy Machinery factory, four amateur poets—Zhu Hongxia, Liu Chuanfu, Li Xiangyang, and Jiang Shicheng

—were accused of having formed a 'literary three-family village' and thus became the main targets in their factory. Later they became leading figures in the Workers' Headquarters, the largest radical organization in Wuhan. At the No. 2 Machine Tool factory, the work team labelled two workers as 'anti-Party elements' and 36 others as 'anti-Party pawns'. Nineteen of them participated in founding the first secret workers' radical group in the city on 17 August.[57]

The list, when kept secret, was a tool for the Party leadership and work team to use to guide the movement. But the measures could backfire if the list were to be made public. The leftists would of course have nothing to complain of, since their positions could not be better; and the rightists would not dare to complain because they usually had long been the objects of attack. Leftists and rightists, however, were few. Most people fell into the other three categories. Those who were placed in the middle three categories would not be happy about the classification. Activists would object to being placed in the category of 'middle leftist'. The middle elements would feel they were not trusted by the leadership which had classified them as such. Even acknowledged backward elements would think it unfair to be classified as 'middle rightists'.[58] A few months later, the publication of such secret lists indeed became an effective means for the rebel organizations to enlist the support of those who were furious about the classifications.

In units where the work teams and the former leadership were antagonistic to each other, the situation was more complicated. Typically in such a case, the former leadership was also under fire. Distrusting former activists, the work team would attempt to foster its own activists. Because of this realignment in the internal power structures at the initial stage of the movement, factionalism in such a unit was likely to deviate from the standard pattern in later stages. If the work team chose new activists from among former middle and backward elements (by accusing the former leadership of having mistreated those people who were from good class backgrounds) and depended on them in attacking the former leadership and former activists, later the old activists were likely to become rebels and the new activists to become conservatives.[59] If the work team brought in outside forces to replace the old establishment, later there would likely be at least two separate rebel organizations, with those who had been suppressed under the old leadership mainly attacking the former power holders, and the former leaders and activists attacking the work team and the new leaders.[60] If the work team succeeded in winning over a large percentage of the former leading cadres and activists, those cadres and activists who were excluded were likely to join the rebel organizations.[61]

However, not every unit was deeply involved in the movement at this time. For various reasons, some factories were almost untouched by the storm in the first two months of the Cultural Revolution. Those were usually units where the Socialist Education Movement had just finished or where the overwhelming majority of employees were from good class backgrounds. Since those units were clean enough or had just been cleaned up, the local authorities allowed them to be exempt from the Sweeping out Monsters and Ghosts Campaign, at least for the moment.[62] Those units thus missed this eventful period which caused a great deal of dissension. As a result, those units later tended to have much less factionalism than others.[63]

Nothing really changed during the first two months of the Cultural Revolution. While the political atmosphere was becoming increasingly fanatical, the old rules of the game remained essentially intact. People were reminded of the pattern of former political campaigns: the driving forces, the targets, the strategies used by the local authorities, and so on.[64] In particular, any person with good sense could see the resemblance between the present movement and the Anti-Rightist Campaign of 1957–8. Since the risks attached to any defiant action were high, people generally had little incentive to act contrary to the rules of the game. Most of the activities taking place during this period were those permitted, encouraged, or even required by the authorities. Spontaneous activities seldom occurred. No one, except a few politically naive college and senior high students, dared to defy the existing rules of the game, and such trouble-makers paid dearly for their actions. Meanwhile, a large number of individuals became victims in June and July, even though they had never thought to defy the work teams or Party authorities. In any case, the Cultural Revolution of June and July 1966 apparently deviated from the direction that Mao had expected it to take, namely, to rectify the Party. The position of the power holders was as secure as ever before. Mao reached the conclusion in mid-July that the movement was unlikely to change the existing power equilibrium unless some of the rules of the game were altered.

4

A New Game with New Players,
August to December 1966

To THE great surprise of the leaders in Wuhan, Mao denounced the work teams soon after he returned to Beijing from Wuhan on 18 July.[1] In Mao's judgement, the controlled mobilization, as practised by work teams during the first two months of the Cultural Revolution, hindered the healthy development of the movement. In order to achieve his radical goals, he decided to upset the existing political equilibrium by relaxing some of the old rules of the game. The first change he introduced was the principle of allowing free mobilization of the masses. The new principle had three significant implications. First, it deprived the Party organization of the power to restrict mass mobilization. In previous political campaigns, the Party organization had always been entrusted with the task of exercising its leadership over the mobilization process. But now, it could no longer legitimately claim the authority to select the participants for mobilization, to deny participation by certain social groups, and to arbitrarily pick the targets for attack.

Second, the individual citizen was for the first time given the right to make his or her own judgements, a right that the Party organization had in the past arrogated to itself in name of Leninist organizational principles. Third, the free mobilization principle could be used as a weapon against the Party organization, if it was found guilty of attempting to suppress the masses' revolutionary initiative, to stifle opinions differing from its own, or to throw obstacles in the way of mass mobilization. According to Mao, a Party official's attitude towards the free mobilization of the masses was an important criterion for determining whether he was a 'revolutionary cadre' or a 'counter-revolutionary revisionist' in the gigantic class struggle of the Cultural Revolution. By significantly reducing the risks of spontaneous political actions, the introduction of the free mobilization principle thus fundamentally changed the political opportunity structure for potential insurgents.[2]

As the zone of permissible behaviours was being gradually widened, individuals with low participation thresholds could be expected to come forward first and become the political forerunners; they, in turn, might head up the process of mass mobilization.

The Rise of the Red Guards

Mao's condemnation of the work teams at first gave Wuhan's power élites a jolt. However, they soon calmed down when Wang Renzhong, a rising political star, was transferred to Beijing. Wang had been promoted to the position of deputy head of the newly established CRSG, the supposed headquarters of the Cultural Revolution. He was also one of the few officials assigned the job of drafting the Sixteen Articles, which were to be the guidelines for the movement. With such a powerful patron in Beijing, the Wuhan Party leaders felt reasonably secure. If anything were to go wrong, they trusted Wang, who was still the First Secretary of the HPPC, to tell them first.

The local leadership, nevertheless, had to alter its policy to conform to Mao's latest instructions. Work teams began to withdraw from the schools in early August.[3] In their place, Cultural Revolution committees were established in all colleges and middle schools.[4] Only students and teachers with good class backgrounds were eligible to be members of such committees. Their claim to political monopoly was based on the so-called theory of blood lineage. The phrase 'a hero's child is a brave man and a reactionary's child is a bastard' began to gain currency in the city at this time. The slogan disheartened and alienated both bad- and middle-origin students, and elevated those with good class backgrounds.

According to the Sixteen Articles, Cultural Revolution committees were also set up in units of other sectors than education. There too they were generally dominated by political activists from good class backgrounds.[5]

Before the Cultural Revolution committees could consolidate their power, a new form of mass organization emerged in Beijing and quickly spread throughout China. It was the Red Guards. The Red Guards first came to the attention of people in Wuhan when Mao received one million young militants at Tiananmen Square on 18 August. The Red Guards were conspicuously linked with Mao, who himself wore a Red Guard armband.[6]

Next morning, Wuhan's first self-styled Red Guards were already marching on the city's streets. The local authorities were taken aback by such an extraordinary development.[7] There had not been a voluntary mass organization such as the Red Guards in Wuhan since the early 1950s. If Mao had not shown his support of the Beijing Red Guards, the local authorities would have imprisoned those who set up political groups without official permission irrespective of their professed programme. But the signal from Beijing seemed unmistakable. Their only safe course of action was to echo Mao's words, even though they were still puzzled by Mao's tolerance, indeed his promotion, of such an autonomous mass organization. On 19 August the provincial authorities visited eleven colleges and middle schools to show their support of the 'revolutionary young militants'. Being a Red Guard instantly gave one honour, respect, and prestige, and since there was no risk or cost involved everyone wanted to be a member of the privileged group. In the days that followed, Red Guard organizations sprang up like mush-rooms in the city, and the local authorities had to go from school to school acclaiming the establishment of new Red Guard organizations.[8] Meanwhile, the HPPC and the WMPC held meetings for Red Guards from the various schools to 'exchange experiences'.[9] The real purpose of those meetings was to bring the Red Guards into line with the local Party leadership. Once released, however, the evil could not be easily put back into Pandora's box.

On 22 August the news that Beijing Red Guards had set out to smash the 'four olds' (old ideas, old culture, old customs, and old habits) reached Wuhan. The Smashing the Four Olds Campaign soon swept the city. As Crane Brinton has pointed out, nothing is more simple or more conspicuous than a change in outward appearances to herald a so-called revolution.[10] The first action the students took was to revolutionize the face of the city, particularly unrevolutionary street names and shop names.[11] For instance, any street or shop whose name contained char-acters such as '*fu*' (lucky), '*shou*' (longevity), '*lu*' (emolument), '*he*' (harmony), '*yu*' (rich), or '*tai*' (prosperity) was rechristened as 'east is red', 'red flag', 'worker-peasant-soldier', 'east wind', 'red guards', or the like.

The students did not confine their efforts to place names. Since 1964, tight-fitting jeans, pointed shoes, high-heeled shoes, Western-style coats and ties, and long hair had been regarded as symbols of a bourgeois life-style. Now they were prohibited. The students ordered barbershops, tailors, and photo studios not to do any work that ran counter to prole-tarian styles. Moreover, checkpoints were set up throughout the city, at which anyone whose appearance did not conform to what the students understood to be a proletarian style was made to conform (long hair was cut, for instance, or high heels were removed from a woman's shoes).

In a few days, all traces of the four olds disappeared from the streets. Students then began to search the houses of the old élites, confiscating or smashing any items which they considered met the criteria. In the hope of showing that they were willing to forsake their original classes, students of bad class backgrounds even invited their classmates to search their own homes. Victims often gave those who searched their houses the names and addresses of other possible targets, especially their personal adversaries. Some families of the exploitative classes destroyed the four olds themselves before the students would do so. Valuables, such as gold bars, jewellery, antiques, and rare books were usually confiscated, and less valuable items were destroyed. However, as the judgement as to value was made by teenagers, many real treasures were destroyed. When the children of workers and low-level cadres found that the living standard of many 'old bloodsuckers', as they were termed, was so much higher than theirs, their envy often led them to associate all items of material comfort with the four olds, and to destroy them on the spot.[12]

Violence against the old élites had erupted at other times since 1949. But unlike the violence in the past, which had always been initiated and co-ordinated by the local authorities, the violence of August 1966 was conducted by spontaneous mobs. As a result, it was more arbitrary and more brutal. In all, 21,000 houses in Wuhan were searched, and 17,845 ounces of gold, 28,936 ounces of silver, 267,000 silver dollars, and 4.4 million yuan in cash were confiscated.[13] The students also held accusation meetings against 'monsters and ghosts', paraded them through the streets, or even forced them to leave the city. Physical abuse became a common practice. Altogether, 32 persons were beaten to death in Wuhan. In addition, 112 persons attempted suicide, of whom 62 died.[14]

Why were Wuhan students so ardent in taking part in the Smashing the Four Olds Campaign? First, there were no risks involved. Since Mao and the CRSG had applauded the Beijing Red Guards' activities in smashing the four olds,[15] Party leaders in Wuhan had no choice but to take a *laissez-faire* attitude towards the otherwise intolerable behaviour of the students. When discussing the chaotic situation with other leaders, Zhang Tixue, the governor of Hubei Province, allegedly said,

> Whatever the students want to do, we should not interfere. Are they going to set up Red Guard organizations? Fine! Are they setting out to smash the four olds? No problem! Do they hope to go to Changsha or Beijing? Give them permission! Do they want to destroy a temple? We have no objection. If we do not take such a tolerant attitude, we will find ourselves in a passive position.[16]

After all, the excesses of the Red Guards would not pose an immediate threat to the local authorities. The central and local authorities' connivance at the initial Red Guard excesses made the students aggressive.

Second, there were no costs, except time. And the students had plenty of time, as they had been told that classes would be suspended for half a year so that they could devote themselves to the Cultural Revolution. Their problem, therefore, was not the scarcity of time but an over-supply of time.

Third, there were benefits. Unlike adults, the students could be easily motivated by expressive benefits to take part in political activities. Indeed participating in the group action of smashing the four olds was exciting and fun for most students. The experience of acting together brought them a great deal of pleasure. Moreover, many students expected some rewards from their activism. In late August, although there were self-styled Red Guards in most schools, the Red Guard organization had not yet formally started recruiting students. Non-Red Guard students believed that their participation in smashing the four olds was a way of demonstrating their determination to be in the vanguard of the Cultural Revolution. They hoped that their performance in such a revolutionary action would be taken into consideration when the Red Guard organization in their school started to recruit. Thus, the non-Red Guard students were just as eager as the Red Guards to go out and smash the four olds.[17] In sum, the seemingly mad Smashing the Four Olds Campaign had its basis in the students' rational, albeit subconscious, action.

The excesses of the Red Guards, while threatening public order, missed the main targets Mao had in mind for the Cultural Revolution, namely, the capitalist roaders. At the end of August, Party officials in Beijing started to cool down the Red Guards.[18] Because the local social control apparatus was still reasonably effective, the massive violence was soon brought under control. But this period set a precedent for the use of violence. When the social control apparatus became paralyzed, violence would become a prominent feature of the Cultural Revolution.

During the Smashing the Four Olds Campaign, the Red Guard organizations began to recruit members. Who was eligible? In a statement carried by the *People's Daily* of 26 August, a group of Beijing Red Guards set the criteria:

> Why can we be the Red Guards of Chairman Mao? Because we are the children of workers, poor and lower-middle peasants, revolutionary cadres, revolutionary soldiers, and revolutionary martyrs.... If you don't belong to the five red categories, you must rebel against your own families, remould yourselves, and come over to the side of the Red Guards.[19]

The principle of the five red categories was of course enthusiastically welcomed by students with good class backgrounds, and was adopted as the criterion of the Red Guards in Wuhan as well. The Red Guards thus became an exclusive organization, with only students of the five red categories being eligible to join. In some schools, students from outside the five red categories were allowed to join a Red Guard peripheral organization called 'Red Periphery' (*hong waiwei*). The issue then became how exclusive the Red Guard organizations should be. If all students of the five red categories were to be accepted, the Red Guard organizations would be very large and thus could hardly be regarded as privileged groups. Some students, namely the children of high-ranking cadres, had an interest in keeping the Red Guard as exclusive as possible. In Beijing, where the children of political élites were relatively concentrated, the criteria were often so restrictively defined that only the so-called most revolutionary elements were eligible to join the Red Guards. Here one's potential for being a revolutionary was measured by the official rank of one's parents.

In Wuhan, high-ranking cadres' children constituted only a tiny minority among high school students, and they were concentrated in a few schools in Wuchang District where the provincial government and the headquarters of the Wuhan Military Region (WMR) were located. While they enjoyed the privilege of being accepted as the first Red Guards, they could not afford to adopt the very strict Beijing criteria. Otherwise, only a handful would be eligible to be Red Guards in a few élite schools, and many schools would have no Red Guards at all. As a result, the recruitment pattern of Red Guards in Wuhan was very different from that in Beijing. In Wuhan's élite schools the criteria of recruitment were relatively modest as compared to those used in Beijing.[20] In other schools the criteria were even less restrictive.

Nevertheless, students with bad class backgrounds were excluded from Red Guard organizations outright, however good their political performance had been. Students of middle-class origins were in a difficult position. In theory, they were eligible to become Red Guards, but the decision as to whether they would be accepted was in the hands of those whom they had previously held in contempt. These middle-class students, especially those from intellectual families, had been the cream of the crop in their classes, and the favourites of teachers. It was painful for them to be reduced to a subordinate status.

Even worse, students with bad or even middle-class backgrounds were often subjected to public humiliation. A former senior high student who came from an intellectual family recalled one night in late August 1966:

> That night, an all-school gathering was held on the football field at my school. Everyone was required to participate. In the past, whenever there was an all-school gathering, the students always sat with their classmates.

This time, however, classes had been disbanded and the students were divided into three blocks. Those with good class backgrounds sat in the front. They shouted loudly, 'A hero's child is a brave man, while a reactionary's child is a bastard' and sang 'East is Red'. We, the middle-origin students, sat in the middle, singing 'Sailing the Seas Depends on the Helmsman'. The poor- or bad-origin students were ordered to be quiet and to sit at the back. Many teachers from exploitative family backgrounds were dragged to the rostrum and forced to sing 'We are Monsters and Ghosts'. That night marked a turning point in my life. I had sensed discrimination for quite some time before the Cultural Revolution. Back then, the discrimination had been subtle. But now the veiled discrimination was replaced by a public humiliation, and the dormant contradictions among students by open confrontation. The students literally split, though no one dared to protest at that moment. We were filled with fury.[21]

Similar scenes could be seen almost everywhere. As noted in the previous chapter, students from good class backgrounds accounted for less than half of the student body in Wuhan's high schools. Their exclusivism and their imperious and despotic behaviour inevitably alienated the others.[22] This was a silent volcano that might erupt at any moment.[23]

The rise of the Red Guard and the Smashing the Four Olds Campaign were significant in two senses. First, the Red Guard set a precedent for people with the same interests to organize themselves into groups against others. Although in August and September 1966 only good-origin students were allowed to do so and only one Red Guard organization was supposed to exist in each school, the Red Guard was the first real mass organization not subject to the direct control of the political hierarchy in China since 1949. Unlike the Trade Union, the Communist Youth League, and the Women's Association, which had no autonomy from the Party committee at the same level, the Red Guard was independent from the outset. Its establishment, recruitment, composition, programme, strategies, and activities were decided by the members themselves. Because of their autonomy, they were more likely to confront than to co-operate with the authorities. Moreover, the principle of the Party leadership was now interpreted as 'the leadership of the party centre headed by Chairman Mao',[24] and this could be used to justify actions running counter to guidelines specified by the local authorities.

Second, trans-unit activities began to take shape. In the past, social forces had been vertically segmented and all political activities confined to individual units. Only the CCP had had the capability to mobilize trans-unit actions through its hierarchical networks. The Red Guards set a precedent for people with the same interests to form trans-unit alliances in order to pursue their common goals.

These breakthroughs were the prerequisites for a spontaneous mass movement. Mao was so preoccupied at the time with gaining enough popular support to crush his enemies within the Party leadership that he did not fully understand the far-reaching implications of the rise of the Red Guards. Nor did he realize that the Red Guards were in fact moving in a direction he had tried to avoid. What the Red Guards did in August was to strike yet another blow at those who had been the targets of various campaigns over the last seventeen years and again in the first two months of the Cultural Revolution. However, they were not going to attack the capitalist roaders as Mao expected.

The Spread of Rebellion

The Smashing the Four Olds Campaign overshadowed another important development in August—the growing number of students who were travelling between Beijing and the provinces to 'exchange revolutionary experiences' (*chuanlian*). The rumour that Chairman Mao would receive more Red Guards attracted a large number of students from the provinces to Beijing. At the same time, the desire to kindle the flames of the Cultural Revolution in the stagnant provinces and to see the outside world drove many Beijing students to other parts of the country.

In late August the first group of Beijing students arrived in Wuhan.[25] They brought some extraordinary news to the city: every student had the right to go *chuanlian*; Liu Shaoqi had been criticized by the Party leadership; and local Party committees could be 'bombarded'. Such news made the local leaders very nervous, partly because of the substance of the news and partly because of the way in which it was disseminated. The news was potentially detrimental to the social order they were trying to preserve. Moreover, if an alternative channel of information was allowed to exist, the local authorities' information monopoly would be undermined.

Before the local leaders were able to do anything, the Beijing students began to attack the HPPC directly. Coming from the national capital, many of the Beijing students had a superiority complex. One way to demonstrate their superiority was to do something the locals would not dare to do. The first issue they picked was rather trivial. When the *Hubei Daily* published the Sixteen Articles on 9 August, it did not follow the example of the *People's Daily* by printing the paper in red ink. The Beijing students asserted that printing the Sixteen Articles in black was an intentional insult to the guidelines of the Cultural Revolution and that the provincial leaders should take at least some responsibility for the incident.[26] The provincial leaders, however, considered the Beijing students captious, and had no intention of yielding to a bunch of teenagers.

The provincial and municipal leaders adopted three strategies to deal with the students from Beijing. The first was a preventive measure. On 29 August the HPPC announced that the head of its propaganda department, Zhen Chun, had been ferreted out. A week later, a vice governor, Chen Yixing, was publicly denounced. Both men were members of the standing committee of the HPPC. This was a trick the Chinese call 'giving up pawns to save the knight'. By sacrificing these two persons, the provincial leaders hoped to show that the hidden enemies within the HPPC had all been identified and dealt with.

The second strategy was a defensive one. The local leaders attempted to impress on both the Beijing students and local residents how successful the HPPC and the WMPC had been the during past seventeen years as well as in the first two months of the Cultural Revolution. Zhang Tixue never missed an opportunity to defend the record of the HPPC. On more than one occasion, he declared with pride, 'Holding high the banner of Mao Zedong Thought, the HPPC has never failed to implement the general and specific policies of the Party Centre.... Our general orientation has always been correct.'[27] This was a strategy of using defence as a means of silencing the attackers and winning sympathy.

The third was an offensive strategy. In order to maintain their monopoly on information and to destroy the Beijing students' credibility, the local leaders told the residents of Wuhan that the Beijing students had brought nothing but hearsay to the city. The only reliable information source was still the formal channels operated through the Party hierarchy.[28]

Furthermore, the HPPC and the WMPC secretly mobilized forces to launch counterattacks against the rebels from Beijing. On 30 August a letter of appeal drafted by the HPPC was published under the name of 'The students of Hubei University'. The letter maintained that Beijing students represented an 'adverse current' that was blocking the development of the Cultural Revolution in Wuhan. It also asserted that any attack on the HPPC was an indirect attack on Mao and the Party leadership. The next day, the WMPC formulated another urgent letter of appeal, also under false pretences, calling for a resistance against 'a handful of students from Beijing'.[29] To prove that those who were making trouble in Wuhan were really just 'a handful', the local leaders needed to find some sympathizers among the Beijing students.[30] Wang

Renzhong assisted in this. Taking advantage of his position as a deputy head of the CRSG, Wang sent several groups of Beijing Red Guards that he had carefully assembled to Wuhan. Led by Pu Dahua and Song Yaowu, two nationally well-known Red Guards at the time,[31] the mission of those groups was to defend the HPPC and the WMPC. Acting as 'real' Beijing Red Guards, they praised the Wuhan leadership and condemned those who were attacking the HPPC and the WMPC. The Wuhan power élite regarded them as relief troops and treated them with special care.[32]

The efforts of the HPPC and the WMPC were effective, at least for the moment. Local residents, including the local Red Guards, had from the beginning regarded the attack on the HPPC and the WMPC as outrageous. They now began to launch a counterattack against the students from Beijing, who soon found that they were unwelcome in Wuhan.

However, they were not prepared to give in. On 31 August, Mao received Red Guards in Beijing for the second time, and the Beijing students in Wuhan demanded an interview with the governor. Zhang Tixue, however, declined the request, on the ground that he did not want to appear to be at the beck and call of students. The two sides were thus headed for a collision. On the night of 2 September, forty Beijing students staged a sit-in in front of the HPPC building. The next day, when the number had increased to over 2,000, they decided to go on a hunger strike. This was an unprecedented event and caused a sensation throughout the city. The majority of ordinary workers and cadres objected to the disturbance of civil order, and local residents flocked to the site of the sit-in to condemn the students for attacking the Party leadership.[33] This popular support strengthened the uncompromising stand of the local authorities.

On 4 September the HPPC held a welcome meeting for students from Beijing and other provinces at Wuchang Stadium. In his speech, Zhang Tixue indicated that he had no intention of offering an apology to the striking students.[34] When asked if he supported the sit-in, Zhang replied, 'I support only leftists, not rightists.' This statement enraged the hunger strikers. In protest, they staged a demonstration march in the city and sent some students back to Beijing to lodge a complaint about the HPPC with the CRSG. That night, the head of the HPPC Secretariat, Wang Shucheng, delivered an urgent speech over the local broadcasting networks. He claimed to give an objective account of what was happening in the city. But the words he chose, and the way he described the events, hinted that the sit-in students were responsible for the disturbances.[35]

As expected, Wang's speech gave rise to a new wave of popular

protest against the students from Beijing. At that moment, local authorities in all the provinces were facing challenges from *chuanlian* students.
In some places, the tension resulted in physical fighting between *chuanlian* students and local residents. By comparison, the situation in Wuhan
was relatively stable, so stable that Zhang Tixue could proudly proclaim,
'We have won the first round.'[36]

On 7 September, Mao severely criticized some local leaders for
having incited the workers and peasants against the rebellious students.[37]
As an insider, Wang Renzhong telephoned Zhang Tixue the next day,
advising him to make a self-criticism to *chuanlian* students.[38] But Zhang
thought Wang was being overcautious. Since 5 September, many handbills extolling the HPPC had appeared in the city. Someone had even
composed a song, 'The HPPC is Really Good.'[39] The pro-HPPC forces
were largely spontaneous, which made Zhang believe that the situation
in Wuhan was different from the places Mao had criticized.[40] He failed
to realize that the rules of the game were undergoing a dramatic change.

On 12 September, those Beijing students who had gone back to
Beijing on 4 September returned to Wuhan. They had met Tao Zhu, the
number-four man of the central Party leadership, on 8 September. On
their return, posters appeared throughout the city, claiming that Tao had
instructed Zhang Tixue to make a self-criticism. The *chuanlian* students
also put forward a provocative slogan, 'Down with the HPPC'. This
shocked the city. If the *chuanlian* students' claim were true, it would
explode the myth that the provincial leadership was inviolable. The citizens of Wuhan were so anxious that about one million people gathered
in the streets over the following days to debate whether the HPPC had
made any mistakes. The predominant opinion was that it had not. Most
local residents simply could not believe that a few students would be
able to change the rules of the game established over the past seventeen
years. In direct opposition to the slogan put forward by the *chuanlian*
students, 'Defend the HPPC' became the slogan of the pro-HPPC
forces.[41]

On 15 September the HPPC invited representatives of both the *chuanlian* and local students to a so-called consultative meeting. The meeting
turned into another battle. The *chuanlian* students insisted that Tao Zhu
had instructed Zhang Tixue to make a self-criticism. But according to
the HPPC, Tao had condemned the slogans 'Down with the HPPC' and
'Down with Zhang Tixue'. The pro-HPPC students believed the story
given by the Party authority. They protested that the Beijing students
had shamelessly distorted Tao's instruction. Moved by the enthusiastic
support of the local students, Zhang momentarily lost his head. He made

an emotional, impromptu speech, in which he said, 'In the name of myself and thirty million Hubei people, I condemn Zhao Guilin [a student from the People's University who was the leader of the Beijing students in Wuhan at the time].' The meeting broke up in discord.[42]

Over the following days, numerous mass rallies were held to denounce the Beijing students. At the same time, a great number of pro-HPPC posters and handbills appeared. The rebellious Beijing students thus were put in an awkward predicament. Everywhere they went, they were surrounded by hostile crowds. On 19 September, Zhang Tixue once again proudly declared, 'We are the winners.' Fourteen days before, he had said this only in a closed meeting room of the HPPC, but now he made the statement at a mass rally.[43] On 25 September, Zhao Guilin left Wuhan for Beijing, which was taken as a sure sign that the *chuanlian* students' challenge had failed.[44]

At about this time, Mao decided to completely rewrite the rules of the game. By late September, he had realized that the original Red Guards were the force of the *status quo*. But rebellious forces he could rely upon were only a tiny minority, even in Beijing, not to mention in the provinces. What had made the situation so difficult for the minority students were the rules of the game established during the past seventeen years. In an attempt to move the seemingly stagnant Cultural Revolution forward, Mao decided to take a clear-cut stand to support the minority. At the beginning of October the CRSG made an earth-shattering announcement: wrong political labels imposed on students during recent months must be removed, wrong classifications must be declared invalid, and individuals who had been wrongly treated must be rehabilitated. The implications of this action were twofold. On the one hand, it broke a myth previously held by both the power élites and ordinary citizens: that the local authorities represented the Party leadership and Mao, and so were untouchable. On the other hand, it was a licence, as well as an encouragement, for individuals who had been victimized in recent months to demand remedies from the local authorities. In a phrase, it was right to rebel.

When Mao made this about-face, Wang Renzhong did not forget to telephone his clients in Wuhan. He advised the HPPC to be more careful in dealing with *chuanlian* students and the local 'minority'. But the leaders in Wuhan were complacent about their recent victory over the *chuanlian* students and did not catch the urgency in Wang's message. It took another phone call from Wang to gain the Wuhan leaders' attention. This time Wang dictated in unequivocal terms that the HPPC must acknowledge Zhao Guilin as a 'revolutionary path breaker' and make a self-criticism for what it had done to the *chuanlian* students and the local 'minority'.[45] This was a crucial turning point for the Cultural Revolution in Wuhan, after which the authority of the HPPC and the WMPC began to crack.

The *chuanlian* helped to upset the existing political equilibrium and to create a situation favourable for the emergence of rebels. They did this in three ways. First, the *chuanlian* could turn conservatives into rebels. In August 1966 the original Red Guards made public one of Mao's quotations: 'The essence of Marxist principles in the final analysis can be summed up in one phrase, that is, it is right to rebel.' Now everyone wanted to appear rebellious. However, whereas those who really wanted to see changes did not dare to challenge the seemingly mighty local authorities, those who were most active in August and September were people who had no desire to see fundamental changes. The latter would do whatever they could to preserve the existing power relations in their work units and in the localities in which they lived. In such a situation, there seemed little hope of upsetting the existing political equilibrium. The *chuanlian* changed the equation. When conservative elements travelled to other places where they had no relations with the local power networks, there was a possibility that they might act as rebels. This was exactly what was happening.

In late August and early September, only good-origin students were allowed to go for *chuanlian*. The majority of Beijing students who initiated the attack on the Wuhan authorities thus must have been conservatives in their own schools.[46] The slogans put forward by Beijing students revealed their true nature. The three most controversial slogans they were advocating at the time were 'Bombard the HPPC', 'Suspect Everything', and 'Long Live the Principle of Born Red'. The third was a conservative trade-mark. More interestingly, the Beijing students rarely raised the issue of the work team when they attacked the Wuhan authorities. This could not be accidental. A more plausible explanation was that most of the rebellious Beijing students had once been the work teams' 'fair-haired boys' in their own schools. It was ironical that those who first kindled the flames of revolution in Wuhan were conservatives from Beijing. Zhang Tixue was probably the first person to realize this irony. At a meeting in September, he questioned why the children of high-level cadres from Beijing were so hostile to high-level cadres in Wuhan.[47] The *chuanlian* thus worked as a mechanism to turn conservatives in one place into radicals in other places.[48]

Second, the *chuanlian* helped to bring about organized local opposition forces. When confronting the Wuhan authorities, *chuanlian* students looked hard for local allies.[49] They did have some local sympathizers, but those sympathizers were still wavering, scattered, and unorganized. It was too risky for them to show their support of *chuanlian* students in public.[50] As the scope of the *chuanlian* expanded in mid-September, more information about what was going on in other places began to flow into Wuhan. Moreover, by the end of September, a large number of local students had begun to return from their trips to other places.[51] Either through personal experiences in Beijing and in other cities or through news brought back by a steady stream of *chuanlian* students from other parts of the country, more and more Wuhan residents began to become aware that the rules of the game they had been familiar with in the past were undergoing significant changes. They learned that it was no big deal to 'bombard' local authorities, that one school could have more than one Red Guard organization, and that the 'minority' students should have the same right as the majority to set up their own organization. In effect, the risks attached to being a rebel were not as high as many had previously believed. Thus, late September 1966 saw the emergence of the first minority organizations in some colleges in Wuhan. As a way of distinguishing themselves from the original Red Guards, those small groups usually called themselves Mao Zedong Thought Red Guards.[52] That the monopolistic position of the original Red Guard organization was broken was a crucial development in the Cultural Revolution, which opened the door to factional conflicts.[53]

Third, the *chuanlian* helped to change the balance between the conservatives and the rebels in colleges and high schools. In September, almost all good-origin students went out for *chuanlian* and their absence relieved the pressure on students from middle and bad class backgrounds. In October, however, middle- and even bad-origin students were allowed to go *chuanlian*. When they were away from Wuhan, no one knew their identities, so they could act in the way everyone else did.[54] More significantly, they quickly realized that the main target of the Cultural Revolution was capitalist roaders, rather than people like their parents. The *chuanlian* thus offered them a chance to re-evaluate their position in society and their role in the movement. When they returned to school with new ideas in November and December, the so-called bourgeois reactionary line had been thoroughly refuted and they joined radical organizations in large numbers.

The Breakdown of Local Authority and the Emergence of Rebels in the Schools

One of the most significant turning points in the Cultural Revolution occurred in October 1966. Mao and the CRSG opened fire at what they called 'the reactionary bourgeois line', which in effect reversed the course of the movement. The local authorities were ordered to rehabilitate all those who had been branded 'counter-revolutionaries', 'anti-party elements', and 'rightists' in the first months of the movement, and to destroy in public all 'black materials' contained in their dossiers.[55] Then, on the motion of Mao, a central work conference was convened, at which provincial officials were criticized for having been passive, defensive, and restrictive in dealing with rebellious students.[56] The conference was a nightmare for the Hubei officials in particular. From Wang Renzhong, Zhang Tixue learned that Mao had criticized him for 'having fallen behind the situation', and he had to make a self-criticism.[57] Unexpectedly, Wang Renzhong himself soon became a victim. Immediately after the conference, Wang was ordered to leave Beijing for Hainan Island, which signalled his fall from power.[58]

In Wuhan, the movement also took a sudden turn in October. Until 4 October, local officials were still confident that they had made no 'line mistakes'.[59] As the pressure from Beijing grew, however, their confidence dissipated. At first, they tried to survive the storm by playing the same old trick—'giving up pawns to save the knight'—again. The deputy director of the Provincial Culture Bureau, Ren Qing, and the deputy secretary general of the WMPC, Shi Yu, were publicly denounced.[60] But such attempts now produced no effect. Local officials thus were left with no choice but to admit their 'mistakes' and to make apologies to *chuanlian* students and to local minority students.[61] Wang Renzhong's fall from power wiped out their last gleam of hope for a quick recovery.

The power structure of the Chinese political system was like a pyramid, in which power élites at every level derived their legitimacy from upper levels of power, and ultimately from Mao. In the first seventeen years of the People's Republic, those power élites had become used to unified leadership and unchecked authority. With the support from above, they could suppress challengers from below with little effort. But they had had no experience of dealing independently with challengers. In the first few months of the Cultural Revolution, the Wuhan officials had Wang Renzhong as a powerful patron in Beijing, so they felt secure and acted with confidence. Now their patron had gone and Beijing was turning its back on them. Without support from above, the local leaders were at their wits' end.

While the radical ideas brought into Wuhan by *chuanlian* students paved the way for the emergence of local rebel groups, the decline in authority of the local leadership further reduced the risk of collective action. Moreover, many attributed the enfeeblement of the local power organs at least partially to the heroic efforts of the rebel forerunners. The local authorities' increasing pusillanimity in dealing with the minority students was seen as proof that collective action could be efficacious and fruitful. The initial success of the nascent rebel movement thus decisively altered potential rebels' calculations of the marginal benefits of collective action, making it even more attractive than before.

In the middle of October, when Zhao Guilin returned to Wuhan from another trip to Beijing,[62] he found that *chuanlian* students were no longer able to play the leading role in the fight against the local authorities. By then, the monopoly of the original Red Guard organization had been broken, and the alienated students had begun to set up their own organizations. Criticism of the 'reactionary line' enabled those who had been excluded from the original Red Guard organizations to make their presence felt. For the first time, all students, regardless of their family origins, were given the freedom to set up political groups in schools. Practically anyone who wanted to set up an organization could do so. All that was needed was a catchy name with which to recruit members.

Organizations were not required to be registered with the authorities. Even if there were no followers, it could be a one-person organization. The founders of such organizations were called generals without soldiers (*guanggan shilin*). Once a group was formed, it was entitled to receive financial aid, in one form or another, from its school. All groups wanted to have their own mimeographs, stencils, stencil steel boards, papers, and broadcasting equipment, but the schools were unable to meet all their demands. There were numerous reports in October and November of groups stealing or taking by force equipment that belonged to other groups. In any event, individual members did not have to spend any of their own money to keep their organizations functioning, which made the formation and operation of mass organizations financially viable. The same was true of non-student organizations in the later period of the Cultural Revolution. This factor made collective action relatively easy.

As a result of the free-wheeling formation of associations, October 1966 saw the emergence of countless organizations in every school. These new groups all had one thing in common: their members resented the exclusiveness of the original Red Guard organizations. In the fanatical political atmosphere of the Cultural Revolution, the sense of belonging to a group was very important. Since the original Red Guard organizations were very exclusive, once their organizational monopoly was broken, the first reaction of those who had been excluded was to set up their own organizations or join other newly established groups. In this way they achieved self-realization, self-respect, and other forms of psychological satisfaction.

In order to compete with the original Red Guards, the new groups were generally more willing to co-operate with one another and form loose coalitions. By the middle of October, students had been largely divided into two camps in most schools: the original Red Guards and the Mao Zedong Thought Red Guards (referred to as Thought Guards). Since the former had already set up a headquarters to co-ordinate the city-wide activities of branches in individual schools in mid-September,[63] the latter quickly moved to build their own city-wide networks.[64] In late October the Thought Guards underwent a rapid expansion. Two strategies contributed to its success. First, its criteria for membership were much more flexible than those of the original Red Guards. Whereas the Red Guards accepted only students of the five red categories, and in extreme cases only children of high-level cadres, the Thought Guards welcomed virtually everyone.[65] Second, the Thought Guards were adept at prodding those who remained on the fence to join their ranks. One way of doing this was to publish so-called black materials, especially the secret lists prepared by work teams and Party committees that classified people into five categories. Many people joined radical organizations simply because they discovered they had been put into categories worse than they had expected.[66]

The organizational expansion boosted the Thought Guards' courage. In the last ten days of October, the Thought Guards began to assume the offensive. They took over public announcement systems in some schools, seized archives in others, and ousted Cultural Revolution committees in still others.[67] In the meantime, they were preparing to establish a headquarters to co-ordinate the city-wide activities of all Thought Guards. Every college was invited to send a few delegates to participate in the preparation. Because the Thought Guards first emerged at the Central China Institute of Technology and at Hubei University, the delegates from these two schools expected the others to recognize them as the natural leaders. They also wanted to impose the declaration and constitution of the organization they had drafted on the other participants. Their arrogance, however, evoked a strong aversion among the delegates, who insisted that only CCP members with pure backgrounds might be elected as leaders, for none of the delegates from the two schools met this criterion. As a result, Yang Daoyuan, a student at Wuhan Institute of Topography, was chosen as the leader of the future headquarters, despite his apparent unsuitability to lead a large organization. Disappointed by the result of the election, the Thought Guards from the Central China Institute of Technology and Hubei University withdrew from the united Thought Guard organization to set up their own headquarters. Thus when the Wuhan Thought Guard Headquarters (the Second Headquarters, as it was called) was formally established on 26 October, the Thought Guards from those two schools were not included. Later their independent headquarters were commonly known as New Central China Institute of Technology and New Hubei University. The failure to form a united organization did not immediately lead to open conflict among the Thought Guards, because they were still facing formidable foes—the local authorities and conservative forces. During this time of uncertainty, what they needed was a strong coalition. However, the latent internal contradictions resulting from this incident would surface, as we shall see, when their common enemies were gone.[68]

The establishment of the Second Headquarters was a significant event. Some provincial leaders attended the inaugural meeting of the Second Headquarters. This gesture signified that the local authorities, for the first time, had to recognize the right of existence of opposition forces. Compared with the situation during the preceding seventeen years, this was a sea change in politics.

The Thought Guards quickly grew into a formidable force. On 1 November, when the Thought Guards disrupted an important meeting of the HHPC, the provincial power holders felt almost helpless. They no longer dared to restrain local opposition, for any attempt to do so could be condemned by Mao and the CRSG as 'suppressing the revolutionary masses'. All the local authorities could do was to open negotiations with the rebellious students on an equal footing.[69]

The most important result of the criticism of the bourgeois reactionary line was that it destroyed the legitimacy of the local authorities. As radical central policies chipped away at the legitimacy of the local authorities, the latter's main function—social control—was paralyzed. This development gave rise to a question: Could Mao control and direct the social forces he had unleashed without the support of adequate mechanisms of social control?

In the past, the local authorities had served as 'gatekeepers' monitoring communications between the power centre and the grassroots, and as enforcers executing Mao's directives. The hierarchical structure of power could minimize the possibility of deviations among the masses by standardizing the interpretation of messages from Beijing, and by punishing non-compliant behaviours. Of course, there was a danger in this model that the local authorities might either deliberately or unintentionally misrepresent messages from Beijing, as had happened during the first few months of the Cultural Revolution. Nevertheless, it was much easier for the Party leaders in Beijing to deal directly with a few gatekeepers than with millions of people. Now, the old authority structure was disintegrating, and no new structure was in sight to replace it. All that remained was Mao's personal authority, and this was strengthened during this period. There was no doubt that the cult of personality could serve as a tool of popular mobilization. However, it was not clear whether the cult as such could substitute for the mechanisms of social control. An effective leadership is supposed to have two functions: energizing and directing.[70] If a leader succeeds only in energizing but not in directing, he will see the followers he has energized move in directions other than what he intends. As the following chapters will show, the cult of personality *per se* could not help to realize Mao's will, however faithful millions of people might claim themselves to be, because Mao destroyed the social control mechanisms that were necessary for him to dictate to and co-ordinate the popular forces.

The Proliferation of Mass Organizations

The most significant development in the last two months of 1966 was that the movement went beyond the bounds of cultural and educational institutions to enter virtually every quarter of society.

Since the very beginning of the Cultural Revolution, factories had been largely untouched by what was happening in the schools and in society generally. The Sixteen Articles stated: 'The cultural and educational institutions, and the leading bodies of the Party and government in large and medium-sized cities are the focal points of the ongoing Cultural Revolution movement.' It further specified that for workers, the movement meant merely a campaign 'to foster proletarian ideology and to eliminate bourgeois ideology'. In September, the Party centre attempted to confine the scope of the movement by stipulating that political activities in factories should not take place during working hours.[71] Thus, the workers did little more than attend political study sessions and discuss central directives. Regular production was not disturbed, and most workers never imagined that they would one day be allowed to act like riotous students.[72]

Some factory workers—those who had been branded as 'rightists', 'elements of local three-family villages', 'counter-revolutionaries', and the like in June and July—envied the students. Since student victims of 'the bourgeois reactionary line' had been rehabilitated, they wanted their honour redeemed too. But they had to weigh the potential risks before making a move. By watching carefully every turn of the movement, they became very sensitive to subtle changes in the official line. In August and September, when they still could not openly pursue their goals, some workers established secret ties within their units to assess the situation, to exchange opinions, and, more important, to give each other moral support.[73] New information was extremely valuable to them, and to get the latest news they looked beyond official channels. For this reason, they were attracted to the *chuanlian* students. In September, Hubei University, an assigned reception centre, was the base camp for *chuanlian* students in Wuhan. A number of discontented workers went there after work to quietly gather information, and they soon got to know one another. Various secret networks thus developed, which were the embryos of future radical worker organizations. Among those workers, many would become famous over the next ten years.[74]

In October 1966, inspired by the victory of the minority students, the alienated workers became a little more aggressive. If the grievances of student 'rightists' could be redressed, they figured that the labels imposed on them might also be removed. They therefore stepped up their activities. The first thing to be done was to win the sympathy of rebellious students. Their stories of how they had been persecuted by the bourgeois reactionary line quickly drew the attention of the students. The latter saw that the workers' cases could serve as new evidence against the HPPC and the WMPC. Some rebel students made frequent contact with workers, and encouraged them to look for more comrades and to organize collective efforts to put pressure on those who held power. In this sense, those students played the role of political entrepreneurs. Gradually, a number of informal networks developed between the worker activists and rebellious students, among which the most extensive one emerged in Wuchang. In September and October, Wuchang was the main battlefield in the fighting between the *chuanlian* students and local minorities on the one hand and the local authorities on the other. It was not surprising, therefore, that the alienated workers in Wuchang were able to develop a closer tie with radical students than their counterparts in other districts.[75]

In late October, when the situation became unmistakably favourable to the radical students, the worker activists finally dispelled their misgivings and decided openly to declare their existence. On 28 October the Wuchang network held its first independent rally to criticize the reactionary line implemented by the HPPC. A week later it joined forces with the Second Headquarters and some other student radical organizations in staging a mass gathering, which put forward the slogan, 'Bombard the HPPC'.[76] A worker rebel organization called Workers' Headquarters came into being in Wuhan on 9 November, the same day that the famous Headquarters of Rebellious Workers was formally established in Shanghai.[77] Mao did not lift the ban on worker mass organizations until a number of such organizations had emerged in several cities. After some hesitation, Beijing finally removed the ban on 13 November.[78]

The legalization of autonomous worker organizations was one of the most important turning points of the Cultural Revolution. If workers were allowed to set up their own organizations, it was felt that people in other sectors should be entitled to enjoy the same right. For the first time, Chinese were free to organize themselves into whatever groups they wanted, as long as they claimed to be loyal to the supreme leader of the state—Mao. However limited this freedom might be, it awakened people's consciousness of self-interests or group interests that had long been suppressed, and provided the opportunity to pursue those interests. Multifarious mass organizations thus emerged in the following months. For instance, there were groups of artists, contract workers, apprentices, cooks, veterans, elementary school teachers, middle school teachers, teachers in schools run by communities, policemen, judges, prosecutors, street cleaners, doctors, militias, members of the Socialist Education Movement work teams, blind persons, and so on.

Soon after its establishment, the Workers' Headquarters experienced a 'palace coup'. The original leader, a worker at a medium-sized factory, was forced to resign from his position by some of his comrades from large enterprises, who justified their action on the ground that persons from large enterprises were in a much better position gain popular support. In the following months, four more 'coups' took place. As a result, the power of the Workers' Headquarters was gradually concentrated in the hands of a group of young workers from a few very large factories, such as Wuhan Heavy Machinery, Wuhan Boiler, and Wuchang Shipyard. This process caused rebellious workers to split into several factions. For instance, after being forced to resign, the former head of the Workers' Headquarters formed, with his followers, the 17 August Corps, which for the next two years didn't get along with the Workers' Headquarters.[79]

While the Workers' Headquarters was being established in Wuchang, another rebel worker organization was taking shape in Hankou. Its birthplace, Wuhan Electronic Device, was a medium-sized factory. In

October the factory became well-known when some of the workers waged a vigorous offensive against the Socialist Education Movement work team stationed there. The workers' actions quickly attracted the attention of both rebellious students and alienated workers in other factories. With the help of students from the Central China Institute of Technology, these workers formed a small core group, which in turn sent people to support workers in other factories. Over time, a network developed, culminating in the Workers' Rebel Headquarters which formally declared its existence on 8 December.[80] Four days later, another radical workers' organization, the 13 September Corps, emerged in Qingshan District, where two giant enterprises, Wuhan Iron and Steel and the First Metallurgical Corporation, were located.[81] The Workers' Headquarters, the Workers' Rebel Headquarters, and the 13 September Corps henceforth became leaders among the numerous smaller radical workers' organizations in Wuhan. Later, the Workers' Headquarters managed to penetrate many enterprises in all six districts of Wuhan, whereas the Workers' Rebel Headquarters and the 13 September Corps had little influence outside the regions where they originated. The 13 September Corps recruited its members mainly from Wuhan Iron and Steel and the First Metallurgical Corperation, and the Workers' Rebel Headquarters drew its forces largely from small and medium-sized factories in Hankou.[82]

The proliferation of mass organizations opened the door for rebels to strike at the roots of China's bureaucratic structure. Before November 1966, although the provincial and municipal authorities had come under increasingly fierce attack and the authority of school officials had almost completely crumbled, the power relations that had existed prior to the Cultural Revolution had remained largely intact in all sectors except education, because adult mass organizations were still considered illegal. The proliferation of mass organizations thus threatened to break the power equilibrium in all sectors and to throw society as a whole off balance.

The Conservatives versus the Rebels

Radical workers began to gain momentum in December, but in most cases they were still a tiny minority in each unit.[83] Most cadres, CCP members, CYL members, activists, and senior workers were perplexed by the rise of radical workers' organizations. In their eyes, good people would not be rebellious, and rebels could not be good people. They could not understand why the rebels seemed to have support from Beijing, why the provincial and municipal Party committees were under fire, and why Beijing tolerated the increasingly chaotic situation.[84] They gradually came to the end of their patience when the rebels began to run rampant.

On 9 November the Second Headquarters and other radical organizations occupied the offices of the *Hubei Daily*, the organ of the HPPC, and threatened to close the paper. The Central Southern Bureau, a Party organ that supervised Party activities in China's central southern region, including Hubei, Henan, Hunan, and Guangdong provinces, intervened, but the rebels ignored the warning. A week later, the paper was closed.[85] It was probably the first instance in China of this sort of thing happening.[86] The closure incurred the wrath of a great number of local residents. In the days that followed, workers, cadres, students, and people from all walks of life surrounded the *Hubei Daily* building, shouting, '*Hubei Daily* is the tool of the proletarian dictatorship and the organ of the CCP' and 'We want to read the *Hubei Daily*'. They tried to force the rebels to leave the building. Unexpectedly, however, Zhang Tixue made a statement recognizing the rebels' action as a revolutionary action on 18 November. Both the editorial board of the paper and the HPPC made public self-criticisms for the 'mistakes' the paper had allegedly made in recent months. But the concession pleased no one. After being given an inch, the rebels tried to take a mile. While continuing their occupation of the newspaper office, they made more claims to the HPPC. The concession also disillusioned supporters of the HPPC. Protesting the committee's 'capitulationism', they decided it was time to set up their own organization.[87] Initiated by a group of workers from the Wuhan Machine factory, the Federation of Revolutionary Labourers took shape on 2 December. It quickly expanded into an organization of 400,000 members.[88]

A conservative organization in nature, the Federation of Revolutionary Labourers was moderate in action. Thus, when caught in the crossfire between the rebels and the conservatives, the HPPC would rather please the former than the latter. On 15 December the HPPC officially decided to stop publication of the *Hubei Daily*, which was widely considered a shameful submission to the rebels' pressure. The rebels, as a result, became wilder, and on 18–19 December they raided the headquarters of both the Red Guards and the Federation of Revolutionary Labourers.[89]

While the rebel organizations were getting the upper hand in dealing with the provincial and municipal authorities, individual rebellious workers became emboldened to make personal claims within their units. The so-called black materials were the hottest issue. According to a definition given by Zhou Enlai, premier of the State Council, 'black materials' were materials compiled by work teams and Party committees in the period between 16 May and 8 August 1966 (the date when the Sixteen Articles were made public). The CRSG ordered that self-criticisms written by victims must be returned to their authors, and that other forms of black materials should be publicly destroyed.[90] The rebels wanted to know, in addition to the materials compiled after 16 May, what else was in their dossiers. Unit leaders, however, preferred to hand out as few materials as possible, for they thought that some materials were too valuable to give to the rebels, even if they had been collected after 16 May.[91] Former activists also objected to the rebels seeing their dossiers, as there might be some materials that were based on their exposures. Besides, the unit leaders and activists did not believe that the rebels, many of whom had long been considered villains, would be in the ascendancy for long.

When one side wanted more materials to be released and the other side declined to hand them out, tension grew. The problem was that neither Beijing nor the HPPC and the WMPC had ever made it clear who had the right to decide which material was 'black' and which was not, who had the right to verify whether all black materials had been presented, and who had the rights to arbitrate the disputes that arose in the process of sorting out black materials.[92] Without rules and rule enforcers, rebels from many units simply seized all personal dossiers by force. Such actions often led to violent conflicts.[93] One such incident resulted in the death of a female archivist, who happened to be a member of the Federation of Revolutionary Labourers. Seizing on the incident, the Federation launched a counterattack against the rebels. On 25 December, a snowy day, workers from all over the city gathered at Xinhualu Stadium, the largest stadium in Wuhan, to hold a memorial rally for the woman. Following the rally, they staged a mammoth demonstration. Many units even flew the national flag at half-mast. The whole operation was quite successful in itself, but the rebels pointed out that it took place just one day before Mao's birthday (26 December). They accused the Federation of attacking Chairman Mao, on the grounds that some of the portraits of the deceased woman carried by marchers during the rally and the demonstration were larger than those of Mao. When a handbill distributed by the Federation, containing a floral border around a quotation from Mao, was found to be composed of plane-shaped marks, the rebels charged that the Federation meant to 'bomb' Chairman Mao. To outsiders, the rebels' accusations may sound ridiculous, and the whole episode may seem patently silly. But every Chinese at the time knew that even an unpremeditated insult to Mao's image was unpardonable. The Federation of Revolutionary Labourers thus found it hard to vindicate itself.[94]

Misfortunes never come singly. Before the incident of 25 December had quieted down, more bad news came in from Guangzhou, where the Central Southern Bureau was located: under the pressure of a group of Wuhan rebels, Li Yiqing, a leader of the Central Southern Bureau, had stated that the Federation of Revolutionary Labourers was a 'conservative organization'. 'Conservative' was considered a dirty word in Communist China. Calling someone or some organization 'conservative' was an indignity, especially in a feverish revolutionary context like the Cultural Revolution. The Federation considered Li's remark an outrageous insult. Most of its members had long been the backbone of the socialist revolution and construction. How could they be conservatives? In the first few days of 1967, thousands of workers surrounded the HPPC, demanding that it retract Li's assertion. Unfortunately, the weather let them down. An unseasonable blizzard brought the temperature down to below zero, and it was impossible to keep up an outdoor protest for long under such conditions. As a result, the operation was aborted.[95]

Even worse than the weather was the political climate. Beijing was taking an increasingly hostile attitude towards conservative forces in the nation. Conservatives were those for whom respect of authority had been a moral code. Without official recognition, their organizations could not hold out.

In contrast to the conservative organizations, radical organizations were advancing at full steam by the beginning of 1967. With the support of the radical leaders in Beijing, they were now in a position to dismantle all the symbols of the old power relations. Their targets were the organs of power, individual power holders, and conservatives. Under pressure from the rebels, the HPPC and the WMPC made a number of self-criticisms in December. But the rebels were no longer content with apologies. On the last day of 1966 they closed down the *Wuhan Evening News*, the official newspaper of the WMPC. The *Hubei Daily* and the *Wuhan Evening News* had been the city's only two newspapers. With both of them now shut, the HPPC and the WMPC not only lost their mouthpieces but also had difficulty in proving their existence. Indeed, after this episode, the two organs of power in effect stopped functioning. As far as individual power holders were concerned, no one in Wuhan had been more powerful than Wang Renzhong. On 25 December, Wang was brought back to Wuhan from Guangdong by a group of rebels. Two days later, nineteen rebel organizations founded a United Command Post for Struggling against Wang Renzhong. In the first three days of 1967, three mass rallies were held to denounce the former First Secretary of the HPPC. As the prestige of the city's former number one man was destroyed, the rebels no longer had scruples about attacking the power holders in their units. Almost all of the Party cadres were 'kicked aside'. The rebels held criticism- and struggle-sessions against them, and paraded them in the streets in order to humiliate them. Moreover, the rebels launched a fierce attack on the conservatives. The headquarters of the Red Guards was raided on 29 December. On 5 January the Workers' Headquarters even set out to bust the leaders of the Federation of Revolutionary Labourers. As a result, 3,100 people were taken into custody.[96] Wuhan fell into the hands of the rebels.

The story of the rise of rebel forces in Wuhan illustrates how important political opportunity is for mass mobilization. In the first few months of the Cultural Revolution, because the old rules of the game remained largely unchanged, the high risks involved in defiant action effectively deterred potential rebels from coming to the fore. The first groups of local student rebels did not declare their existence until students from Beijing had shown them the vulnerability of the local authorities. Even then, adult rebels kept a low profile. It was only after Mao had decisively crippled the social control apparatus and the students had further tested the limits of rebellion that adult rebels began to cast aside their misgivings and jump on the bandwagon. The people had had little incentive to act when action was likely to beget suppression. Their decision to take part in the Cultural Revolution was thus based mainly upon careful calculation of the possible individual pay-offs.

5

The Anatomy of Factionalism

The Composition of Conflicting Factions

THE FIRST six months of the Cultural Revolution was a phase of mobilization. By the end of this period, Wuhan residents had been divided into two extremely loose groupings: the rebels and the conservatives. As suggested above, those who suffered during the first two months were most likely to become rebels. However, not every such victim was in the ranks of the radical organizations and not every rebel was a former victim. And the rebels themselves were internally divided, though these tensions had not yet surfaced. Personal experiences in the opening stages of the Cultural Revolution alone, it seems, do not tell the whole story of the movement's factionalism. Chen Yi, the Foreign Minister, hit the nail on the head when he pointed out, 'Some have suggested that the factionalism was caused by the wrong policy of dispatching work teams. But there is a strong factionalism in Shandong Province where no work team was sent at all. In my judgement, the factionalism is a reflection of underlying conflicts between classes and strata in our society.'[1]

What was the relationship between factionalism during the Cultural Revolution and the social structure in China in the years leading up to it? Several observations are noteworthy.

The Composition of Conservative Organizations

Generally those who had enjoyed a comparatively close relationship with the authorities before the Cultural Revolution tended to become conservatives during the movement. This was the case not only in schools but also in industries; not only in Wuhan, but also in other places. In fact, this tended to be the case throughout the decade of upheaval. During the course of the movement, conservative organizations often attacked radical organizations on the ground that the latter were the hideouts of 'monsters and ghosts'. The rebels, however, could not use the same accusation against their adversaries. The conservatives were proud of the 'purity' of their family backgrounds and of their political performance before the Cultural Revolution. The rebels could hardly deny that their claim was well founded. Mao also noted that the majority of CCP members, CYL members, activists, and ordinary workers were affiliated with conservative organizations, but he attributed this phenomenon mainly to the capitalist roaders' alleged efforts to mislead them.[2]

This was not the case. With the collapse of the old power structure, the Cultural Revolution provided an opportunity for everyone to make a choice between radical and conservative organizations. 'Whether one participated and with which faction was completely voluntary. There was no longer a need to show off one's activism in order to win institutionalized approval.'[3] The majority of people voluntarily joined conservative groups, not because they were afraid of, or had been mislead by, former officials, but because they sincerely believed that the old structure was basically sound. The economic, social, and political status of most workers had improved after 1949. Moreover, in their view, most Party cadres were trustworthy, because they had enjoyed little economic privilege, rarely abused their power for personal pecuniary gains, and generally were on good terms with their subordinates. Although there had been a number of political campaigns in which some people were victimized, most workers had always been relied upon as activists or allies. They therefore saw little reason to rebel against the basically sound system and its operators.

The Composition of Rebel Organizations

What kinds of people were likely to be rebels? In schools, the rebels were those who had been excluded from the original Red Guards. In factories and other units, they were people who had been alienated before the Cultural Revolution or during the first few months of the movement.[4] It was not surprising, therefore, that many more people of non-proletarian origins were in radical organizations than in conservative ones.[5] In an attempt to turn their political liability into political capital, some rebel theorists put forward a theory of 'changed class relationship' to explain the phenomenon. According to them, the class structure of China had changed since 1949. Many people from good class backgrounds had degenerated into 'aristocrats of labour,' and formed new vested interests, while the former semi-proletariat, petit bourgeoisie, and bourgeoisie had become proletariat. During the first seventeen years of the People's Republic, the latter group had been often unjustly persecuted in political campaigns. They constituted a new oppressed class, and thus they were justified in rising against the establishment.[6] Furthermore, those radical theorists argued that there were

now two basic classes in contemporary China: the rebellious class represented by them, and the conservative class represented by their enemies.
The struggle between the two classes would continue throughout the
entire period of socialist development. This theory was very attractive
among rebel rank-and-filers.[7]

Class background, however, was not the sole variable of factional
alignment. For instance, the leaders of the Workers' Headquarters were
all from good family backgrounds and three of them were CCP members
(see Table 5.1). Why did they become rebels? A closer look at their past
experiences reveals that they were not as 'pure' as their class labels
suggested. In other words, all had reasons for discontent with society.

Most of the leaders of the Workers' Headquarters had been disciplined at least once, for one reason or another, before the Cultural Revolution.[8] Zhu Hongxia had allegedly joined a secret society before 1949.
In 1955 he was disciplined for having been involved with a group that
planned to defect to Hong Kong. In 1957 he was criticized for sympa-
thizing with the rightists. At the beginning of the Cultural Revolution
he was branded as a member of a local 'three-family village' along with
Jiang Shicheng and two other colleagues.

Hu Houming, an ambitious young man, often said, 'If I cannot leave
a good name for a hundred generations, I would rather have my name
go down in history as a byword of infamy.' In 1961 he was accepted by
the CCP, but he did not immediately become a full member after the
one-year probationary period, because many people considered him too
ambitious, too crafty, and too lazy. During the Socialist Education

Table 5.1 The Chief Leaders of the Workers' Headquarters, 1966

Name	Sex	Age	Class Origin	CCP/CYL
Zhu Hongxia	Male	34	Urban Poor	No
Hu Chongyuan	Male	31	Poor Peasant	CCP
Jiang Shicheng	Male	29	Poor Peasant	No
Hu Houming	Male	29	Independent Labourer	CCP
Li Hongrong	Male	39	Lower-middle Peasant	CCP
Yu Keshun	Male	33	Poor Peasant	No
Liu Qun	Male	23	Poor Peasant	No
Hou Lianzheng	Male	33	Independent Labourer	No
Zhou Guangjie	Male	34	Urban Poor	No
Li Chenghong	Male	24	Staff	No

Source: Guanyu Ganggongzong Wenti Diaocha Baogao [Report on the Case of
Workers' Headquarters], July 1967.

Movement, he attempted to gain the position of director of the workers' club in his unit, but the Party secretary and the work team prevented his election. These two incidents nourished Hu's resentment against the establishment. In the early stages of the Cultural Revolution, he was also labelled as a member of a minor 'three-family village' in his factory.

Li Hongrong was another CCP member. During the Socialist Education Movement he was placed on probation within the Party (an inner-Party disciplinary measure), because he was found to have had affairs with several women, to have illegally resold clothing and food coupons at a profit, and to have practised usury.

Yu Keshun was sentenced to seven years' imprisonment for swindling in 1957. Hou Lianzheng was labelled as a 'bad element' and expelled from his factory in 1958. Zhou Guangjie was twice dismissed from his post, once for helping a capitalist make a forged tax report in 1951 and the other time for corruption.

It is not important whether the charges brought against these individuals were well founded. What is important is the fact that they felt they had been victimized. Therefore, despite their good family backgrounds, they wanted to see changes in the existing power structure.

Some individuals from good family backgrounds who themselves had never been chastised also joined radical organizations. There were two possible reasons for this. First, they were 'backward elements'. Distrust, criticism, and discrimination had long made them uncomfortable. Before the Cultural Revolution, they were angry but had to bottle it up. Now they could let it out.[9] Second, they might have relatives who had been punished as 'monsters and ghosts' at the beginning of the movement. In ancient China, an individual could be implicated if one of his relatives was found guilty. This practice continued after 1949 and was carried to extremes during the Cultural Revolution. Thus a person's identity could be involuntarily changed as a result of someone else's malefaction. Once one's identity changed, one's behaviour was likely to change accordingly. For this reason, many people who would have otherwise joined conservative organizations joined rebel organizations. Their affiliations with the radical groups often surprised their friends, who had expected them to be on the conservative side. For instance, one young worker was the secretary of the Youth League branch of his unit and had been active in various campaigns before the Cultural Revolution. But at the high tide of 'sweeping out all monsters and ghosts', his uncle, who worked in the same unit, was exposed as a 'rightist who had slipped through the net in 1957'. Because of his uncle, he himself fell into an inferior category. He knew that he would never be able to regain the trust of his leaders and colleagues, however sincere he was in making a break from his uncle. To clear his own name, he would have to clear his uncle's name first. The young man later became the leader of the Workers' Headquarters branch in his unit.[10]

It is not difficult to understand why people from bad and middle class backgrounds became rebels, but it is sometimes difficult to explain why a large number of people with good class designations joined radical groups. However, those who were caught up in the movement were generally able to identify the specific reasons why members of their units chose to be a rebel.[11]

Complications

The omnibus labels 'rebels' and 'conservatives' were sometimes misleading. It was not uncommon for people who protected the power holders within their unit to affiliate themselves with a city-wide radical organization; or, conversely, for those who attacked their superiors in the unit to be associated with a city-wide conservative organization. Such cases often occurred in units where a dual power structure had existed during the Socialist Education Movement, with one led by the work teams and the other by the Party branches. The supporters of the former were necessarily at odds with the supporters of the latter. They were likely to form different groups during the Cultural Revolution, one attacking the work team and the other the Party branch.

In order to strengthen their bargaining power at the level of intra-unit politics, all unit-based groups reached out to tie themselves to powerful city-wide organizations. It was unlikely for groups that were at odds with one another on internal issues to be associated with the same city-wide organization. It thus was possible for supporters of Party branches to become rebels and for challengers of work teams to align themselves with conservative organizations, and vice versa.[12]

In discussing the factionalism of the Cultural Revolution, it has been a common practice to categorize people simply by identifying their formal affiliation with the main city-wide organizations. Thus, in Wuhan, those who joined the Second Headquarters or the Workers' Headquarters were called 'rebels' and those in the original Red Guards or the Federation of Revolutionary Labourers were called 'conservatives'. This categorization is useful but could be deceptive. It has been suggested by some of those who took part in the movement that it is better to categorize people according to their positions on the internal affairs of their units. Although this appears to be an impossible task for researchers, the advice nevertheless can keep us sober-minded when we use such omnibus labels as 'rebel' and 'conservative'.

The term 'conservative' needs some further qualification. Conservatives (*baoshoupai*) were often called 'loyalists' (*baohuangpai*), implying that they were loyal to the power holders, from Liu Shaoqi down to the Party secretaries of their work units. Indeed, when the news that Liu was a target of the ongoing movement first reached Wuhan, the conservatives were shocked. But so were the rebels. Once it was confirmed that Liu really had 'made mistakes', the conservatives were no less critical of the former head of state than were the rebels.[13] In the case of Wang Renzhong, before he was ousted by the CRSG, the Wuhan rebels generally ignored the former number one man of the province. The rebels were as shocked as the conservatives when they first learned that Wang had been ousted from the CRSG.[14] And it was the conservatives who held the first mass rally in the city to denounce Wang.[15] The conservatives' attitude towards the HPPC and the WMPC was more interesting. When the two power organs led the fight against *chuanlian* students and the local 'minority', the conservatives were their enthusiastic supporters. However, once they came under pressure from Beijing to make concessions to the rebels, the conservatives themselves became contumacious in dealing with the provincial and municipal power holders. At the grassroots the conservatives shared a common fate with the power holders of their units. They tended to defend those cadres to the very end, for the patron–client relationship formed before the Cultural Revolution had bound them and the power holders so closely that any attack on the latter amounted to a blow struck against them. To defend themselves, they had to defend those power holders. That the conservatives cared much less about the fate of higher-level cadres than about that of their immediate superiors suggests the participants in the movement were motivated not so much by concerns over grand ideological issues as by concerns over their own vital interests. Essentially, what the conservatives tried to protect was not individual power holders but the existing power distribution structure, from which they had benefited.[16]

The Stand Aloof Faction

It needs to be noted that not everyone was actively involved in factional struggles during the Cultural Revolution. There were bystanders, called *xiaoyaopai*. In the early stage of the movement, *xiaoyaopai* were mainly composed of three types of persons: the excluded, the free rider, and the disinclined. 'The excluded' referred to individuals who were politically handicapped because of very bad family backgrounds. No organization wanted to be condemned as 'a hideout for monsters and ghosts', so they generally rejected obvious 'monsters and ghosts' as members. Besides, it was too risky for such people to take a clear-cut stand in factional conflicts. Individuals thus excluded were involuntary *xiaoyaopai*. 'Free riders' were those who formally registered as members of various organizations but rarely or never participated in collective action. They wanted to benefit from others' collective efforts but had no incentive to make a contribution. 'The disinclined' were those who were politically apathetic because they felt they had nothing either to lose or gain from the Cultural Revolution, or because they were simply ignorant. Middle-of-the-road workers, for instance, were very likely to fall into this category. They were voluntary *xiaoyaopai* in the sense that not only did they not join any organization, but also they cared little about which side was right or wrong, hoping only that the movement would not disturb their lives too much.[17] With the exception of the third type, *xiaoyaopai* took sides in the factional fighting. Although they did not take part in collective action, they nevertheless were averse to doing anything that would harm the faction they favoured. *Xiaoyaopai* were by no means merely a small segment of the population. In many units, they accounted for one-fourth to a half of the total employees. And as time went on, the number of *xiaoyaopai* tended to grow even larger.

Participation in Collective Action

It is clear from the above section that the factionalism that emerged in the Cultural Revolution was rooted in latent contradictions that had existed for some time in China. But the mere existence of those latent contradictions was not enough to cause an insurrection. It was one thing for a person to be desirous of something; it was quite another for him to join a collective action to pursue that goal. Why did so many Chinese throw themselves into factional struggles during the Cultural Revolution? How could they overcome the action and collective action problems discussed in the introduction to this book?

The Action Problem

Contrary to the conventionally held view that the Chinese all threw themselves into the Cultural Revolution without hesitation, Chapters 3 and 4 showed that spontaneous actions did not occur until Mao had largely removed the institutional constraints on political action.

Mao first expanded the zone of permissible action by legitimizing the development of freely constituted and autonomously operating groups formed by certain kinds of people (that is, the Red Guards by students of good class origins). He then enlarged the circle of permissible actors by allowing social groups holding grievances against the *status quo* to demand a voice in politics. Finally, he disarmed the existing rule-enforcing institutions by withholding his support of the lower levels of government. His emphasis on 'it is right to rebel' not only legitimized challenges against the establishment but also delegitimized social control. By rewriting the rules of the game, Mao created a new political arena whose gate was thrown open to people long accustomed to being excluded from politics. This was the precondition for spontaneous political action to take place.

This observation was supported by the following facts. First, the rebels did not become a viable political force in Wuhan until 'criticism of the bourgeois reactionary line' had greatly debilitated the authority of the HPPC and the WMPC and thereby significantly lowered the risks of being challengers. Second, the rebels first became apparent in places where social control was first impaired. This was why student rebels emerged earlier than did worker rebels. Third, the power structure in China disintegrated in a top-down fashion: central leaders such as Liu Shaoqi and Deng Xiaoping first, the regional authorities next, and power holders at the grassroots last. Due to the pyramid structure of authority in Chinese society, the whole organizational hierarchy soon disintegrated once it lost its mandate from its supreme leader. The rebels on their own would never have been able to bring down the mighty social control system.

The Collective Action Problem

The participants in the movement still needed to overcome the collective action problem before they took part in group action. Those who joined the original Red Guard organizations did not face the collective action problem at all. At the time when the original Red Guards was formed, membership did not involve any cost or risk. On the contrary, it was an honour to belong to such a privileged group.

Other mass organizations came into existence in a different political environment. None of them was a privileged group. If what they were pursuing was either the provision of a public good (to preserve the *status quo*) or the elimination of a public bad (to change the existing power distribution structure), why would anyone take part in collective action? There might be six reasons.

First, during the early period of the Cultural Revolution, everyone felt obligated to join an organization, for not doing so could be interpreted as being 'inactive in a great political movement', a serious charge most people wanted to avoid.[18] In addition, one's failure to be a member of a group was often taken as an indication that one had serious problems that made one unacceptable for membership.[19] Since everyone was compelled by the prevailing political atmosphere to join a group, people of course tended to take the side that served their interests. Here the social pressure functioned as a special form of selective incentive impelling Chinese to take part in at least some collective actions.

Second, the distinctions between collective and non-collective goods were often blurred. For the rebels, seeking to change their social status was both a collective and a non-collective good. It was a collective good in that it was impossible for them to change their individual status if they could not collectively break the old power equilibrium and bring about a political transformation. It was a non-collective good in that a favourable political environment would not automatically lead to the change of a particular person's social status if he did not press hard for it himself.

For many conservatives, what they were pursuing also had a dual nature. They were fighting to preserve the existing patterns of power distribution because their advantageous positions in their units would be endangered if the rebels were to gain the upper hand. With their future at stake, they had an individual incentive, other than saving the *status quo* in general, to join in the conservative collective action, especially when the threat from the rebels was seriously endangering social order. Moreover, having learned from experience that those who challenged the regime would come to no good end and that those who showed their loyalty to the regime when it was under attack would be rewarded, they tended to see membership in conservative organizations as an investment. Investment, of course, involved risk. But to gain a high return, it was worthwhile to take the risks. In short, the conservatives as well as the rebels had selective incentives for doing what they did.

Third, all organizations, both radical and conservative, adopted a federated structure with a grand city-wide organization made up of numerous small groups based in individual units. The multicellular structure of organizations had two advantages. On the one hand, in a small group where the members who already knew one another were pursuing immediate tangible benefits, 'free riders' could be readily detected and social sanctions could be effectively administered by the members themselves. In this way, conditional co-operation was more likely to occur. On the other hand, only city-wide networks were able to provide the necessary organizational support for small groups to survive the fierce factional struggle within their units, and to bring about a favourable macro-political environment in which small groups could achieve their local goals.

Fourth, movement initiators played an important role in facilitating nascent mobilization. Movement initiators were not necessarily political entrepreneurs. The first initiators of the rebel movement, for instance, were students from Beijing who were neither rebels in their own schools nor had a personal interest in Wuhan politics. The Beijing students cultivated groups of local 'minority' students, who in turn mobilized their alienated schoolmates into a rebel student movement. Soon after the student movement had consolidated, student activists developed connections with 'minority' workers, encouraging them to rouse alienated workers to action. In the process, some students and workers became political entrepreneurs and helped to swell the rebel ranks.

Fifth, collective action entailed little or no financial cost to the participants. *Chuanlian* was free. For several months in late 1966, students were allowed to travel free of charge on trains and buses. They could go anywhere in the country they wanted to go. Later, workers were given the same privilege. Inter-city and intra-city *chuanlian* was essential for mobilization. However, it was the government budget that, to a large extent, bore the costs of mobilization. Similarly, the funds and equipment necessary for group action were, directly or indirectly, financed by the government budget. The only cost for participants in the mobilization was time. However, as pointed out above, the students had an oversupply of time and thus were inclined to participate in the collective action. Workers and others had their salaries guaranteed, whether they stood fast at their posts or left to take part in political activities. Since the participants did not have to personally bear the costs of communication and organization, and the opportunity costs of their action were about zero, they were inclined to act collectively once the risks of political action were removed.

Sixth, the successful achievement of goals and successful mobilization could make collective action more attractive to prospective participants. Many rebels began to take part in collective action because such unanticipated successes as concessions from the HPPC and the WMPC 'proved' to them that collective effort was efficacious.[20] Less-dedicated rebels followed them once the size of a group had passed a certain threshold and the new participants no longer faced individual risks of any significance.[21]

Features of Factionalism

Intensity of Factionalism

Latent contradictions in society were the primary reason why millions of Chinese threw themselves into the unprecedented movement. This observation can be carried a step further to suggest that factionalism tended to be more intense in units where the latent contradictions had been more acute before the Cultural Revolution. In Wuhan there were three types of work units—homogeneous, heterogeneous, and polarized units—which differed in the severity of the hidden conflicts. In the homogeneous units, employees were to a great extent from similar backgrounds. For instance, the Party and government agencies in charge of confidential or important works and munitions factories usually employed only people from good class backgrounds. Because of their purity, those units had rarely been treated as focal points in previous political campaigns. As a result, internal conflicts usually were much less evident in those units than elsewhere. During the Cultural Revolution, the conservative majority in those units was usually so overwhelming that a small number of rebels could not stir up much trouble.[22]

The polarized units drew their employees from diametrically different groups. Among the best examples were cultural, educational, and scientific research institutions, where most employees were intellectuals of non-proletarian origins, and a small proportion of the employees were revolutionary cadres and odd-job workers from good class backgrounds. In the years leading up to the Cultural Revolution, those groups had been involved in continuous conflict with one another. During the movement, the rebel forces usually dominated those units and thus the factionalism tended to be more intense in those units than in others.[23]

The heterogeneous units lay somewhere in between the homogeneous and polarized units. Before the Cultural Revolution, the latent antagonism in such units had been less apparent than in the polarized units but more acute than in the homogeneous units. As a result, neither the conservatives nor the rebels could build up absolute superiority, and the factionalist politics in those units were likely to be more complicated.[24]

Internal Division within the Rebel Camp

Since people became rebels for different reasons, there could not be a homogeneous rebel group. In fact, the rebels were divided into smaller factions, conflicts among which could be as violent as those between the rebels and the conservatives. The following four cases might help to explain why this was so.

Case 1. In one key school, the rebellious students were divided into two groups. One was affiliated with the Second Headquarters, and the other with the Third Headquarters. The former was composed mainly of students from non-proletarian families, while the latter was made up largely of students from good backgrounds but who had been considered 'backward'. They all had been excluded from the original Red Guards, because of either their 'impure' family backgrounds or their inadequate political performance. The exclusion was the basic reason for their becoming rebels. However, the two groups of rebels had different targets in mind. Since the members of the branch of the Second Headquarters had been good students favoured by teachers and school leaders for their excellent academic achievements and good behaviour, they were reluctant to criticize those teachers and leaders. The branch of the Third Headquarters, however, attacked not only school leaders and teachers but also what they called 'minor power holders within the student body', namely the former good students. Although the Third Headquarters in general was much more moderate than the Second Headquarters in city politics, in this particular school, the situation was reversed.[25]

Case 2. The teachers at one middle school were divided into three groups: a conservative organization composed of former political activists with good class backgrounds; an affiliate of the Workers' Headquarters, whose members were mostly teachers with good backgrounds who had not been trusted by school leaders; and a group calling itself Red Teachers, whose members were mainly from non-proletarian backgrounds. The second was most radical because its members did not like that the former school leaders had relied upon activists in dealing with political affairs and upon teachers with non-proletarian backgrounds in academic matters. They felt that they constituted a group that had been ignored. The members of the third group did not like political activists, and at the same time they looked down on those in the second group for their inadequate academic abilities. While the branch of the Workers' Headquarters concentrated its attack on the principal, who was concurrently the Party secretary, the Red Teachers had ambivalent feelings about this power holder because he had treated them fairly well.[26]

Case 3. In one particular hospital, there were two radical groups. One consisted mainly of good-origin odd-job men who had been regarded as backward, while the other consisted primarily of non-proletarian-origin doctors and other professionals. The former focused its criticism on the director of the hospital, while the latter took the Party secretary as the main target. They chose different targets because the former believed that the director had represented the interests of professionals and held the odd-job men in contempt, and the latter thought the Party secretary should be responsible for discriminatory practices against non-proletarian-origin intellectuals in the hospital.[27]

Case 4. A large transport company was considered to have 'rotted' during the Socialist Education Movement. Many cadres were dismissed from their posts and replaced by members of the work team who were from other units. When the Cultural Revolution broke out, the so-called dismissed cadres during the Socialist Education Movement and their sympathizers (mostly office clerks) rose against the new power holders, holding the former work team members responsible for their suffering. Their action, however, received little support from another rebel group, which consisted for the most part of backward workers. The latter group focused its attack on cadres who had run the company before the Socialist Education Movement, because, unlike the new leaders who had been around for only a brief period of time, the former leaders had for many years kicked around the backward workers.[28]

These four cases suggest that the composition of rebel groups, as well as the internal conflicts within the rebel camp, were intimately connected with the principal social divisions in society, namely, the tensions between the cadres and the masses, between people with good and bad class backgrounds, and between political activists and backward elements. The different elements within the rebel ranks did share some goals and attitudes—after all, both backward elements and people with bad class labels had suffered prior to the Cultural Revolution. However, when they were attacking power holders and former activists, their suspicions of each other didn't disappear. They might form expedient coalitions when facing formidable pressure from the conservatives, but their different or opposing motives would ultimately lead them to the battlefield.

Internal Organizational Problems

While the federated structure of mass organization had the advantage of keeping members highly motivated, it had its disadvantages as well. Because both the vertical relationship between the central group and its constituent groups and the horizontal relationship among the small groups were loose, the decentralized, segmented network was ultimately incompatible with sustained large-scale mobilization and often hindered its strategic effectiveness. The central group might occasionally issue guidelines, but it was up to the constituent groups to decide whether they would follow the directions issued. The small groups might help each other occasionally, but they were not obligated to do so. Without a system of rewards and sanctions, it was impossible for such an organization to operate in a cohesive way.[29] Rebel organizations were generally more slack in internal co-ordination and more lax in discipline than were the conservative organizations, and they often had difficulty in controlling the actions of their subsidiary groups. The conservative organizations were relatively more centralized, because their leaders generally possessed a very important asset not available to the rebels—advantageous positions in the pre-existing socio-political organizations. They could use those connections to mobilize and organize their constituents.

At the grassroots, the warring factional groups were not in a position to impose strict discipline on their members either. An individual might belong to more than one group. Some members might never take part in group actions. In the anti-bureaucracy environment of the Cultural Revolution, many rejected any kind of leadership and discipline. As a result, some groups were merely little more than disorderly bands.

When social control was paralyzed and internal control within the newly established mass organizations was lacking, the possibility of accidental conflicts was multiplied. This was so not because the participants were 'bad' or 'innately aggressive', but because there was nothing to prevent people from resorting to force. In normal times, the government monopolized the use of force. Organized violence as a strategy was ruled out—or at least, made prohibitively costly—by the government, which threatened to punish any individuals or groups who used force against others without authorization. Now, however, no agency existed that could credibly threaten reprisal if force were used to settle disputes. The absence of rules and rule enforcers allowed even good people to come to blows when their interests clashed. In this hostile atmosphere, even minor strife in a particular unit was likely to be interpreted as part of a large organization's scheme to harm its opponent. Thus, hostile sentiments and aggressive actions tended to escalate. A single spark could start a prairie fire.

Micro-politics and Macro-politics

What really mattered for most participants in the movement were issues within their respective units, not grand ideological issues. For instance, most rebels were concerned mainly with seeking remedies for individual grievances. Animosities were personally directed at some leaders and activists of their units. This personalization of conflict was a direct outgrowth of the old system of officially organized patronage that personalized social control and rewards to an extent unusual in other social settings.[30] It deflected resentment away from the system and focused it on to specific individuals.

If the gravity of factionalism was in individual units, why did small unit-based groups affiliate themselves with city-wide organizations? The primary reason was to deter or match the opposing groups within their units. It would be foolish for a group not to establish external connections if others were doing just that. Once it became part of a city-wide organization, however, a local group would have to share a common fate with its patron group. For the sake of its own interests, it had to be in agreement with the patron on issues of city politics. That is to say, it was alignment that led to agreement, not the other way around.

Furthermore, the rebels had two reasons for preferring to operate outside their own units. First, many of them had 'impure' personal records. If their activities were to be confined within their units, their unsavoury records would be embarrassing labels that their adversaries could use against them. Operating outside, their identities were somehow concealed and they could act just as others did.[31] Second, in most cases, the rebels were the minorities in their units. External connections could help them to appear much stronger than they really were. When the minorities from various units bound themselves together, they were able to overpower the majority of any single unit. The rebels understood that only when the rebel faction gained the upper hand in city politics could individual rebels realize their goals in their units.

As the majority, the conservatives did not feel a desperate need to tie themselves to outside forces. If the movement were to be circumscribed within the boundary of each unit, their superiority over the minority would bring the latter to their knees. For this reason, city-wide conservative organizations, except the original Red Guards, tended to emerge later than did their radical counterparts.[32] Despite the conservatives' preference for not going beyond the boundary of individual units, however, whenever they felt that the rebels were getting out of hand they would unite to fight them.

Mao and His Followers

Mao's instigation of rebellion and his efforts to delegitimize the existing power structure were the necessary conditions for millions of

Chinese to throw themselves into the Cultural Revolution. But it does not follow that Mao, as the initiator of the movement, could direct the forces he had called into being. In fact, criticism of the bourgeois reactionary line created a situation in which Mao would not be able effectively to communicate with his followers and to exercise his leadership.

The new model of communication which emerged after the criticism of the bourgeois reactionary line contained four important changes. First, the prevalence of the personality cult reduced normal public discourse to a set of dogmatic clichés. Although behind the linguistic veneer of revolutionary rhetoric there was a constant tug-of-war over resource redistribution, the participants' real motivations were rarely expressed in public. Messages in the information flow were thus tainted to begin with.

Second, after the well-established hierarchical communication channels were destroyed, messages from Beijing had to be relayed to the masses mainly by pronouncements in the media, by mass organization tabloids, and by word of mouth. The multiplication of information channels reduced the probability of a single leader or a small group of leaders monopolizing the communication.

Third, after the local authorities were deprived of the role of gatekeeper, no one was in a position to claim that his or her interpretation of a message from Beijing was more authoritative than others'. Without the help of a hierarchical structure of gatekeepers, the communication between Mao and his followers became extremely unstable, which made it possible for people to interpret messages from Beijing in whatever way they liked, and to behave according to their own understanding of the messages.[33] This enabled them to exploit the high-level generality of official ideology to pursue their own interests, consciously or subconsciously. Even worse, the absence of any checks by the local authorities made it more likely that someone might fabricate messages from Beijing to serve factional interests.[34]

Fourth, the disintegration of supporting agencies at the provincial level and below put Mao in the position of an imposing head without a torso, arms, or legs. The removal of the rule-enforcing institutions made it difficult for Mao to rectify trends that were deviating from the path he desired. Later, he would face a dilemma: to pursue radical goals, he would have to rely on the free mobilization of rebels, which always resulted in chaos; to resume even a minimum degree of law and order, he would have to re-establish the organs of authority at the local level, which, without exception, would lead to a tendency to restore the old power relations. For Mao, neither outcome was desirable, but over the course of the next decade he was unable to resolve the dilemma. Instead, the movement would oscillate from 'left' to 'right' to 'left' with increasing frequency.

6

Conflicts between Conservatives and Rebels, January to April 1967

Power Vacuum

THE REMOVAL of the ban on free association of workers was one of the most daring decisions Mao made during the Cultural Revolution. If the student groups alone had been allowed to mobilize freely, civil order might have been disturbed but could be easily restored. But once workers also were granted the right to revolt, the very foundations of society were shaken.

At the beginning of 1967, China hovered on the verge of anarchy. Since the local authorities had been in effect castrated, there were no institutional constraints on people's behaviour. In the absence of coercion, no one would voluntarily refrain from doing things that threatened social order.[1] As a result, lawlessness and disorder ensued. The absence of government soon gave rise to what contemporary Chinese news media called 'rampant economism'.[2]

Contract and temporary workers of state-owned enterprises were among the most aggressive in advancing their economic interests through organizational means. In contrast to permanent workers, contract and temporary workers not only received lower salaries but also were denied many fringe benefits. More important, without the job security enjoyed by permanent workers, they might be fired for minor misconduct, which made them especially vulnerable to retaliation by power holders. Their first demand, therefore, was to obtain job security. Under the pressure of contract and temporary workers, the HPPC agreed that all those who had been discharged after 1 June 1966 should be allowed to return to their original units and that henceforth contract and temporary workers should not be fired.[3]

The success of the contract and temporary workers put spurs to the expansion of 'economism'. Unemployed youth demanded jobs. Employees of collective enterprises extorted the upgrading of their firms to state-owned status. Educated urban youth working in the countryside returned to the city without permission. Workers and cadres who had been persuaded or forced to move to rural areas in the early 1960s laid claim to the jobs they had given up.[4] Even some permanent workers of state-owned enterprises took the opportunity to try to gain higher salaries or more bonuses and benefits. Private pedlars also seized the opportunity to pursue their interests. They attacked tax collectors, pressed them for the return of the taxes they had already paid, and demanded a reduction of tax rates and reform of the tax system. In addition, people forcibly occupied the empty rooms in former capitalists' houses and public houses. Some even went so far as openly to rob public warehouses.[5]

'Economism' put an enormous financial burden on China's fragile economy. But it was just one of the dangerous trends that had resulted from the absence of authority. In order to end the anarchy, Mao found it necessary to rebuild the public authorities that had sufficient power to restore restraint. He had two options, either to restore the old power structure or to establish a new power structure. Mao, of course, did not want to give up his revolution half-way. He therefore chose the latter, that is, to push the Cultural Revolution one step further towards power seizure.

Power Seizure, Factional Realignments, and Disorder

The power seizure was not a well-planned stage of the movement.[6] Rather, it was an expedient measure to which the Party leaders had to resort in order to avoid the collapse of the Chinese economy.[7] When the leaders agitated for a power seizure, they did not anticipate that this might create more problems than it could solve. The basic questions concerning power seizure were who, under what conditions, had the right to seize power; whose power and what power were to be seized; how the seizure should proceed; and what the new power structure should look like. Messages from Beijing about all those questions were ambiguous and conflicting.

As a result, the power seizure became a game without rules and rule enforcers. Mao's idea of having a power seizure was based on the assumption that the rebels could easily be united to take over power from the capitalist roaders. This proved to be a wrong calculation. Although the different rebel groups had united with one another to fight against the old establishment in recent months, that was when holding power was beyond their wildest dream. Now, rebellion became a possible stepping-stone to social respectability. At least some rebels could have a career in local politics. The lucrative prospect of becoming the new power holders decisively altered the rebels' pay-off scheme, which in turn changed their strategies and behaviours. Since every group wanted to wield power as exclusively as possible, internal struggle was inevitable. The call from Beijing for a seizure of power thus immediately set off factional warfare between the rebel organizations in Wuhan.

The Workers Headquarters was the first rebel organization in Wuhan to respond to Beijing's appeal to take over power from the so-called capitalist roaders. On 14 January it invited thirteen other groups to discuss how to seize power in the city. It did not take them long to reach an agreement on an 'Open Letter to the People of the City'. But discussion of the detailed plan on how to carry out the power seizure, and how to cut up the pie, soon led to a deadlock. The negotiations broke down and the letter was never made public.

While negotiations had ceased, behind the scenes the preparations for the power seizure were being speeded up. Each organization was looking for allies while keeping an eye on its adversaries' activities. The Red Building in Wuchang, where the Workers Headquarters, the Second Headquarters, the 13 September Corps, and a few other rebel organizations had located their headquarters, became a centre of conspiracy. With the intention of performing good deeds to atone for his 'misdeeds', Zhang Tixue, on his own initiative, sent his representative to the Red Building to express his willingness to co-operate with the rebels there in the power transition. This gesture indicated that the former power holders were not planning to throw obstacles in the way of the rebels. The problem remained, though, of who would take power.

On 20 January, at the suggestion of the Workers' Headquarters and the Second Headquarters, negotiations resumed in Wuchang. Fourteen organizations participated in the negotiations. After haggling with each other for three days, they declared on 23 January that an agreement to form a 'great alliance' had been reached. The new super-organization was called the Wuhan Revolutionary Rebel General Headquarters, with the Workers' Headquarters as its chair. Presumably, the General Headquarters was to handle all the matters arising from the power seizure and to serve as an interim government at both the provincial and municipal levels during the period of power transition. This proved to be wishful thinking, however. It was found that one of the participant organizations, the Workers' Rebel Headquarters, was secretly organizing another 'great alliance' in Hankou, which was composed of some twenty groups based on the north bank of the Yangtze. The Workers' Rebel Headquarters was plotting to arrogate the municipal authorities to itself while sharing the provincial authorities with others.

During the following three days, the negotiations became heated.

Three issues divided the participants. The first was whether conditions were right for a seizure of power. The Workers' Headquarters, the Second Headquarters, the 13 September Corps, and the other groups located in the Red Building, the so-called Red Building coalition, insisted that the conditions were ripe, because they were reasonably certain that they would have no problem dominating the power seizure. The Workers' Rebel Headquarters had by then finished making its arrangements to take over the municipal power, and knew that no one could legitimately exclude it—the second largest rebel worker organization in the city—from participating in the power seizure at the provincial level. It therefore agreed that the time was right. However, organizations that needed more time to improve their bargaining positions, such as the Third Headquarters, the New Central China Institute of Technology, and New Hubei University, asserted that the power seizure should be postponed.

The second issue was which organizations would become members of the standing committee of the General Headquarters. The Second Headquarters proposed that the standing committee should be composed of five members—four worker organizations plus one student organization. Moreover, it saved the only seat for a student organization for itself. This suggestion was, of course, rejected by the other student groups. After heated debate, four worker organizations (the Workers' Headquarters, the Workers' Rebel Headquarters, the 13 September Corps, and the Red Worker Army) and three student organizations (the Second Headquarters, the Third Headquarters, and the New Central China Institute of Technology) were elected to serve as members of the standing committee.

The third issue was the relationship between the General Headquarters of Wuchang and the ghost general headquarters of Hankou. Previously, the Workers' Headquarters and the Workers' Rebel Headquarters had had a tacit understanding about the division of territory: Wuchang was the former's sphere of influence and Hankou the latter's. For this reason, the Workers' Headquarters was not in a position to condemn the Workers' Rebel Headquarters' attempt to gain power on the north bank of the Yangtze. Therefore, the Second Headquarters led the criticism against the Workers' Rebel Headquarters, in an attempt to force the latter to disband its ghost general headquarters immediately. The Workers' Rebel Headquarters refused. On 25 January the General Headquarters decided that the power seizure at the provincial level would formally take place at 3 p.m. on the following day, but the Workers' Rebel Headquarters, enraged by the Second Headquarters' insistence that the general headquarters of Hankou must be dissolved, announced its withdrawal from the 'great alliance'.

In an attempt to keep the power seizure plan from miscarrying, the General Headquarters urged the return of the Workers' Rebel Headquarters. The latter insisted that it would not take part in the power seizure unless the Second Headquarters was kicked out of the standing committee. The other student groups, who had been displeased by the Second Headquarters' 'single student organization' plan, supported the proposal. A compromise was not reached until the final minutes: the Second Headquarters was to maintain its membership in the standing committee, but its current chief negotiators were to be replaced. Thus, when the provincial power changed hands on the afternoon of 26 January, the Second Headquarters had no representatives on the scene.

Hubei Radio immediately broadcast the news that the provincial power had been taken over by the rebels. Zhang Tixue, the former governor, asked the former heads of the municipalities, prefectures, and counties of the province to co-operate with the new authorities.

Co-operation from former power holders, however, could not prevent the new leadership from falling apart from within. Realizing that the absence of the Second Headquarters would decisively weaken its influence in the standing committee, the Red Building coalition made a joint statement declaring the power seizure invalid five hours after the power transition had taken place. Thereafter the rebels in Wuhan split into two camps.

Neither side gave up hope of obtaining power, but they could no longer work together. On 30 January the Workers' Headquarters and its allies held a public accusation rally against Zhang Tixue and Song Kanfu. Two days later, Zhang Tixue became the subject of another public accusation rally organized by adversaries of the Workers' Headquarters. On 2 February the Workers' Headquarters and twelve other organizations founded the Hubei Revolutionary Rebel Headquarters for Grasping Revolution and Promoting Production. The next day saw the establishment of the Hubei Red Rebel Headquarters for Grasping Revolution and Promoting Production by the Workers' Rebel Headquarters and forty-three other groups. On 5 February the Revolutionary Rebel Headquarters published an 'urgent notice' against 'economism' in the *Yangtze Daily*. On the next day, another 'urgent notice', with almost identical contents, appeared in the *Hubei Daily*, signed by the Red Rebel Headquarters.[8] This type of competition caused relations between the two camps steadily to deteriorate.

On 8 February the Workers' Headquarters, the Second Headquarters, and ten other organizations issued a statement in the *Yangtze Daily*, attacking by name the Workers' Rebel Headquarters and its allies as 'Trotskyists', 'splittist groups', and 'the secret agent squad of the HPPC'. This statement added fuel to the flames. For the rest of the month, the '8 February Statement', as it was called, was the hottest issue in the city. Its opponents cursed the statement as 'a piece of poisonous weed'. They surrounded the offices of the *Yangtze Daily* every day, accusing the paper of 'inciting the masses to struggle against the masses' and of 'supporting one faction while suppressing the others'. The proponents of the statement, however, praised it as a 'beautiful fragrant flower', justifying it on the ground that the revolutionaries must clear 'Trotskyists' out of their ranks. The issue was so important that crowds gathered all over the city to debate the statement.[9]

Interestingly, many of those who were involved in the debate did not read the text of the statement. And even more interestingly, many outwardly die-hard advocates of the statement admitted privately that personally they did not like it, and vice versa. A former rebel leader explained this seeming paradox by saying, 'While one's position in society before the Cultural Revolution had to a large extent predetermined whether one became a rebel or a conservative, one's factional affiliation predetermined which side one took in the debate about the 8 February Statement.'[10] What was at issue in essence was not the statement *per se* but one's factional identity. Such a debate would not change one's attitude towards the subject-matter, but it worked as an effective mechanism to reinforce one's identity with the group with which one had already affiliated. Previously, the disputes about the January power seizure had concerned only the top leaders of the rebel organizations. The debate about the 8 February Statement helped to spread the factional antagonism to the grassroots. Thereafter the two factions of rebel organizations received new names: the 'Fragrant Flower Faction' and the 'Poisonous Weed Faction'. The distrust between the two factions was never really dispelled until the very end of the Cultural Revolution, though occasionally they might form a tactical coalition against the conservatives.

Mao's expectation that the power seizure would bring about a revolutionary order turned out to be an illusion. To his great disappointment, the power seizure played havoc with almost every aspect of Chinese society. First, the power seizure did not lead to the establishment of new authorities. In most cases, it succeeded only half-way. That is, while having formally sounded the death-knell of the old power structure, the rebels failed to provide an effective substitute. The ruin of the old authorities was thorough in Wuhan. Former power holders, from the governor and the mayor to workshop foremen and production group heads, were all removed from their posts. In some cases, even cadres of neighbourhood committees, who were not on the state's payroll, and policemen in charge of household registration were considered power holders.[11] In some units the rebels went still further. Regarding Party membership as a symbol of power, non-Party member rebels claimed the right to expel Party members from the CCP.[12] Mao often said that one had to begin by destroying; construction would come later. In the case of the power seizure, however, the destruction fed on itself and engendered an authority crisis. Lacking the pillars of public authorities, society was left in imminent danger of disintegration.

Second, the power seizure split the rebel ranks from within. It might have been expected at first that the power seizure would encounter resistance from former power holders. However, the expected struggle did not materialize. Having lost the mandate from the supreme leader, the power holders readily gave up their power. The rebels' enemies were not the power holders but one another. The power seizure fomented a power struggle among the rebels.

Third, one of the reasons that Mao had resorted to the power seizure was to restore civil order and normal production, but the situation in fact worsened after the ill-prepared seizure. The power vacuum that resulted provided an opportunity for the victims of past political campaigns to redress their grievances and to wreak revenge on Party cadres and former activists. In order to justify their demand for the 'reversal of past verdicts', they preached that 'all the political campaigns of the past seventeen years must be re-evaluated'; 'the proletarian dictatorship must be thoroughly remoulded'; and 'the Cultural Revolution has changed class relations'.[13] Because there were no longer any public authorities that could regulate their behaviour, their vindictive actions were usually more brutal than what the original Red Guards had done to them several months before.[14]

Fourth, it was impossible to maintain normal production when the country was in anarchy. January 1967 was the worst month for industrial production in Wuhan since the beginning of the Cultural Revolution. Statistics showed that, at best, factories fulfilled only 60 per cent of their production quota; most of them filled only 40–50 per cent, and some only 20 per cent.[15]

Finally, following their victory in dismantling the civilian authority structure, the rebels tried to bring down the last pillar of the old establishment—the army. Before the Cultural Revolution, relations between the civilian and military authorities had traditionally been very close. The First Secretary of the HPPC, Wang Renzhong, was concurrently the First Political Commissar of the Wuhan Military Region (WMR): and the Commander of the WMR, Chen Zaidao, was a member of the standing committee of the HPPC. When the civilian government was in danger, the central Military Affairs Commission (MAC) instructed the military regions in the provinces to accept any secret archives and documents the local governments asked them to save, and to provide shelter for local leaders. For this reason, the rebels regarded the army as the 'last hideout of power holders taking the capitalist road'.[16]

The Restoration of Order: The February Adverse Current

The urgent situation facing Wuhan and, for that matter, the whole country forced Mao to take immediate and drastic counter-measures to hold the frenzied rebels in check.

First, the People's Liberation Army (PLA) was called in. The army had always been the key element in the state's power, and at the beginning of 1967 it was the only organized force that remained largely intact. Mao attempted to stabilize the perilous situation by playing this trump card. On 21 January he ordered the army to step in to 'support the forces of the left.'[17] In order to ensure that the army had the prestige and solidity needed to deal effectively with the warring factions, Mao authorized a MAC ordinance on 28 January which forbade civilians from trespassing on military installations or attacking military personnel.[18] Before long, the army's power was expanded from the passive mission of supporting the leftists to the broader missions of maintaining law and order, administering the economy, and re-establishing the power structure.[19] The problem was that no specification was given about how to distinguish true leftists from false ones. The task of supporting the leftists thus entitled the army to support whoever it thought were revolutionaries.

Second, the role of veteran cadres was emphasized. The unexpected disorder which derived from the ill-prepared power seizure must have reminded Mao that the rebels alone could not build up a functioning new power structure. Mao began to make use of the veteran cadres' administrative skills by stressing the indispensability of their participation in the new power structure. According to him, revolutionary cadres constituted a majority of cadres. Even those who had made mistakes should be given an opportunity to return to the fold.[20] This new policy was a shot in the arm to thousands of despondent Party cadres.

Third, in order to overcome the pronounced tendency towards anar-chism that had characterized the behaviour of the rebels in the first month of 1967, Mao initiated a campaign to reorganize them.[21] The rebels were criticized for the excesses they had committed during the January power seizure, and this punctured their arrogance.

In the course of the restoration of order, a formula called 'three-in-one combination' began to take shape.[22] The 'three-in-one combination' referred to an equal sharing of power by the representatives of the army, the Party cadres, and the rebels within each revolutionary committee. The participation of soldiers and Party cadres in the power seizure was expected to balance the rebels' extremism. Later events would demon-strate that the formation of an alliance among these diametrically opposed forces was an impossible task.

Although Mao was attempting to curb the excesses of radicalism and spontaneity, he had no intention of discrediting the rebels altogether. At most, he wanted to rectify the rebels' behaviour somewhat so that the Cultural Revolution could proceed in a more balanced way. In the view of the regional military leaders, however, Mao's goal in pushing his deradicalization policy was to debilitate and even demobilize the rebel organizations. Due to miscommunication, Mao's strategy thus would once again bring about something he had not anticipated, that is, the 'February Adverse Current'.

When the 8 February Statement attacking the Worker's Rebel Head-quarters was published in the *Yangtze Daily*, stirring up a great distur-bance in Wuhan, Chen Zaidao and Zhong Hanhua, the Commander and Political Commissar of the WMR, were attending a MAC conference in Beijing. Chen and Zhong were most impressed by Mao's remark at the conference that there must have been some 'evil-doers' among the rebels who raided the army compounds. Mao advised the army to 'give way to the attackers first in order to avoid conflict' while being assaulted. But Chen and Zhong thought that what Mao meant was a tactic of 'retreating in order to advance'. If the rebels reached for a yard after taking an inch, they believed the army should strike back in self-defence.[23]

On 11 February the WMR's Headquarters Supporting the Leftists, which had been set up just ten days before, was raided by the Fragrant Flower Faction of the rebels.[24] By then, backed by the MAC, Chengdu, Fuzhou, and Guangzhou Military Regions had all initiated counterat-tacks against those who had attacked the army.[25] Following the exam-ples of other military regions, the WMR issued a 'solemn statement' on 18 February denouncing the 8 February Statement and the Fragrant

Flower Faction.[26] The next day, the army in Wuhan staged an unprecedented armed march in central Wuhan as a display of strength. Meanwhile, military compounds placed cordons at their gates so as to deter trespassers.[27]

The WMR's statement was understandably welcomed by the Poisonous Weed Faction. Although this faction did not particularly like the army, and some of its members had criticized it, it was glad to have the army on its side against the powerful Fragrant Flower Faction. The essence of the power struggle game was to keep the number of legitimate claimants to power as small as possible. The Poisonous Weed Faction believed that its alignment with the local military authorities could help it to drive the Fragrant Flower Faction out of the game. For this reason, the rest of February saw the Poisonous Weed Faction enthusiastically supporting the WMR's position by issuing statements, holding mass rallies, and staging demonstrations denouncing the Fragrant Flower Faction.[28] For the moment, the interests of the WMR and the Poisonous Weed Faction seemed to coincide.[29] Under the pincer attack, many members of the organizations belonging to the Fragrant Flower Faction dropped out. The Fragrant Flower Faction thus quickly lost its superiority over the Poisonous Weed Faction.

Around the end of February, Chen Zaidao and Zhong Hanhua returned to Wuhan. Before they left Beijing, they had a private meeting with Zhou Enlai, who advised them to pay special attention to three things: industrial production, the resumption of classes in schools, and the formation of alliances along the lines of trade, profession, or unit. Zhou's instructions led the two military leaders to conclude that the restoration of order would be their primary task. Meanwhile, their worries about possible resistance by the rebels, especially by the Fragrant Flower Faction, were removed by the CRSG's criticism of the 8 February Statement. On 27 February a member of the CRSG pointed out to representatives of the Second Headquarters' liaison office in Beijing that the 8 February Statement was wrong. He also warned the Wuhan rebels not to direct their spearhead of attack against the PLA.[30]

With the support of both moderate and radical leaders in Beijing, Chen and Zhong were confident that they could quickly restore order in Wuhan. Soon after they returned to the city, a high-handed policy was adopted in dealing with the rebels. The first victim was the Fragrant Flower Faction. The weapon the WMR used against the faction was the CRSG's criticism of the 8 February Statement.

During the Cultural Revolution, although the Chinese people were encouraged to rebel, rebellion was not their legal right. In a sense, it was merely a privilege bestowed by Mao. It could be taken away at any time. When a group had the privilege, it might act freely and did not have to bow to the local authorities. When it lost the privilege, however, its very existence could be in danger. In theory, every factional group had this privilege. But once Mao showed the slightest distaste for a particular group, its rivals could take the opportunity to deprive it of its privilege and even destroy it.

When the news that the CRSG had denounced the 8 February Statement arrived in Wuhan, the rebels of the Fragrant Flower Faction realized that they had lost in the battle against the Poisonous Weed Faction and the army. Their only choice was to take a low-key position and wait for the next turn of events. On 27 February the heads of the Workers' Headquarters went to the WMR to ask for forgiveness. The following days saw a continuous stream of Fragrant Flower Faction rebels in the streets of Wuhan carrying placards expressing their apologies for their 'mistakes'. While the Fragrant Flower Faction submitted to humiliation, the WMR became swollen with arrogance. It ordered all organizations belonging to the Fragrant Flower Faction to clear away any posters in the city which ran counter to the WMR's 18 February statement. It also prohibited any criticism of the WMR's policies. On 1 March, Chen Zaidao declared, 'Counter-revolutionaries must be suppressed. Their only choice is to behave themselves. Unruliness in their word or deed will not be tolerated.' The WMR knew that appeasement would bring disaster. It therefore planned to show no mercy to the rebels.

In order to cut off the local rebels' connections with Beijing and with rebels in other provinces, the army imposed military control on the Telecommunications Bureau on 1 March. Mass organizations were no longer allowed to send telegrams to Beijing unless they got approval in advance from the military control commission of the bureau. Censorship was also secretly applied to correspondence between local and outside rebels. The Fragrant Flower Faction's capacity to influence public opinion was crippled when the WMR shut down the *Yangtze Daily*. After depriving the Fragrant Flower Faction of its communication channels, the army began to attack the faction's footholds. Between 3 and 10 March the army took over five buildings which the Fragrant Flower Faction rebels had occupied since the end of 1966.[31] This was a fatal blow to the rebels. Most of them were in the minority in their respective units and they usually had vulnerable points that could be capitalized on by their conservative colleagues. The rebels could dominate in city politics only when they were allowed to operate outside their units. Once forced to confine their activities to individual units, they could be easily subdued even if the conservatives were not well organized.

A political offensive was also staged to shake the rebels' morale. Directed by Chen Zaidao, local newspapers and radio stations published and broadcast items condemning the 8 February Statement. This campaign aimed at intimidating the members of the Fragrant Flower Faction. As a further means of smearing the rebels' reputation, the buildings recaptured by the army became the setting for exhibitions which depicted the rebels as a bunch of scoundrels. Thousands of visitors left the exhibitions with the impression that the rebel organizations were nothing but criminal gangs.[32]

Meanwhile, a secret investigation against the Workers' Headquarters was being undertaken. For this purpose, a special group was set up by the WMR, and the scouting force of the Wuhan Public Security Bureau was mobilized to conduct a reconnaissance against the heads of the organization. The investigation led the army to conclude that the Workers' Headquarters was indeed a sink of iniquity that had sheltered 'monsters and ghosts'. The WMR then decided to disband the organization altogether. Although the CRSG did not affirm the WMR's suggestion, it did not overrule it either, and Beijing's noncommittal attitude was taken to be tacit consent to the proposal. In the small hours of 17 March the WMR arrested 485 heads and activists of the Workers' Headquarters. On 21 March it published a report on the crimes allegedly conducted by counter-revolutionaries in the Workers' Headquarters. Condemning the Workers Headquarters as an organization manipulated by a clique of counter-revolutionaries from behind the scenes, the WMR ordered it to disband immediately.[33]

If the army had not been prohibited from dismissing student organizations by the Sixteen Articles, it would also have forced the Second Headquarters to disband. Given the restriction imposed by the Sixteen Articles, it had to adopt a different strategy in dealing with the largest student rebel organization in Wuhan—that is, to increase the risks and costs of staying in the organization. The Second Headquarters was said to have made 'serious political mistakes'. It was also alleged that the leadership of the Second Headquarters had been penetrated by counter-revolutionary elements. By making such accusations, the army hoped that the rank-and-filers' determination to ferret out 'hidden class enemies' and to rectify their mistaken leaders would ruin the Second Headquarters. This tactic seemed very effective. The enormous political pressure from the army threw the leaders of the Second Headquarters into a great panic. They paraded through the streets imploring the army to forgive their past wrongdoings. The three main leaders even started to accuse each other, trying to shift the blame. Claiming to have been fooled, some branch leaders set up a 'rectification office' and took over the headquarters.[34] At the grassroots, ordinary members went even further. Public accusation meetings were held in many schools to struggle against their division heads. Thousands of rank-and-filers formally resigned from the organization, and more simply abandoned their membership by not coming to group activities. If in the past they had expected some social and psychological benefits from their participation in the rebel movement, such prospects now appeared to be gloomy. The increasing risks attached to membership suggested to them that it was time to leave. As the leadership at every level was being paralysed and ordinary members were deserting, the Second Headquarters in effect ceased to exist in late March of 1967.[35]

In much the same way, the other mass organizations of the Fragrant Flower Faction, such as the 13 September Corps and the Red Teachers, collapsed under the pressure.[36] At first, the rebel organizations of the Poisonous Weed Faction supported the army's suppression of the Fragrant Flower Faction. They hoped that such actions would eliminate their rivals in the unfinished power seizure. When the army collected evidence against the Workers' Headquarters, the rebel organizations of the Poisonous Weed Faction co-operated by supplying information.[37] Before long, however, they realized that the conservatives could take advantage of the criticism of the 8 February Statement and the Fragrant Flower Faction to stage a counterattack. On 4 March the *Hubei Daily*, which was under the control of the Poisonous Weed Faction, published an editorial warning the conservatives not to expect restoration of the old order. But the army charged that the editorial was no less 'poisonous' than the 8 February Statement. The next day, the *Hubei Daily* was forced to countermand the editorial. After the paper carried a long self-criticism for the 'serious political mistake' reflected in that editorial on 9 March, the army removed all the rebel elements from the editorial board of the paper and reinstated the former editor-in-chief.[38] The 4 March editorial affair marked the end of the short honeymoon between the rebels of the Poisonous Weed Faction and the WMR, and the Poisonous Weed Faction soon began to decline. By the end of March, some organizations within the faction had broken down, and the others were struggling desperately to survive.[39]

The disintegration of both the Fragrant Flower Faction and the Poisonous Weed Faction rebels was cause for celebration by the army and by all those who had been subjected to the rebels' insults over the past months. A deputy commander of the WMR commented on the development as follows:

> Good will be rewarded with good, and evil with evil. It is time to return
> evil for evil. Some are accusing us of trying to settle accounts after the
> autumn harvest. They are wrong. We would like to settle accounts right
> now in the spring.

The director of the WMR's Headquarters for Supporting the Leftists
added:

> The purpose of the Cultural Revolution is to rid the country of 'monsters
> and ghosts'. Over the past few months, we have given them the chance
> to assert themselves. Now it is our turn. If they do not behave them-
> selves, we shall punish them. It is what the proletarian dictatorship is
> meant to be.[40]

Conservatives and cadres shared the army's view. Recent events
which they had had difficulty in comprehending now began to make
sense to them. Again, the Cultural Revolution was seen as a trap. Mao's
encouragement of rebellion, they believed, was a way of encouraging
hidden 'monsters and ghosts' to show their true colours. Many conservatives and Party cadres admired Mao's 'brilliant scheme': 'Chairman
Mao is indeed wiser than Liu Shaoqi. Liu catches fish with a net,
while Mao simply picks up the fish after draining the water from the
pond'.[41]

As the rebels' influence faded under pressure from the army, the
conservatives began to revive. While they had been down on their luck,
they had adopted two strategies to conserve their forces. The first strategy was to regroup themselves into new organizations. For instance, the
Red Armed Guards, an organization mainly composed of core members
of the old militia, was established on 26 January 1967. Within two
months its membership had grown to 50,000. A dozen similar organizations also emerged between January and March. Among them were
the Rebel Army, made up mainly of former members of the Socialist
Education Movement work teams, and the Red City Commune, consisting of Party cadres and activists from the neighbourhood committees.
Those organizations bore strong vestiges of the old institutional framework, which enabled them to operate smoothly and efficiently.[42]

The other strategy was to join the weakest rebel organizations in their
units collectively. A large number of worker conservatives, for instance,
enrolled in the Workers' Rebel Headquarters to continue their fight
against the Workers' Headquarters, while a large group of student
conservatives joined the ranks of the Third Headquarters to maintain

their independence from the Second Headquarters. The Workers' Rebel Headquarters and the Third Headquarters at first warmly welcomed these 'defectors' from the conservative groups, because new forces were vital in their power struggles against the rival rebel organizations. However, they gradually realized that the large inflow of former conservatives threatened to turn some of their branches into the cat's-paw of those 'defectors.'[43]

Thousands of conservatives simply withdrew from politics, content to watch the factional struggles from the sidelines. No matter which strategy they chose, however, the conservatives all tried to avoid associating with hostile rebels in their units.

The WMR's redefinition of the concepts of 'leftist' and 'rightist' helped to reinvigorate the conservatives. One WMR chief put it in these terms:

> Who are leftists? Who are rightists? Those who act in accordance with the centre's policies are leftists, whereas those who act wildly in defiance of the laws are rightists. Some claim that they are revolutionary rebels, but they have imposed the label 'conservative' on a large number of revolutionary masses, and treated the so-called conservatives ruthlessly. They are counter-revolutionaries, Nationalist elements, fascists, and bandits. Even the bourgeoisie are better than them, for at least the bourgeoisie are not as barbarous as those rebels are. Those whom they call 'conservatives' are real leftists.[44]

Propped up by the army, the conservative organizations revived and soon launched a vindictive counterattack against the rebels. In many units the heads of rebel groups and even rank-and-file rebel members were forced to make self-criticisms. When committees were set up in the factories to propel the revolution forward and to promote production and in the schools to resume classes, as the army had instructed, the rebels, especially members of the Fragrant Flower Faction, were generally excluded from the election process. Overnight, 'rebel' became a derogatory term in Wuhan.[45]

At the same time as the army was suppressing the rebels, it attempted to re-establish public authority. Immediately after Chen Zaidao and Zhong Hanhua returned to Wuhan from Beijing, the Hubei Military Region convened a conference of three-level cadres (province, prefecture, and county). Chen told the participants that something must be done to improve the stagnant economy. This goal could only be achieved, he insisted, by setting up an umbrella production body at every level and in every unit. After the meeting, the Provincial Office for Grasping Revolution and Promoting Production was founded. A week later, a similar institution was established at the municipal level. Before long, such offices appeared in almost every unit.[46]

Thereafter, the Office for Grasping Revolution and Promoting Production became a standard form of public authority. All power seizures at the grassroots, whether successful or not, were declared to be null and void. It was hoped that by setting up such offices at every level and in every unit, a unified, coherent, and effective system of authority could be installed to fill the power vacuum that had existed since the end of 1966.[47]

According to Mao, the Office for Grasping Revolution and Promoting Production should be based on the principle of 'three-in-one combination'.[48] However, the army dominated such offices everywhere.[49] Representatives of mass organizations were included at best merely for show, if they were included at all. For instance, the provincial office initially had about forty representatives from the rebel organizations, but they were told that once they started working in the office they were no longer representatives of any particular mass group. Furthermore, they were warned that 'rebellious behaviours' were prohibited within the office and that any leakage of office secrets to mass organizations would not be tolerated. Even with such restraints, the army still could not trust the rebels, and in late March all the mass representatives were expelled from office.[50]

Party cadres played a crucial role in the Offices for Grasping Revolution and Promoting Production. They were the only group with the skills needed to restore social and economic order. The army announced that former unit chiefs would retain their authority and that the masses should submit to their leadership. Except in a few cases, most of the former officials were reinstated. The former governor of Hubei, Zhang Tixue, was asked to nominate the members of the Provincial Office for Grasping Revolution and Promoting Production, though he himself was in Beijing and not included in the office. The former mayor of Wuhan, Liu Huilong, was appointed to be the first deputy director of the office at the municipal level. At the grassroots, the reinstatement was more complete.[51]

By late March the old power structure seemed to have been largely restored. Cadres were reinstated. Workers returned to their production posts. Students resumed classes. The public security system began to function again to maintain social order. The roles of Party members, Youth League members, and activists were re-emphasized. The stagnant economy took a favourable turn.[52] On 28 March, when making a speech to a cadre meeting, Liu Huilong comforted his audience by saying:

You all have been wrongly treated and suffered a great deal in the past few months. It does not matter. What matters is that by giving 'monsters and ghosts' an opportunity to manifest themselves, we now can round them up at one fell swoop.[53]

Chen Zaidao was more sanguine about the future. He said:

We have successfully crushed a counter-revolutionary adverse current. At present, the proletarian revolutionaries are forming a great alliance, the rightist groups are falling apart, and the power usurped by a handful of careerists is being seized back. The progress of the Cultural Revolution in Wuhan is very good.[54]

Rebels' Counterattack and Stalemate

Dizzy with success, Chen failed to note that the wind was blowing in another direction in Beijing. In mid-March, Mao and the CRSG began to realize that the pendulum had swung too far in the direction of order and stability. In order to put the movement back on the right track, they initiated a counterattack against the so-called February Adverse Current. Tan Zhenlin, the Minister of Agriculture, was chosen as the symbol of the 'adverse current of counter-revolutionary restoration'.[55]

On 19 March the Beijing Red Guard Congress sent a group of delegates commissioned by the CRSG to Wuhan to collect information about the status of local rebels.[56] On the basis of a 100-page report prepared by the group, the *People's Daily* published an editorial entitled 'Correctly Treat Revolutionary Young Militants' on 2 April. According to the editorial, the main characteristics of the adverse current were:

By seizing on the revolutionary young militants' minor mistakes and attacking them for trivial faults, some people have totally repudiated the revolutionary young militants' general orientation. Worse still, some have gone so far as to impose the label 'counter-revolutionary' once again upon the revolutionary young militants and to help the conservatives to reconstruct their dead organizations.[57]

Who were the people being referred to? Beijing's decisions on the situations in Anhui, Sichuan, Inner Mongolia, Fujian, and Henan made it clear. In each of those cases, the local military authorities' actions in February and March were criticized. On 6 April the MAC issued a Ten-point Ordinance, which severely circumscribed the army's power in its dealings with the mass organizations. The army was now forbidden to declare mass organizations 'reactionary', to disband them, to retaliate against those who had assaulted soldiers, and to make any arrests except when the people concerned were unquestionably guilty.[58]

The *People's Daily* editorial and the MAC's Ten-point Ordinance snatched the Wuhan rebels from the jaws of death. The first half of April saw tremendous changes in the situation in Wuhan and even in the city's outward appearance. The streets, which had been quiet for about a month, were once again filled with people; and the walls of buildings, which had just been washed, were covered by colourful big-character posters and slogans. The rebels were once again in high spirits.

But while politically naive student rebels were visibly pleased, the older rebels tended to keep their rejoicing to themselves. Except for those who felt they had nothing else to lose, most of these older rebels preferred to take a wait-and-see attitude until they could be sure they would not be at further risk. Some had learned from the experiences of the past two months that they could at best gain very little but might lose a great deal from their involvement in rebellious activities. Those rebels decided to end their affiliation with any organizations and to watch the movement from the sidelines from that time on.[59]

As in the early period of the Cultural Revolution, the student rebels spearheaded the attack in the battle against the February Adverse Current. On 1 April the New Central China Institute of Technology, the New Hubei University, and the New Central China Agricultural College (often referred to as the Three News) and the Second Headquarters separately held mass rallies and parades. When the contingents of marchers met on the streets, they joined forces and praised each other's 'revolutionary rebellious spirit'. Facing powerful common enemies who had indiscriminately suppressed all rebels, these rivals for power realized the necessity of co-operation. Their number one enemy was Chen Zaidao of the WMR, or in their words, the 'Tan Zhenlin of Wuhan'. (Tan had been singled out as one of those responsible for the February Adverse Current.) From that day on, 'Down with the Tan Zhenlin of Wuhan' became a slogan that united all the rebels in Wuhan. In a bid to extricate themselves from the army's control, the rebel students launched a campaign to drive out the army's military training teams, which had been stationed in the schools since March. Under pressure from the rebels, the WMR was forced to withdraw the teams on 9 April.[60]

The army's concession further boosted the rebels' courage. A group of rebels boldly put up a poster entitled 'We Challenge a Handful of Scoundrels in the WMR's Headquarters for Supporting the Leftists' outside the office of the headquarters. This action caused a sensation throughout the city.[61]

Viewed from the conservatives' standpoint, the situation was becoming implausible again. When the term 'adverse current' first appeared in official Party newspapers, they believed it meant the excesses committed by the rebels. They, of course, had no sympathy with that kind of adverse current.[62] It soon became clear, however, that 'adverse current' meant the suppression of the rebels. Boosted by Beijing's call for a counterattack on the adverse current, the rebels were becoming increasingly arrogant and militant. The conservatives could not understand why the rebels had again found favour with Beijing.

The army was similarly unprepared for the change. The WMR had made an extraordinary effort to restore public order, but Beijing's new policy ruined the new order before it could take root.

There were signs that the disbanded Workers' Headquarters was planning to create a disturbance even though its leaders were still in prison. On 8 April, several dozen former members of the Workers' Headquarters held a torch march. The next day, in two of the city's largest factories, rebel workers announced the reinstatement of branches of the Workers' Headquarters. A few days later, a liaison centre of the Workers' Headquarters was founded. The liaison centre declared that its purpose was to seek rehabilitation of the Workers' Headquarters and the release of its leaders. The student rebels were more savage. Every day there were reports that Second Headquarters' branches had raided conservative or moderate groups' offices in schools and seized their broadcasting equipment. On 11 April a group of rebels from the No. 1 Middle School made excessive demands to the Municipal Office for Grasping Revolution and Promoting Production. After their claims were turned down, they went on a hunger strike for four days. On the day after the strike ended, a group of rebel students occupied the Hongqi Building, the office building of the *Yangtze Daily* and the *Hubei Daily*.[63]

Chen Zaidao and Zhong Hanhua, who were attending a meeting of the MAC in Beijing from late March to late April, were vexed by the setback in Wuhan. They believed that the problems stemmed from the support given to Wuhan rebels by the CRSG, whose decisions were based on faulty information. At a session of the MAC meeting, Chen complained:

> The CRSG does not know what is really going on in the provinces. It heeds and trusts only the rebels and some special correspondents it has sent out, but rarely listens to the army. Our reports and suggestions are often treated as merely a scrap of paper. Even when we ask the group for instructions about a matter of urgency, it often turns a deaf ear to us. We thus are often left in an awkward position.

Chen proposed two alternative means of remedying the faulty communication system: the CRSG could set up 29 sub-groups, each of which would be designated to lead the Cultural Revolution in a specific province; or the local army could be authorized to send delegates regularly to the CRSG to receive specific instructions. In any case, he hoped that a direct channel could be established between the CRSG and the local army: 'If we just do what the CRSG tells us to do, we won't make any further mistakes.'

The CRSG once again turned a deaf ear to Chen's suggestions. At about this time, the hunger strike in Wuhan came to the attention of Jiang Qing, Mao's wife and the deputy head of the CRSG. She was told that at least 50,000 people were taking part in the strike. When interviewing representatives from the rebels on 16 April, Jiang pointed out, 'The situation in Chendu and Wuhan is relatively more complicated and more grave. Therefore, the rebels of the two cities may need to launch a charge (*chongyichong*) to puncture their opponents' arrogance'. In Chinese, the term *chong* can mean 'criticism' or 'raid'. Chen Zaidao could imagine how serious the consequences might be if Jiang's remark were to reach the rebels in Wuhan. At Chen's request, the CRSG held a session on 19 April to hear the WMR's account of the situation in Wuhan. According to Chen, only 300 or so students had participated in the hunger strike, and the strike was now over. This put Jiang Qing in the position of having been misinformed. The session came to four conclusions. First, the original Red Guards should be allowed to exist. Second, the Workers' Headquarters should not be reinstated, because it had been dissolved before the MAC's Ten-point Ordinance of 6 April. Third, the WMR was not wrong to arrest about 500 persons in March, but the arrests needed to be reviewed case by case. The innocent should be released from custody. And finally, the WMR had made no 'orientation or line mistakes'. In addition, it was decided that Qi Benyu, a member of the CRSG, would meet on 21 April a group of Wuhan rebel representatives to dissuade them from attacking the WMR.[64]

Delighted by these unexpected results, Chen Zaidao and Zhong Hanhua immediately relayed the good news to other leaders of the WMR by telephone. Although they had been sworn to secrecy, the WMR leaders, who were under growing pressure from the rebels, could not resist sharing the news with their intimates. Before long the news had spread all over Wuhan. The next day, 20 April, the conservative organizations set their propaganda machinery in motion to publicize and hail 'the most welcome news from the centre;' the rebels, meanwhile, were perplexed.[65]

That afternoon, Jiang Qing learned of this development from a report by CRSG's special correspondents in Wuhan. She was furious at Chen and Zhong who, she believed, were trying to bully the rebels in the name of the CRSG. Chen and Zhong were ordered to hand over their copies of the minutes of the 19 April meeting, and were warned never to mention the matter again. The scheduled meeting between members of the CRSG and the Wuhan rebel representatives was cancelled. Jiang Qing even threatened to withdraw all future offers of help to the WMR from the CRSG. After this episode, the already tense relations between the CRSG and the WMR deteriorated further. The CRSG deliberately turned a deaf ear to the WMR's requests for instructions, which made the WMR particularly vulnerable in the highly volatile situation that developed in the following months.[66]

A more direct result of this episode was the mystery surrounding Beijing's instructions of 19 April. The conservatives firmly believed that those instructions, coming from reliable sources, could not be false, whereas the rebels asserted that the so-called instructions were fabricated by the army and the conservatives. Since there was no way to verify the existence of the instructions, each side simply held what was in keeping with its best interests to be the truth, which in turn led them to believe that Beijing was on its side. Such a conviction created a dangerous balance. Should one side be told by Beijing that it was in the wrong, the conflict between the two camps would end up with the unlucky side withdrawing from the competition. If both sides were convinced that they were backed by Beijing, however, the chances of them becoming involved in a life-or-death confrontation would increase significantly. As pointed out above, it was a rule of the game played out during the Cultural Revolution that no group would withdraw from the competition unless Beijing unequivocally denied its eligibility (for example, by declaring it a reactionary or conservative group). The ambiguity of the official position allowed full play to all sides of the conflict and thus was very likely to lead to a full-scale clash.

7

Conflicts between Conservatives and Rebels, May to July 1967

The Formation of Conservative and Rebel Grand Coalitions

The Conservative Coalition

WHEN Chen Zaidao and Zhong Hanhua returned to Wuhan on 28 April,[1] two grand alliances were taking shape in the city, one comprising all the conservative organizations and the other the rebel groups. The two alliances were not the kind of 'great alliance' Beijing had expected. Rather, they were the products of an ominous presentiment that there would soon be a decisive battle between the two camps.

The February Adverse Current had enabled the conservatives to regain their strength over the past three months. Many new organizations had come into being and quickly expanded their forces. The Red Armed Guards was a notable example. When the group was founded in mid-January 1967 it had only several hundred members. By 20 April, however, its membership had reached 240,000, becoming one of the largest mass organizations in Wuhan. Even more impressive than its rapid growth was its closely-knit structure. Based on the pre-existing institution of the official militia, the Red Armed Guards was organized like a paramilitary organization. Its leaders were mainly former militia officers, who had developed an extensive web of institutional and personal relationships in the years before the Cultural Revolution. The leaders managed the huge organization through two mechanisms. Along geographical lines, the members in an administrative district constituted a 'corps'; and, along occupational lines, the members in the units under an administrative bureau made up a 'column'. There were ten corps and twenty-five columns. The headquarters could operate the organization in either way when dealing with routine or potential problems.[2] The Red Armed Guards thus stood head and shoulders above the poorly organized rebel groups.

As pointed out above, after the collapse of the Federation of Revolutionary Labourers and the Red Guards, their members were scattered among the several dozen new organizations, and some joined relatively moderate rebel groups. By April 1967 the latter no longer found it necessary to put up under others' roofs. They therefore dropped their membership of the rebel organizations and rejoined the conservative ranks.[3]

When the rebels were down on their luck in February and March, the conservatives did not feel pressed to form a united grand alliance, for they could easily subdue the rebels once the latter were scattered among the individual units. But the revival of the rebels in April forced the conservatives to reconsider their strategy of how to deal with the rebels. The lack of a strong leadership and an effective operational system was an important cause of the failure of the Federation of Revolutionary Labourers. This lesson reminded the leaders of the various conservative organizations of the importance of unity and leadership. On the basis of a few fortuitous contacts, the conservative groups quickly developed both formal and informal trans-organizational communication channels.[4] In late April all the conservative groups in the city reached an agreement to hold a massive parade on 1 May, Labour Day, to show their solidarity and strength. This plan fell through when Beijing banned the demonstration. However, the idea of unifying all the conservatives endured. The necessity for unity was justified by a renaissance of class theory. In early May a conservative theorist was invited to address various organizations on the subject of 'How to Analyse the Situation in Wuhan'. What struck the audience most was the theory of class he put forward:

> In doing any analysis, the most important tool is the concept of class. At present, there seems to be a great deal of confusion about the concept, that needs to be clarified. Class relations should never be confused with the relations between the 'rebel' and the 'conservative'. Neither rebels nor conservatives constitute a class. Class is class. The Cultural Revolution does not change people's class identities. Workers are still workers, poor and lower-middle peasants are still poor and lower-middle peasants, capitalists are still capitalists, and landlords are still landlords.[5]

What this theorist was saying, in effect, was that the Cultural Revolution should not change the substance of social (power) relations. A handbill circulated at around this time made this point more vividly:

> Just as a proper temperature may incubate an egg into a chicken but no temperature is proper to hatch a rock into a chicken, landlords, rich peasants, counter-revolutionaries, bad elements, rightists, and other types of 'monsters and ghosts' will never come over to the side of Chairman Mao's revolutionary line, whichever mass organizations they may affiliate themselves with in the Cultural Revolution.[6]

This theory not only strengthened the self-confidence of the conservatives, but also pointed out the common ground on which a great conservative alliance might be founded. It helped to hasten the parturition of such an alliance.

Finally, on 16 May, a coalition liaison centre was created. Because the total membership of fifty-three constituent organizations of the coalition allegedly exceeded one million, the umbrella organization called itself the 'Million Heroes'.[7] Initially, the Million Heroes was a loose coalition, and the participant organizations were still rather independent. Each was limited to sending a liaison officer to the liaison centre, and the liaison officers worked together to co-ordinate actions in fighting against the rebels. The liaison centre did not have the power to deploy forces unless it had the approval of the participant organizations. This form of leadership obviously couldn't be efficient when coping with emergent situations. Thus, when the conflict between the conservatives and the rebels escalated, there was a cry to reshape the organizational structure and the leadership of the Million Heroes.

The change took place on 3 June. The fifty-three participating organizations agreed to give up their independence and to pool their resources to build up a thoroughly united organization. Correspondingly, the liaison centre was replaced by a headquarters.[8]

The leaders of the headquarters were carefully selected. First, incompetent candidates were excluded. A large percentage of the new leaders were low-level Party cadres rather than workers. Second, the candidates' political backgrounds were carefully examined. The Wuhan Public Security, a conservative organization made up of policemen, was asked to investigate each candidate's family origin and past political performance.[9]

The nucleus of the headquarters was its standing committee. Under the committee, there was an office to handle the day-to-day business, and seven departments in charge of internal security, communication, logistical support, propaganda, organizational work, strategic planning, and operational co-ordination.

The combined forces of the participating organizations were now subject to assignments given by the headquarters. In order to manage one million members efficiently, headquarters set up sub-headquarters in ten administrative districts (including suburban districts) and appointed leaders for each. The internal structures of sub-headquarters were modelled after those of the headquarters, so that the various departments at headquarters could readily identify their counterparts at the lower level and instruct them to carry out their orders.[10]

In general, by forming a coalition, the member organizations expected to gain more in combination than the sum of the pay-offs they would receive by pursuing their independent strategies. This rule apparently applied in the case of the Million Heroes: the coalition would enable them to deal with the rebels more forcefully than otherwise. However, the case of the Million Heroes seems to be at odds with William H. Riker's 'size principle'. According to Riker, while rational coalition makers have an incentive to create an effective ruling bloc, they have no intention of making their coalition as large as possible since the more coalition partners are included, the less each partner would gain from the victory of the coalition. Riker believes that rational coalition makers will try to create a coalition that is just large enough, they believe, to ensure a win and no larger—or, simply put, a minimum winning coalition.[11] However, the Million Heroes was a coalition that included almost all the conservative organizations in Wuhan. Does this fact suggest that the Wuhan conservatives were not rational? Not necessarily.

The common goal of the conservatives was to preserve the existing structure of power distribution, in which they had enjoyed some vested interests. While fighting to prevent the rebels from ruining their opportunities in life, they expected nothing less and nothing more. Since there would be no spoils for them to divide up in the event of victory, they did not have to worry about the size of their winning coalition. In other words, a maximal coalition could in fact serve their interests better than a minimal coalition.

It is much easier to build a maximal coalition than a minimal coalition. Whereas in the latter case the coalition-forming groups are uncertain of what constitutes the minimum, in the former case, the maximum means to include as many as possible. There is little uncertainty about the size of the coalition. For this reason, the conservative organizations were able to form a grand coalition without much haggling.

The Rebel Coalition

While the conservatives were building up their alliance, the rebels were attempting to form their own. But theirs did not come as easily as the conservatives'. The rebels all hoped that the Cultural Revolution would help to realize their interests, but their goals were different. Some expected material gains, others wished to change their socio-political status, and still others hungered for power. Even if they had shared the same aims, the scarcity of resources would have forced them to compete with one another over the distribution of whatever might come to them if they gained the ascendancy. The power seizure in January was a good example. While all the rebel organizations wanted to create a coalition that was strong enough to secure a victory, they hoped to keep its size to a minimum. In their calculations, if too many organizations took part in the power seizure, there might not be sufficient positions to be allocated. Given such a consideration, what the rebels tended to form could only be a minimum winning coalition.[12]

As pointed out above, building a minimal coalition is a very delicate process. The coalition makers have constantly to consider who is to be included while at the same time avoiding being excluded from the game. Even if a coalition is already in place, the partners need to keep an eye on each other (as potential competitors) while fighting together against their common enemies. Distrust thus tends to make the building of a minimal coalition time consuming and to make an existing minimal coalition unstable. Since a minimal coalition could best serve the interests of the rebels, underhanded competition was inevitable, which hampered the rebels' capacity to create an all-embracing alliance.

In the volatile political situation of the Cultural Revolution, information was imperfect and incomplete. There was no way for the coalition-forming groups to be certain of how one or more of the partners to their coalition would act in a time of crisis. (Would this or that partner desert the coalition and leave it to face defeat?) Therefore, it would be unwise for them to form a coalition without at least some extra margin of security. A coalition greater than the minimum size would at least have a chance of winning, while attempts to build nothing more than a minimum winning coalition might in effect create a coalition that was too small to have any chance at all of winning.

Under the stress of the circumstances in April and May 1967, the rebels nevertheless needed some form of coalition to survive their confrontation with the conservatives. In units where the rebels had been completely put down, the first task was to rally the rebel forces. This was not an easy job. Having suffered in February and March, most of the former rebels still had a lingering fear. Although April saw the first sign of the revival of the Workers' Headquarters, less than half of the former rebels dared to join the re-established branches. In most units, the branches of the Workers' Headquarters did not formally redeclare their existence until late May and early June, and in some units not until after the Wuhan Incident in late July. That many rebels did not formally rejoin the rebel organizations did not mean that they were no longer rebels. In May a so-called eighth headquarters emerged in Wuhan. The eighth headquarters was not an organization. Rather, it was a phrase

referring to individuals who did not join any organization but enthusiastically supported the rebels' cause. Because of the obscurity of their
identities, those people became the most violent forces on the rebel side.
In addition to taking part in demonstrations, mass rallies, and hunger
strikes, they often made raids on conservative organizations and physically attacked individual conservatives. The main components of
the eighth headquarters were former members of the Workers'
Headquarters.[13]

Other rebellious worker organizations began to recover at around the
same time. The Workers' Rebel Headquarters managed to recoup its
strength after the conservative elements had split off. In some large
enterprises, rebels set up new independent organizations, among which
the most influential were the United Headquarters of the Planning and
Research Institute of the Yangtze River Valley Development, the New
Zhongyuan Machine Factory, and the New Wuchang Shipyard. Even in
government agencies where the rebels' influence had been generally
weak, some rebel sympathizers set up for the first time their own organizations, such as the Red Headquarters of the Government Functionaries and the United Headquarters of the Public Security Officers. In
addition, some discontented high-level cadres founded the Liaison
Centre of the Revolutionary Cadres, openly expressing their sympathy
and support for the rebels.[14]

Relations between these various rebel organizations were loose,
although informal communication channels had long existed. In the face
of increasingly assertive conservative forces, the rebels started to build
up their great alliance through actions.

Their first action was to demand Xia Bangyin's release from prison.
Xia, a branch leader of the Workers' Headquarters at Hanyang Steel
Rolling, was one of 485 persons who had been arrested on 17 March.
Unlike many leading members of the Workers' Headquarters, Xia's
record was quite clear. From a poor urban family, he was a Party
member and had been honoured with the titles of 'advanced labourer'
and 'enthusiastic student of Chairman Mao's works' several times
before the Cultural Revolution. Since the army had very little evidence
to support its accusation against Xia, his case could be used to win wide
sympathy for the rebels and to put the military authorities on the defence.
On 22 April the Three News and the Second Headquarters organized a
sit-in in front of the Hanyang Branch of the Wuhan Public Security
Bureau where Xia was believed to be held. Soon, thousands of rebels
from all over the city joined the sit-in in support of the 'revolutionary
action'. This well-calculated strategy proved to be successful. In the

face of growing pressure, the army conceded: Xia was set free on 14 May.[15]

Before the end of this sit-in, the rebels took another action. On 10 May an incident occurred involving rebel students from the Public Security School and conservative policemen from the Jianghan Branch of the Wuhan Public Security Bureau; both sides suffered injuries. The students insisted that the Military Control Committee of the Public Security Bureau should take responsibility for the incident, and demanded that the committee punish their 'assailants'. The rebel students attempted to force the committee to meet their requests by staging a hunger strike in front of the bureau's building on 13 May. This event quickly drew considerable attention, giving the rebels another chance to show their 'militant solidarity'. Rebels from all trades were mobilized to support the rebel students from the Public Security School. Within a few days, the WMR found that people were taking part in hunger strikes in virtually every district of the city, especially in the downtown areas and at the sites of power organs, including its own headquarters' compound. The total number of hunger strikers reportedly exceeded 40,000. On 19 May, Zhong Hanhua was forced to enter into negotiations with the strikers. After eight hours of bargaining, the strikers declared that Zhang had agreed to meet all of their demands, and they held a rally to celebrate their victory. But the WMR denied that any concessions had been made.[16] Even if the WMR did not make any concessions, the rebels emerged as the winners, since the incident had helped to expand their influence and to draw their forces close together.

While these two events were in progress, more concerted actions were taken to pull the rebel organizations together. On 6 May, six influential student organizations jointly founded the United Headquarters of the Revolutionary Rebel Students of Wuhan. Two days later, fifteen worker organizations set up a parallel organization, the United Headquarters of the Revolutionary Rebel Workers of Wuhan. Finally, on 1 June, the United Headquarters of the Wuhan Revolutionary Rebels was brought into being, which was supposed to be the ultimate command centre of all the rebel forces in Wuhan.[17]

In reality, however, none of those umbrella organizations had real power over the constituent organizations under their command. In fact, no tangible headquarters ever took shape. At best they were quasi-formal communication networks through which the rebel organizations might co-ordinate their strategies and actions. But there was no guarantee that the headquarters could exercise control over the participants' strategies and actions. The rebels' alliances thus could not be efficient.

Nevertheless, the establishment of those networks was better than nothing. Faced with formidable foes, the rebels needed such mechanisms to reduce internal strife and to hold their forces together.

Issues Dividing the Conservatives and the Rebels

Throughout the period between April and July 1967, two main issues divided the conservatives and the rebels in Wuhan. One was whether the case of the Workers' Headquarters should be redressed, and the other was how to evaluate the WMR's record of 'supporting the leftists'. The issues were actually two sides of the same coin. If one asserted that the Workers' Headquarters had been wrongly treated, it might be concluded that the general orientation of the WMR was incorrect. Conversely, if one believed that the Workers' Headquarters had been a 'hotchpotch of monsters and ghosts', one would naturally side with the WMR.

The WMR itself, of course, insisted that its decision to disband the Workers' Headquarters was correct. Since the CRSG had taken a clear-cut stand against the reinstatement of the Workers' Headquarters on 19 April, Chen Zaidao and Zhong Hanhua maintained that Beijing's criticisms of the army in Qinghai, Anhui, Sichuan, Inner Mongolia, and Fujian did not apply to Wuhan. However, to be prudent, the WMR set up a special group to re-examine the case of the Workers' Headquarters on 22 April. By 15 July the group had compiled three volumes of evidence against the organization. The contents of the volumes reaffirmed Chen and Zhong's conclusion that the Workers' Headquarters was a 'bad organization manipulated by a handful of counter-revolutionaries'. They therefore had no intention of giving in to the rebels. On 4 June the WMR made a proclamation reiterating its con-sistent stand: 'The Workers' Headquarters must not be reinstated.'[18]

The tougher the stand the army took on the issue of the Workers' Headquarters, the more respect it obtained from the conservatives. In fact, the conservatives were more anxious than the army to prevent the Workers' Headquarters from reviving. They knew that in the zero-sum game of the Cultural Revolution, if the Workers' Headquarters returned from the grave, they might be buried in its place. More precisely, the conservatives worried that if the rebels were to gain the upper hand, the entire power structure of China might be turned upside down. They could not believe that Mao would do that to them, the very social forces Mao had relied on for decades. They were confident that the Workers' Headquarters comprised mainly three types of persons: people of bad origins, backward elements, and opportunistic careerists. In their view, there was nothing wrong in calling the Workers' Headquarters 'a sinister crew of old and new counter-revolutionaries'.[19] In an attempt to prevent such an organization from being rehabilitated, they supported the WMR, proclaiming themselves the 'pro-army faction'.

All the rebel organizations pressed the WMR to redress the case of the Workers' Headquarters, but their purposes were different. The former Fragrant Flower Faction demanded a thorough reinstatement of the disbanded organization. Obviously, the organizations of that faction would not be able to redeem their own honour unless the Workers' Headquarters could be reinstated. Such a thorough reinstatement was not in the best interests of the former Poisonous Weed Faction, however. The case of the Workers' Headquarters was useful in so far as it served as an issue around which all the rebels could be united. But the former Poisonous Weed Faction had no intention of bringing a strong rival back to life. Thus, while the Fragrant Flower Faction praised the Workers' Headquarters as a 'revolutionary organization', the Poisonous Weed Faction was only willing to go so far as to deny that it was a counter-revolutionary organization. In other words, it was necessary to remove the label 'counter-revolutionary' from the organization, but it was not necessary to restore the organization. Due to the differences in evaluating the nature of the Workers' Headquarters, the rebel groups' positions on how the cases of February Adverse Current victims should be redressed diverged. Whereas the Fragrant Flower Faction demanded the release of all those who had been arrested, the Poisonous Weed Faction asked only for the release of those who would prove to be innocent after case-by-case investigations. The subtle difference was an obstacle to the unity of the rebels.[20]

The confrontation between the rebels on the one hand and the army and the conservatives on the other hand overshadowed the differences within the rebel camp. However discordant the rebels' stands might be, in the face of powerful resistance from the army and the conservatives, they had no choice but to fight together. Since they were attacking the local army, they were regarded as the 'anti-army faction'.

Anarchy and Violence

The views of the conservatives and the rebels were so divergent on the issues of the Workers' Headquarters and the army that the tension between them was gradually aggravated. On 29 April, in a small textile factory, the conservatives and rebels resorted to violence in a minor dispute. This event marked the beginning of large-scale violent conflicts in Wuhan.[21]

Three factors created the fertile soil for collective violence to occur. First, messages from Beijing were so ambiguous that both the rebels and the conservatives believed they had the support of Mao. On the one hand, there were reports from 'well-informed sources' that the rebels' struggle against 'the Tan Zhenlin of Wuhan' was endorsed by the CRSG. On the other hand, news was circulating that 'some leading comrades of the central authorities' had denounced the Wuhan rebels.[22] Since there was no way to check the reliability of such information, people tended to believe the news that fitted their best interests, while asserting that those that ran counter to their interests were rumours or sheer fabrications. Thus, neither side was willing to give ground. As a result, the possibility of collision increased.

Second, in the present hostile environment, factions had insufficient information about their adversaries' capabilities, strategies, and willingness to use force. There was no channel for the rebels and the conservatives to communicate with each other, which prevented them from obtaining such information through diplomatic exchanges. Even if there had been communication channels, the factions had strong incentives to misrepresent their willingness to fight.[23] Uncertainty created fear. As a consequence, those factions faced a security dilemma.[24] Because they did not know what their rivals would do to them, they felt compelled to arm themselves. Yet, in doing so, they did not necessarily increase their own security, because their rivals would also resort to the same means. Such a spiral of insecurity tended to make all the factions less secure, since it increased the level of potential threat to which all were exposed.

Third, and most important, there were no rules and rule enforcers to mitigate conflicts. The army was supposed to be the mediator in the rebel—conservative strife. But the rebels viewed the WMR not as a mediator but as an adversary. Moreover, the WMR's capability to use coercion had been significantly enfeebled by the MAC's Ten-point Ordinance of 6 April. Without a mechanism for propitiating the contentious factions, oral insults could easily turn into physical clashes, and small-scale fisticuffs could quickly escalate into city-wide factional warfare.

Some commentaters believe that the collective violence which characterized the Cultural Revolution was an indication of human irrationality (or evil, or innate aggression). In fact, violence was a rational yet deplorable form of action. Under normal conditions, when the state, who monopolized the use of force, could threaten to punish groups or individuals who used force against others, organized violence as a strategy was ruled out or, at least, made extremely dangerous. Under anarchy, however, the provision of social order became a problem. Because there was an important element of social order that was a 'public good', individuals would not voluntarily refrain from doing things that might threaten the social order. Without an authority that could credibly threaten reprisal for the use of force to settle disputes, even good and rational people might come to blows when their interests conflicted. Thus, the strategy of violence must have always been kept in mind by the factional leaders, even if they themselves had no truly aggressive intent.[25] Recognition of the problem of anarchy makes possible a better understanding of why armed clashes often occurred during the Cultural Revolution, even though the participants were not foolish, ignorant, or evil.

Late May saw the first signs of large-scale fighting. On 21 May, when the organizations of the Million Heroes staged demonstrations in various parts of the town, the eighth headquarters harassed the parades. The two sides then engaged with each other in donnybrooks. This was the first incidence of city-wide physical conflict between the two factions, and it triggered a wave of violent clashes in the following days. On 27 May the conflict at the No. 20 Middle School took the life of a member of the Second Headquarters; it was the first death to result from factional struggle in the city. The seventeen-year-old boy's comrades carried his body to all corners of the city in a bid to mobilize support. The rebels were outraged and vowed to avenge the martyr.[26] The situation thus was becoming more explosive, and a full-scale war could break out at any moment.

In order to be prepared for the worst, both sides began to amass forces for action. The rebels had already occupied many public buildings and schools in the downtown area of Hankou. Now they moved more forces to those strongholds so as to control vital communication lines. The conservatives, who had not intentionally built up any strongholds, now realized the importance of arming themselves. The main aim of the reorganization of the Million Heroes on 3 June was to strengthen the conservatives' fighting capacity. The day after the reorganization, the Million Heroes took over the WMPC building and moved its headquarters there. Soon after, the Million Heroes gained complete control over most of the factories in three districts—Jiang'an, Qiaokou, and Hangyang—and drove the rebels from those factories to their strongholds in the city centre. Meanwhile, a number of blitz units were formed. Organized like the army, the units were composed of young men in their twenties and early thirties, many of whom had served in the army.[27]

On 6 June Beijing issued a general order to all the provinces, strictly forbidding the use of force in factional disputes.[28] However, no one took the order seriously. On 8 June the conservatives staged a march in the city centre, allegedly to 'promote the resumption of classes in schools' and to 'propagate the importance of forbidding violence.' Behind those noble slogans, however, was a plan to teach the rebels a lesson. It was calculated that when the parade passed through the downtown area, the rebels would make trouble, which then could be used as an excuse to confront the rebels. In fact, before the action started, the Million Heroes had already set ambushes in the neighbourhoods near the city centre. The plan was to ambush the rebels when they revealed themselves. As expected, the rebels fell into the trap, and the well-organized conservative forces easily put them to rout.[29]

This crushing defeat shocked the rebels. In the past, the conservatives had been timid and easy to bully, but the 6 June incident revealed that they were now becoming strong and aggressive. The changing nature of the conservatives made the rebels extremely nervous, and they decided to arm themselves with new defensive and offensive weapons. In the following days they fortified their strongholds and readied their weapons. Some even tried to develop explosive devices. These preparations restored the rebels' confidence. Wearing rattan helmets and carrying their home-made weapons, they staged armed marches around the city as a display of strength.[30]

The Million Heroes' strategy was to go about their task steadily. Hanyang District, which was then under the complete control of the conservatives, was called the 'liberated area'. Hankou was called the 'guerrilla area' because its two industrial districts, Jiang'an and Qiaokou, were under the Million Heroes' thumb, except for a few factories and schools, while its commercial district, Jianghan, was largely under the control of the rebels. The rebels dominated Wuhan's cultural district, Wuchang, which was called the 'enemy occupied area'. Faced with such an uneven power distribution, the Million Heroes decided to adopt Mao's famous tactic of using a superior force to destroy the enemy forces one at a time. First, the backyard must be cleared up. On 9 June the Million Heroes captured the Jurenmen Middle School, and three days later they stormed Wuhan Auto Parts, both of which were the rebels' last strongholds in Qiaokou District.[31] They then turned their attention to driving all the rebels out of Hankou.

The WMR was ineffectual in preventing violent clashes. After 6 June the WMR issued three strongly worded statements warning that anyone involved in violent activities would be punished, but neither the conser-

vatives nor the rebels paid them any heed. On 14 June the CRSG telephoned Chen Zaidao and urged him to stop the violence in Wuhan.
Without coercive power, however, Chen's hands were tied.[32]

On 17 June the Million Heroes launched a general offensive to 'liberate' the downtown area of Hankou. Thousands of members equipped
with lances and knives engaged in the operation. The conservatives were
superior not only in number but also in organization. A commander of
this operation proudly pointed out:

> Our people were well-equipped. In the battle of 12 June, we found that
> the rebels had been armed with lances. Therefore, we decided that we
> should have lances to protect ourselves too. Since most factories were in
> our hands, it was a piece of cake for us to do that. Within a few days,
> we were armed with much better weapons than the rebels were. Our
> people also had high manoeuvrability. Wuhan's six motor transport corps
> and five public transit companies were all under our control. We there-
> fore could deploy them at will. In addition, trucks from other units that
> we dominated were also at our disposal. Whenever there was an opera-
> tion, the leaders of the headquarters only needed to make a few phone
> calls to muster enough troops and conveyances. And after each opera-
> tion, we could provide sufficient good food to reward our fighters. With
> such an efficient organization, we didn't lose a single life in fights with
> the rebels throughout June and July.[33]

The rebel defenders, on the other hand, were in disarray. Most of them
were so-called eighth headquarters fighters in their late teens and early
twenties. Lacking a command system, they fought without tactics and
co-ordination. It was easy, therefore, for the conservative attackers to
break them up into small groups and then to wipe them out.[34]

The battle of 17 June was fiercely fought, lasting from the noon of
the seventeenth to the next morning. The rebels claimed that nearly one
hundred of their people were killed and about a thousand wounded. The
Million Heroes, however, denied this charge and insisted that it was
responsible for only one man's death. The truth might lie somewhere in
between. There was solid evidence that at least a dozen people were
killed in this incident.[35]

Outraged by their loss, the rebel organizations issued a number of
mobilization orders over the next few days, instructing their members
to prepare for an 'all-out counterattack' against the 'Tan Zhenlin of
Wuhan' and the conservatives. Slogans such as 'sword against sword
and spear against spear' and 'an eye for an eye and a tooth for a tooth'
created a stir in the city. The Wuchang rebels even issued an ultimatum
declaring that they would cross the Yangtze and wipe out all the conservatives unless the WMR disbanded the Million Heroes immediately. The

rebels' plan to conquer Hankou was of course wishful thinking, since they were inferior to the conservatives in almost every respect except propaganda. However, the rebels' war clamours evoked a strong reaction from the conservatives.

On 23 June the Million Heroes began to encroach on the so-called enemy occupied area—Wuchang. The first targets were the Xianfeng Building and the Fourth Institute of Railway Design, two rebel fortresses. The targets were not randomly chosen. The former was located at the only gateway to Wuchang from Hankou and Hanyang, and the latter was in a vital position which controlled the strategic pass between Wuchang and Qingshan. By taking over these two key positions, the Million Heroes attempted to ease the movement of its troops, a prerequisite for conquering Wuchang.

While the siege of the two fortresses was still under way, rebels from the Wuhan Water Transport Institute accidentally caught seven branch leaders of the Million Heroes. Holding those men as hostages, they demanded that the Million Heroes abandon its sieges immediately. The conservatives refused. Instead, after capturing the Xianfeng Building and the Fourth Institute of Railway Design, the Million Heroes moved its troops and besieged the Water Transport Institute. Two hundred of the encircled rebels fought desperately, but they were hopelessly outnumbered by the conservative attackers. The institute fell into the hands of the Million Heroes the next day.[36]

The Million Heroes tolled the death-knell of the rebels in Wuhan on 24 June. In Hankou it stormed the headquarters of the Workers' Rebel Headquarters. In the process, twenty-five rebels were killed.[37] Why were the conservative raiders so cruel? The commander of the operation described it as follows:

> Since the day of the Federation of Revolutionary Labourers, whenever we were trodden upon by the rebels, we bore and forbore. Now we were driven beyond the limit of forbearance. It became our belief that only when all the rebel fortresses were wiped out could peace prevail again in Wuhan. More specifically, the headquarters of the Workers' Rebel Headquarters was located in an area largely under our control, and its loudspeakers swore at us and stirred up trouble by rumour-mongering all the time. It was a thorn in our side. When we besieged it, therefore, we gave the rebels there no mercy.[38]

The fall of the Workers' Rebel Headquarters terrified the rebels. By the next day, all of the rebel strongholds in Hankou and many in Wuchang were deserted. Some of the former defenders retreated to colleges in Wuchang, which were still controlled by the rebels; others retreated to private life; and still others left the city in order to avoid further trouble.[39]

The defeat of the Wuhan rebels immediately drew Beijing's attention. On the night of 24 June, Chen Boda, the head of the CRSG, personally telephoned Chen Zaidao, urging him to prevent further violence. On 26 June the CRSG and the PLA Cultural Revolution Group sent a joint telegram to the WMR. The full text reads as follows:

> Recently, some large-scale violent conflicts have taken place in Wuhan. This is an unusual phenomenon. We hope that the WMR will adopt effective measures to stop the violence. The Million Heroes must stop its sieges of schools and factories. Those who were directly involved in the killing must be punished according to the General Order of 6 June. The centre will soon invite the representatives of the WMR and of mass organizations on both sides to Beijing in order to hear their respective accounts of the situation in Wuhan.[40]

After being criticized by name by Beijing, the Million Heroes adopted a low-key position. The very next day, it moved its headquarters in the WMPC building to a military supplies factory and dissolved its department of operational co-ordination. Although the conservatives stated publicly that 'the circular of 26 June shows the CRSG's concern for the Million Heroes' progress', inwardly they complained that 'the telegram fosters the arrogance of the bourgeoisie and dampens the spirits of the proletariat'. It was hoped that the Beijing meeting would provide a forum for them to pour out their grievances against the rebels and to justify their actions on the grounds of self-defence.[41]

The telegram of 26 June saved the rebels from extinction. A special correspondent dispatched by the CRSG told representatives of the Wuhan rebels in Beijing that central leaders needed information about the WMR and urged them to collect such information and to report it to Beijing. Such a gesture indicated that Beijing did not trust the WMR. The rebel leaders took the hint and became cocky again. On 28 June the WMR ordered that all organizations, conservative and rebel alike, must withdraw from their fortresses, all students and workers must return to their own units, and all weapons must be surrendered. The rebel organizations refused to abide by this regulation. Instead, some rebels returned to the strongholds they had abandored only a couple of days earlier.[42] Nevertheless, the rebels' vitality was greatly sapped. Terrified by the bloody violence, many decided it was wiser to avoid the trouble spots, at least for the moment. Many of the formerly crowded strongholds now were very quiet. Most of those who dared to return were middle school students.[43]

From 27 June to 15 July the city was relatively peaceful. There were no reports of serious clashes.[44] Both the conservatives and the rebels were waiting for the promised meeting in Beijing. If they were to gain at the bargaining table what they had failed to gain on the battlefield, they would have to exercise restraint. Both sides knew that they must avoid making any unwise move at this crucial time.

The WMR was also busy preparing for the upcoming Beijing meeting. In a report it prepared for central leaders, the WMR did not conceal the revulsion it felt towards Wuhan's rebel organizations. The rebels were accused of having defied the PLA. Between 6 January and 30 June, it was estimated, 342 soldiers had been attacked, among whom 226 were wounded and 38 severely injured. In every incident, the assailants were the rebels. Moreover, the rebel organizations were described as 'hotchpotches of monsters and ghosts'. The New Central China Institute of Technology was said to have been manipulated by a group of teachers, most of whom were from families of landlords, rich peasants, and capitalists.

In the WMR's view, the best organization in Wuhan was the Third Headquarters. It was a rebellious group in that in late 1966 it had played an important role in fighting against the HPPC's 'bourgeois reactionary line'. Unlike the other rebel groups, however, it had rarely committed excesses and always stood on the army's side. The only problem with the Third Headquarters was that its influence was shrinking in the increasingly volatile political environment.

The WMR asserted that popular sympathy lay with the Million Heroes. For one thing, the members of the Million Heroes had 'pure' political backgrounds. It was estimated that 85 per cent of the Party members in the city had joined the organization. Moreover, the conservatives had in general been moderate in their behaviour. Only when their restraint was mistaken by the rebels for weakness did they launch counterattacks. Cruel as the events after 8 June were, those operations were described as necessary to restore civil order. The WMR held the rebels responsible for most of the violence.[45]

The rebels' explanation of the violence was very different from that of the WMR. According to the rebels' statistics, 174 violent clashes took place between 29 April and the end of June, among which 130 occurred between 4 and 26 June. Those events involved 70,000 persons; 158 people died and 1,060 were seriously wounded. The conservatives were charged with provoking those conflicts.[46] The Third Headquarters, however, reported that during the period mentioned above, there were 107 incidents of violence, only 6 of which were started by the Million

Heroes.[47] As to who fired the first shot, the Third Headquarters' account was probably closer to the truth. Unorganized and undisciplined rebels, especially the so-called eighth headquarters fighters, tended to be more bellicose than the well-organized conservatives. Even the rebels themselves acknowledged that 'the eighth headquarters had great destructiveness but little real fighting capacity'.[48] As to which side caused most of the injuries and deaths, however, the rebels' charge might be legitimate. Since the conservatives were superior in number, equipment, and organization, once they decided to launch counterattacks, they could easily crush the rebels.

The violence not only cost lives and jeopardized public security; it also damaged production and disrupted the residents' daily lives. The gross value of industrial output dropped 6 per cent in May and 16 per cent in June. Labour productivity fell 6 per cent in the first half of the year. The crippling of production resulted in shortages of many daily necessities.[49] The WMR held the rebels responsible for the consequent economic difficulties. Because the conservatives generally dominated industrial firms, it was they who kept up production in most factories. But there were exceptions. In units where the rebels were in charge, or where the antagonism between the conservatives and the rebels was not tense, the rebels also played a role in maintaining production.[50] However, the exceptions could not change the WMR's perception of the rebels.

The Wuhan Incident

On 10 July, Zhou Enlai notified Chen Zaidao that the Wuhan negotiation would take place in the city itself rather than in Beijing as previously planned.[51] The reason for the change, which Zhou did not tell Chen, was that Mao decided to make an inspection tour of several southern provinces, and his first stop would be Wuhan.

Mao arrived in Wuhan on 13 July. Among his entourage were Zhou Enlai, Xie Fuzhi (the Minister of Public Security), and Wang Li (a key member of the CRSG). For the personal safety of Mao, even Chen Zaidao and other local leaders were not informed of his arrival. Only Zhou, Xie, and Wang were assigned the task of dealing with local problems, and only the latter two were supposed to appear on public occasions.[52]

Around midnight on 13 July, Xie and Wang, in plain clothes, went to Hubei University, a rebel stronghold, to gather information. However, they were recognized by students, and the news that Beijing had sent a delegation to Wuhan soon spread among the rebel organizations.

The next day, the rebels staged mammoth demonstrations to express their welcome to 'the beloved delegation sent by Chairman Mao', and the conservatives were at a loss. They could not understand why no one had informed them of the arrival of the central delegation. This was exactly the effect the rebels had hoped to create, that is, to bully the conservatives by putting up a façade which implied that they had special connections with Beijing. As a display of courage, the rebels intentionally paraded through areas under the control of the Million Heroes. They shouted 'Disband the bandit gang of the Million Heroes', and the Million Heroes' loudspeakers responded, 'Smash the black Workers' Headquarters and suppress counter-revolutionaries' and 'Mop up the Three News and the Second Headquarters'. The exchange of invectives soon triggered a clash. However, the Million Heroes was well prepared for surprise attacks. Its highly manoeuvrable blitz units had been on the alert for any possible aggression, and the rebels were soundly defeated. Ten were killed, thirty-seven were seriously wounded, and eighty were slightly injured.[53]

The renewed violence demonstrated the urgency of solving the factional conflicts in the city. On 15–16 July, Mao twice called in Zhou, Xie, and Wang to discuss how to solve Wuhan's problems. Mao made three suggestions: first, the Workers' Headquarters should be reinstated and the arrested rebel leaders released; second, the Million Heroes should be allowed to exist, even though it was a conservative organization; and third, the WMR should stop its discrimination against the rebels.[54] Following Mao's instruction, Zhou, Xie, and Wang convened a meeting of local high-ranking military officers from 15 to 18 July. The meeting was said to be a chance for local military leaders to express their opinions about the situation in Wuhan. But, with Mao's instructions in mind, the three central leaders ignored the advice given by the local leaders. Presenting the evidence gathered by the WMR, Chen Zaidao tried to prove that the Million Heroes was a 'genuine' revolutionary organization, but Mao's envoys refused to listen to him. Instead, the three central leaders pressed him to admit that the WMR had made mistakes in the past months. Unaware that Mao was present in Wuhan and that it was Mao who had set the tone for settling the local conflicts, Chen denied the charge.[55]

On the night of 17 July, Xie and Wang visited the headquarters of the Million Heroes. Wang reproached the leaders of the Million Heroes for having involved the organization in violent actions, and appealed to the Million Heroes to surrender its weapons and abandon its fortresses. The Million Heroes' leaders replied that their organization was willing to lay down its arms, if the rebels would do the same at the same time. Wang then criticized them: 'It is wrong to put forward such a prerequisite. You should restrain yourselves first.' His excoriation infuriated the Million Heroes' leaders, who retorted, 'We will not lay down our arms unilaterally. You have no right to force us to do so. All mass organizations are equal. The central delegation should treat them equally.' The meeting thus broke up in discord.

After leaving the headquarters of the Million Heroes, Xie and Wang went to the Wuhan Institute of Topography, where the headquarters of the Second Headquarters was located. They told the rebels there that Mao had recently said that no large mass organization should be forsaken even if it was conservative in nature. Although Xie and Wang said nothing about Beijing's position on local factional disputes, they hinted that the Party centre favoured the rebels but hoped they would show magnanimity towards members of the conservative organizations.

On 18 July, Zhou Enlai announced Beijing's decisions to the participants at a meeting of military officers: (1) The WMR had made serious political mistakes in the past months, for which Chen Zaidao and Zhong Hanhua should make self-criticisms. It was wrong to disband the Workers' Headquarters. The Workers' Headquarters should be vindicated and reinstated, and all the arrested rebel leaders released. (2) The Second Headquarters, the Three News, the 13 September Corps, and the Workers' Headquarters were genuine revolutionary organizations. They should form the core of the future great alliance. (3) No mass organization, including conservative ones, should be banned or disbanded. (4) The Million Heroes was a conservative organization. After the Workers' Headquarters was reinstated, its members might make reprisals against those in the Million Heroes. Efforts should be made to dissuade them from doing so. (5) The Third Headquarters was an organization whose orientation was inclined towards the conservative side. (6) The WMR should persuade peasants not to come to the city to help the conservatives attack the rebels. (7) The WMR should encourage the units under its command to support the rebels. (8) All mass organizations must rectify themselves and change their perception of the PLA.[56]

Chen Zaidao and Zhong Hanhua remained unconvinced. Zhou Enlai then sent them to see Mao. Only then did Chen and Zhong realize that behind the scenes it was Mao who had made all the decisions. Chen might have the nerve to contradict Xie, Wang, and even Zhou, but he did not dare challenge Mao's authority. Chen thus had no choice but to agree to make a public self-criticism.

After Mao's interview with Chen and Zhong, Zhou Enlai left Wuhan

for Beijing. Since the two top local leaders had accepted Mao's decisions, he assumed that there were no more obstacles to a peaceful settle-
ment of the local problems. How the masses of ordinary people would
react to those decisions was ignored.

In the small hours of the next morning, Xie and Wang made Mao's
decisions public to a group of rebels at the Wuhan Institute of Hydroelectric Engineering. Those rebels could not keep the good news to
themselves, and all the propaganda machines at the rebels' disposal were
set in motion. Before long, the news had spread to every corner of the
city, but it was distorted. In their propaganda, the rebels deliberately
emphasized four points made by Mao while overlooking the rest: the
WMR's general orientation had been wrong; the Workers' Headquarters must be reinstated; the rebels were genuine leftists; and the Million
Heroes was a conservative organization. All this sounded as if Beijing
would be content with nothing less than the destruction of the WMR and
the Million Heroes.

The news that Beijing had decided to support the rebels reached the
conservatives through another channel—Unit 8201, the garrison of
Wuhan. When the WMR set up the Headquarters for Supporting the
Leftists on 1 February, the unit was assigned to support the leftists in
the city.[57] After the Million Heroes was established, the unit developed
a close relationship with the conservative organization. It was an open
secret that the unit had strong sympathy for the Million Heroes. On the
night of 18 July the commander and commissar of the unit relayed Zhou
Enlai's speech to the officers and the rank-and-filers. Not convinced
themselves by the central decisions, the two leaders simply told their
perplexed subordinates that 'whether you agree with the centre's position or not, it is our job to implement the decisions'. Unit 8201 had a
large number of officers and rank-and-filers who were serving as military representatives in various industrial, communication, commercial,
and government units. Through this network, Mao's decisions reached
the conservatives, who at first had thought that the decisions were merely
the rebels' lastest fabrication. Interestingly, when the military representatives passed on the central decisions, the same four points the rebels
had stressed were emphasized.[58] Indeed, those four points were vital to
both sides.

On 19 July the leaders of the WMR began to implement the decisions.
In the morning, Chen Zaidao and Zhong Hanhua drafted their self-criticisms. In the afternoon, the meeting of military cadres was resumed, at
which Xie Fuzhi and Wang Li were invited to help those officers to
straighten out their 'muddled thinking'. Wang took the opportunity to

lecture the ideologically unsophisticated army officers on the importance of the Cultural Revolution. His talk lasted from 4 p.m. until 11 p.m. It was not clear how effective Wang's lecture was in changing the audience's perceptions of the local factional conflicts. However, it soon became evident that even if all the high-ranking officers decided to turn over a new leaf, which was unlikely, the events of the following days could still not be stopped. While Wang Li was lecturing at the WMR's auditorium, a political storm was gathering in the city.

The members of the Million Heroes were outraged by the news that they were officially labelled as 'conservatives'. Just a week earlier, a research group from the Red Guards had presented a report to the headquarters of the Million Heroes, which anticipated that Beijing's decisions on Wuhan would be unfavourable to the conservatives. This judgement was based on observations and analyses of the patterns reflected in Beijing's decisions on factional conflicts in the surrounding provinces. At best, the report forecast, Beijing would give the Million Heroes the ambiguous label 'mass organization' and allow it to persist. The leaders of the Million Heroes took the report very seriously but thought it sounded too pessimistic. The report therefore was kept from ordinary members so as not to shake their morale.

Wang Li's unkindly excoriation of the Million Heroes on 17 July was another evil omen. However, most of the leaders and members of the Million Heroes still could not believe that Mao would forsake them, the long-standing power base for Communist rule. Wang's criticism was considered to represent his personal prejudice.

The Million Heroes' worst nightmare now came to pass. The rebels, of course, emphasized that Wang came to Wuhan on behalf of the Party leaders in Beijing and that his four-point instructions represented Beijing's viewpoint. But the conservatives doubted this. At that moment, except for a few top local leaders, no one knew that Mao and Zhou were in Wuhan pulling strings behind the scenes. Only Wang and Xie had frequently appeared in public, and Wang had made most of statements. Therefore, the conservatives tended to believe that Wang represented only himself and that the so-called four-point instructions merely manifested Wang's personal hostility towards the Million Heroes. The conservatives worried that Beijing might be deceived by Wang and endorse what he had done in Wuhan.[59] If they were to avoid coming to a sticky end, as their counterparts in other provinces had done, the Million Heroes thus had to do something extraordinary to demonstrate to Beijing how broad its mass bases were and how strong the popular opposition was in Wuhan to Wang's arbitrary decisions.

On 19 July the city was in turmoil. Infuriated by 'Wang's decision', even those conservatives who were usually conciliatory became irritated.[60] Popular resentment among the members of the Million Heroes ran so high that the situation in Wuhan became very explosive.

The flames of uprising were kindled by soldiers of Units 8201 and 8199. At dusk, some sixty soldiers gathered at the gate of the compound of the WMR's headquarters, demanding that Wang Li explain what he was trying to achieve by issuing the four-point instructions. Their request, however, was ignored both by the central envoy and by the leaders of the WMR. They then decided to bring heavier pressure on Wang by seeking popular support. Around 8 p.m., dozens of officers were sent out to make contact with the Million Heroes and the Wuhan Law Enforcement Officers (a conservative organization made up of functionaries of the Wuhan's public security organs, the procurators' offices, and courts).[61] Four hours later, hundreds of trucks loaded with angry conservatives and law enforcement officers rushed to the WMR's headquarters to search for Xie and Wang. However, Xie and Wang had left for the East Lake Guesthouse, where they were staying. The intruders then questioned the leaders of the WMR: 'The army's general orientation in supporting the leftists has been correct. Why did Chen Zaidao and Zhong Hanhua admit that the WMR has made mistakes?' Some even called Chen and Zhong 'capitulators'.

The WMR leaders reported at once to Wang what was happening at its headquarters compound and suggested that he meet the conservatives' representatives before the situation got out of hand. But Wang dismissed the events as undeserving of serious attention. He and Xie retired for the night without making any effort to ease the situation.

As dawn broke, about two hundred conservatives entered the East Lake Guesthouse and confronted Xie Fuzhi and Chen Zaidao. Because Xie, unlike Wang, was a veteran cadre and rarely criticized the Million Heroes and the WMR in public, negotiations between him and the conservatives went fairly smoothly. It was agreed that he and Wang Li would meet a group of conservatives and that the conservatives would withdraw from the guesthouse. When Wang Li came out of his room, however, several hundred more people, mostly soldiers from Units 8201 and 8199, burst into the guesthouse and confusion broke out once were. At first, some mistook Chen for Wang and beat him with their rifle butts. After they realized their mistake, they set upon Wang.[62] At this point Zhong Hanhua reportedly fell to his knees and begged the agitaters to release Wang.[63] The situation was so confused, however, that his pleas were ignored and Wang Li was dragged back to

WMR headquarters, where thousands of members of the Million Heroes were waiting.

While these events were going on in Wuchang, exciting 'news' began to spread throughout the city. The following are some examples:

Chairman Mao said that he has had four great discoveries in the Cultural Revolution: first, Nie Yuanzi's poster; second, the Red Guards; third, Shanghai's January Storm; and fourth, the Million Heroes.

Chairman Mao's instructions concerning the Million Heroes: 'The Million Heroes is a good and pure organization with broad mass bases. We should cherish it.'

A telegram from the MAC (received at 4 a.m. on 20 July): (1) The WMR's general orientation in supporting the leftists has been correct. (2) Wang's four-point instructions reflect neither the centre's position nor the CRSG's viewpoint. (3) If Wang's instructions run counter to Mao Zedong Thought, the masses have the right to criticize him.

A telegram from the CRSG: (1) The CRSG knows nothing about the so-called four-point instructions. (2) Premier Zhou Enlai and comrade Chen Boda will fly to Wuhan shortly. (3) Xie Fuzhi and Wang Li were sent to Wuhan merely to find out about the situation there. The decision will be made by Zhou and Chen.

What matters is not who fabricated those rumours but the effect that those rumours had on local residents. It may be that rumours are likely to be accepted and circulated by those whose interests are served by the rumours. In this case, the conservatives spared no effort in spreading the rumours because they voiced their expectations.

The rumours quickly boosted the conservatives' morale. Donning rattan helmets and carrying spears, clubs, and knives, tens of thousands of them took part in large-scale demonstrations either by truck or on foot. It was estimated that between 1,000 and 1,500 trucks were requisitioned for this purpose. More people massed along the streets to cheer on the parades. Meanwhile, big-character signs and posters were put up everywhere, all saying the same thing: 'Wang Li's four-point instructions are poisonous weeds', 'Oust Wang Li from the CRSG', 'Drive Wang Li out of Wuhan', and 'Welcome genuine envoys of Chairman Mao—Premier Zhou and comrade Chen Boda—to Wuhan'.Throughout the city, the conservatives' loudspeakers broadcast all day long a song based on a poem by Mao, 'Congratulate the PLA's Capture of Nanjing' written in 1949, because it contained the phrase 'million heroes'.[64]

The feverish atmosphere caused many soldiers from Units 8201 and 8199 to get carried away by the excitement. Armed with rifles, they

joined in the actions of the Million Heroes and the Wuhan Law Enforcement Officers.[65] Not since they had undertaken the task of supporting
the leftists had the army openly associated with the conservative organizations, although it had had a strong sympathy for them all along. Now
the mask was stripped off. In an 'extra urgent appeal' issued on that day,
the officers and men of Unit 8201 declared:

> The notorious Workers' Headquarters is doubtlessly an organization
> manipulated by counter-revolutionaries. To rid the people of the scourge,
> we are determined to smash the Workers' Headquarters without
> mercy.... The Million Heroes is a genuine revolutionary leftist organi-
> zation. Its spearhead of struggle has always pointed to a handful of capi-
> talist roaders within the Party. It has played an exemplary role in carrying
> out and defending the Party line, in grasping revolution and promoting
> production, in supporting the army, in preventing violence, and in strik-
> ing relentless blows at 'monsters and ghosts'. If anyone dares to touch
> a single hair on the heads of the Million Heroes, we will wipe them out
> to a man.[66]

In response to the appeal, the Million Heroes put out an 'extra urgent
statement' on the same day, which swore:

> Sharing the same destiny, we, the members of the Million Heroes, are
> determined to fight side by side with the officers and men of Unit 8201
> against our common enemies.... A handful of counter-revolutionaries in
> the notorious Workers' Headquarters must be suppressed. Whether those
> intellectuals within the Three News and the Second Headquarters are
> revolutionary must be judged by us, the workers, peasants, and soldiers,
> rather than by few imperial commissioners.... And time bombs hidden
> in the centre [namely, Wang Li] must be removed.... We are prepared
> to sacrifice everything in order to crush the ongoing adverse current of
> capitalist restoration.[67]

The Third Headquarters also promulgated a statement, but it was
couched in much less harsh terms. Wang Li was still called a 'comrade'.
Though his four-point instructions were considered to run counter to
Mao Zedong Thought, they were criticized merely as 'an outcome of the
bureaucratic way of doing things'. The Third Headquarters joined the
protest mainly because it thought that Wang Li had given the Third
Headquarters an unfairly low quota of delegates to the negotiations
concerning Wuhan's future.[68] It had no idea that it had been classified
as conservative by Beijing. If it had known of this, it might have been
as militant as the Million Heroes.

Wuhan was in turmoil, when Mao was still in the city, staying in a
building very close to that from which Wang Li had been removed.
There was no sign of any threat to his safety. At Mao's request, the

WMR's leaders managed to rescue Wang Li from his captors and to move him to a safe place. However, the Party leaders in Beijing thought Wuhan was now too dangerous for Mao to remain in the city. On Lin Biao's advice, Mao left Wuhan for Shanghai early on the morning of 21 July. Before Mao's departure, Zhou Enlai flew back to Wuhan. In an attempt to cool down the situation, he suggested that the WMR select 100 delegates from both the rebel and conservative organizations to attend open negotiations in Beijing. Chen Zaidao saw this proposition as a sign that Beijing might soften its verdict on Wuhan. He promptly issued an order: 'Do not mention Wang Li's instructions any more. The final decision will be made in Beijing.'[69]

On 21 July the conservatives' demonstrations continued, and the city was still in ferment. Wherever the Million Heroes paraded, the rebels fled before them. When they encountered resistance, the Million Heroes troops simply swept it away. More than a dozen rebel fortresses were taken by storm. By 23 July, only four or five of the city's colleges were still in the hands of the rebels.[70]

Buoyed up by their successes, the Million Heroes began to contemplate seizing provincial and municipal power. While the rank-and-filers were parading on the streets, the top leaders held a meeting to discuss the power transition. Excited by the release of an enormous energy among their fellow conservatives during the past two days, the participants agreed that conditions were right for a power seizure. The Million Heroes had embraced the majority of the revolutionary masses, and most of the leading cadres had either publicly declared their support of, or stealthily felt sympathy for, the Million Heroes. In addition, the WMR much preferred to work with the Million Heroes than to deal with the disorganized rebels. With all the components of the three-in-one combination in readiness, the leaders of the Million Heroes were confident that they would be able easily to seize power.[71]

While the conservatives were jubilant over their victory in Wuhan, Beijing was reaching the conclusion that the events in Wuhan constituted a 'counter-revolutionary rebellion'. On 23 July the Central Broadcasting Station repeatedly aired the news that Xie Fuzhi and Wang Li had returned safely to Beijing.[72] The next day, huge demonstrations were held all over China to condemn the 'Wuhan reactionaries'. These demonstrations climaxed on 25 July when the CRSG held a mammoth mass rally at Tiananmen Square in Beijing. On 27 July the Party leaders in Beijing issued an open letter to the residents of Wuhan, calling on them to point the spearhead of struggle at 'three handfuls'—'a handful of evil leaders of the WMR, a handful of evil leaders of the Million

Heroes, and a handful of evil leaders of the Wuhan Law Enforcement Officers'.[73]

When the conservatives in Wuhan first learned from the radio that Wang Li had been greeted at Beijing airport, they were shocked. In the days that followed, the message became clearer when the Beijing authorities openly denounced the Million Heroes and supported the Wuhan rebels. Thousands of critical telegrams from all over the country streamed into the headquarters of the Million Heroes, which put enormous pressure on the chief leaders of the organization. They cared little about Chen Zaidao's personal fate. But they could not understand why Beijing was treating the Million Heroes, the largest mass organization in Wuhan, so harshly. The only interpretation they could think of was that Mao and Lin Biao had been somehow deceived.[74]

At first, the headquarters of the Million Heroes decided that as long as Mao and Lin did not openly declare their positions, the organization would not surrender. Lin Biao's presence at the meeting at Tiananmen Square on 25 July, however, cast a pall over them. Although a few individuals, who surmised that Mao might have been put under house arrest by Lin, swore to fight to the bitter end unless Mao personally arraigned the Million Heroes, most people accepted that the new development had been endorsed by Mao himself.[75] For many years, the Chinese people had been inculcated with the belief that Chairman Mao could do no wrong. Since the beginning of the Cultural Revolution, most of the authorities had been crippled, but Mao's personal authority had been enhanced. Anyone might be suspected and disowned, but not Mao. Nevertheless, Mao's repudiation of the Million Heroes and recognition of the Workers' Headquarters as a 'revolutionary organization' bewildered the conservatives. The conservatives' feelings were ambivalent, as illustrated by the following excerpts from the minutes of a meeting held by a sub-headquarters of the Million Heroes:

> A: I cannot accept that we, poor and lower-middle peasants and workers, are the followers of Liu Shaoqi and Deng Xiaoping, whereas those so-called rebels are true believers of Chairman Mao.... Whether or not we are to make a statement endorsing the centre's decision, we are losers. It seems to me, however, that if we make such a statement, we can prevent our rank-and-filers from resorting to excesses while being exasperated; and thereby we may have a better chance of keeping our organization. Now the headquarters [of the Million Heroes] has declared that it upholds the centre's decision, but our sub-headquarters has not. We should probably keep in step with the headquarters. After all, what is important for us now is to enhance the internal unity of our organization and to pull it through the current crisis.

B: If we make such a statement, it amounts to admitting that what we have done in the past few days are counter-revolutionary actions. I would rather die on my feet than live on my knees. What I am trying to say is that we should make such a statement under no circumstances.

C: I am baffled by the centre's decisions. First, in doing class analysis, we all know that the Workers' Headquarters is full of impure elements, but the centre calls it 'a revolutionary organization'. I think that the Workers' Headquarters should never be allowed to wield power. We are pure. We have never committed evil deeds. We have made a great contribution to the Cultural Revolution in Wuhan. Second, Chairman Mao always stresses the importance of uniting 95 per cent or more of the masses and cadres, but the centre's decisions in fact favour the minority at the expense of the majority, which makes me wonder whether Chairman Mao's mass line is still valid. Third, in responding to Chairman Mao's call to 'support the army', we have stood by the army's side. But now the centre accuses us of having been loyal to Chen Zaidao. It is not true. What we have supported is the army as an institution created by Chairman Mao rather than Chen Zaidao as an individual.

Conclusion: Whether or not we are convinced, we must observe and implement the centre's decision without reservation.[76]

First put forward by Lin Biao, 'Whether you are convinced, you must follow Mao's instruction' was a prevalent phrase during the Cultural Revolution. By encouraging blind faith on the one hand and implying a threat on the other, Beijing was able to compel some disobedient individuals or groups to submit. For ordinary people, it was a way to avoid questioning the justness and sanctity of Mao's instructions, when they found that such instructions contradicted their interests. During the Cultural Revolution, whenever Beijing's instructions were too general, the factions in the provinces tended either to pay lip service to those instructions or to interpret them in accordance with their own interests. If the instructions were sufficiently specific, especially when Beijing decided to disown a particular group, however, few dared to dispute that the judgements were sound.

On 27 July the Million Heroes finally disintegrated. The rebels were wild with joy. Because the conservatives had once asserted that 'The Workers' Headquarters cannot be reinstated unless cocks are going to lay eggs', they posted big pictures of cocks everywhere and added the slogan, 'Wuhan's cocks have laid eggs, and the Workers' Headquarters has been reinstated'. The leaders of the Workers' Headquarters were released and greeted as if they were generals returning in triumph. From 25 July on, the rebels staged daily demonstrations to celebrate the 'second liberation of Wuhan'. On 31 July, Beijing named the new leaders of the WMR. Zeng Siyu, former deputy commander of Shenyang Military Region, was appointed to be the commander of the WMR; and Liu Feng, former deputy head of the Wuhan Air Force, was named the commissar.[77]

The rebels won the city, but they did not win the hearts of the former conservatives. Although the conservative organizations crumbled, the conservatives as a social force did not vanish.[78] Thus, the conflict between the conservatives and the rebels was likely to continue in a new form. In the case of the rebels, it was questionable whether the partnership formed among the various rebel organizations in adversity could be sustained. Nevertheless, with the fall of the conservative Million Heroes, the Cultural Revolution in Wuhan entered a new phase.

8

Conflicts between Rebels, August to December 1967

The Great Tumult

SINCE neither the military leaders of the WMR nor the supporters of the Million Heroes intended to defy the central authorities, the Wuhan Incident was quickly brought under control. But the events in Wuhan triggered off a dangerous nation-wide campaign of 'pulling a handful of capitalist roaders from the army'.[1]

An article published in Wuhan in early August 1967 expounded on the strategic implications of the rebels' triumph in the city:

> The lesson of the Wuhan Incident is that a prerequisite for seizing power from the handful of capitalist roaders in the Party is to take over the military power usurped by the handful of bourgeois representatives in the army. Otherwise, the power seizure would be just empty talk.[2]

In their fight against 'the handful in the army', the rebels were convinced that they needed to arm themselves. For the first time, the PLA's weapons were seized by the warring mass organizations in many parts of the country. The restrictions imposed upon the army about using force against civilians made it impossible for the army to resist. In late July and early August, almost all the mass organizations were attempting to arm themselves. Thousands of army depots and barracks were raided around the country.[3] This spontaneous militarization of the mass organizations alarmed Beijing, which adopted a two-fold position in an effort to maintain a minimum of public order. On the one hand, it advised the masses not to seize the army's weapons by themselves; on the other hand, it promised to distribute firearms to leftist organizations in an orderly way.[4] In Wuhan, the new leadership of the WMR began to arrange the distribution of weapons to the rebel organizations in mid-August.[5] While the rebels cheered Beijing's decision to arm the leftists, few paid attention to the Party's appeal that they cease the spontaneous seizure of weapons from the army. Since Beijing did not, and could not, specify which groups were leftist and which were not, its decision to arm the leftists accelerated the arms race among the mass organizations.

Many organizations set up quasi-military groups and started military training programmes. In most cases, however, the rebels armed themselves simply by raiding the army's arsenal without making any effort to discipline such behaviour. For a while, it became fashionable to carry guns on public occasions, and students and young workers were fascinated by firing shots into the sky and throwing hand grenades into open areas. The possession of firearms by undisciplined rebels increased the possibility of armed clashes between the opposing factions.[6]

Compared with the situation in many other cities, the situation in Wuhan was relatively calm in August. There were two reasons for this state of affairs. First, the leadership of the WMR had recently been reshuffled, and the local army units which had suppressed the rebels had been relieved by other units. The rebels had no excuse to attack the army. Second, the rebel organizations had recently been forced to form a united front in the fight against the powerful conservative forces. Even if their common enemies no longer existed, it took some time for the latent contradictions among them to deteriorate to the point of open conflict. As a result, the army in Wuhan did not face as serious a challenge as did its counterparts in Guangzhou, Fuzhou, Nanjing, Shenyang, and many other places, and there were no reports of major armed clashes in the city after 25 July.[7] However, the rest of the nation was still largely adrift in a sea of chaos. Pitched battles between heavily armed factions were reported in nearly all of the provinces. Even Beijing witnessed an unprecedented wave of violence.[8] China was on the brink of civil war in the summer of 1967.

By late August, Beijing began to realize that in a Hobbesian 'state of nature', it was unlikely that the warring factions would sit down and negotiate a way out of the 'war of every man against every man' unless a common power was re-established. It therefore took a series of harsh measures in a bid to restore order. The general orientation of the rebels in late July and August was repudiated, the programme of 'arming leftists' was terminated, and various restrictions were imposed on the rebels' behaviour. More important, the rebels were ordered to return their weapons to the army.[9]

As always, when Beijing explicitly prohibited something, its directives were fairly effective. In early September the rebels in Wuhan began to return their weapons to the army. But it was by no means a genuine political *détente*. What the rebels returned to the army were in most cases old, bulky weapons that could not be easily hidden. New and small weapons such as pistols and grenades were often kept. Thus, the truce between the rebels and the army on the one hand, and between the rival factions on the other, was likely to be short-lived. Nevertheless, due to Beijing's intensified efforts, the movement weathered the storm and was entering calmer waters by autumn.

Searching for New Identities

The Wuhan Incident gave the participants in the Cultural Revolution in Wuhan a new identity and thereby changed their expectations and calculations of the value of collective action.

Impenitent Conservatives

After the Wuhan Incident, the conservatives were urged to acknowledge their faults and to cross over to the side of the rebels.[10] Mao assumed that they had been hoodwinked into being conservatives and that once they realized this, they would join the ranks of the rebels. But as the preceding chapters have shown, which side one took during the Cultural Revolution was not randomly determined, and thus the conversion did not occur as easily as Mao had expected. It was not difficult to make the conservatives believe that Chen Zaidao was an 'evil man'. After all, they knew little about him. However, it was very difficult to convince them that the rebels were real 'revolutionaries'.[11] Thus, although the Million Heroes fell apart without much resistance, most of the conservatives maintained a degree of independence after the Wuhan Incident, refusing to co-operate with the rebels of their units.

If the conservatives were to survive in this generally hostile environment, they had three choices. The first was 'physical exit'. Afraid of retaliation from the rebels, a great number of the conservatives reacted to Beijing's denunciation of the Wuhan Incident by fleeing the city to take refuge in their home towns or other safe places. Thus, the first thing the rebels did after the Wuhan Incident was to issue thousands of wanted circulars. Among the most wanted men were thirteen leaders of the Million Heroes and the Wuhan Law Enforcement Officers. After an intensive search, they were arrested by mid-August. Except for one captive who was beaten to death at a public accusation meeting by rebels in August 1967 and another who died of illness in prison, the rest were to stay in gaol until March 1972.[12]

As a result of the rebels' threat to suspend the salaries, or even to terminate the employment, of those who had left the city, the conservative fugitives slowly returned to their units. However, students generally were less afraid of being expelled from school, and some of them did not return to their schools until the end of 1967.[13]

The second choice was 'organizational exit'. From the very beginning of the Cultural Revolution, there had been people known as *xiaoyaopai*, or the 'stand-aloof-faction'. Many conservatives now decided not to join the rebel organizations, thus becoming a new type of involuntary *xiaoyaopai*. The very choice was a manifestation of their unwillingness to co-operate with the victorious rebels. Although those former conservatives no longer had their own organizations, they still banded together, openly or secretly, to exchange information and opinions. These intractable conservatives were considered a nuisance by the rebels.[14]

The conservatives' third choice was 'transmutation'. A large number of conservatives joined the rebel organizations with the express purpose of continuing their fight against the rebels in their units. For instance, many conservatives joined the 13 September Corps. This was a deliberate and clever choice. An organization based at Wuhan Iron and Steel Corporation in Qingshan District, the 13 September Corps had been a small organization until mid-July 1967. Because of its alliance with the Workers' Headquarters, however, it had some influence in city politics. There were two advantages for the conservatives in joining the 13 September Corps: they would be safe while remaining independent of the 'genuine' rebels in their units, who could not take action against the former without offending the 13 September Corps as a whole.[15]

The 13 September Corps was not the only choice of the conservatives. In many cases, they joined the weakest rebel groups in their units in hopes of somehow changing the composition and even the leadership of those groups.[16] For instance, in one hospital there had been two rebel organizations: one, an affiliate of the Workers' Headquarters, consisted mainly of odd-job men; while the other, an affiliate of the Red Rebel Headquarters, was made up largely of medical staff. After the Wuhan Incident, both attempted to expand their forces by recruiting former conservatives. Most of the conservatives eventually enrolled in the Workers' Headquarters. This may appear odd to outsiders, because the Workers' Headquarters was more radical than most of the rebel organizations in city politics. The conservatives chose to join the Workers' Headquarters because its branch in that particular hospital was much weaker than the Red Rebel Headquarters' branch. Later the branch of the Workers' Headquarters came under the control of the former conservatives, even though its leaders largely remained the same. This type of realignment took place in many units after the collapse of the conservative organizations.[17]

Of course, there were opportunists who changed their allegiance and threw in their lot with the winners. And there were also those who joined rebel organizations in the hope that their affiliations would shield them from revenge by individual rebels. After the conversion, the opportunists often acted more radically than the genuine rebels as proof of their sincerity. The cravens, on the other hand, generally had no interest in the rebels' cause.

Recalcitrant Rebels: Retaliation

Retaliation is probably a natural human instinct. In normal times, this instinct is circumscribed by social norms and laws. But the Cultural Revolution broke down all social norms and laws, along with public authority. It was not surprising, therefore, that retaliation became a pervasive phenomenon. Beijing had anticipated that the rebels would seek revenge against the members of the Million Heroes after their victory. After the Wuhan Incident, it made a series of efforts to exhort the Wuhan rebels not to retaliate against the former conservatives.[18] What Beijing failed to do was to take concrete measures to stop the rebels from doing so. In the anarchy of late July and August, retaliation became a part of the 'war of every man against every man'.

Indeed, the first thing the rebels set out to do after the Wuhan Incident was to make reprisals against the former conservatives in their units. Given the pain and humiliation they had endured, they relished the opportunity to seek revenge. In late July and August, public accusation meetings were held in every unit, and thousands of people were paraded through the streets. The scenes resembled those during the Smashing the Four Olds Campaign except that people's roles were reversed. Many of the victims of that campaign were now cocky 'revolutionary rebels' who were in a position to punish those who had maltreated them just a year ago. Their victims included not only the leaders of the Million Heroes' headquarters but also its branch leaders and even ordinary members. The rebels were not interested in merely returning like for like. Rather, in giving vent to their accumulated rancour, they often acted more ruthlessly towards their victims than those people had done towards them. Many conservatives were tortured, their homes seized, and their family members abused.[19] According to incomplete statistics, in Wuhan alone more than 600 people were beaten to death and over 66,000 were injured or crippled as the result of being tortured after the Wuhan Incident.[20] The retaliation of one faction against the other seems to have cost more lives and human suffering than the armed conflict between the two factions.

Retaliation took a different form in different types of units. Students were usually not very sophisticated politically, and they knew that after graduation they would all go their own way. Therefore, they had little to fear from beating up their conservative schoolmates.[21] Retaliative actions took place more frequently among adults than among students. Factory and office workers, however, had to be more careful. In the Chinese system, once one was employed, one was very likely to stay in the same unit for the rest of one's life. Thus, it was politically risky to beat up one's colleagues. Such concerns did not stop the rebels from avenging themselves on their conservative colleagues. But they often asked their rebel comrades from other units, especially middle school students and young workers, to do the actual dirty work so that the victims would not be able to identify the hidden instigators. To an extent, this tactic worked. Many of those who suffered such reprisals could not name the assailants who had injured them. But in another sense, the tactic was a complete failure. Because the tactic was widely used, no victim would assume that an attack on him by outsiders was an accident. Instead, the victims tended to believe that the rebels in their units had planned the attacks and should be held responsible for their suffering. They therefore were unwilling to forgive either the abettors or the assailants. As a result, their hostility towards the rebels in their units, instead of abating, actually spread to include rebels in society as a whole. They might have to hide their hatred for the moment, but in due course they would retaliate against the rebels should there be an opportunity.[22]

Even though revenge and retaliation typically took place in a group context, they were essentially private acts. While such reckless acts of violence might serve personal desires, they could result in some unwanted external effects and create 'public bads', thus harming the rebel movement as a whole. Of course, individual rebels would not be able to strike out against their personal adversaries if they had not succeeded in their collective cause. But the pervasiveness of the retaliative activities at this time seemed to suggest that, after having triumphed over the conservatives, the rebels' individual calculations of the value of collective action had begun to change. In the eyes of many rebels, the marginal utility of further collaboration was diminishing. It was ironic that the very success of collective action reduced its value.

Recalcitrant Rebels: New *Xiaoyaopai*

The high tide of retaliation lasted about two months. As public order was gradually restored in mid-September, the rebels' excesses receded. Suddenly, a large number of rebels found themselves at a loss as to what to do next. When reassessing the role of the rebels in the Cultural Revolution, a former rebel theorist pointed out that the rebel was a destructive force that had enormous capacity to disturb and paralyse the existing system but had little thought about how to reform it. In seeking to liberate themselves from all forms of oppression and restrictions, the rebels had their immediate superiors and conservative colleagues as the targets. For many rebels, vindictiveness thus was a main, if not the only, force that kept them active in politics. Once they, as victors, had vented their spite on those whom they hated, there was little more to be individually gained from collective action. With no tangible targets to fight against, a large number of rebels, especially former backward elements, lost interest in collective action. They began to remove themselves from politics, becoming 'new *xiaoyaopai*'.[23]

Since the schools were closed and the factories severely affected, the problem for the new *xiaoyaopai* was how to spend their time. Junior high students found that it was more fun to play with their friends in the neighbourhood than with comrades from their rebel organizations at school. They wandered the streets seeking excitement from childish games such as cockfighting and raising carrier pigeons. Senior high and college students had more sophisticated ways of entertaining themselves. Some played card games and chess. Others read novels, Chinese and foreign, modern and classic. Books that had been subjected to burning a year ago were now in vogue. Still others engaged in romantic relationships with other young people, which helped to divert their attention from the turbulence going on around them. Some people devoted themselves to learning a foreign language, or studying mathematics, physics, and the like. Others were more practical, taking up knitting, sewing, or cooking, or learning to repair radios or to play a musical instrument, or developing other skills.[24]

Workers were even more pragmatic. They spent their time trying to improve the quality of their daily life. Many took up fishing, hunting, carpentry, or home repairs. In late 1967 a rumour circulated in Wuhan that regular injections of cock's blood would prolong one's life. For a short time, this became a hot topic of conversation in the town. Some people tried it out, while most people just enjoyed talking about it.[25] It was ironical that while hundreds of people were killed and injured during the factional strife, others were looking for magical ways of prolonging life. A further irony was that many films that had been labelled as 'poisonous weeds' were being shown again under the pretext that if the rebels were to criticize them, they first needed to view or review them. In fact, people were tired of watching the same few boring 'revolutionary' films and wanted broader choices. Some rebel organizations tried to make a profit out of showing the old films to audiences long deprived of such fare. Organizations reportedly even stole copies of the films from one another.[26]

Recalcitrant Rebels: Cashing in on Economic Returns

Following the rebels' triumph in July, a new tide of economism engulfed Wuhan. Some rebels raised an agitational call, 'We want to stand up not merely in a political sense, but also in an economic sense.' Taking advantage of the absence of public authority, economically dis-advantaged groups tried to force their demands upon terrified former power holders.

A large number of educated youth who had been sent to the country-side returned to Wuhan and demanded permanent residence permits and employment opportunities in the city. Demobilized soldiers who were dissatisfied with their assignments demanded better jobs. The 1966 and 1967 graduates of special or technical secondary schools who were unhappy with their appointments and remuneration demanded better positions and higher pay.

Temporary and contract workers in state enterprises demanded to be made regular workers or at least to be treated as regular workers in terms of pay and other benefits. Some regular workers in state enterprises demanded promotions, pay rises, better fringe benefits, and more bonuses.

Economism ran most rampant in collective enterprises. Instead of just putting forward their demands, workers in these enterprises began to make changes without authorization. Some merged small enterprises into large ones, and declared them 'state enterprises'. They then granted themselves pay and benefits equivalent to those enjoyed by regular workers in state enterprises. Some restructured their enterprises into smaller organizations and announced that each was an independent accounting unit whose members had the right to decide how to distrib-ute its profits and how much to distribute. Some, though making no structural change, raised their own salaries anyway. It was reported, for instance, that in one small factory with fifty-eight employees, fifty-one got a 22.5 per cent increase in pay. In addition to efforts to increase their monthly salaries, workers in many collectives tried, under a variety of pretexts, to line their pockets with the accumulated funds of their enter-prises, which, according to government regulations, could only be used for reinvestment. It was not uncommon for such funds to be divided and distributed as 'shareout bonuses' among the employees. In some extreme cases, funds were quickly exhausted. Some workers even turned their enterprises into 'underground factories or shops' which engaged in speculation, profiteering, tax evasion, and other illegal activities in order to reap staggering profits.

Although those economic demands were, almost without exception, made by the rebels, none of the major rebel organizations supported them. The leaders of the main rebel organizations cared more about the redistribution of political power. People from different organizations but sharing similar interests in one aspect of economic life thus often found it necessary to form an expedient 'single-issue' alliance so as to press their demands. Rarely did such alliances take the form of a new organization. The people involved simply acted together whenever action was needed.

Social psychologists and theorists of collective behaviour have observed that casual crowds are more likely to be involved in violence than well-organized groups. This observation is supported by the case of those who seized the opportunities provided by the Cultural Revolution to pursue their own economic interests. There were frequent reports of mobs raiding the finance and accounting sections of enterprises, municipal or provincial financial organs, tax bureaux, and banks. The targets the mob attacked were not limited to former power holders. Anyone who blocked their way would almost certainly come under attack. They often clashed with rebels of institutions they were raiding.[27]

Recalcitrant Rebels: Cashing in on Political Returns

The triumph over the conservatives in July emboldened many rebels to try to cast off the labels imposed on them in the past. Some former capitalists, landlords, rich peasants, and bad elements complained that they had been forced by 'Liu Shaoqi's reactionary revisionist line' to bear humiliating labels. Asserting that the Anti-Rightist Campaign of 1957 had been initiated by Liu Shaoqi and Deng Xiaoping, some rightists called for the abolition of the label 'rightist'. They appealed for redress of 'wrongs' and demanded the return of their properties confiscated during the Smashing the Four-Olds Campaign.[28]

Officials who had been designated as the targets of attack in the early stages of the Cultural Revolution also came out to demand rehabilitations. Li Da, the supposed head of the 'three-family village' of Wuhan University, had died, but professors and administrators implicated in the case did not want the matter to end. After the Wuhan Incident, they set up a powerful organization which worked to redress the case.[29] Cheng Yun, the head of the 'black gang of Wuhan's literary and art circles', who had been publicly denounced by local official newspapers in July 1966 and taken into custody subsequently, now spoke out to claim his innocence.[30] Zeng Chun, the former director of the Propaganda Department of the Hubei Provincial Party Committee who had been accused of being 'the backstage boss of Li and Cheng', also pleaded his case. He claimed that Wang Renzhong had used him as a scapegoat in order to safeguard himself.[31]

In the autumn of 1967, a self-styled Committee of Re-examination and Rehabilitation (*zhenbie pingfan weiyuanhui*) was established to handle appeals for re-examining miscarriages of justice in the past and to reverse unjust verdicts. For a short time, the committee attracted a large number of people seeking help. The growing influence of the organization in turn boosted the morale of those who believed they had been wrongly treated.[32] This 'evil wind of seeking restoration' obviously diverged from the general orientation of the struggle set by Beijing.

Politics of Power Distribution

The mainstream rebels did not degenerate into new *xiaoyaopai*, economic interest hunters, or individualistic freedom fighters, but they did not follow Mao's instructions either. In fact, they became a real headache for Beijing.

Despite the Party leaders' repeated requests that the rebels form a great alliance, the relationship between the various rebel organizations soured soon after the Wuhan Incident. The formation of a great alliance was a prerequisite for the establishment of the future power structure. Obviously, it was a process of distributing power. The experience of the power seizure of January 1967 convinced the faction leaders that the only way to ensure good positions for themselves in the forthcoming revolutionary committees was to gain the upper hand when the great alliance was being formed.

The rebel faction leaders wanted to be in power, not so much because they needed power to realize noble goals such as reforming the existing system, as because they wanted power as such. Initially, they had sought only to take advantage of the Cultural Revolution to vent their personal spite. Mao's call for a seizure of power nourished their ambition for power. They began to perceive the movement as a lucrative opportunity to replace the old power holders. Few questioned whether an old structure with new leaders would be able to make any fundamental changes.

None thought to develop new institutions to overcome China's social maladies. They simply wanted to be the new power holders.[33]

Power cannot be shared by contenders unless there is a set of enforceable rules to regulate the contenders' conduct. The rules should contain at least three elements: the criteria for selecting candidates from the thousands of ambitious men and women who covet power; a procedure for choosing the power holders from the candidates; and a principle for distributing power among the selected power holders. None of those rules was laid out when the rebels were urged to seize power in January 1967. It is not surprising, then, that the power seizure resulted in tangled warfare between the rebel factions. This time, Beijing wanted to avoid that kind of disastrous result. Rather than laying out the rules of the game, however, it only set a prerequisite for playing the game: the rebels must form a great alliance before power was to be allocated.

The formation of a great alliance was by no means an easy task. When the rebels were fighting against the conservatives, they needed each other to win the game. But now they had a new game, one which would divide power among themselves. They had played this game before (during the power seizure in January), but only for a very brief period of time. Now the game restarted. In such a game, the participants needed to form coalitions in order to gain control over the new power organs, but they wanted to keep the coalitions as small as possible, for two reasons. First, for each coalition partner that was added in order to win, there would inevitably be an additional price to pay.[34] Second, unlike the life-and-death struggle between the rebels and the conservatives, the distribution of power was not perceived as a zero-sum game, at least not at that moment. Even if a coalition turned out to be smaller than necessary, its constituents could still expect some seats in the new power organs. They therefore could afford the risk of forming a coalition smaller than the optimal size. This desire to keep the winning coalition as small as possible prevented the voluntary formation of a great alliance.

Soon after the Wuhan Incident, the prospects of holding power from the provincial level down to the grassroots again split the Wuhan rebels along the old lines of the Fragrant Flower Faction and the Poisonous Weed Faction, now called respectively the Strong Faction and the New Faction.[35] Each side tried to dominate the great alliance under consideration at the expense of the other.

At first, the Strong Faction asserted that only the seven organizations mentioned by name in the letter of 27 July from Beijing to the residents of Wuhan (the Workers' Headquarters, the Second Headquarters, the

13 September Corps, the New Central China Institute of Technology, the New Hubei University, the New Central China Agricultural College, and the Revolutionary Committee of the Third Headquarters) were eligible to participate in the formation of the great alliance at the provincial and municipal levels. Other organizations were left with one choice, that is, to disband themselves and to merge into one of the seven. This proposal obviously aimed at minimizing the number of power contenders. However, it failed to get the support of the three New Faction organizations included in the list. From the New Faction's point of view, the proposal was a tactic by the Strong Faction to ensure its dominant position in the bargaining process. The rebel forces in Wuhan were distributed in such a way that the three Strong Faction organizations listed above embraced almost all the students and workers belonging to the faction, while the three New Faction organizations included in the list represented only three colleges. The Revolutionary Committee of the Third Headquarters took a somewhat neutral position in the conflict between the two factions. If the Strong Faction's proposal were to be accepted, New Faction forces in other colleges, middle schools, and factories would be excluded from the negotiations about the future great alliance. The Workers' Rebel Headquarters, the second largest rebel worker organization in the city and the backbone of the New Faction, was especially outraged. On 8 August, when a group of central leaders met the heads of the major Wuhan rebel organizations, the representatives of the New Faction expressed their strong aversion to the plan. In order to pacify the New Faction, the central Party leaders declared that all existing rebel organizations had the right to play a part in the formation of the great alliance.[36]

When its first ruse failed, the Strong Faction tried another. This time it proposed that the great alliance would need a 'core leadership', and that the Workers' Headquarters should be that core. It soon became clear that by advocating the core theory, the Strong Faction hoped to annex the entire New Faction. First, it suggested that all other workers' organizations should disband themselves and their members should join the Workers' Headquarters. The leaders of those organizations might be reappointed to positions in the Workers' Headquarters if such positions were available and if they were judged 'suitable' by the leaders of the Workers' Headquarters.

Second, the Strong Faction advocated the 'Wuhan way' of forming the great alliance. In Beijing the student movement had overshadowed the workers' movement, whereas in Shanghai the workers movement had dwarfed the student movement. By the 'Wuhan way', the Strong

Faction meant an integration of the student and worker movements, with the Workers' Headquarters as its core. Accordingly, it proposed that not only all worker organizations but also all student organizations should merge into the Workers' Headquarters.[37]

Third, while the Workers' Headquarters claimed to be the core of the great alliance at the provincial and municipal levels, its branches made similar claims at the grassroots, regardless of their relative strength in particular units. At Zhongyuan Machine Factory, for instance, the New Zhongyuan was the dominant rebel organization with several thousand members, while the branch of the Workers' Headquarters was a tiny group with a few dozen members. But the latter held that, as the representative of the most revolutionary organization in the city, it was entitled to wield power in the factory. Similar cases were reported in many units.[38]

The New Faction, of course, had no desire to bow to the Strong Faction. It countered the Strong Faction's plan by proposing a different model for forming the great alliance, 'the model of united headquarters'. According to this model, various mass organizations in each unit should merge first and then set up a united headquarters without a preset core. The great alliance at the provincial and municipal levels should be based on thousands of such independent united headquarters, rather than on a few giant city-wide organizations. This was a carefully calculated proposal. As pointed out above, the Strong Faction forces were concentrated in a few large organizations, whereas the New Faction's forces were scattered. The model of a united headquarters ensured that the New Faction forces, which were generally weaker than their Strong Faction counterparts, would at least get fair representation in the great alliance at the grassroots as well as at the provincial and municipal levels.

Politics at this time was basically a contest of strength. The New Faction knew that its proposal would be rejected by the Strong Faction unless it could show that it had the strength to compete. On 17 August, fifty-seven organizations of the New Faction declared that they were amalgamating into a grand union, the New Wuhan. It was hoped that the merger would significantly strengthen the New Faction's bargaining position in the power struggle with the Strong Faction.[39]

On 19 August the *People's Daily* published an editorial entitled 'The Core of Leadership of the Revolutionary Great Alliance Can Take Shape Only in the Process of Mass Struggle', which explicitly criticized 'self-centring claims for power' of any sort.[40] This provided the perfect opportunity for the New Faction to attack the Strong Faction. The *People's Daily* article was featured prominently in all the major publications of the New Faction over the next day or so. The editorial, however, did not intimidate the Strong Faction. Resorting to sophistry, it insisted that the Workers' Headquarters was the core of leadership of the great alliance that was taking shape in the course of the mass struggle. It further charged that those who refused to accept the leadership of the Workers' Headquarters had their eye on the leadership position themselves.[41]

By late August it had become very clear that neither the Strong Faction nor the New Faction would compromise in matters of power distribution. In order to obtain a better bargaining position, both sides sped up their efforts to expand their forces. Former conservatives, and those with no organizational affiliation, were fair game in the competition to win new members.[42] For the reasons discussed above, a fairly large number of former conservatives joined the rebel organizations. The number of registered members of almost all the rebel organizations soon increased sharply—so sharply, in fact, that armband making and related printing became a flourishing business, while production in general stagnated. One organization, for instance, reportedly ordered 200,000 armbands in late August.[43] The dramatic expansion of the rebel organizations was partially due to the fact that many people simultaneously joined more than one organization. According to statistics provided by four organizations at the Wuhan Boiler factory, their total membership exceeded 6,000. But there were only 4,000 employees.[44] The strategy of joining two or more competing organizations might help individuals to survive the volatile political environment, but those with dual membership were unlikely to commit themselves to the cause of any single organization.

The two factions did not appear to care much about their new recruits' loyalty. What they cared about was the size of their organizations. They deliberately inflated the numbers of their registered members. The Workers' Headquarters claimed to have 600,000–700,000 members, the 13 September Corps, 100,000–200,000, and the Workers' Rebel Headquarters 360,000.[45] The former head of the Workers' Rebel Headquarters later admitted that his organization had at most 60,000–70,000 members at that time. He added that organizations overstated their membership because people believed that power would be distributed roughly in accordance with the relative strength of each organization. The exaggeration, like the irresponsible recruitment, was a strategy to contend for more seats in future power organs.[46]

Early September saw the exacerbation of tension between the two factions. On 4 September the Strong Faction forces jointly established the General Headquarters of Proletarian Revolutionaries.[47] This was a countermove to the constitution of the New Wuhan. With the two giants confronting each other, the danger of a clash increased. Fortunately, in mid-September, Beijing made a push to build up the great alliance in the provinces, which temporarily arrested this perilous tendency.

Beijing's method for creating a 'high tide' of the great alliance was to publicize some phony examples.[48] The response of the rebels in the provinces was to establish phony alliances in order to please Beijing.

In Wuhan, the 'high tide' of forming great alliances occurred between 22 and 24 September. On 22 September, rebels from Qiaokou and Jiang'an districts declared that they had reached an agreement to form alliances at the district level. And on 24 September, rebels from Jianghan District made a similar claim.[49] In the meantime, thousands of people went to the WMR and the newly established Wuhan Garrison Command to report the 'good news' that rebels in their units had achieved unity. The major mass organizations then vied with one another to demonstrate their goodwill in 'keeping in step with Mao's strategic plan'. The Workers' Headquarters and the 13 September Corps declared that they were merging into a single Workers' United Headquarters and invited the Workers' Rebel Headquarters to join them. The Workers' Rebel Headquarters in turn spread a smoke screen, as if it was preparing to disband itself and to form an alliance with the other workers' organizations. The Second Headquarters penned a slogan, 'Dissolving the Second Headquarters to bring about a great alliance', while the New Central China Institute of Technology, one of the New Faction's major strongholds, proposed 'No New Faction, no Strong Faction, let's build up a unity of proletarian revolutionaries together'.[50]

To an outsider, it might have appeared that the great alliance at the municipal and provincial levels was just around the corner. But the participants knew that all these endeavours were merely for show. Before Beijing was able to get excited about the 'good news' from Wuhan, the inorganic alliances began to fall apart, and the unctuous expressions of goodwill were quickly replaced by a renewed exchange of accusations between the various factions. By the last week of September, a factional war was in the making.[51]

Again, fortunately, these dangerous developments were arrested, or more accurately, interrupted by Zhou Enlai's visit to Wuhan on 8 October with an Albanian delegation. On his arrival he learned that the rebels who had come to welcome him had just engaged in a battle at the airport and that both sides had suffered some casualties.[52] The incident convinced Zhou of the deep-rooted division among the rebel organizations in Wuhan. Zhou met with the faction leaders every day the following week in an attempt to press them to form a great alliance as soon as possible.[53] He told the faction leaders that, according to 'Chairman Mao's great strategic plan', the process of setting up a new government structure (the revolutionary committee) in all the twenty-nine provinces and major cities must be completed before February 1968. Wuhan should not be an exception. He also said that none of the faction leaders would be appointed as chiefs of the future provincial and municipal revolutionary committees, however prominent their roles had been in the past year. These positions would be reserved for veteran military or civilian officials. Further, he announced that the great alliance should take the forms of the Workers' Congress and the Red Guard Congress respectively for workers and students, and that no mass organization should be excluded from the preparation process.[54] By setting a deadline, lowering the rebel leaders' expectations about their opportunities in the new government structure, and specifying the form of the alliance and its legitimate participants, Zhou hoped that the way would be smoothed for the rebels to reach unity.

On the surface, all the organizations warmly applauded Zhou's speeches.[55] Behind the scenes, however, factional struggle was raging. The only difference was that the battlefield had shifted from the street to the conference room.

On 13 October the negotiations for setting up both the Workers' Congress and the Red Guard Congress at the municipal level began. The two key issues of both negotiations were which organization should get seats in the leading bodies of the two congresses and how many seats, and which organization heads should assume the top positions. Before those questions could be discussed, it had to be decided first which organizations were eligible to have representatives in the preparatory committees of the two congresses. Obviously, whichever faction had more say in the preparation process was likely to gain more power in the congresses. In the case of the Red Guard Congress, Zhou Enlai avoided quibbles over which organizations should be on the committee by naming six major student bodies as members. The preparatory committee of the Red Guard Congress thus came into being on 14 October.[56]

What Zhou did not realize was that the situation in Wuhan was quite different from that in Beijing. In Beijing, the rebel worker organizations had been underdeveloped from the outset, so that as long as the rebel students could be brought under control the situation there would be more or less stable. In Wuhan, however, both the student and worker movements had kept pace with each other and had been well integrated. Because of this complicated situation in the city, it was not sufficient to focus attention solely on the student organizations. As a result of Zhou's failure to designate the member organizations of the preparatory committee of the Workers' Congress, the negotiations for setting up the Workers' Congress were stuck on the issue of the composition of the preparatory committee.

The Workers' Headquarters and the 13 September Corps insisted that the committee should consist only of themselves plus the Workers' Rebel Headquarters and that the three organizations should be given respectively seven, five, and three seats. The Workers' Rebel Headquarters refused this proposition. In a move to counter the Strong Faction, the Workers' Rebel Headquarters made two suggestions. First, the three biggest organizations should have equal representation on the committee. Second, the preparatory committee should also include representatives from the other worker organizations. After intense bargaining from 13 to 15 October, the Workers' Headquarters and the 13 September Corps finally accepted the first demand: each of the three giants would have three negotiators participating in the preparatory work. But they flatly refused to consider the inclusion of representatives from other organizations. Thus the negotiations reached an impasse.[57]

On 17 October, Beijing issued a short but important circular, which stated: 'Factories, schools, government agencies, and other institutions must build revolutionary great alliances on the basis of trade, profession, and class.... Accordingly, all organizations consisting of people from more than one trade should make necessary adjustments.'[58] The prime objective of the announcement was to regain control over the movement by breaking up organizations into small components that would presumably be easier to control.

As always, Beijing's new directive was cheered by all the organizations involved, and the suspended negotiations were resumed on 18 October. But none of the parties was interested in discussing how to carry out Beijing's instructions about dissolving the giant mass organizations. Rather, attention was still focused on the issue of the composition of the preparatory committee. Pointing out that the circular used the phrase 'all organizations', the Workers' Rebel Headquarters asserted that its proposal to include minor organizations' representatives on the committee was in keeping with what Beijing was intending to achieve. The Workers' Headquarters and the 13 September Corps disagreed. They pointed out that most of the organizations which the Workers' Rebel Headquarters suggested be included were those whose members came mainly from a single unit. Those organizations might be eligible to prepare the great alliances in their own trades, but they should not be included in the preparatory committee of the Workers' Congress at the municipal level. Neither side intended to give in. The negotiations thus came to a deadlock again on 20 October.

The WMR and the Wuhan Garrison intervened at this point. After intensive behind-the-scenes activities for three days, on 24 October the Workers' Rebel Headquarters made a surprising statement that 'due to enlightenment by the WMR leaders', it was willing to compromise with the Workers' Headquarters and the 13 September Corps. It agreed that the preparatory committee of the Workers' Congress would be made up of the delegates of only the three largest worker organizations. There were reports that the Workers' Rebel Headquarters had made this concession under pressure from the army. The army pressed the Workers' Rebel Headquarters to give in, not because it was partial to the Strong Faction, but because it assumed that monitoring negotiations among a small number of contenders was much easier than dealing with a large number of contenders.

On 25 October the preparatory committee of the Workers' Congress was formally established. The committee, however, was immediately caught in a cross-fire. On 29 October, when it called the first meeting to discuss what should be done next, an unexpectedly large crowd poured into the conference room. Representing organizations that had been excluded, they came to express their indignation at the Strong Faction's attempt to arrogate all powers to itself. More important, they came to demand representation in the preparatory committee. Some people got carried away by the tumultuous atmosphere and revealed their true motives. One man, for instance, stated, 'Yes, I am ambitious. I want to be a member of the preparatory committee. You may call me selfish. In this regard I do not think there is much difference between you and me. What does make me different from you is that I dare to openly acknowl-edge this, but you don't.' When Zhu Hongxia, the head of the Workers' Headquarters who was chairing the meeting, tried to extricate his comrades and himself from the predicament by announcing that the meeting was adjourned, the crowd became angry, and blows were exchanged. Zhu himself was hit.[59] Noting that the head of the Workers' Rebel Headquarters had not come to the meeting, the Strong Faction concluded that the incident was a premeditated action by the New Faction. In revenge, its forces immediately stormed 155 strongholds of the New Faction, injuring hundreds of people.[60] The negotiations between the two factions broke off again. All that had been achieved was lost.

The preparatory work of the Red Guard Congress was also in trouble, though the issue of the composition of the preparatory committee had been settled. Here the trouble was that the Second Headquarters disagreed with the other five organizations about how to select the leaders of the future Red Guard Congress. The Second Headquarters suggested that the leaders should be selected in three steps. First, the various rebel organizations in each school should form a great alliance; then the schools should send delegates to attend the Red Guard Congress; and finally, the leaders of the congress should be elected by the delegates.[61] This scheme was exactly what the worker organizations of the New Faction called 'the road of united headquarters'. At first glance, this might seem puzzling: why did the students of the Strong Faction advocate a scheme which their worker comrades vigorously opposed? An analysis of the relative strength of the Second Headquarters could help us to answer this question. The Second Headquarters was the largest rebel student organization in Wuhan. Its membership was larger than that of all the other student organizations combined, and with the exception of a few colleges and middle schools its forces had the whip hand on most campuses. In the preparatory committee of the Red Guard Congress, however, the Second Headquarters was in the minority. The other five member organizations were all part of the New Faction. If the leaders of the congress were to be selected by the six organizations in the committee, the Second Headquarters could be easily reduced to an inferior position in the congress. The only way to avoid losing the game, therefore, was to adopt a set of favourable rules.[62]

In a bid to further enhance its chances of winning, the Second Headquarters suggested that only those schools in which a great alliance had been established should be given the right to send delegates to the congress. By that time, six colleges had established revolutionary committees. Five of them were schools under the control of the Second Headquarters. The Central China Institute of Technology was the only exception. Hubei University was about to announce the establishment of the revolutionary committee, but the Second Headquarters refused to recognize its legitimacy, because the committee excluded a tiny group from the Strong Faction of the university. At the Central China Agricultural College, another component of the Three News, the Second Headquarters had a small branch which was attempting to block the establishment of the revolutionary committee there. If the Second Headquarters' proposition were to be adopted, the New Hubei University and the New Central China Agricultural College would have no right to send delegates to the Red Guard Congress, nor the opportunity to have their people take up leadership positions, even though they were member organizations of the preparatory committee of the congress.

The New Faction member organizations of the preparatory committee, of course, did not want to lose their superiority in the committee. They insisted that the members of the committee should be the members of the leading body of the future Red Guard Congress.[63]

The two sides could find no way to reconcile their differences. As relations among the worker organizations of the Strong Faction and New Faction steadily deteriorated, the negotiations between the student organizations also reached an impasse in early November.[64]

Compared to recent months, November 1967 seemed monotonous in Wuhan, as well as in other parts of China. There were no reports of violence, no conspicuous events, no heated debates, and no general excitement. Neither was there much talk of the great alliance. Describing the situation during this period, some observers asserted that the Cultural Revolution had weathered the storm and was entering calmer waters.[65] But stalemate should not be mistaken for calmness. In Wuhan, after the breakdown of the negotiations for setting up both the Workers' Congress and the Red Guard Congress, the rift between the Strong and New Factions was widening.[66] In the words of a local publication, 'The antagonism between the two factions has taken a turn for the worse.'[67] Each side started to launch personal attacks on the other's leaders,[68] and embarrassing facts about the former relationship between the two factions were dredged up. The Strong Faction condemned the New Faction as an 'accomplice' of Chen Zaidao in putting down the Fragrant Flower Faction after the 8 February Statement, while the New Faction ridiculed the Strong Faction for having servilely petitioned Chen Zaidao for amnesty when the Workers' Headquarters was outlawed in March. The reopening of those old sores aggravated the tension between the two factions, and both feared that the tension might trigger armed conflict. In preparation for the worst, they started to organize their own semi-professional armed forces.[69] The Workers' Headquarters set up the Armed Working Team for Joint Defence and the Guards Regiment; the 13 September Corps, the Dare-to-Die Brigade; and the Workers' Rebel Headquarters, the Iron Army. Beijing was new peddling 'order' and 'unity' in the nation, which gave the two factions no excuse to rekindle the flames of violence. They thus had to restrain themselves at a time when they would have preferred to destroy each other. What they were waiting for was an opportune moment to take action. But that moment was some time in coming.

9

Conflicts between Rebels, 1968

Imposed 'Alliance'

I N September 1967 Mao had stipulated that all China's twenty-nine provinces should have established their revolutionary committees before the Spring Festival of 1968.[1] Despite Beijing's painstaking efforts, however, by early December only nine provinces had set up the new power structure. The disappointingly slow pace must have frustrated the central leaders, who began to realize that the great alliance would be an unobtainable goal if the rebel factions were left to negotiate the agreements on power distribution among themselves. This assessment was probably right.

What the opposing factions were in fact playing was a game called 'prisoners' dilemma'. In the game, both sides of the conflict will be better off if they agree to co-operate, but non-cooperation is the dominant strategy for each player, 'dominant' in the sense that following this strategy will leave each player better off whatever the opponent does. For instance, if one side chooses to co-operate, non-cooperation provides the other side with a higher pay-off than co-operation. Similarly, if one side chooses not to co-operate, then non-cooperation is still a better choice than giving in to the other side. Consequently, despite the fact that if both players choose the non-cooperative strategy, they will end up with a suboptimal outcome in which they will find themselves worse off than if they had chosen the co-operative strategy, in an environment where external pressure for co-operation is absent, the independent choices of both players tend to lead both to adopt the non-cooperative strategy, as long as the number of plays of the game remains small. Here, one way for the co-operative solution to emerge is to introduce external intervention. By increasing the costs of defecting, such external intervention could dispel the players' temptation to choose the non-cooperative strategy and thus force them to co-operate with each other.[2] Mao might not have understood the game theory, but he had by the begining of 1968 come to the conclusion that a solution to the deadlock of power distribution in the provinces must be imposed from above, if his deadline for setting up new power organs was to be met at all.

Beijing attempted to facilitate the formation of the great alliances and the establishment of the revolutionary committees in the provinces by trying out a new formula—'Mao Zedong Thought study programmes'. Local representatives from the various provinces were summoned to Beijing, where they were quartered in separate military compounds and negotiated, under Mao's supervision, every issue concerning the distribution of power in their own provinces. Only after an agreement about the composition of the revolutionary committee in a province was hammered out would the study programme of the province be ended.[3]

In the case of Wuhan, the study programme was held not in Beijing but in the city, presided over by the WMR and the Wuhan Garrison. The programme began in early December, and the leaders of all the major mass organizations were required to participate. Backed by Beijing, the army adopted a 'stick and carrot' policy in dealing with the rebels. On one hand, it threatened the rebels that they should not try to boycott the negotiations, whatever the result might turn out to be. The rebel leaders were told that the formation of the great alliance was the most important part of Mao's strategic plan. Whoever put obstacles in the way of the army's implementation of the plan would be excluded from the leading body of the Workers' Congress or the Red Guard Congress. On the other hand, the army tried to work out a power distribution scheme that would satisfy the minimum expectations of the two factions.[4] The scheme the army came up with was to let the Strong Faction dominate the Workers' Congress and the New Faction dominate the Red Guard Congress. Under increasing pressure from Beijing and from the local military authorities, the two factions had no choice but to accept this arrangement.[5] On 17 December the New China News Agency jubilantly declared, 'Wuhan rebels have formed a revolutionary great alliance.'[6] A month later, the Red Guard Congress and the Workers' Congress of Wuhan were formally established.

The alliance was merely nominal. Neither the Strong Faction nor the New Faction was satisfied with the results.[7] The student organizations on the Strong Faction side (such as the Second Headquarters) and the worker organizations on the New Faction side (such as the Workers' Rebel Headquarters) were very unhappy about being in the minority in their respective congresses. But there was little they could do at the moment, because the political climate was changing in a direction favourable to the army. In December 1967, Beijing instructed the army to 'support leftists but not any particular faction'.[8] Who were the leftists? The key criterion of leftist in this new phase of the Cultural Revolution was said to be one's willingness to co-operate with the army in forming and consolidating the great alliance.[9] The new year, 1968, started with an all-out campaign against factionalism. 'Whether or not one is willing to overcome factionalism', asserted the new year editorial of the *People's Daily*, 'is the most important sign of whether or not one is willing to be a real revolutionary under the present circumstances.'[10] In such a daunting atmosphere, the rebels had to restrain themselves.

The Issue of Party Cadres

The formation of the great alliance, however, met only one of the prerequisites for the establishment of the revolutionary committee. The revolutionary committee was supposed to be based on a three-in-one combination. The army's representatives in the revolutionary committee rarely became a problem because Beijing prohibited the rebels from poking their noses into the army's internal affairs.[11] The cadre representation, however, was a hot issue.

Mao had never intended to remove Party cadres from their posts on a massive scale, especially at the lower levels. Indeed, at each phase of the consolidation he had appealed to the rebels to 'treat cadres correctly'. But the rebels were reluctant to reinstate cadres whom they had insulted. On the one hand, they were anxious that if former officials were restored to their posts, conservatives who had defended those officials would regain ground. On the other hand, the rebels were afraid that the rehabilitated cadres might one day take revenge on them. Besides, it was obvious that the greater the number of seats allocated to cadres, the fewer the rebels would have in the revolutionary committee. Based on those considerations, the rebels were generally inclined to have as many cadres continuing to bear the label 'capitalist roader' as possible.[12]

From the Beijing's perspective, however, the cadres' administrative experience was indispensable, so that the new governmental structure—the revolutionary committee—must reserve posts for them. A central Party circular issued on 7 November 1967 provided that no revolutionary committee would be recognized as legitimate unless cadres were fairly represented.[13] This transmitted an unmistakable message to the rebels that they had to share power with some cadres. The crucial question for rebel factional warriors now became with whom they would agree to work in the revolutionary committees.

In selecting future partners, the rebels' first choice was cadres who they believed would be easy to deal with. It was a manifest phenomenon of the Cultural Revolution that dedicated Party cadres who had faithfully carried out official policies before the Cultural Revolution generally drew heavier criticism from the masses than those cadres who were known as 'old benign persons'. This type of cadre was characterized by an avoidance of responsibility, an indifference to matters of principle, and a manner to please everyone. Since these cadres had rarely offended anyone, few sought to square accounts with them during the course of the Cultural Revolution. As a result, they were often considered as 'educable cadres', while others were labelled as capitalist roaders. By recommending this type of cadre as a suitable partner in the revolutionary committees, the rebels could present themselves as complying with Beijing's guidelines while using the 'old benign persons' as their puppets.[14]

The rebels' next choice was cadres who had transferred into their units from outside shortly before the Cultural Revolution. Since those cadres had been new in the units, grievances had not had time to mount against them. Therefore, they were often let off while other cadres were tormented. The rebels preferred to work with these recent arrivals rather than to deal with cadres who had been in the units for a long time. The new arrivals might not be as easily manipulated as the 'old benign persons', but at least they had less enmity against the rebels than others.[15]

The 'old benign persons' and the new arrivals were usually acceptable to all the rebel factions, because they were unlikely to be harmful to their interests. For other types of cadres, however, even those who had supported the rebels' cause, the situation was more complicated.

From the outset of the Cultural Revolution, there had been cadres who stood on the rebel side. They were acclaimed as 'revolutionary cadres' by the rebels. Their organization—the Federation of Revolutionary Cadres—was founded in May 1967.[16] The reasons why those cadres affiliated themselves with the rebels varied. As the following profiles of forty-nine outstanding members of the federation show, they could be roughly put into four categories: those who were disciplined before the Cultural Revolution; those who were suppressed by their superiors; those who failed to get the promotion they believed they deserved; and those who staked their future on the victory of the rebels (see Table 9.1). Four representative cases, one example from each of the four categories, are discussed below.

(1) Wang Shengrong joined the Chinese Communist Party (CCP) in 1926 and was among the most senior Party members in Hubei province in the 1960s. While studying in the Soviet Union in the 1930s he became a member of Wang Ming's clique known as the 'Twenty-eight-and-a-half'.[17] As a result of Wang Ming's fall from leadership in the Party,

Table 9.1 A Profile of Forty-nine 'Revolutionary Cadres'

Name	CCP Standing	Position in 1966	Record
A			
1. Wang Shengrong	1926	Deputy Section Chief in a Provincial Bureau	Disciplined in 1943 and 1952
2. Pu Shengguang	1933	Vice Chairman of the Provincial CPPCC	Disciplined in the early 1950s
3. Li Shouxian	1927	Deputy Director of the Provincial Commission of Science	Disciplined in 1957
4. Mei Bai		Chief Correspondent of Hubei Daily in Huanggang Prefecture	Disciplined in 1957
5. Tu Gongbo		Deputy Director of the Municipal Bureau of Cultural Affairs	Disciplined in 1957
6. Chong Guoquan		Deputy Magistrate of Hongshan District	Disciplined in 1957
7. Zhu Hanzhu	1932	Deputy Magistrate of Wuchang District	Quite the CCP in 1936
8. Li Ming	1929	Director of the Provincial Hydrological Station	Disciplined in 1954
9. Zhao Mingzhen		Deputy Director of the Provincial Bureau of Foreign Trade	Wang Shengrong's wife
10. Liu Zhanbiao	1929	Deputy Director of the Municipal Office of Population Control	Disciplined in 1951
11. Ding Li	1939	Deputy Director of the Provincial Economics Commission	Disciplined in 1952

Table 9.1 *continued*

Name	CCP Standing	Position in 1966	Record
B			
12. Xie Jingjie	1938	The First Party Secretary of Hangyang District	Had strained relations with the chief leaders of Wuhan since 1959
13. Yang Guanghua	1927	Vice Chairman of the Provincial CPPCC	In a Soviet Union prison between 1935 and 1956
14. Yang Youshan	1937	Director of Wuhan Telecommunication Bureau	Had strained relations with party secretary in the bureau
15. Xu Jinbiao		Vice Chairman of the Provincial CPPCC	
16. Xie Pusheng		Vice Chairman of the Provincial CPPCC	
17. Liu Dexi		Party of Secretary of Hubei Medical College	Labelled a 'member of a black gang' during the first stage of the Cultural Revolution
18. Cui Fengmin		Deputy Director of the Municipal Bureau of Statistics	
19. Chen Gang		Deputy Director of Wuhan Auto Parts	
20. Qi Huanmiao		Deputy Party Secretary of Wuhan Construction Machine Factory	
21. Zhao Xianzhang		Deputy Party Secretary of the First Cotton Mill	
22. Wu Yungong	1941	Deputy Director of Hangyang Rolling Mill	Had strained relations with the chief leaders of the factory

Table 9.1 *continued*

Name	CCP Standing	Position in 1966	Record
23. Feng Yiying	1941	Secretary General of the Department of United Front of Wuhan	Had strained relations with the chief leaders of the department
24. Li Zhenxing	1938	Member of the Supervisory Committee of the Agricultural Commission	Had strained relations with the chief of the commission
25. Wei Tinghuai	1929	Deputy Mayor	Had long been ignored by the chief leaders of the municipality
26. Song Feishi	1937	Deputy Secretary of the Municipal Supervisory Committee	Had strained relations with the chief of the committee
27. Zhang Bin	1938	Deputy Director of the Political Department of Municipal Industry and Communication Commission	Had strained relations with the chief leaders of the municipality
28. Zhang Lianqi	1941	Deputy Director of the Municipal Agricultural Bureau	Had strained relations with the chief of the bureau
29. Zhao Xueguang	1938	Deputy Director of the Inspection Office under the Municipal Government	Had long been ignored
30. Ren Aisheng c	1935	Director of the Political Department of Provincial Agricultural	Had offended Wang Renzhong in 1958
31. Liu Zhen	1938	Deputy Secretary General of the HPPC	

Table 9.1 *continued*

Name	CCP Standing	Position in 1966	Record
32. Mao Yuanyao	1929	Party Secretary of Wuhan Topographic Institute	
33. Cheng Fangqiu		Deputy Section Chief of the Provincial Bureau of Industry	
34. Zhang Min	1931	Secretary General of the Municipal People's Commission	
35. Li Jingru	1935	Deputy Director of the Provincial Grain Bureau	
36. Li Zhoushi	1933	Director of the Provincial Meteorological Bureau	
37. Wang Shun	1937	Section Chief of the Provincial Geological Bureau	
D			
38. Xue Puruo		Deputy Mayor	
39. Zhang Hua		Secretary General of the HPPC	
40. Meng Futang		Deputy Governor	
41. Su Ping		Magistrate of Qingshan District	
42. Yang Chunting	1936	First party Secretary of Yichang Prefecture	
43. Zhang Ruping		Party Secretary of Wuhan Water Transport Institute	

Table 9.1 *continued*

Name	CCP Standing	Position in 1966	Record
44. Zhang Yuhang		Deputy Director of the Provincial Bureau of Education	
45. Liu Ang		Party Secretary of the Municipal School of Foreign Language	
46. Zhang Zhaoyi		Deputy Party Secretary of Wuhan Topographic Institute	
47. Liu Suxian		Deputy President of Wuhan University	
48. Zhao Wenhua	1938	First Party Secretary of Enshi Prefecture	
49. Sun Deshu		First Party Secretary of Huangshi Municipality	

Sources: Wuhan Shi Sanjiehe Ganbu Jianjie [The Profiles of Cadre Candidates for the HPRC and WMRC], 20 January 1968; *Shengshi Geming Sanjiehe Ganbu Jianjie* [The Profiles of Cadre Candidates for the WMRC], February, 1968; and *Xinhuda* [New Central China Institute of Technology], 26 June 1968.

Wang Shengrong was criticized during the period of the Yan'an Rectification Movement. In 1952, he was dismissed from the post of vice minister of the Industry Ministry of the Central South Region and sentenced to one year's imprisonment for allegedly divulging state secrets and taking bribes. After serving the sentence, he was made a deputy section chief in a provincial bureau.[18]

(2) Xie Jingjie was regarded as a very promising young cadre in Wuhan in the early 1950s. In 1956 he was appointed as the First Party Secretary of Hanyang District at the age of thirty-two. In the fervour of the Great Leap Forward (1958–60), the WMPC put in place an industrial development programme that proposed to build 200 large industrial enterprises in the city within the next few years. Xie criticized the plan as unrealistic, on the grounds that insufficient raw materials and transport facilities were available. As a result, he was labelled as a 'right deviationist', and his rank was reduced from the eleventh grade to the fifteenth grade. In 1962, the label was removed, but he continued to have some brushes with Wang Renzhong and Song Kanfu. He was made a mere figurehead in his district, having no real power.[19]

(3) Liu Zhen had joined the CCP in 1938. In 1951 he was disciplined for harbouring his brother, a despotic landlord. Thereafter he was rarely promoted. Liu was especially unhappy about the fact that many of his former colleagues and even subordinates had become his superiors. In 1966 he was a deputy secretary general of the HPPC, a high position for someone who had joined the Party in 1938. But he still nursed a grievance against the leaders of the province. In his own words, 'I pretended that I was satisfied with my position, but I was not. Therefore, once I had an opportunity, my hidden discontent would begin to surface.'[20]

(4) Xue Puruo was promoted to be a deputy mayor of Wuhan in 1964. In spring 1967 he was appointed by the WMR as a deputy director of the Wuhan Municipal Headquarters for Grasping Revolution and Promoting Production. But on 15 May he resigned from this position and made a public statement in support of the rebels. Why did he defect? In a confession written in December 1967, Xue acknowledged that the desire to protect himself had been the prime motive. When most cadres thought that it was safe to follow the army, Xue sensed that the movement was developing in a direction favourable to the rebels. He therefore decided to stake his fortune on the rebels. 'Concern for defending Chairman Mao's revolutionary line alone', he admitted, 'was not strong enough to push me to take that decisive step.'[21]

After the Wuhan Incident, when the rebel mass organizations publicly split into two factions, the Federation of Revolutionary Cadres fell apart from within. The majority of cadres allied themselves with the Strong Faction, calling themselves the 'left wing' of the federation; the rest associated with the New Faction.[22]

By November 1967 it had become clear that Beijing wanted the revolutionary committee to be an institution in which the military representatives performed the role of guardians and the rebel representatives the role of surveillants, while the day-to-day decision-making power would be wielded mainly by the cadre representatives. Thus, a faction's influence in a revolutionary committee would, to a large extent, depend on how many cadres it favoured were on the committee. The focus of factional politics therefore shifted quickly to the issue of cadres in the last days of 1967. The two factions in Wuhan waged vigorous attacks against the cadres who had been nominated by one another at all levels.

The fiercest battle occurred at the provincial and municipal levels. The two factions called upon all their resources, because whichever faction was able to control the revolutionary committees at those two levels would be in a good position to influence politics at the lower levels.

The situation was to the advantage of the Strong Faction at the provincial level. Most of the former leading cadres of the HPPC who had supported the rebels, such as Meng Futang, Zhang Hua, Liu Zhen, and Ren Aisheng, also happened to support the Strong Faction. One probable reason for this was that all three major organizations of the Strong Faction originated in Wuchang where the provincial government was located. But at the municipal level, the two factions were evenly matched in strength. If the municipal revolutionary committee fell into the hands of the New Faction, there would be two hostile authorities confronting each other in the city. Without simultaneously controlling the municipal revolutionary committee, the Strong Faction was afraid that its control over the provincial revolutionary committee would be merely nominal, because it (and the New Faction, for that matter) had little influence beyond Wuhan in the seventy-two counties of the province. For this reason, the Strong Faction was determined to capture the municipal revolutionary committee at all costs.

On the pretext that only a handful of former leading cadres of the WMPC were rebel sympathizers, the Strong Faction proposed that the pool of candidates for the municipal revolutionary committee should be broadened by allowing cadres other than former officials of the WMPC into the race.[23] The New Faction had no objection to breaking the bounds between cadres of different origins, but it insisted that Xue Puruo was the best candidate for the position of first vice chairman of the municipal revolutionary committee. As for the provincial revolutionary committee, the New Faction had to look for cadre candidates elsewhere. One choice was cadres from outside of Wuhan. The other was former chief leaders of the HPPC who had *not* been known as rebel sympathizers, such as the former governor, Zhang Tixue.[24] In the New Faction's view, although it was unpredictable how those cadres would behave once they were included in the provincial revolutionary committee, they were still better choices than cadres recommended by its rival, because the latter would certainly help the Strong Faction in future politics.

On 20 December the WMR leaders hinted that they wanted Zhang Tixue to be considered as a candidate for a key position in the future provincial revolutionary committee. The news caused great indignation in the Strong Faction. Before long, however, the Strong Faction learned, to its great surprise, that Chairman Mao had personally nominated Zhang. No one dared to defy Mao's authority. But Mao's nomination of Zhang worried the Strong Faction. If Beijing could accept Zhang, it might also accept other former HPPC leaders recommended by the New Faction. If that were to happen, the Strong Faction might not be able to achieve superiority in the provincial revolutionary committee, as it had previously expected. The situation was so complicated that the Strong Faction decided to throw its whole might into the battle to select the provincial and municipal revolutionary committees. Heartened by Mao's instruction in its favour, the New Faction was not to be outdone. Both sides thus were ready to enter the finals of the race for power.

In mid-January 1968 the WMR accelerated the formation of its revolutionary committees. Formal negotiations over cadre candidates for the municipal and provincial revolutionary committees began, and the leaders of thirteen major mass organizations were invited to participate in the process. For the municipal revolutionary committee, the New Faction nominated nineteen candidates and the Strong Faction twenty-one; and for the provincial committee, the New Faction nominated fourteen and the Strong Faction eighteen candidates. In the case of the municipal committee, there were only three overlaps between the two lists of nominees, while in the provincial case there were six. Bargaining over the rest was bitter. Neither side was willing to give in before the other did. At the same time as the rebel leaders were wrangling behind closed doors, their supporters waged a propaganda war on the streets to create pressure on the negotiation from outside.[25] Each of the two factions produced a vast number of publications whitewashing its own nominees while vilifying the nominees of the opposition. If a nominee was desirable, he (all the nominees were male) would be deemed acceptable on the ground that Lin Biao had once stressed that any cadre who supported Chairman Mao's political line in the Cultural Revolution was a good cadre, even if he had made serious mistakes in the past.[26] If a nominee was not desirable, however, his past misconduct would be exaggerated and cited in order to discredit him.[27] A local paper correctly pointed out:

> [For those who are maddened by factionalism], what is important in nominating cadre candidates for the revolutionary committee is neither nominees' political records in the past seventeen years (1949–66) nor nominees' performances in the first fifty days of the Cultural Revolution (from June to July 1966), but whether or not those cadres are siding with their own factions at present.[28]

The two factions set up half a dozen broadcasting stations in close proximity to the building in which the negotiations were taking place and proceeded to wage psychological warfare against each other's negotiators by invectives around the clock.

The Revolutionary Committee

Despite the army's painstaking efforts, no agreement was reached on the composition of either revolutionary committee after a week-long negotiation. In the past, such a failure of negotiation would have deferred the establishment of the revolutionary committee. However, Beijing was becoming anxious, and lowered its expectations accordingly. No longer did it insist that disputes on important issues between the opposing factions must be resolved before the revolutionary committee could be established. Instead, Beijing reluctantly concluded that it might be better to set up the revolutionary committee first and then use the new government structure to settle the strife between the factions. In order to accelerate the process, however, it would be necessary to impose solutions from above when the mass organizations were unable to reach agreements about the composition of the committee on a voluntary basis.[29]

In Wuhan, after having failed to hammer out agreements between the Strong Faction and the New Faction, the army took over the task of determining the composition of the municipal and provincial revolutionary committees. Things then began to change quickly. Within a few days the WMR had not only put together the final lists of candidates for the two committees but had also obtained Beijing's approval of their proposals.[30] On 20 January, the Wuhan Municipal Revolutionary Committee (WMRC) was formally established; and on 5 February the Hubei Provincial Revolutionary Committee (HPRC) also came into being.[31]

Both revolutionary committees were headed by army officers. The commander and commissar of the Wuhan Garrison were appointed to be the chairman and the first vice chairman of the WMRC; and the commander and commissar of the WMR were named as the chairman and the first vice chairman of the HPRC. The other seats on the two committees were distributed evenly between the two factions. Almost all the leaders of the major mass organizations were appointed to the committees, an arrangement obviously intended by the army to appease those factionalist warriors. Both factions had an approximately equal number of cadre representatives, with each side successfully placing some of its nominees on the two committees while failing to secure places for the others.[32] Interestingly, almost all the seats reserved for rebel representatives in the HPRC were allotted to people from the Wuhan area, leaving only a few positions for people from the seventy-two counties of the province. In its bid to calm the 'cry-babies' of Wuhan, the army apparently forgot to feed the relatively 'quiet babies' in other parts of Hubei, despite the fact that Wuhan accounted for less than 10 per cent of the population of the province.[33]

With the establishment of the HPRC and the WMRC, a period of uneasy truce followed in the city. Revolutionary committees were formed at the grassroots level, but there were no reports of major conflicts. However, the establishment of the revolutionary committees did not end the factional confrontation. Indeed, factional activity was simmering just below the surface. A constant source of friction was the fact that neither faction was satisfied with its share in the WMRC and the HPRC. In terms of rebel representatives, the New Faction thought that the Strong Faction had too many seats in the HPRC, whereas the Strong Faction complained that the WMRC was in effect controlled by the New Faction. The Strong Faction was especially upset by the composition of cadre representatives in the two committees. Among the twenty-one cadres it had recommended for the HPRC, only five had been accepted; and among the eighteen put forward for the WMRC, only ten had been accepted. This compared unfavourably with the New Faction, thirteen of whose nineteen cadres nominated for the HPRC, and eleven of the fourteen nominated for the WMRC, had been approved. What particularly enraged the Strong Faction was that none of the three cadres it favoured most, namely, Meng Futang, Zhang Hua, and Liu Zhen, was appointed to either committee.[34] The WMR might have thought that it had done its best to divide the pie as evenly as possible, but both factions wanted to maximize their own share. Even a fifty–fifty result would not have pleased either. Moreover, each faction suspected that its rival received more sympathy and support from the army than it did. Many believed that the WMR was the New Faction's patron, and the Wuhan Garrison the Strong Faction's.[35] Such speculations affected both factions' assessments of the distribution of power in the city.

Mao hoped the revolutionary committee would represent an impartial government authority, but the committee members tended to continue to act as representatives of their own factions. Thus the factional confrontation was brought into the revolutionary committee itself. Due to the WMR's predominant role and its internal unity, the factional activity in Wuhan did not go so far as to create a dual authority structure at the provincial and municipal levels, as was happening in Shanxi.[36] However, at lower levels it was common for hastily established revolutionary committees to run into trouble as soon as they were set up. Unlike at the upper levels, it was common for one faction to absolutely outweigh the other in a grassroots unit. If that was the case, the dominant faction often unilaterally set up the revolutionary committee regardless of the other's opposition.[37] Not to be outdone, the depressed faction tended to try to harass the dominant faction and to wreck the committee, often by appealing for help from the faction's trans-unit network. Condemned as 'factional committees', the revolutionary committees in many units thus were paralysed. Even in units where the two factions shared power, the revolutionary committees usually existed in name only. Since the factions were ever-present, such committees were usually unable to pass resolutions; and even if a resolution was adopted, the committees usually had difficulty in implementing it.[38]

But for the moment, factional fighting had to take cover from an ongoing anti-ultraleftist campaign initiated by Beijing. In fact, the first task of the newly established WMRC and HPRC was to build up an anti-ultraleftist momentum in the city. Orchestrated by the WMR, the two committees passed numerous resolutions and held a number of mass rallies over the next two months to denounce factionalism. Local newspapers were full of articles criticizing anarchism. Everyone was required to participate in 'Mao Zedong Thought study sessions' in their unit and to make self-criticisms. This intensive criticism of factionalism and anarchism put an enormous pressure on the rebels. The rebel leaders, in particular, were subjected to severe attack. They were accused of having scrambled for power for themselves and of inculcating factionalism and anarchism in their followers. Such a tense situation forced the rebels to be guarded in their speeches and cautious in their deeds.[39] As a result, in February and early March 1968 the mass organizations were in general dispirited and inert.

Radicalism Rebounds

The moderate period came to an end in late March when Beijing suddenly stopped the anti-ultraleftist campaign. Mao considered the campaign had gone too far, so far that it had led the Cultural Revolution towards the right. He responded by launching a counterattack on rightist trends.

The counterattack on rightist trends rekindled the flames that had been dying out among the rebels in Wuhan.[40] The first reaction of the two Wuhan factions was to assess the significance of this policy shift. Interestingly, both the Strong Faction and the New Faction reached the same conclusion: the Cultural Revolution was entering the stage of a decisive engagement.[41]

In preparation for the battle that lay ahead, the rebel organizations had to rally their forces. But this was not an easy task. In late 1967 and early 1968, many of the rebel activists had begun to distance themselves from politics. Having experienced the excitement of fighting the power holders and conservatives, they found the infighting between the rebel organizations of little real interest. Hard-core faction leaders might come out of the infighting with powerful positions on the revolutionary committees, but what would the rank-and-filers gain? Since there was little to be gained from further collective action, many chose to retire from active involvement. The new campaign against rightist trends aroused little enthusiasm among those new *xiaoyaopai*.[42]

In an effort to prod their members into action, the rebel organizations of both factions tried to strike terror in them by suggesting that the Million Heroes was preparing to stage a comeback. Indeed, when ultraleftism had been denounced, some former conservative activists took the opportunity to voice their grievances against the rebels. In most cases, however, they dared to grumble only over instances of physical abuse carried out by individual rebels in their units. Only a very small group of former conservatives were bold enough to plan to regroup the Million Heroes force in order to challenge the rebels' ruling position. Before this group could take any concrete action, however, its conspiracy was uncovered in early January 1968. Rebel newspapers called the group an 'underground headquarters of the Million Heroes'. In fact, only about a dozen people were involved in the plot, and none of them had ever worked for the headquarters of the Million Heroes.[43]

This minor incident was seen as a sign of a growing threat from the conservatives. Rebel publications asserted that the 'underground headquarters' had developed an extensive network throughout the city and was preparing to stage a *coup d'état*.[44] In addition to appealing for revolutionary vigilance, the rebels attacked the conservatives, especially those who had been heads of the Million Heroes at various levels. Wuhan once again saw a reign of terror. Tens of thousands of conservatives were denounced at public accusation meetings and paraded through the streets, and thousands were taken into custody. The newly established 'Wuhan Outpost' under the Workers' Headquarters played a special role in the new wave of suppression. The self-styled mass dictatorship group turned the Wuhan Gymnasium into a large prison. Upon receiving blacklists prepared by rebels within individual units, the Wuhan Outpost sent its teams to the units, where people whose names were listed were either beaten on the spot or taken back to the gymnasium. Those who were locked up in the gymnasium were cruelly tortured. Some were beaten to death.[45]

A former rebel theorist admitted:

> It was a trick to say that the Million Heroes was going to start something again. In fact, at that time the Million Heroes posed no threat to the rebels. By exaggerating the threat, the faction leaders wanted to terrify disinterested members into becoming active again. By victimizing former conservatives, the two factions aimed to outdo each other in showing that they had not been infected by the 'rightist trends', because at the time, it was widely accepted that 'moderate' was tantamount to 'right'. To prove itself revolutionary, an organization thus had to act ruthlessly; and to prove itself more revolutionary than others, it had to act even more ruthlessly.[46]

The 'crying wolf' tactic was not totally successful. In most units, only a few committed rebels responded to their leaders' call; and in some units, no one was interested in taking part in the new campaign. Tired of the twists and turns of the Cultural Revolution, many rebels had grown cynical. A popular aphorism among them was 'take whatever stand the centre is taking, and you will surely be acclaimed as a true leftist'. 'Take whatever stand the centre is taking' meant taking no stand and doing nothing except paying lip service to the official line.[47]

The few who were still active tended to be rebel leaders at the grassroots. They had a stake in continued involvement—their positions in the revolutionary committees and the opportunity for advancement this provided. Furthermore, because of the extent of their previous involvement, they were in a sense locked into a part of the social fabric from which escape was undesirable, if not impossible. Even if they became disillusioned with the cause they had committed themselves to, they would find that the costs and rewards were balanced in such a way as to make the decision to end their commitment a traumatic one.[48]

Lacking popular support, the two opposing factions had to rely heavily on special forces. These were the semi-professional storm troops that had been raised by major organizations in previous confrontations, among which the most powerful were the Wuhan Outpost of the Workers' Headquarters, the Dare-to-Die Brigade of the 13 September Corps, and the Iron Army of the Workers' Rebel Headquarters.[49] In the past, those groups had at best played a supplementary role in the factional struggle. Now, however, they were expected to play a leading role. These groups were combat-worthy not so much because their members shared the same goals as their leaders as because they were fond of action. A large percentage of the members of these groups were young men in their twenties, who loved brawling and action but hated discipline. Many of them were recruited from street gangs. Rival gangs often threw in their lot with opposing factions. Thus they could settle old grudges under the guise of factional struggles.[50]

In April, brawls broke out between the Strong Faction and the New Faction. Echoing a popular slogan of the time, both factions insisted that 'power must be redistributed' in Wuhan. What they meant by 'redistribution' was to kick out the representatives of the other faction from revolutionary committees at all levels and place their own men into the organs of power. In order to justify its claim, the Strong Faction condemned the New Faction rebels as 'old-line right opportunists' and demanded that the HPRC and the WMRC be free of 'right opportunists'. The New Faction responded by censuring the Strong Faction groups as 'right splittist organizations consisting of a large number of hoodlums' and insisted that 'only when the Strong Faction is eliminated could peace prevail in Wuhan'.[51]

The issue of the cadres was raised again. The Strong Faction asserted that 'the exclusion of Liu Zhen and Zhang Hua from the HPRC is a manifestation of the rightist trends'. Arraigning Zhang Tixue as 'the chief culprit of the rightist wind' in the province, it attempted to bring down Zhang and all the cadres in the HPRC and the WMRC who had been nominated by the New Faction. The New Faction, on the other hand, set out to strike down the so-called shadow government planted by Wang Renzhong, by which it meant all the cadres in the HPRC and the WMRC recommended by the Strong Faction.[52]

By the end of April the tension between the two factions had become so great that both the Workers' Congress and the Red Guard Congress fell apart.[53] The very existence of the HPRC and the WMRC was also in danger. Busily engaged in factional struggles, the rebel leaders simply had no time for the routine activities of the two organs.[54]

Meanwhile, both factions began to collect arms again, including rifles and pistols the rebel organizations had hidden the previous autumn. It was estimated that about 100,000 weapons were left in the hands of the various rebel organizations after the events of the summer of 1967. Squads were also sent to Sichuan, Guangxi, Shanxi, and other places to purchase more weapons. They took with them such highly prized commodities as newsprint, cigarettes, pork, and trucks; and brought back grenades, semi-automatic rifles, and machine guns. Both factions were anxious to obtain more weapons because they believed that a bloody, decisive battle was inevitable.[55]

Their anxiety was confirmed by the 3 May Incident. In its simplest terms, the incident can be outlined as follows. In April the New Zhongyuan Machine Factory, a New Faction organization, charged several men with hooliganism and took them into custody. Those men were members of a tiny Strong Faction group within the factory. The Wuhan Outpost retaliated by kidnapping one of the heads of the New Faction organization. An exchange of hostages was negotiated but soon came to an impasse. The Wuhan Outpost then issued an ultimatum demanding the release of the men of the Strong Faction before 3 May. The New Zhongyuan Machine Factory did not give in. On the afternoon of 3 May, the Outpost encircled the factory and blocked all roads leading to it with thousands of troops in full battle array. Before long, an all-out offensive was launched. The battle resulted in three deaths, fifty-seven injuries, and property damage worth several million yuan. Only after the Wuhan Garrison sent twenty-three companies of soldiers to the spot did the battle cease.[56]

The incident convinced the two factions that a decisive engagement was imminent, and that they must hasten their preparations if they were to emerge as the victor. The Strong Faction first held a summit meeting to assess the exigent situation. Then the leaders of the major Strong Faction organizations were summoned to Wuhan from all over Hubei to discuss how to meet the challenge from the New Faction in the province at large. Finally, at a huge gathering convened on 11 May, the faction leaders briefed thousands of branch leaders on the strategies they had decided to adopt. In addition, the participants were told that the New Faction was plotting to assassinate leaders and activists of the Strong Faction. This was a poorly veiled attempt to evoke the rank-and-filers' resentment against the New Faction.[57]

Those moves alarmed the New Faction. It held its summit conference from 15 to 18 May, which was attended by about a hundred leading figures of the faction from all over the province. In the face of the growing threat from the Strong Faction, the summit concluded that the New Faction must prepare to avert the peril. In order to meet the challenge of the Strong Faction head-on, the meeting decided that special attention should be paid to propaganda, organization, and armaments. Following the meeting, the New Faction launched a campaign to mobilize its rank-and filers. A New Faction publication told its rank-and filers: 'In the past, we have exercised self-restraint in dealing with the Strong Faction. As a result, the Strong Faction has always tried to bully us. From now on, we should no longer act like Martin Luther King, Jun., because nonviolent resistance does not work here.'[58]

At the same time as they were whipping up factional sentiment, the two factions stepped up their war preparations. Dozens of high buildings were occupied as command points. There were also widespread rumours that some organizations were conducting reconnaissance of armouries they planned to loot.[59] In such a climate, brushes between the forces of the two factions became more frequent.[60] Finally, two incidents brought the already perilous situation to the brink of a real war. On 18 May, Lu Li'an, a well-known rebel theorist favoured by the Strong Faction, was kidnapped by the New Faction. In an attempt to force the New Faction to release Lu, the Strong Faction formed the United Delegation for Rescuing Lu Li'an and staged armed demonstrations around several of the New Faction's strongholds. Before these protests could produce any result, however, another incident occurred. On 26 May, two leaders of the Workers' Headquarters drove their car through an area under the control of the Workers' Rebel Headquarters, and the Iron Army opened fire on them. Although neither man was hurt, the incident seemed to confirm the Strong Faction's assertion that the New Faction was planning to assassinate its leaders. The next day, the Strong Faction held mass rallies in various parts of the city to denounce the New Faction.[61] Convinced that the Strong Faction would strike a vindictive blow, the Workers' Rebel Headquarters issued a secret order to all its strongholds the same day: 'You must be on the alert against any possible aggression tonight. If anyone approaches your building and provokes a conflict, you should first fire warning shots. If the invaders deliberately disregard the warning and continue to make trouble, you have the right to open fire on them.'[62]

On 27 May there were no reports of friction between the two factions, but only because they were busy seizing arms. The three days between 26 and 28 May saw a feverish race to seize arms by both factions in

Wuhan. Almost all of the armouries in the city and nearby counties were looted, and in some cases weapons were taken straight from soldiers' hands. On 27 May alone, it was estimated that about 80,000 guns were stolen. A total of more than 100,000 guns and more than 10,000,000 cartridges were seized over the three days, which, according to Lin Biao, made Wuhan the number one city in terms of arms seized from army arsenals.[63]

On 28 May the MAC and the CRSG sent a telegram to the two factions in Wuhan: 'The centre orders you to stop seizing arsenals immediately. What is happening in Wuhan is against the law and the centre's ordinances. The centre will soon invite your delegates to Beijing and open negotiation here. You may begin to select your representatives now.'[64]

As always, both factions claimed that they wholeheartedly endorsed Beijing's instructions. That night, all the major organizations issued urgent ordinances prohibiting their members from seizing arms. But everybody knew that this was for show. Privately no one took the telegram seriously.[65]

In order to show their 'sincere endorsement of the centre's instructions', the next day, many organizations began returning weapons. But, as they had done a year before, they returned only broken or worn rifles, which accounted for only a small portion of what they had taken. This was understandable. In the words of a leader of the Workers' Headquarters, 'We have to prepare for the worst'.[66]

For many rebels, rifles, pistols, and grenades were amusing toys. Even uncommitted rebels who would not willingly have engaged in a real battle enjoyed playing with guns. For a while, shooting bullets into the air or throwing grenades into open areas became a popular game. In the last few days of May and the first few days of June, the sound of rifles being fired was common in the city. But some rebels became bored with merely shooting into the air and began to entertain themselves with marksmanship contests. Power poles and electric cables were often chosen as targets. Within a few days there were sixteen incidents in which electric cables, including cables used by the military and to link Hankou and Wuchang, were hit. Those who were not good marksmen shot at large targets such as aircraft on the ground. On 3 June alone, five planes were damaged. Although people were rarely chosen as targets, by the middle of June there were fifty-seven fatal shootings and 327 cases of wounding by stray bullets.[67]

Arms also became a commodity. Since many organizations in Wuhan now had surplus weapons, and arms were in short supply in places like

Beijing, Guangzhou, and Henan, a long-distance arms trade emerged. Many people came to Wuhan from other provinces with pork, soap, cigarettes, matches, or cash and left with rifles, pistols, and grenades. The parties engaged in this trade profited enormously, having invested only the time they had spent in looting state warehouses and military armouries.[68]

Nevertheless, arms were used primarily for fighting and deterrence. The rebels' possession of modern weapons greatly increased the possibility of armed conflict. On 30 May, to support the Second Headquarters' branch at the Wuhan Metallurgical Institute, troops of the Wuhan Outpost surrounded the institute and bombarded the building in which New Faction forces were entrenched. About thirty people were killed or wounded in the battle. On 5 June, forty truckloads of troopers from the Workers' Headquarters and the Second Headquarters forcibly occupied the First Metallurgical Corporation, a stronghold of the New Faction, causing one death. Three days later, another stronghold of the New Faction was besieged by the Guards Company of the 13 September Corps.[69] All of these incidents occurred in Qingshan District. The New Faction suspected that the Strong Faction had a grand plan to eliminate the opposition district by district. The New Faction, as various newspapers reported, claimed that it had evidence that the Strong Faction had drawn up a programme to 'fight the decisive battle [with the New Faction]' and to 'achieve final victory [dominating the province and the city]'. The Strong Faction countercharged that the New Faction was clamorously advocating that Wuhan 'follow the example of Sichuan' (contending for power by armed force) and was making preparations to do so. Both accusations seemed to be valid, for neither denied the charge levelled against it. And both factions quoted a famous phrase from Mao as their watchword: 'Cast away illusions as to peace, prepare for struggle'.[70]

As the atmosphere became more tense, the residents of the city were seized with panic. Few dared to leave home, being afraid of being hit by stray bullets. Many left the town to seek refuge with their relatives in the countryside.[71] Even those committed factional forces who were quartered in fortresses became anxious. If the anticipated all-out war was to break out, they might not be able to secure a regular food supply. In order to make provision against the worst-case scenario, they looted state warehouses to obtain food, pork, vegetables, briquettes, and other daily essentials. Some even robbed banks to get cash.[72] The situation was much more tense and chaotic than when the rebels had fought against the Million Heroes a year earlier.

Demobilization

While the situation in Wuhan deteriorated, the top leaders of the WMR, Zeng Siyu and Liu Feng, who were concurrently the chairman and the first vice chairman of the HPRC, were in Beijing.[73] Partly because of their absence, the other leaders of the HPRC were reluctant to take harsh action against the rebels' excesses.[74] Before Zeng and Liu left Beijing, they met with Lin Biao, Zhou Enlai, and other central leaders who invested them with discretionary power to restore order in Wuhan. Upon their return to Wuhan on 15 June, Zeng and Liu immediately adopted a series of drastic measures to restore order. In the second half of June, the heads of all the major mass organizations were summoned to participate in numerous conferences held by the HPRC and the WMRC. Extravagances committed by the rebels were condemned. The rebel organizations were exhorted to surrender all the arms they had seized, to disband all the storm troops they had established, and, more important, to dissolve themselves altogether.[75]

At first, the rebel leaders did not take the criticisms and warning seriously. Apart from making token self-criticisms, they did nothing to draw in their horns. The last ten days of June saw endless armed parades in commemoration of the first anniversary of the rebels' victory over the Million Heroes. But the fact that such activities were conducted in June rather than in July indicated that their real purpose was to enable the rebel organizations to intimidate their rivals by making a show of force. The crack of rifles could still be heard throughout the city, and occasionally a massed volley broke out, indicating that another bloody battle was unfolding between the two hostile factions somewhere in the city. The situation was so tense that some organizations thought guns and grenades were not powerful enough for offence and defence. Rebels from some of the factories and colleges then started to develop 'new' weapons such as tanks, chemical weapons, high-explosive packages, and mines. The tension between the opposing factions thus went from bad to worse.[76]

The renewed outbreak of violence triggered by Beijing's call for a campaign against rightist trends was by no means unique to Wuhan. Many other provinces were transformed into battlegrounds in the period between April and July 1968.[77]

In the face of increasingly unrestrained civil chaos, Beijing was compelled to call off the campaign against the rightist trends and turned its attention to restoring public order. It published a peremptory circular demanding the cessation of violent conflict in Guangxi Province on 3 July, and yet another order about the situation in Shaanxi on 24 July.[78]

The two circulars marked a turning point in the Cultural Revolution, after which the flame of what had been known as 'revolutionary extensive democracy' was gradually extinguished. Beijing's new orientation was echoed by most people, because they wanted an end to the violence.[79] A more enthusiastic response came from the provincial military authorities, who had long been irritated by the rebels' ruleless behaviour but had to appear sympathetic, or at least not hostile, to the troublemakers. Now they had a licence to squelch the rebels.

The first reaction of the Wuhan military authorities to the circular of 3 July was to make it known to as wide an audience as possible. On 7 July the HPRC issued an urgent order of its own, which was worded more imperiously than that issued by Beijing which had urged only that the mass organizations return their seized weapons. The provincial order empowered the local army to take weapons from the rebels by force, and warned that anyone who hid weapons would be severely punished.[80] The military leaders soon got even tougher with the rebels. At a joint meeting of the HPRC and the WMRC held on 13 July, Zeng Siyu criticized by name Zhu Hongxia, Yang Daoyuan, and Zhang Likuo, three vice chairmen of the HPRC, who represented the rebels and whom he had never dared to affront. On 18 July, Mao instructed that the propaganda of the circular of 3 July be pushed one step further. Accordingly, Beijing decided to set in motion a massive propaganda campaign.[81] This decision further emboldened the provincial military authorities. On the night of 22 July the Wuhan army ransacked 118 hotels and hostels throughout the city, searching for arms dealers from other provinces. As a result of this operation, more than 2,700 persons were deported and 270 arrested. When Beijing's circular of 24 July was issued, the HPRC held a mass rally urging the rebels to surrender all the arms they were still holding.

Despite their discontentment with the new policies, the rebels were not able to stage a counterattack. All they dared to do was to condemn in private the two circulars issued by Beijing as 'poisonous weeds' and to surreptitiously tear down the posters carrying the two circulars.[82]

In the remaining months of 1968, life became harder for the rebels. In August, editorials in the *People's Daily* came out strongly against the so-called theory of polycentrism.[83] The term 'polycentrism' was just another way of saying 'factionalism'. Because Mao had recently issued instructions requiring people to 'make a class analysis of factionalism', Beijing invented the new term to avoid sounding self-contradictory. The criticism of factionalism thus was resumed, a task that Beijing had abandoned four months before.

The HPRC attempted to eliminate the impact of factionalism by summoning the leaders of the major mass organizations from all over the province, especially from Wuhan, to participate in an extensive Mao Zedong Thought study programme in the middle of August, at which once arrogant rebel leaders were put in the dock. Around this time, the chief military leaders of the WMR were recalled to Beijing. Mao received them, and Lin Biao heard their report about the situation in Wuhan. They left Beijing confident that this time they did not have to be polite to the rebels.

Upon their return to Wuhan, the military authorities set about three tasks. First, workers' propaganda teams were to be sent into all schools. At first, the workers' propaganda team was merely Mao's expedient measure to put an end to violent confrontations among the fractious student rebels in Beijing, particularly at Qinghua University. But by the middle of August, Mao had come to the conclusion that if universities were to cease to be permanent sources of unrest, the workers' propaganda team should be institutionalized.[84] On 25 August, Beijing issued a circular to the provinces, dictating that such teams should be set up and sent to all schools, especially to colleges.[85] Two days later, Wuhan's first workers' propaganda team was dispatched to Wuhan Metallurgical Institute, where two factions of students had divided the campus, erected fortifications in each other's territory, and frequently engaged with each other. In the following months, virtually all schools came under the control of the workers' propaganda teams. The teams' task in the schools was first to disarm the rebels and then to dissolve the rebel organizations. But what was more devastating for the rebels was that the teams in effect cut off their connections with their comrades in other schools and sectors. Once such connections were cut off, the isolated rebels became very vulnerable to attack.[86]

The final blow came to the rebel students when they were called on to 'go up the mountains and down into the countryside to receive re-education from the poor and lower-middle peasants'.[87] By the end of the year, the campuses of Wuhan's colleges and high schools were almost empty. All students with the exception of the 1969 junior high class were sent to the countryside. Since the students who were old enough to care about politics were now dispersed, the threat posed by troublesome and unruly student rebels was removed once and for all.

The second task carried out by the military authorities was to gradually disband the mass organizations. On 6 September, at a conference attended by the chairpersons and vice chairpersons of revolutionary committees at all levels in Wuhan, Zeng Siyu read a resolution concerning the 'thorough dissolution of all mass organizations' passed by the HPRC. The resolution outlawed all mass organizations and declared that 'feigned compliance' would not be tolerated.[88] Under pressure, the Workers' Headquarters held its farewell rally on 10 September. Three days later, the Workers' Rebel Headquarters closed its office. Finally, on 20 September, the 13 September Corps ceased all activities. Other minor organizations all demobilized themselves around the same time. Along with the dissolution of the mass organizations, their publications were banned and their broadcasting equipment confiscated.[89] After two years of existence, all traces of the Cultural Revolution's 'great democracy', except for the rhetoric, were gone overnight.

The military authorities' third task was to tear apart the 'hornets' nests'. On 25 August, the *Red Flag* carried an article entitled 'Hornets' Nests Must Be Torn Apart'. By 'hornets' nests' it meant units where the influence of factionalism had been strong. In order to overcome factionalism in those units, the article suggested, the public authorities must use coercive measures.[90] In Wuhan, the slogan gained a new meaning. Many individual rebels were labelled as 'hornets' and made into targets in special 'study programmes'. For instance, Hu Houming, the number two man in the Workers' Headquarters and a member of the standing committee of the HPRC, was accused of having directed many of the Workers' Headquarters' violent operations. He was condemned as a 'conspirator' and 'careerist'. Following the public denouncement of Hu, rebel leaders of many units were labelled as 'Hu Houming, Jun.' and given a hard time. Some were even taken into custody. Peng Zulong, the number two man in the Workers' Rebel Headquarters, for example, was imprisoned by the Wuhan Garrison for seven months, though he was still a member of the HPRC in name.[91]

The workers' propaganda team, the dissolution of the rebel organizations, and the campaign to 'tear apart hornets' nests' all worked to puncture the arrogance of the rebels. The suppression of the rebels continued and grew in intensity in the last two months of 1968.

In October a campaign to 'purify class ranks' began to unfold in Wuhan. By its very nature, the campaign was to work to the advantage of former conservatives. The officially designated targets of the campaign included 'landlords', 'rich peasants', 'counter-revolutionaries', 'rightists', 'bad elements', 'renegades', 'spies', and 'incorrigible power holders taking the capitalist road'.[92] In reality, the range of attack was much broader.[93] Except for capitalist roaders, the campaign targeted exactly the same people whom the conservatives had called 'monsters and ghosts'. The declared purpose of the campaign was to drag out 'impure' class elements from all units regardless of which faction they had joined in the previous stages of the Cultural Revolution. But it was the rebels who were vulnerable to such a campaign, because many of them or their family members had bad class backgrounds or inglorious historical records. The cases of capitalist roaders were different and were usually handled with extreme caution. In fact, thousands of cadres who had been indiscriminately called 'capitalist roaders' during the previous two years began to be 'emancipated' during the campaign.[94]

In a bid to push the campaign forward, the WMR sent PLA Mao Zedong Thought propaganda teams (the members of which were called 'military representatives') to all units. Like the Workers' Mao Thought propaganda teams, wherever the PLA teams went, they assumed over-all control, setting the revolutionary committees aside. The members of both teams were carefully selected in accordance with the criteria set by Beijing.[95] The first criterion was that they had to be from good class backgrounds. They thus were very likely to be conservatives or conser-vative sympathizers. It was not surprising that the two teams tended to rely upon former conservatives as the backbone of the campaign in the renewed attack against 'monsters and ghosts'. Former conservatives thus were given a chance to stand up again.

Most former conservatives, however, were at first hesitant to lay bare their hostility towards the rebels. They had observed more than once in the past two years that a temporary decline of the rebel force was followed by their comeback. It was too risky for them to make any move against the rebels. The rebels, on the other hand, believed that the current downturn would not last for long. They often warned, explicitly or implicitly, former conservatives against seeking revenge.[96]

In order to expedite the campaign, the PLA teams attempted to dispel the former conservatives' misgivings. The most effective way of doing so was to use the mass media to discredit the rebels. Throughout Octo-ber and November, the *Yangtze Daily* carried reports that the rebel groups of certain units were revealed to have been manipulated by 'hidden class enemies'. Some institutions were even categorized as units where 'evildoers are in power, while good people are suffering'. As a result of the PLA teams' unremitting efforts, former conservatives grad-ually cast aside their fears and became active in helping the PLA to carry out the campaign. Their first targets were, of course, the rebel leaders and activists in their units. They conducted investigations against those rebels. If damaging materials were unearthed from the rebels' own or their family members' records, those rebels would be condemned as 'alien-class elements'. In most cases, such investigations were unnecessary, as the conservatives generally knew the background of the rebels in their units. Those with 'impure' records could hardly escape unnoticed. Charges brought against them varied. But the charge used most often at that time was that those class enemies had exploited the opportunity provided by the Cultural Revolution to inflict 'class vengeance on revolutionary cadres and masses'.

Rebels from good class backgrounds were urged to expose 'impure elements' within the rebel organizations. Their strategy of coping with the pressure was to expose people who had previously belonged to rival rebel organizations. Because of their reluctance to harm their comrades in their own faction, they were often criticized as 'obstacles' or 'stumbling-blocks' in the campaign to purify the class ranks.

As the campaign moved forward, some former conservatives became elated again and began to harp on the same old string they had accentuated throughout the course of the movement: all rebel organizations were 'shelters of evil people' or 'sinks of iniquity'.[97] Accordingly, they asserted that 'the rebels should never be allowed to wield power'.[98]

By the beginning of 1969 the rebels had lost much of their power in the revolutionary committees from the grassroots up to the provincial level in Wuhan. At first, rebels who were considered as impure class elements were discharged from their posts. Then, under the pretext of consolidating or reorganizing the revolutionary committees, the power organs in many units were reshuffled. In some units, the revolutionary committees were suspended altogether and replaced by what were called 'the leading group for grasping revolution and promoting production', or 'the leading group for struggle–criticism–transformation', or simply 'the revolutionary leading group'. Whatever form these changes took, the outcomes were essentially the same: the rebels were replaced by the former conservatives, and the cadres who had supported the rebels by the cadres who had not.[99]

Those rebels who still held positions in the revolutionary committees felt threatened as well. In November 1968 the HPRC convened a twenty-one-day conference for representatives of revolutionary committees at the county level and above. Ren Aisheng (a vice chairman of the HPRC) and Yang Chunting (a vice chairman of the WMRC) were castigated. Both Ren and Yang were veteran Party cadres who had sided with the rebels since early 1967. They were now criticized for having 'unprincipledly' supported the rebels, and labelled as 'sinister hands' and 'right opportunists'. Cadres who had sided with the rebels in revolutionary committees at lower levels were also caught in the cross-fire. After the conference, the rebels' representatives in the HPRC and the WMRC functioned at best merely to maintain an outward show of the 'three-in-one combination'.[100] Some of them were driven out of the two committees altogether. The Workers' Congress and the Red Guard Congress also existed only in name.[101]

After two-and-a-half years of the Cultural Revolution, it seemed that as 1969 began, the pendulum was taking a discernible swing back to where it had been in 1965.

10

Factionalism from 1969 to 1973

The Resurgence of Factionalism in 1969

BY THE beginning of 1969 the Cultural Revolution, as a tumultuous, revolutionary, violent upheaval, seemed to have come to an end in Wuhan. Troublesome and unruly students had been driven out to the countryside. Spontaneous mass organizations had been demobilized. Revolutionary committees had been established in virtually all units. According to the *People's Daily*, the Cultural Revolution was entering a 'stage of struggle–criticism–transformation'.[1] Beneath the calm sea, however, another storm was brewing.

Soon after the Purification of Class Ranks Campaign started in Wuhan, rebels began to remonstrate that the campaign represented a 'new bourgeois reactionary line'. The Workers' Mao Thought propaganda teams were called 'conservative teams' and the military representatives 'sympathizers of the conservatives'. They were accused of helping former conservatives to stage a comeback. Such private murmurings, however, could not help to reverse the direction of the seemingly irresistible campaign.

In an effort to overcome the communication barrier between rebels in different units, some rebels tried to restore trans-unit connections in early January 1969. Before long, many underground networks were formed, and exciting rumours started to circulate in the city. According to one rumour, a new central directive had criticized that the general orientation of the Purification of Class Ranks Campaign was incorrect. Beijing was alleged to have ordered the rehabilitation of those rebels who had been wrongly purged during the campaign. There was also talk that there were no military representatives in Shanghai, and that the Shanghai rebels were urging the Wuhan rebels to rise in rebellion against 'restorationist activities'. Such seemingly encouraging news emboldened some rebels to take more tangible action. Some of those who still held positions in the revolutionary committees began to defy the military representatives in their units. Some even went so far as to state publicly, 'Although our organizations have been disbanded, there is still the Workers' Congress. The Workers' Congress is the core of leader-

ship for us. We do not acknowledge the authority of military representatives. We do not acknowledge the authority of the puppet revolutionary committee.'[2]

In late January and early February, many high school graduates who
had gone to the countryside returned to Wuhan to join their families for
the traditional Chinese Spring Festival. The die-hard rebels among them
quickly re-established connections with the secret networks set up by
the rebel workers. Dauntless and aggressive as they were, those rebel
students put up big-character posters on the streets, declaring that they
would square accounts with the conservatives after the Spring Festival
and thereby make the rebels' might felt once again. The students' action
boosted the morale of rebels in other sectors. In some units, they began
openly to demand the reversal of verdicts against them or their comrades
imposed by military representatives during the Purification of Class
Ranks Campaign. There were even attempts to re-establish rebel organizations.[3] But a protest movement did not really take shape until April.

At the beginning of April the Ninth National Congress of the Chinese
Communist Party opened in Beijing. 'Unity' was the watchword of the
congress.[4] Many Chinese believed that the Ninth Party Congress would
be the mark of the formal closing of the Cultural Revolution.

While Mao was trying to act as a unity-makēr in Beijing, a new
upheaval broke out in Wuhan. This storm had been brewing for some
time. It finally arrived in April when local leaders were attending the
congress in Beijing.

Four factors might have emboldened some frustrated rebels to rise in
rebellion while Mao was making efforts to create stability. First, if they
had learned anything from the experiences of the past three years, it was
that misfortune never lasted long. In April 1967 and April 1968 the
rebels had twice narrowly escaped and staged strong comebacks. They
believed that April 1969 would be another fortunate month for them.
Second, open factional conflicts had continued in several other
provinces.[5] Factional conflicts in other provinces assured the Wuhan
rebels that one more uprising would not cost them too much.

Third, the news from elsewhere was encouraging. There was a rumour
that Zhang Chunqiao had called the rebels in Shanghai to counterattack
the so-called tendency to restore old ways.[6] A report approved by Beijing
also condemned this tendency.[7] The most heartening news was brought
back from Shandong Province by Hu Houmin. Hu had been sternly
denounced in September 1968 and had been looking for a way to stage
a comeback. For this purpose, he went to Shandong in early 1969. The
Shandong rebels, like their counterparts in Wuhan, had been repressed

in the Purification of Class Ranks Campaign. What impressed Hu was that Wang Xiaoyu, the chairman of the Shandong Provincial Revolutionary Committee, initiated a counterattack against the tendency to restore old ways.[8] Hu's account of what was happening in Shandong heightened the morale of the Wuhan rebels.

Fourth, the rebels still had some political resources, which enabled them to rise again. Although some rebels had been purged, most rebels had only been repressed rather than formally persecuted. Some rebels still held positions on revolutionary committees, at least in name. In some units, the rebels still had the upper hand.[9] With so many former comrades-in-arms having been purged as 'monsters and ghosts', they were afraid that the tendency to vilify all rebels would ruin their political careers. There were two choices for them: either put up a last-ditch struggle, or resign themselves to extinction. Many felt that they could not afford to sit back and watch what remained of their political resources being taken away. Moreover, at the municipal level, the Workers' Congress and the Red Guards Congress, though impaired, still existed and could provide the leadership necessary to mobilize the discontented.

The insurgency started with some amorphous activities. In mid-April, when the Ninth Congress was still in session, the Workers' Congress of Wuhan finally came to the fore. In order to turn the inchoate resistance into an organized protest movement, on 18 April it put out a proclamation declaring its support of the increasingly widespread wildcat strikes in the city. Moreover, it called on workers' congresses at the grassroots level to lead the struggle against the restorationist manoeuvres. It also urged the rebels to rebuild workers' congresses wherever they had been dissolved. The role of the workers' congress was emphasized because, unlike the revolutionary committee in which rebels at their best had to share power with army officials and Party cadres, the workers' congress was the exclusive domain of the rebels. To ensure that no other force would have a hand in this domain, the 18 April proclamation further dictated that 'workers' congresses at the grassroots must subject themselves to the dual leadership of the revolutionary committees at the same level and the workers' congresses of the higher level'.[10] This was a bold revision of the principle put forward by Mao in the joint 1969 new year editorial of the *People's Daily*, the *Red Flag*, and the *PLA Daily*: 'The revolutionary committee must exercise a unified leadership.'[11] In fact, 'dual leadership' was a façade. What the authors of the proclamation really wanted was a 'unified leadership' exercised by the workers' congress.

During the rest of April and May, Wuhan was thrown into turmoil again. *Wuhan Workers*, the organ of the Municipal Workers' Congress, which had published only eight issues in four months from 1 January to 23 April, put out nine issues within a single month from 23 April to 25 May. Not only did the frequency of its publication increase but its content also underwent a dramatic change. Since 26 September 1968, *Wuhan Workers* had done nothing but dance to the tune of the HPRC and the WMRC. After mid-April 1969, however, the paper became captious and radical, directly attacking the HPRC and the WMRC and the military authorities behind them. The issue of 23 April, for instance, carried an article that listed 'ten manifestations of the tendency to restore old ways', among which were the following:

(1) Due to the fact that all mass organizations had been disbanded, the power base of rebel representatives in the HPRC and the WMRC had been vitally attenuated.

(2) A number of 'revolutionary cadres' (namely, those who had sided with the rebels all along) in the HPRC and the WMRC had been denounced as 'evil backstage manipulators' or 'right opportunists' and excluded from decision making.

(3) During the campaign to purify class ranks, a great number of rebels were labelled as 'intriguers', 'careerists', 'counter-revolutionaries', or simply 'monsters and ghosts', and many rebel leaders were called 'stumbling-blocks' or 'obstacles' in the way of the campaign.

(4) Under the pretext of 'preventing factionalism from corroding the newborn red political power', rebels in many units were barred from holding positions in revolutionary committees.

(5) Under the pretext that 'it is time to redefine who are the real leftists', former conservatives were propped up and former power holders rehabilitated.

(6) Revolutionary committees in which rebels had considerable influence were often suspended and replaced by 'leading groups for grasping revolution and promoting production'.

The article concluded:

> The present situation is one in which those who tried to overturn [the pre-Cultural Revolution establishment] are overturned and those who once seized power [from the capitalist roaders] are divested of their power. Yesterday's revolutionary pioneers today are treated as criminals. After three years of the Cultural Revolution, the pendulum is swinging back to the place from where it started.

To 'reverse the reversal of history', the paper asserted that the rebels must be united as one in order to seize back the power usurped by 'the bourgeoisie', namely, former conservatives, former power holders, and army men.[12]

Having suffered the same bitter experiences in recent months, rebels from the different factions once again joined forces. Hu Houmin rationalized the necessity of unity between the rebels by admonishing:

> The present situation, in many aspects, resembles the one we saw after the publication of the 8 February Statement in early 1967. We are rebels. No matter which faction we used to belong to, we share a common destiny. We will all be eliminated unless we close ranks to fight the common enemy together.[13]

Zhu Hongxia, Li Xiangyu, and Wu Yanjin, the heads of the Workers' Headquarters, the 13 September Corps, and the Workers' Rebel Headquarters, published in late April a joint statement urging the rebels to 'combat restorationism, combat the tendency to restore old ways, and repulse the assaults of a new February Adverse Current'.[14]

Reproduced as big-character posters and handbills, the joint statement was made known to all residents of the city overnight. It became an order for the general mobilization of the rebels. When the Workers' Congress held a mass rally in the downtown area of Hankou on 27 April, 500,000 people reportedly attended the event. Of course, not everyone present was a rebel and not every rebel was present. Nevertheless, the large attendance indicated that the efforts of the three rebel magnates had begun to take effect. The rally was held under the pretext of 'celebrating the successful close of the Ninth Congress', but the topic of 'unity', the watchword of the Ninth Congress, was ignored. The word 'unity' was used only in the context of unity within the rebel ranks, which was obviously at odds with what Mao meant. The real purpose of the rally was to gather the rebels together to demonstrate their strength, solidarity, and determination to win back the prestige and power they had lost. In his speech, Zhu Hongxia claimed: 'With the support of Premier Zhou, Jiang Qing, Chen Boda, Kang Sheng, Yao Wenyuan, and Zhang Chunqiao [the latter five all key members of the CRSG], we are confident that we will win the battle.'[15] This was, however, wishful thinking. Zhu and his audience did not know that at a session of the Ninth Congress, when Zeng Siyu reported to Mao what the Wuhan rebels were currently up to, the Chairman instructed him to stabilize the situation and showed no sympathy for the rebels.[16]

Since most college and high school students had been either assigned jobs or sent to the countryside, the Red Guards' Congress had ceased to exist, except in name, in late 1968. Most of its standing committee members, for instance, had already left Wuhan.[17] Nevertheless, the Congress managed to hold an enlarged meeting of its standing committee on 30 April and passed a resolution entitled 'Combat Restorationism, Combat the Tendency to Restore Old Ways, and Fight to Win Still Greater Victories'. According to the resolution, 'the tendency to restore old ways' was characterized by the reinstatement of the old power structure and the resumption of the old style of work. In order to counter this tendency, the resolution asserted that the rebels should criticize and repudiate the following 'absurdities':

(1) The two-line struggle had finished with the victory of Mao's revolutionary line. Therefore, the distinction between the rebels and the conservatives no longer made sense.

(2) The rebels were made the targets of attack in the campaign to purify class ranks, because there were too many 'monsters and ghosts' in the rebel ranks.

(3) The rebels had committed acts of 'smashing and grabbing' (*daza-qiang*) over the past two years. The time had come to square accounts with them.

(4) The rebels were generally too selfish and too undisciplined to wield power. They ought to step down on a voluntary basis or be driven out of the revolutionary committee.

The Workers' Mao Thought propaganda team was a major obstacle to the student rebels' instigating a new insurrection on campuses. The resolution therefore insisted that activities hostile to particular Workers' Mao Thought Propaganda Teams should not be interpreted as actions against the working class at large.[18]

On 7 May the Workers' Congress and the Red Guard Congress jointly held a mass rally allegedly to celebrate the fourth anniversary of Mao's '7 May Directive', which reportedly attracted some 200,000 people. In fact, it had nothing to do with the 7 May Directive. Rather, it was a meeting to pledge mass support for the rebels' cause.[19] On the same day, the two congresses published a strongly worded joint open letter addressed to the HPRC and the WMRC. The letter contended that 'some chief leaders' of the two power organs had made several gross mistakes since the fall of 1968. First, the two revolutionary committees had become mere playthings for a few top leaders. The rebels' representatives and 'revolutionary cadres' had been made into mere figureheads and were largely excluded from decision making. Decisions on important issues had been made by a small group of chief leaders without consultation with most of the members of the two committees. Examples included the guidelines for the campaign to purify class ranks, the plan to dispatch the

Workers' Mao Thought propaganda teams to schools, the criticism of Ren Aisheng, the denouncement of Hu Houmin, and the imprisonment of Peng Zhulong.

Second, both the HPRC and the WMRC had been considerably expanded and reshuffled. Initially, neither committee had had more than 100 functionaries. But by early 1969, the staffs of each exceeded 1,000. Furthermore, the majority of new staff members were former conservatives. In the department of economic production under the WMRC, for instance, only 6 per cent of the staff were former rebels.

Third, the local official newspapers, the *Yangtze Daily* and the *Hubei Daily*, had been used to vilify the rebels.

Based on those accusations, the open letter made seven claims:

(1) All Party cadres must subject themselves to 're-education' monitored by rebel workers.

(2) Any cadre who refused to accept the rebels' paramountcy must step down from their posts.

(3) The chief leaders of the HPRC and the WMRC must make public self-criticisms about the mistakes they had committed in recent months.

(4) The Workers' Congress and the Red Guard Congress must be strengthened rather than weakened, and their role in local politics should be upheld.

(5) Rebels who had been wrongly criticized or purged in the Purification of Class Ranks Campaign must be rehabilitated, and the power they had lost must be restored.

(6) The HPRC and the WMRC must stand in the forefront of the struggle against the tendency to restore old ways.

(7) The Workers' Mao Thought propaganda teams must be placed under the leadership of the Workers' Congress, and conservative elements in those teams must be replaced by rebel workers.[20]

Together, those claims amounted to nothing less than a total repudiation of the practices of the HPRC and the WMRC in the previous half year or so. Four days after the publication of the open letter, the rebels showed in action their contempt for the provincial and municipal authorities: more than 100 truckloads of rebel workers charged the office buildings of the two committees.[21]

The rebels' Fight against the Tendency to Restore Old Ways Campaign disturbed Wuhan. But the rebels were more a spent force than a force in the ascendant. The deportation of almost all college and high school students from the city had banished the rebels' most energetic elements. The students who remained in middle schools were too young to care much about politics. Meanwhile, with Mao's sanction, the high-handed policy implemented by the Workers' and the PLA's Mao Thought propaganda teams at educational and cultural institutions had effectively demoralized the rebels among school teachers and other types of intellectuals. As a result, while other sectors of society were caught up in the upheavals of April and May, educational, cultural, and scientific research institutions, which the rebels had previously dominated, were largely quiet.[22] Party and government institutions were also generally placid, not only because the rebels had never controlled these organizations but also because most of the functionaries of those bodies, especially rebels, had been sent to the countryside to 'undertake the tasks of struggle–criticism–transformation'.[23]

Even in the industrial and commercial sectors, most former rebels were apathetic about the Fight against the Tendency to Restore Old Ways Campaign. Some, growing sick of politics, adopted an indifferent attitude. Some, persecuted in the Purification of Class Ranks Campaign for their problematic records, were still badly shaken. Although the rebels in general had been suppressed in recent months, there were exceptions. In some units, particularly those units in which the rebels had opposed the work teams rather than the power holders at the very beginning of the Cultural Revolution, the rebels had been able to retain their predominance. Rebels in those units had little incentive to risk their political careers for someone else's sake. They therefore tended to stand aloof from the battle their former comrades were fighting, though they might feel sympathy for them. Only those rebels whose records were fairly clean and who believed that their participation in the new uprising would cost them a little but might enable them to benefit a great deal were active in the campaign. Those who held formal posts in revolutionary committees but had little real power were among the most enthusiastic in giving impetus to the struggle. They hoped that the campaign would result in a decisive improvement of their power positions.[24]

In the Fight against the Tendency to Restore Old Ways Campaign, the role of four units was particularly conspicuous. They were the Post Office, the Telecommunications Bureau, the Power Supply Bureau, and the People's Bank. Although the names of the four units bore such terms as 'bureau' or 'office', they were not administrative agencies and their staff were not government bureaucrats. But due to the local military authorities' ignorance about civil affairs, the four units were mistakenly categorized as administrative agencies. As a result, a large number of the employees of the four units, including mailmen, telephone operators, maintenance workers in the power system, and bank tellers, had been sent to undertake 'struggle–criticism–transformation' in the countryside.

Separated from their families and suffering from the hardships of life in
the country, these people hoped to return home as soon as possible. The
Fight against the Tendency to Restore Old Ways Campaign provided an
opportunity for them to pursue this goal. The rebels in the Power Supply
Bureau published a statement asserting that 'it is against Mao Zedong's
Thought to force workers to undertake struggle–criticism–transformation in the countryside'.[25] Rebels in the Post Office and the Telecommunications Bureau claimed that because the city was short of mailmen
and phone operators, the already low quality of postal and telecommunications service might take a turn for the worse. Under the pretext of
participating in the Fight against the Tendency to Restore Old Ways
Campaign, many returned to Wuhan. Interestingly, some former conservatives in the four units joined with their rebel adversaries. Like most
rebels in the four units, those former conservatives cared little about the
Fight against the Tendency to Restore Old Ways Campaign. What they
really cared about was family reunion. In the four units, again only those
rebel leaders who were afraid of being kicked out of the power structure were really zealous in supporting the campaign.[26]

To sum up, all those rebels who remained active during the spring of
1969 had what Mancur Olsen calls 'selective incentives' to keep them
fighting.[27] Because their estimates of personal benefits from continued
activism still outweighed their calculations of possible costs, they were
convinced that it was worthwhile for them to maintain their commitment
to the cause they had fought for over the past two-and-a-half years.
Nevertheless, most of the former rebels had become disheartened for
one reason or another. While the mass base of the rebel forces had
shrunk, their ranks had become more select, more devoted, and more
combat-worthy. Therefore, although they were fewer in number, their
capacity for manoeuvres had improved and they were still able to stir
up turmoil in late April and May. Altogether, 736 rebel groups re-
emerged in the city; and they took over power from revolutionary
committees in 180 units. The rebels' activities climaxed on 17 May
when a so-called Workers' Investigation Delegation forcefully entered
the building of the WMRC. The Workers' Congress had organized the
delegation, whose mission was to determine to what extent the WMRC
had contributed to 'the tendency to restore old ways'.[28] This was a great
humiliation for the WMRC. If any group of people who opposed the
municipal government were allowed to place themselves above the
government, there would be neither authority nor order. The rebels could
have done this during the early stage of the Cultural Revolution because
Mao had backed them at that time. The Wuhan Workers' Congress must

have counted on Mao's support or at least tolerance when it decided to send the delegation to the WMRC. But now Mao was in a different mood.

The Fight against the Tendency to Restore Old Ways Campaign derailed Mao's plan. At the Ninth Party Congress he called on his fellow citizens to 'unite to win still greater victories', but in Wuhan and several other places, factionalism resurfaced. The factionalism undermined local authorities, disturbed public order, and crippled production.[29] The course of the Cultural Revolution over the past two-and-a-half years had demonstrated that factionalism was an infectious social disease that was hard to cure but easily spread. Therefore, it was crucial to nip factionalism in the bud wherever it germinated. Beijing attempted to keep the factionalism in Wuhan from spreading elsewhere by summoning dozens of local rebel leaders to the capital in mid-May and ordering them to stop their campaign.[30] On 27 May, Beijing issued a directive aimed specifically at dealing with the situation in Wuhan. The so-called 27 May Instruction declared that the general orientation of the Fight against the Tendency to Restore Old Ways Campaign was wrong.[31] The rebel leaders were forced to make self-criticisms in front of the central leaders and local military leaders. Their followers in Wuhan thus were left with no choice but to beat a retreat. There was no point in continuing to fight a losing battle. By early June the tense atmosphere the city had seen in April and May began to relax. The newspapers of the Workers' Congress and the Red Guards Congress were closed, organized rebel forces were disbanded, and the streets became quiet again. The short-lived Fight against the Tendency to Restore Old Ways Campaign thus ended in failure.

Suppression of the Rebels

In the second half of 1969, Beijing made a series of efforts to peddle its theme of unity. In June a joint editorial of the *People's Daily*, the *Red Flag*, and the *PLA Daily* declared that the distinction between rebels and conservatives was no longer valid. Thus the most important political capital that the rebels possessed was removed.[32] In July and August, Beijing issued two decrees authorizing the local army to suppress by force any individuals and organizations that stubbornly continued factionalist activities. In the meantime, all propaganda machines were set in motion to disseminate new notions such as 'unity', 'authority', and 'discipline'.[33]

But factionalism died hard, at least in Wuhan. Although all tangible factional organizations had gone, intangible connections persisted. Some obstinate rebels went underground in order to keep their secret networks running.[34] The fate of Wuhan's rebels was sealed on 27 September 1969, however, when Beijing issued an Instruction Concerning the Plough Society, the *Juepai*,[35] and the *Yangtze Tribune* (which were usually abbreviated as *bei-jue-yang*, the first characters of each name in Chinese) of Wuhan. The Plough Society and *Juepai* were two names for one group and the *Yangtze Tribune* was its organ. This tiny group, consisting of no more than two dozen college and high school students, enlisted some of the city's brightest rebel theorists. Its publications had been influential in local politics, but at the time of the 27 September Instruction the two leaders of the group had been in gaol for more than a year. Hence, *bei-jue-yang* posed no threat to the stability of the situation in Wuhan. The 27 September Instruction singled out *bei-jue-yang* as the primary target of attack, because Beijing, as will be shown, had an axe to grind. According to the 27 September Instruction, *bei-jue-yang* was 'a hotchpotch manipulated by a handful of renegades, spies, and counter-revolutionaries from behind the scenes', whose leaders and activists should be punished without mercy. Another important message conveyed by the 27 September Instruction was that Beijing would soon summon 'the parties concerned' from Wuhan to take part in a Mao Zedong Thought study programme in the capital.[36]

The HPRC and the WMRC knew in advance that Beijing would issue this instruction. A week before the publication of the instruction, twelve persons who were allegedly the leaders, or backbone, of *bei-jue-yang* were arrested.[37]

The 27 September Instruction sounded the death-knell not merely of *bei-jue-yang* but also of Wuhan's rebels at large. A week later, an enlarged conference of the HPRC was convened, which lasted about a month. The participants included members and alternate members of the HPRC and the WMRC, members of the Workers' Congress and the Red Guards' Congress, and members of the revolutionary committees of selected large enterprises and colleges. The conference marked the start of a two-year criticism campaign against the rebels. Local rebel leaders came under rigorous attack from all sides. Under great pressure, some rebel leaders went down on their knees. Trying to give an impression that he was willing to co-operate with the authorities, Zhu Hongxia, for instance, revealed that his comrade, Hu Houmin, had advocated what he called 'a theory of three protracted struggles', namely, protracted struggles between the rebels and the conservatives, between the new and the veteran cadres within the revolutionary committee, and between the

New Faction and the Strong Faction. Such a co-operative gesture, however, failed to save Zhu from severe criticism, and he and the other rebel leaders were admonished not to try any further tricks. They were told that 'nobody would be allowed to get by under false pretenses this time'. The Workers' Congress and the Red Guard Congress were also caught in the cross-fire. The two institutions were charged with having sheltered the reactionary *bei-jue-yang*.

At the end of the conference, Zeng Siyu announced:

> According to the information we have collected so far, the leading bodies of some units have been contaminated by factionalism. And what is worse, in some units, evil-doers are still holding power and riding roughshod over good people. We must settle this matter systematically in accordance with the centre's instructions.[38]

A week after the close of the enlarged conference of the HPRC, the Hubei Mao Zedong Thought study programme began in Beijing. About 600 prominent rebels from Wuhan were called to take part in the programme. Though called the 'Hubei programme', it contained no rebels from other parts of the province. The participants were divided into five 'companies', which in turn were broken up into 'platoons' and 'squads'. One company was composed exclusively of college students; the other four contained people from other sectors. At the top was a Party committee headed by Zhang Zhaojian, the commissar of the Wuhan Garrison. The participants' activities were strictly restricted. For instance, although all the participants were quartered at the Air Force Academy, people from different companies were prohibited from having any contact with one another. This measure aimed to prevent the participants from acting in collusion so as to make their confessions tally. Indeed, the real purpose of the programme was to compel the participants to confess their own guilt and to expose others'. Few participants, however, voluntarily co-operated. When examining their own mistakes, they tended to avoid the important and dwell on the trivial; and when asked to expose their comrades' mistakes, they usually prevaricated, giving indefinite answers. In a bid to overcome the participants' passive resistance, the Party committee adopted the strategy of divide and conquer. Members of the Strong Faction and the New Faction were incited to expose each other. Some rebels saw this as an opportunity to settle old scores, and rose to the bait. They accused one another of having provoked armed clashes, committed acts of 'smashing and grab-bing', and supported *bei-jue-yang*. In this way, the Party committee gradually accumulated 'evidence' against virtually every participant.

Initially, the programme lacked a coherent theme. Anything and everything detrimental to individual rebels and to the rebels as a whole was welcome, but it was not clear how the information gathered should be interpreted and what action should be taken against the people concerned. In January 1970, Beijing offered a theme—finding out who were the members of the 16 May Regiment.[39]

The 16 May Regiment was a small, radical group from Beijing, which had been nipped in the bud in the autumn of 1967. The decision to castigate a shoestring group that had disappeared a long time ago can be explained by Beijing's need for a pretext to get rid of obstinate and unruly rebels. By launching a nationwide campaign to ferret out 16 May Regiment elements, Beijing created a delusion that the 16 May Regiment was a nation-wide organization with which a large number of individuals and groups in the provinces had secretly affiliated themselves. Rebels thus could be purged on a vast scale, on the ground that they were undercover members of this 'reactionary conspiratorial organization'. Without such a rationale the rebels might be criticized but not drummed out, because the charge of factionalism was not sufficient to liquidate them politically.

From January 1970, 'ferreting out 16 May elements' became the theme of the Hubei Mao Zedong Thought study programme. *Bei-jue-yang* was alleged to have been an affiliate of the 16 May Regiment, with an extensive membership. In order to ferret out local 16 May elements, it was necessary to establish the hypothetical 'links' between the 16 May Regiment of Beijing and its subsidiary in Wuhan. Li Li, a college student who had headed the Second Headquarters' intelligence department, was identified as the link, based on his frequent travels between Beijing and Wuhan in recent years. Li categorically rejected the charge as groundless. Under growing pressure, however, Lei Zhimao and Li Sumin, two young men who had once headed the Second Headquarters' liaison office in Beijing made false confessions, admitting that they had helped to build the bridge between the 16 May Regiment and some prominent Wuhan rebels such as Hu Houmin and Yang Daoyuan.[40] The testimonies of Lei and Li not only confirmed the Party committee's hypothesis that the 16 May Regiment had penetrated Wuhan but also provided clues to the identity of other local members of the clandestine group.

The first few suspects were compelled to provide a list of those whom they had supposedly recruited. The list of suspects thus snowballed. Many suspects admitted that they had joined the 16 May Regiment or its peripheral organization, *bei-jue-yang*. They yielded partly because they were told that the official policy was 'leniency to those who confess their crimes and severity to those who refuse to', and partly because they found that confessing was probably the only way to prevent themselves from being subjected to endless interrogation. Some, however, refused to yield, however much pressure was applied. But their insistence on their innocence did not free them from suspicion. Rather, they were regarded as diehards and often suffered more than their relatively recreant counterparts.[41]

While prominent rebels were being interrogated in Beijing, their underlings in Wuhan were being put under great pressure as well. Several campaigns were simultaneously under way.[42] In all the campaigns, former rebels were most likely to be the targets. Few former rebels, apart from those who had completely withdrawn from politics long before, could avoid serious accusation of one sort or another.

Unlike the chaotic and freewheeling campaigns that characterized earlier stages of the Cultural Revolution, under the leadership of the PLA's and Workers' Mao Thought propaganda teams, the campaigns of late 1969 and 1970 were conducted in accordance with guidelines specified by Beijing and in a controlled manner.

The guidelines were embodied in the 'Experiences of the Six Factories and Two Universities' prepared by Mao's guard division—Unit 8341. In 1969 and 1970, at least forty-three reports were compiled by Unit 8341 into booklets and distributed throughout the nation to serve as manuals for those who were directing various campaigns at the grassroots. Most of the reports dealt with ways of ferreting out hidden class enemies.[43] Following Beijing's example, the HPRC also selected several units as local models, which were called the Six Factories and One University of Hubei.[44]

Guided by the national and local models, every unit in Wuhan set up a special investigative group to examine all suspects in the unit. Suspects were often locked in 'study classes' or 'cowsheds'. They were not allowed to leave the compound, to receive visitors, to write letters, or to make telephone calls. They were prisoners in every sense except that they were gaoled in their own unit rather than in state prison.[45]

Corporal punishment was forbidden. In most cases, this prohibition was fairly well observed. Also supposedly forbidden was the use of compulsion and trickery to obtain confessions, but this was in fact a common practice. Various tactics were used. Among the most prevalent were *chelunzhan* (several persons taking turns to interrogate one suspect in order to tire him out) and *jingshenzhan* (forcing a suspect to confess by hinting that he had been exposed by others, especially his intimates). Many of the accused confessed to crimes they had not committed, because they were unable to stand the overwhelming pressure or they were tempted by the 'stick and carrot' slogan, 'leniency to those who confess their crimes and severity to those who refuse to'.[46]

Anyone who confessed would be asked to supply the names of accomplices, especially in the case of people suspected as a 16 May Regiment or *bei-jue-yang* element. Military representatives believed the two secret organizations kept a roster of membership. Under pressure, some began to supply fabricated lists. The number of those falsely accused thus mushroomed.

There were probably more people incriminated in 1970 and 1971 than at any other time in the history of Wuhan. The One Struggle and Three Antis Campaign alone indicted 35,461 persons in the city, among whom a great number were former rebels. Moreover, 33,659 persons were labelled as either 16 May Regiment or *bei-jue-yang* elements.[47] At the Wuhan Telecommunications Bureau, a unit with less than 1,000 employees, 136 men and women were labelled as members of the two clandestine groups. The situation at Wuhan Song and Dance Ensemble was even worse, with about 200 out of the 400 actors and actresses being impeached. All suspected 16 May Regiment and *bei-jue-yang* elements were rebels. There was virtually no unit in Wuhan in which no one was affected.[48] Two factors might have contributed to the excesses. First, military representatives understood that if they had to make a choice, it was much safer for them to mistakenly accuse an innocent person than to allow a possible class enemy to escape. Second, many conservatives and cadres were taking the opportunity to strike a vindictive blow against the rebels. The combination of these two factors caused misery to a great number of former rebels.[49]

In early June 1970 the Hubei Mao Zedong Thought study programme finally ended. With Beijing's approval, Hu Houmin—the soul of the Workers' Headquarters, Yang Daoyuan—the number one man at the Second Headquarters, and Li Xiangyu—the chief of the 13 September Corps, were deposed from their posts in the HPRC and the WMRC and put in gaol. In addition, Ren Aisheng, the only vice-chairman of the HPRC who had supported the rebels (there were eight vice chairmen), was labelled as the 'chief backstage boss of *bei-jue-yang*' and placed under house arrest.[50]

The other participants in the programme were divided into two categories: those holding positions in the HPRC and the WMRC were immediately transferred to a study programme run by the HPRC in Wuhan, while the rest were allocated to dozens of study programmes managed by lower levels of the revolutionary committees. The latter were joined by a large number of grassroots rebel leaders. The local programmes differed from the Beijing one in that each rebel was assigned several colleagues from his own unit as his 'mentors'. With few exceptions, 'mentors' were former conservatives whose role was to identify the rebel's faults, to criticize him, to compel him to confess, and to watch his every move. The programme run by the HPRC lasted about a year, while the duration of the other programmes varied from two to six months. When those programmes finished, the participants were brought back to their own units or assigned to other units. In either case, they were usually forced to do penal labour under public surveillance. Later it was revealed that as a part of the plan to conclude those study programmes, the military authorities once considered sentencing eighty-four well-known rebels to death. For some unknown reason, however, the plan was not implemented.[51] The Ferret out 16 May Regiment Elements Campaign did not end until late 1971 when Lin Biao became the target of a new mass campaign.

The Restoration of Old Power Relations

Political developments between late 1969 and 1972 fundamentally changed the substance, if not the form, of the power structure at the provincial level and below in China, including Wuhan. Most rebels were deprived of their posts in the revolutionary committees. Even those rebels who were lucky enough to keep their seats—for example, Zhu Hongxia, Wu Yanjin, and Zhang Liguo, previously the heads of the Workers' Headquarters, the Workers' Rebel Headquarters, and the New Central China Institute of Technology—had no real power. No one ever announced their dismissal from the HPRC or the WMRC, but they were denied access to the building of either committee.[52] Only in a few units where the rebels had formed alliances with the power holders in the fight against work teams at the beginning of the Cultural Revolution were the rebels able to retain their positions.[53]

The rebels were not only deprived of power but were also discriminated against in everyday life. In institutions that were classified as 'restricted units', attempts were made to oust the rebels. The Telecommunications Bureau, for instance, recruited 800 demobilized soldiers in 1970 and transferred a like number of rebel employees to other units.[54] Rebel students who had gone to the countryside also found that they were treated as second-class citizens. In 1970, industrial enterprises and PLA units began to recruit educated youth in the countryside, but former rebels were usually excluded from these efforts. Even rebels' family members and relatives were often denied the opportunity for upward mobility. In a sense, 'rebel' in the early 1970s was as derogatory a label as 'rightist' or 'bad element'.[55]

As the rebels were silenced, a new social order took shape. The Party organizations gradually resumed their predominance at the grassroots.[56] A new WMPC and HPPC came into existence in early 1971.[57]

The reconstruction of the Party apparatus was accompanied by a renewed vigour in rehabilitating former Party officials. By late 1972 about 95 per cent of veteran Party cadres in Wuhan had been 'emancipated', and over 90 per cent of them had resumed their posts.[58] The pre-Cultural Revolution pattern of power distribution thus was largely restored. In other words, the organizational base of the movement was largely dismantled in the city.

Lin Biao's demise in late 1971 had a great impact on local politics in Wuhan.[59] First, the number one and number two men in both the HPPC and the WMPC were found to have had something to do with Lin's conspiracy. Liu Feng, the Second Secretary of the HPPC, was purged as a 'sworn follower' of Lin Biao. Zhang Zhaojian, the Second Secretary of the WMPC, was chastened. Although Zeng Siyu and Fang Ming, the First Secretaries of the HPPC and the WMPC respectively, were able to retain their posts, they were forced to subject themselves to criticism by the members of the two committees. Their power position and prestige thus were significantly crippled. All four men were military officials. The waning of their influence was accompanied by an increase in influence of the civilian officials in the two decision-making bodies. The demise of Lin Biao also paved the way for an improvement in the power position of civilian cadres at lower levels.[60] Finally, in late 1972, military representatives were ordered to withdraw from all civilian units. Civilian cadres thus regained their lost prestige.

Second, former conservatives thought that Lin Biao and Liu Feng were responsible for using the Wuhan Incident against the Million Heroes. Although the former conservatives had gained the upper hand over the former rebels since 1969, the Wuhan Incident of 1967 had not yet been officially rehabilitated. As long as the case was not redressed, the Wuhan Incident would always be a vulnerable point in their political struggle. The demise of Lin and Liu provided an opportunity for them to press for the Wuhan Incident to be redressed.

In March 1972 the eight leaders of the Million Heroes who had been detained since August 1967 were released. Soon after their release, an informal network was set up among the former heads of the Million Heroes at various levels. In mid-1972 the two alleged 'chief culprits' of the Wuhan Incident, Generals Chen Zaidao and Zhong Hanhua, reappeared in public and were appointed to important positions in other provinces. For former conservatives, this was a sure sign that Beijing now admitted that the Wuhan Incident had been a miscarriage of justice and they began to put pressure on the local authorities for an official rehabilitation of the case.[61]

Third, former rebels who had been persecuted over the past two years saw in the demise of Lin Biao a glimmer of hope that the situation might change in their favour. One good sign was the sudden halt of the Ferret out 16 May Regiment Elements Campaign. Soon, the special group investigating the *bei-jue-yang* under the HPRC was dissolved. There were also reports that in some provinces, rebels who had been detained were being released. These seemingly isolated incidences were seen by some desperate rebels as indications that the recent trend might be reversed.[62]

Indeed, Mao had criticized Zeng Siyu, saying that, under his direction, the Ferret out *bei-jue-yang* Elements Campaign in Wuhan had wrongfully persecuted many innocent persons. Thus the HPPC and the WMPC were forced to re-examine all the cases of 16 May Regiment and *bei-jue-yang* suspects. The re-examination lasted from March 1972 to February 1973, and came to the conclusion that out of 33,659 suspects, only 177 persons could be proved to have joined *bei-jue-yang*. In other words, about 95 per cent of the cases were unfounded.[63] During the process of re-examination, some former rebels closely followed every new development and began secretly to re-establish trans-unit ties in order to exchange information.[64]

11

Factionalism from 1974 to 1976

The Rise and Fall of Factionalism in 1974

A T A B O U T the time the re-examination process was finishing, the criticism of Lin Biao suddenly took a turn in favour of the rebels. In the first year after Lin's death, he was condemned as an ultra-leftist. But as an anti-ultraleftist momentum was building, Mao sensed that a sustained assault on ultra-leftism could fundamentally wreck the *raison d'être* of the Cultural Revolution. In December 1972, Mao came to the conclusion that the critique of ultra-leftism had gone too far. Accordingly, the nature of Lin Biao's crime was redefined as ultra-rightist.[1] If he was to reverse the course of what he believed was a prevailing rightist trend, Mao needed a social force that could be used to counterbalance pressures from the right. He once again called to mind the constituency of the movement—the former rebels. The provinces were now instructed to allow those rebel leaders who had originally had offices in local revolutionary committees to reassume their posts, and to appoint others to positions in official mass organizations that were being reconstructed, such as the Trade Union, the Youth League, and the Women's Federation. Moreover, Wang Hongwen, a well-known rebel leader from Shanghai who had recently been promoted to a position in Beijing, was sent to tour a number of provinces in order to meet former rebel leaders.[2]

The change in Beijing's tune initially went largely unnoticed in Wuhan. What caught the residents' attention was the reappearance in public of a number of former rebel leaders in January 1973. Among the first to make their presence felt were Xia Bangyin and Dong Minghui, two rebels who had been elected as members of the Central Committee at the Ninth Congress in April 1969 but had since disappeared from public life.[3]

When the rebels learned of Wang Hongwen's tour through their channels of information, they realized the significant implications of the redefinition of Lin Biao's problem. In late February, soon after the conclusion of the re-examination of the cases of 16 May Regiment and *bei-jue-yang* suspects, a group of former rebels led by Zhu Hongxia and Wu Yanjin plotted to stage a demonstration in the downtown area of

Hankou to demand the reinstatement of rebel leaders in their former positions in the HPRC and the WMRC. The local authorities uncovered the plot and managed to forestall it, but had to make some concessions.[4] On 1 May, to the great surprise of Wuhan's residents, Zhu Hongxia and a number of other former rebel leaders were invited to attend the official Labour Day celebration and were introduced by their titles in the HPRC and the WMRC. This was their first appearance in public since mid-1969.[5] In mid-May there came yet another encouraging sign for former rebels: among the six secretaries of the newly established Hubei Provincial Committee of the Youth League, two were former rebel student leaders.[6]

The conspicuous return of former rebel celebrities drew the attention of some rebels at the grassroots. The change in the local authorities' attitude towards former rebel leaders was interpreted as a sign that the situation was developing in a direction favourable to them. In order to rally the scattered rebel forces, the underground rebel network planned a demonstration to be held on 26 May. The date, a Saturday, was carefully picked to coincide with the opening of the Fifth Municipal Congress of Trade Unions. Traffic in the city on a Saturday was normally very busy, so the event would attract a great deal of attention. Moreover, staging a demonstration on that day would convey a clear message to the local authorities that the rebels wanted to have proper representation in the future Municipal Council of Trade Unions. However, the plan was leaked, and on 26 May, some 2,000 policemen were deployed on the streets. The demonstration did not materialize.[7] Nevertheless, when the Wuhan Municipal Council of Trade Unions was established on 31 May, Dong Minghui was appointed the chairperson and Wu Yanjin one of the six vice chairpersons.[8]

On 28 June the Hubei Provincial Council of Trade Unions was set up. Four of its ten vice chairpersons were former rebel leaders: Dong Minghui, Xia Bangyin, Zhu Hongxia, and Ping Yi.[9] On 11 July the Hubei Provincial Women's Federation was created. Wang Caizhu, a former leader of the Second Headquarters, was elected as one of its nine vice chairpersons.

In sum, as a result of pressures brought upon the local authorities by Beijing, in mid-1973 a number of former rebel leaders in Wuhan were once again allowed to hold official positions. Compared with the situation over the past few years, it was a momentous change. But such victories at the provincial and municipal levels were not yet reflected at the grassroots. In factories, schools, government agencies, and other institutions, former rebels were still generally excluded from the leading bodies of official mass organizations. Those who had been dismissed from their posts on revolutionary committees were still denied readmission.

By then, most victims of the Ferret out 16 May Regiment and *bei-jue-yang* Elements Campaign (commonly known as the Double-checkup Campaign) had received notices that they were no longer considered as suspects. Many were content with the removal of the label, though they received no apology. After all, life would be much easier for them without such a prejudicial label. For some, however, the mere removal of the label was not enough. The label '*bei-jue-yang* element' had practically ruined their careers and lives. Some had been degraded, some had lost their jobs, and some had been sent into the countryside with their families. They therefore felt they were entitled to some sort of compensation. College students who had been assigned to jobs far from Wuhan also wanted to return to the city, but these appeals for compensation to the leaders of their units were often turned down. Many thus became frequent visitors to the reception centres of the HPPC or the WMPC, which were supposed to handle local residents' complaints against their superiors.

At the reception centres, these former rebels from different units soon became acquainted with one another. At the moment, they were not pursuing any broadly defined 'public good'. Rather, their goal was individual liberation. But there were good reasons for them to act together. First, one person's effort might produce positive results for others. If, for instance, a former rebel was recompensed for his suffering in the past, his case could be used by others as a precedent to advance their own claims. Moreover, acting in concord enabled them to put greater pressure on the local authorities than would have been possible when acting alone. It mattered little who would be the first to receive compensation, since all would ultimately benefit from the initial success.

Second, acting together might reduce the individual participant's risk of acting in an unruly manner and thus enhance the effectiveness of their efforts. Those people who were not averse to taking risks in the first place, because they had lost almost everything anyway and therefore had little more to lose by rebelling again. In their own words, they were 'beasts at bay who would put up a desperate fight'. Nevertheless, acting together was still better than acting separately. Without co-ordination, those former rebels might go to the reception centres on different days. If there were only a few people at the centres each day, they might be ignored or easily subdued. If a large group of people showed up every day, however, simply detaining one or a few was no longer an effective response for the authorities. Hence, if a reasonably large number of people joined forces, the individual participants might face less individual risk, and their endeavours might be harder to ignore.[10]

Third, information that was crucial to their cause was so scarce and so dispersed that they needed some form of information exchange if they were to overcome the problem. Information has a special property: when its owner shares it with others, its value to the owner does not necessarily decline. Thus, when people exchange the information they have, everybody walks away with more information. Of course, information exchange is not without cost. One way for those who are interested in the exchange of information to reduce the transaction cost is to band together. Whether in a formal or an informal manner, such an association facilitates information dissemination and internalizes the cost. In addition, the more competent members of the group can help the less competent ones to better understand the information they have pooled together and to use it more efficiently. Probably due to these three considerations, the rebels gradually forged several informal networks, with smalltime former rebel celebrities as leaders. There were also connections between those networks. Altogether about 100 people were actively involved.

One network deserves special mention because it was to play an important part in the events to be described below. The leaders of the network were Nie Niansheng, Liu Hanwu, Fang Baolin, Xie Miaofu, and Wang Huazhen. Nie, Liu, and Fang had been well-known leaders of rebel college student organizations during the peak years of the Cultural Revolution. Wang and Xie, however, were ordinary workers who had been ciphers in the rebel camp. Together, the five of them made a good team. The college graduates were sensitive to subtle changes in the official line, had many strategic ideas, and were good at conducting propaganda and agitation, not to mention the large circle of acquaintances they had among rebel notables in the city. Wang and Xie, though simpleminded and rash, were dauntless, vigorous, and action-oriented.[11]

Several active organizers of the secret rebel networks were arrested on 28 August 1973, the same day that the Tenth National Party Congress concluded in Beijing. What was conspicuous about the congress was a slogan put forward by Mao: 'A Marxist-Leninist principle is to go against the tide', which reminded former rebels of another of Mao's quotations: 'It is right to rebel.' Some former rebels decided to translate the slogan from words into practice. On 5 September a wall poster entitled 'Why We Rise to Rebel Again' appeared in Hankou. This was the first rebel poster seen in the city since mid-1969. The authorities

responded by arresting Xie Miaofu. While the series of arrests drove the
protesters underground, it did not scare the rebels. They put up more
posters demanding the release of Xie and other detainees, which caused
a stir in the city.[12]

These self-styled 'fighters going against the tide' were still small in
number. When they staged the first march in mid-September, only about
100 people took part.[13] However, they were determined and indomitable.
In the last three months of 1973, more insurgents were arrested, including Nie Niansheng. But they continued to conduct propaganda and agitation in hopes of gaining additional support. As a result of their resolute
efforts, the atmosphere in Wuhan gradually became more fanatical. Sites
which had been used by the various factions to display posters and where
people had gathered to exchange information between 1966 and 1968
once again became crowded. More posters appeared each day.[14]

Despite the expansion of their influence, however, the resistance
posed by the 'fighters going against the tide' remained largely an underground operation before 1974. During the daytime, they usually hid.
When night fell, they came out either individually or in groups to put
up more posters. Occasionally, they staged a rally or a march and then
quickly slipped away when the police arrived on the scene upon receiving reports. In order to avoid being rounded up at one fell swoop, the
core members of the secret networks usually divided themselves into
several teams. It was hoped that even if some of the core members were
caught, there would always be some persons who could take the leadership role.

After four relatively tranquil years, most people had become used to
obedience to authority. They were shocked when a small number of
former rebels again rose to challenge the provincial and municipal
authorities. The former conservatives, of course, resented the insurgents'
action and hoped they would soon be put down. The former rebels might
share the insurgents' grievance, but most of them thought it too risky to
plunge into the struggle. In particular, rebel leaders who had recently
been reinstated in their former positions in the HPRC and the WMRC
or appointed to positions in official mass organizations were very
cautious out of a fear of jeopardizing their own official careers. Their
best strategy was to play it safe. Zhu Hongxia and Xia Bangyin, for
instance, tried to distance themselves from the street insurgents. They
even endeavoured privately to dissuade some of the leaders of the secret
networks, most of whom were their acquaintances, from making more
trouble. However, these attempts were unsuccessful. Soon they would
find that their appraisal of the situation was too conservative.[15]

Two factors helped to change the political climate in the next few months. First, a new mass campaign—the Campaign to Criticize Lin Biao and Confucius—began to unfold in China in the autumn of 1973. The new campaign was an offensive initiated by radical central leaders, whose targets of attack were their rivals in Beijing. But most Chinese failed to discern the practical significance of criticizing two dead men. The Wuhan 'fighters going against the tide' were no exception. Up to the end of 1973, the campaign was still generally considered as an academic debate, or at most an ideological struggle. If they were to kindle the masses' enthusiasm for the campaign, the radical central leaders would have to relate the campaign to issues that made sense to their prospective constituents. In January 1974 they launched an intensive mobilization drive. Now, the masses were told that the real targets of the ongoing campaign were not Lin Biao and Confucius but anyone who was hostile to the Cultural Revolution. They were urged to do away with all outmoded rules and regulations and to throw themselves into the campaign. Furthermore, officials at all levels were warned against trying to dampen the masses' enthusiasm about participating in the campaign.[16] In many respects, the events of January 1974 were reminiscent of those of October 1966. Indeed, Wang Hongwen claimed, 'The Campaign to Criticize Lin Biao and Confucius is the second Cultural Revolution.'[17]

A second factor which contributed to the changing political climate was the leadership shakeup which took place in Wuhan at this time. Zhang Tixue, the Second Secretary of the HPPC since 1972, died of cancer on 3 September 1973.[18] Three months later, as a result of Mao's decision to reshuffle China's eight regional military leaders, Yang Dezhi replaced Zeng Siyu to become the commander of the WMR. Zeng's position as the First Secretary of the HPPC was taken by Zhao Xingchu, a ranking official from Beijing.[19]

In an increasingly radical environment, the new provincial leadership's first action in the new year of 1974 was to release the detained 'fighters going against the tide', which sent a clear message to those fighters that the general situation was turning in their favour. On 6 January, Nie Niansheng reappeared at a mass rally held in Hankou. In his speech, Nie asserted that the transfer of Zeng Siyu indicated that Zeng had made serious mistakes. If the two provincial leaders who had been in charge of the Double-checkup Campaign in Wuhan, namely Zeng Siyu and Liu Feng, had both made mistakes, Nie pointed out, the orientation of that campaign could not have been correct.[20] This sophism proved to be very appealing to his followers, and the 'fighters going against the tide' immediately started a more vigorous offensive to force the provincial and municipal authorities to address their cases.

In late January, Dong Minghui returned to Wuhan after having attended a central study class presided over by Wang Hongwen in Beijing. He first met some former rebel leaders who held official positions and told them what Wang Hongwen had said at the central study class. Two points were emphasized. First, Wang condemned the local authorities in many provinces for having suppressed the rebels. Second, Wang proposed that more 'young cadres', namely, ones coming out of the rebel ranks, should be promoted to higher positions. Those rebels might have been content with their largely symbolic posts in the past. Now they suddenly realized that they could win more important offices, offices that would allow them to wield real power. Wang Hongwen, who had recently been given the position of the CCP's vice chairman at the Tenth Congress, was seen as an example of this. In recent months, those rebel figures had hesitated about 'going against the tide'. With the support they now had from the Party's vice chairman, they now expected more benefits from a renewed rebel movement and no longer worried about its cost. Their recalculation of the payoffs to be gained from various behavioural options thus led them to cast off their misgivings and to throw themselves once again into a factionalist battle.[21]

At the same time as the former rebel leaders decided to jump on the 'going against the tide' bandwagon, the provincial and municipal authorities received a directive from Beijing ordering them to cease their persecution of the rebels. The converging pressures from Beijing and Wuhan thus forced the HPPC to make some concessions to the rebels. During the long weekend of the Spring Festival of 1974, it invited dozens of rebel celebrities to a forum and asked them to make comments and suggestions about its work. Aside from the rebels holding official positions, the HPPC also invited some former leaders of major rebel organizations during 1966–8 who had remained obscure since 1969, and some of those who had led the Going against the Tide Movement since the summer of 1973. At the forum, they all took the opportunity to air grievances they had accumulated over the past four years.[22] Following the forum, the HPPC and the WMPC held a series of mobilization rallies in the city, calling people to join the Campaign to Criticize Lin Biao and Confucius.[23] In the meantime, the leading bodies of the Trade Union, the Youth League, and the Women's Federation at both the provincial and municipal levels staged numerous mass assemblies to push forward the campaign in the city. By making such gestures, the local authorities intended to kill three birds with one stone. The first was to show Beijing that they were following closely the central line. The second was to show potential local challengers that they were willing to make deals. The third goal was more important, that is, to bring the unfolding campaign somehow under their control. If they could win Beijing's trust and please potential local challengers, they believed that the third goal was achievable.

The third goal proved to be unattainable for two reasons. First, what the former rebels demanded went far beyond what the local authorities were willing or able to offer. Second, even if the local authorities were willing and able to meet the rebels' demands, their appeasement policy towards the rebels would provoke strong indignation from former conservatives.

The former rebels' goal was to change the power relations that had crystallized during the last four years. Their minimal objective was to prove that they were innocent and that all accusations brought against them in recent years were unjustified. To do so, they needed to totally repudiate the necessity and validity of the Double-checkup Campaign, rather than seek to redress each case, as the 'fighters going against the tide' had done. If they were able to achieve this minimal objective, they would cease to be second-class citizens. But some former rebels were not content with this minimal objective. They had an intermediary objective, that is, to repay those who had victimized them. There were still a small number of rebels who were not content with this intermediary objective. They were mostly former rebel heads at various levels, and their maximal objective was to regain power.

For former conservatives, especially those who had been active in ferreting out the 16 May Regiment and *bei-jue-yang* elements, none of these objectives was acceptable. The interests of former rebels and former conservatives were diametrically opposed. As a result, soon after the former rebels began to revive, the old factional animosity between the rebels and the conservatives resurfaced. In early February the two basic camps resuscitated under new names. The former rebels called themselves 'Revolutionary Masses' and the former conservatives 'Workers–Peasants–Soldiers'. The conflict between the two sides threw Wuhan into renewed turmoil. Every corner of the city was again covered by big-character posters, and noisy mass rallies were held daily, jeopardizing public order.[24]

In mid-February the Revolutionary Masses staged demonstrations and sit-ins at the offices of the Wuhan Public Security Bureau, demanding the release from prison of Hu Houmin, Li Xiangyu, Yang Daoyuan, and Ren Aisheng. This was a strategy the rebels had used successfully when fighting for the rehabilitation of the Workers' Headquarters in April 1967. The four men were the best-known victims of the Double-checkup Campaign in Wuhan. If the verdicts on those men could be reversed, then the validity of the campaign as a whole could be repudiated; and if the validity of the campaign as a whole could be repudiated, then all victims of the campaign should be rehabilitated. This strategy was obviously better than seeking redress on a case-by-case basis. If an individual demanded that his case be redressed, he ran the risk of being punished if he failed to achieve this goal. It he took part in a city-wide activity, however, his identity was concealed. Even if the operation failed, he would not be at personal risk. This strategy fitted in with the needs of circumspect rebels, many of whom continued to keep a low profile within their units while actively participating in rebel activities once they were out of sight of their conservative colleagues. By now, several provinces had released and rehabilitated key rebels imprisoned after 1969.[25] Since there were precedents, the Wuhan rebels had good reason to believe that they could win the battle.

On 2 March, Hu Houmin and Li Xiangyu were released.[26] They were hailed as returning heroes by the Revolutionary Masses. That the nascent campaign extracted concessions from the local authorities immediately demonstrated two things: its viability and the latter's impuissance, both of which increased the likelihood that future collective action would be fruitful. The success of the initial collective action greatly boosted the morale of the less dedicated rebels, and many of those who had hesitated to side openly with the Revolutionary Masses finally cast aside their apprehension. Thus, on 3 March, the Revolutionary Masses was able to stage a demonstration of unprecedented size: the parade consisted of several hundred trucks fully loaded with supporters. At that time, however, most of the rejuvenated rebels were operating only outside their units, preferring to conceal their partisanship from their bosses and conservative colleagues. Still doubtful that the rebels' cause would eventually win, they did not want to give others a handle against themselves in case the rebels' enterprise should fall through. If their participation in activities organized by the Revolutionary Masses contributed to forcing the provincial authorities to renounce the Double-checkup Campaign, they could settle accounts with their adversaries in their units later.

On 4 March the HPPC put forward a 'Seven-point Proposition' in which the HPPC for the first time officially admitted that the Double-checkup Campaign had wronged many innocent people. It also pledged to rehabilitate all the victims. Who should bear the responsibility for so many persons' suffering? The proposition stated:

It was Liu Feng who was responsible for having wrongly persecuted so many innocent people. Those who handled individual cases during the campaign should not be held responsible for the tragedy, not to mention the mass of the people who took part in that campaign.[27]

Obviously, this was an attempt to placate the increasingly obstreperous rebels on the one hand, and to tranquillize the anxious conservatives on the other. The attempt to please both parties proved to be misguided.

In the rebels' judgement, the Seven-point Proposition was 'a piece of poisonous weed'. They did not concede the argument that Liu Feng alone was responsible for their misfortune. Instead, the rebels insisted that all those who had persecuted the rebels must pay for what they had done. This was not merely a matter of chalking up an excuse to legitimately take their revenge on conservatives and Party cadres. In order to furnish themselves with proper grounds for seeking power, the rebels needed to show that those in power had made grievous political mistakes. If they were able to make Party cadres and conservatives bear responsibility for the misguided Ferret out 16 May Regiment and *beijue-yang* Elements Campaign, the rebels felt that they would be in a much better position to claim power. For those reasons, the Revolutionary Masses increased pressure on the local authorities after the publication of the Seven-point Proposition.

The release of Hu Houmin and Li Xiangyu had already incurred great enmity and bitterness among former conservatives. The Seven-point Proposition further irritated them. In their view, there was nothing wrong with the Double-checkup Campaign. It was right and proper to suppress 'monsters and ghosts' hidden in the rebel ranks. What was wrong was that the Wuhan Incident of July 1967 had never been officially redressed, which made former conservatives and cadres still vulnerable to criticism even though they had been in the ascendant since 1969. The conservatives were particularly outraged by the local authorities' soft line in dealing with former rebels. They believed that what made the HPPC and the WMPC so submissive to the rebels was the rebels' aggressiveness and roughness. In an attempt to prevent the local authorities from making more concessions to the rebels, the Workers–Peasants–Soldiers decided to become aggressive and rough themselves. The municipal and provincial authorities thus were caught in a pincer.

In a political climate that was generally favourable to the rebels, the local authorities found it harder to resist the pressure from the rebels than that from the other direction. In the first half of March, the local authorities made more concessions to the Revolutionary Masses. Arrangements were made to appoint more rebel celebrities to official posts, which then was called 'leadership replenishment'. Four rebels, for instance, were appointed to be vice chairmen of the provincial trade union council and five to its municipal counterparts.[28] Almost all the rebels who had been deposed from the HPRC and the WMRC after 1969 were recalled to office, including Hu Houmin and Li Xiangyu, who had just been released from gaol. Hu was reinstated as a member of the standing committee of the HPRC, and Li as a vice chairman of the WMRC.[29] Some rebels also began to receive compensation for the losses they had suffered as a result of the Double-checkup Campaign.[30]

On 16 March the HPPC revised the Seven-point Proposition and replaced it with a 'Six-point Proposition', which cut out the provision that freed those who had handled cases during the Double-checkup Campaign from responsibility.[31] The implication of the revision was two-fold. The direct implication was that the rebels might pay their superiors and conservative colleagues back blow for blow. The indirect implication was that the harder a faction pressed the local authorities, the more concessions it would attain.

The Six-point Proposition further boosted the morale of the rebels. As the spirit of the rebels ran high in the city at large, some former rebels finally decided that it was time to show their true colours in their own units. In many units, the rebels began to put up wall posters assailing their superiors and conservative colleagues by name. In some units the rebels even tried to force their superiors and conservative colleagues to offer formal apologies.[32]

The main issue at the grassroots was also power. A prevailing slogan at the time was 'power must be wielded by revolutionary rebels'.[33] For those who had once served on the revolutionary committees, things were relatively easier. All they needed to do was to demand reinstatement. However, those who had never previously held an official post needed to be a little more imaginative. One creation of the rebels during this period was the so-called Office of the Campaign to Criticize Lin Biao and Confucius. In March, various such offices were set up in Wuhan's factories, schools, administrative agencies, and so on, and the rebels forced the Party committees of the units to recognize the leading role of these offices in the ongoing campaign. In many units, such offices almost superseded the leadership of the Party committees.[34]

The conservatives were, of course, infuriated by these developments. If the rebels could get compensation for their personal losses and rebel celebrities could be appointed to the leading positions in official institutions, they felt they deserved to be treated at least on equal terms. Accordingly, the Workers–Peasants–Soldiers set out to demand rehabilitation of the Wuhan Incident, compensation for their losses in the days following the Wuhan Incident, and the appointment of conservative personages to important positions at the provincial and municipal levels. At their strong request, a two-day negotiation was arranged between the provincial leaders and the chiefs of the Workers–Peasants –Soldiers. However, they got nothing but vehement criticism from the provincial officials.[35] On 19 March, when two provincial leaders, Zhao Xingchu and Zhao Xiu, were attending a meeting at Wuhan Iron and Steel, a group of frustrated conservatives kidnapped them and demanded an explanation as to why the provincial authorities had made so many concessions to the rebels but none to the conservatives. Although the two Zhaos suffered no abuse and were set free a few hours later, the incident was reported to Beijing by a central newspaper's special correspondent in Wuhan. On 21 March the General Office of the Central Party Committee issued a three-point instruction concerning the situation in Wuhan, which stated among other things: 'The abduction of comrades Zhao Xingchu and Zhao Xiu was wrong; and the verdict on the Wuhan Incident of July 1967 should not be reversed.'

The Workers–Peasants–Soldiers were dismayed at the three-point instruction. However, they had no choice but to be on the defensive.[36] In contrast to the disappointed conservatives, the rebels took the three-point instruction as a sure sign that Beijing was backing their struggle for liberation. As a result, they became even more recalcitrant.

On 23 March a group of former rebel students, who had just returned to Wuhan from the countryside, put up wall posters along the main streets of the city, demanding the release from prison of Yang Daoyuan, the former head of the Second Headquarters. The provincial authorities had refused to free Yang on the ground that, unlike the cases of Hu Houmin and Li Xiangyu, Yang's imprisonment had been approved personally by Premier Zhou Enlai.[37] Two days later, a group of rebel workers blocked a crossroads at which the Beijing–Guangzhou Railway and a busy road intersected, for three hours. This dramatic action was meant to put pressure on the local authorities to release Luo Xiaomao, a young rebel worker who had been convicted of several criminal acts. The incident disrupted the Beijing–Guangzhou Railway—an economic artery of the nation—for several days.[38]

On 26 March the Revolutionary Masses raided the Third Office of the WMR, which was located within the courtyard of the WMR Headquarters. An inside source had informed them that the office had a large quantity of so-called black materials against the rebels. Indeed, they seized quantities of personal files, the minutes of meetings, and documents

relating to the Double-checkup Campaign. The raiders were aston-
ished to find among the materials a list of eighty-four rebel leaders whom
the provincial authorities had at one time planned to sentence to death.
This finding led many rebels, especially those whose names were on the
list, to conclude that the present battle was really a life-and-death
struggle in which their only choice was to fight to the bitter end. The
occupation of the Third Office triggered off a wave of attacks on the
army. Many rebels forcefully took former military representatives
back to their units and subjected them to questioning, criticism, and
humiliation.[39]

In the feverish atmosphere, the *Yangtze Daily*, the organ of the
WMPC, once again escaped its patron's control. It carried reports hostile
to the provincial and municipal authorities, and published a large number
of editorials and articles attacking the Workers–Peasants–Soldiers. The
paper thus became virtually an exclusive forum for the rebels.[40]

The local authorities even began to lose control over their own agencies. In the last few days of March, mass rallies were held in almost
every department and commission under the provincial and municipal
governments. Rebel leaders rather than the heads of those agencies
dominated all those occasions. Although all the gatherings were called
'meetings to criticize Lin Biao and Confucius', rarely were they referred
to. Instead, all the speakers concentrated their attack exclusively on the
local authorities. Provincial and municipal leaders were often 'invited'
to attend such meetings, which gave the rebels an opportunity to humiliate them. On 1 April the HPPC itself staged a mass rally to criticize Lin
Biao and Confucius. The meeting, however, was harassed by rebel
forces. During the next week, the rebels launched several huge demonstrations under the banners of the Workers' Congress and the Red Guard
Congress, two institutions that had ceased to exist in 1969. The rebels
acted as if they had won the day.

Even some provincial leaders began to think of joining the rebels.
Zhao Xiu, a secretary of the HPPC, for instance, became known as a
sympathizer of the rebels within the HPPC. Since Zhao had assumed his
current post in Wuhan after the end of the Double-checkup Campaign,
he did not have to worry about the rebels' attacks on the HPPC. Rather
than hurting him, such attacks might help him to improve his career
opportunities by striking down some of his rivals. At the end of March,
Zhao delivered a speech strongly in favour of the rebels at the First
Metallurgical Corporation. The speech forced the Party committee of the
corporation to make the unusual gesture of vindicating its support of the
rebels: it declared itself to be 'a rebellious Party committee'. No one

understood exactly what the phrase 'rebellious Party committee' was supposed to mean, and no one cared. But perplexed and anxious leading cadres of other units took this action as an evil omen. The events of 1966 remained fresh in their memory. If they failed to appear to support the rebels, there was a risk that they might be struck down in the Second Cultural Revolution. If they were to ride out the crisis, they reckoned they had no choice but to follow the example of the First Metallurgical Corporation. Thus, in the first week of April, Party committees of hundreds of units became born-again rebellious Party committees. Since such events were nothing but symbolic gestures, those official organizations all tried to give them wide publicity. For several days, the main streets of Wuhan were packed with their parading trucks. Production and traffic were halted.

Few really believed that the Party officials were sincere in declaring themselves in support of the rebels. Nevertheless, their actions had the effect of heightening the rebels' morale and dampening the conservatives' spirit. The rebels applauded the development, even though they were aware that the Party cadres' hostility towards the rebels hadn't really subsided. However, as long as those in power were subdued and had to dance to the rebels' tune, it mattered little whether their actions were voluntary or not. The conservatives, on the other hand, opposed the development. In an attempt to control the damage, the Workers–Peasants–Soldiers ordered its men to secretly visit as many leading cadres as possible. Party cadres were advised to avoid any action that appeared to support the rebels. To a limited degree, this tactic worked. Many cadres pleaded illness as the reason for their absence from political activities. But their absence made little difference. The general mood of Wuhan became increasingly propitious to the rebels.[41]

In this atmosphere of triumphs, a group of rebels kidnapped a deputy head of the Wuhan Intermediate People's Court and five judges on 5 April. In the meantime, the court received an ultimatum that demanded the immediate release of all rebels remaining in prison, including those who had been found guilty of murder, arson, robbery, rape, and other criminal activities.[42] In the first three months of 1974, with the gradual paralysis of the public authorities, hooliganism had become rampant in Wuhan. There had reportedly been 32 cases of sexual assault in public places, 103 cases of gang fighting, and 28 cases of robbery.[43] One night, when the Revolutionary Masses were holding a huge gathering at a busy intersection in Hankou, a group of hooligans went so far as to assault a number of women and rape a girl in the crowd. This was the worst crime the city had witnessed since 1949.[44] If the public authorities yielded to the rebels' demand and freed criminals, the city would be thrown into total chaos.

Anarchy was by no means unique to Wuhan. By early April, Zhejiang, Hebei, Henan, Hunan, Jiangsu, Sichuan, Jiangxi, Guangdong, Shanxi, and Shandong provinces were all in chaos.[45] The other provinces were also more or less in ferment. Without exception, the unrest in other provinces all stemmed from the same impetuses as that of Wuhan—the resurgent factionalism. Industrial production in the country was severely disrupted. The disorder must have reminded Mao of the chaotic summers of 1967 and 1968 when the situation had been totally out of control. It was certainly not in his best interests to allow that disaster to be repeated. If public authority were to be kept from falling apart, Beijing had to do something to arrest the spontaneous recurrence of factionalism in the provinces.[46]

Wuhan was the first city to be affected by the change in Beijing's mood. On 7 April the HPPC received a set of instructions from the capital. Almost everything the rebels had done and supported in the past two weeks was condemned. The rebels were ordered to release the deputy head and the judges of the Intermediate Court, to withdraw from the WMR Headquarters, and to return all the materials seized from the Third Office. It was also held wrong to attempt to reverse the verdict on Yang Daoyuan, to occupy public buildings in order to set up propaganda stations, to stage demonstrations in trucks, and to attack former military representatives. Those instructions perplexed the rebels, while delighting and invigorating the conservatives, who had been lethargic for some time.[47] The rebels were further confused when they learned, a few days later, the contents of Beijing's latest document. Issued on 10 April, the No. 12 document of the year 1974 pointed out that the Campaign to Criticize Lin Biao and Confucius had been carried out at the expense of industrial production in a number of provinces. To arrest this dangerous trend, the document stipulated:

> The Campaign to Criticize Lin Biao and Confucius must be carried out under the unified leadership of Party committees at various levels. No spontaneous mass organizations should be set up. And no *chuanlian* (establishing an informal network for information exchange) between units and across regions is allowed.[48]

The reassertion of the primacy of Party leadership, as seen in the previous years, had always been the first sign that Beijing was about to bring order out of chaos. The No. 12 document saved the authorities of Wuhan from a political débâcle. With backing from Beijing, the local authorities attempted to rein in the campaign.[49] Leading cadres at all levels were urged to pay more attention to production and to strengthen Party leadership. The Revolutionary Masses, as well as the Workers–Peasants–Soldiers, were exhorted to dissolve their 'liaison nets', 'petition delegations', 'propaganda stations', and other tangible organizations, and return to their own units. Former student rebels who had come back to Wuhan from the countryside were advised to go back. And those who had seized the opportunity provided by the campaign to make economic demands were condemned and compelled to pay back what they had received. Meanwhile, the police force was ordered to get tough with hoodlums, who had run rampant in the past few months.[50]

The No. 12 document was hailed with relief by the Workers–Peasants–Soldiers and the conservative masses at large. They put up innumerable posters greeting the document throughout the city, which presented a striking contrast to the rebels, who made no such response. The conservatives felt certain that the document would ensure their predominance over the rebels, and they held mass rallies to celebrate their victory.[51] For some of the leading cadres who had been forced to make statements supporting the rebels just a week or so earlier, however, the change was too good to be true. Recalling that the Cultural Revolution had always developed by twists and turns, they were cautious not to become over-confident upon seeing the first favourable sign. Thus, ironically, during the rest of April, more of the leading cadres published articles singing the praises of the rebels and promising to promote 'newborn forces' to leading positions than ever before. The Workers–Peasants–Soldiers blamed the *Yangtze Daily* for carrying those articles. In protest, they raided the office of the newspaper on 5 May and took away that day's printing plates, which halted the publication of the paper for a couple of days.[52]

The rebels were stunned by the change brought about by the No. 12 document. They could not understand how the situation could be reversed so abruptly. Their only way of finding out the reasons for the change and of determining how to cope with it was to send some of their representatives to Beijing, where more information was available. However, there was yet another impetus for the rebels to go to the national capital. In April, Beijing adopted resolutions concerning factional conflicts in Henan and Shandong.[53] This was followed by a rumour that Beijing would soon deal with Wuhan. Attempting to influence Beijing's decision on Wuhan, Zhu Hongxia, Hu Houmin, and some others left Wuhan for Beijing in mid-April.[54]

The departure of those rebel celebrities gave rise to a rumour that

Beijing was considering appointing some leading rebels to more important positions in Wuhan. The rumour made both the Workers–Peasants–Soldiers and some less well-known rebels uneasy. The former felt uneasy about the prospect of seeing any rebels in official posts; and the latter feared they would be left out when the spoils were distributed. As a result, more people rushed to Beijing.[55]

These delegations remained in Beijing until early or mid-May. In late April, some provincial and municipal leaders also arrived in Beijing. But when the future of Wuhan was discussed by the central and provincial leaders, all those factional delegations were excluded.[56]

In comparison with the first four months of 1974, May was relatively calm in Wuhan. It was a strategic stalemate. All sides were waiting for Beijing's final judgement. No party would act rashly at the crucial moment, because any incautious actions could spoil their political prospects. For the first time since the start of the Campaign to Criticize Lin Biao and Confucius, the contending factions began to put up some wall posters criticizing Lin Biao and Confucius.[57] An influential rebel leader later testified: 'Nobody then was interested in criticizing Lin Biao and Confucius. We published posters to criticize them, but all posters were copied from articles then flooding official newspapers and journals. We occasionally did so to fool Beijing, as if we were really responding firmly by to its call.'[58] This is yet another example of how the participants in the Cultural Revolution used Maoist rhetoric to serve their own ends.

On 24 May the provincial and municipal leaders finally returned to Wuhan from the capital. Beijing's resolution turned out to contain nothing advantageous to the rebels. Among other things, it declared:

(1) The general orientation of the Double-checkup Campaign was correct.

(2) Zeng Siyu and other provincial leaders might have made some minor mistakes, but on the whole they were good leaders.

(3) It might be necessary to replenish the leadership, but it should not be conducted at the expense of senior officials. And the matter should not be treated with undue haste.

(4) All non-official mass organizations must disband themselves immediately.[59]

On 26 May the HPPC and the WMR held a grand gathering of unprecedented size, which was simultaneously relayed through the wire-broadcasting network to every unit in the city. At the rally, after Beijing's resolution was read, the First Secretary of the HPPC, Zhao Xingchu, the commander of the WMR, Yang Dezhi, and the commis-

sar of the WMR, Wang Liusheng, made strongly worded speeches warning that old grievances should not be brought up in the current campaign.
In other words, it was no longer acceptable to repudiate the Double-
checkup Campaign.[60] On 28 May, another mass rally was staged.
Twenty-one men were sentenced to death or imprisonment for having
committed crimes during the recent troubled months. This event was
also broadcast live over the wire-network. The message was very clear:
public order must be restored.

But those rebels whose demands had not yet been met feared that once
the situation returned to normal, they might never have another opportunity to redress their grievances. They therefore were unwilling to end
the campaign. Although publicly all expressed their endorsement of the
resolution, privately the Revolutionary Masses were disappointed and
frustrated. When asked to comment on the resolution by his anxious
underlings, Peng Zhulong, the former number two man of the Workers'
Rebel Headquarters, pointed out: 'This resolution *per se* is not what we
have expected. Now what is important is how we interpret it.'[61] Moreover, some rebels questioned how authoritative the resolution was,
because it was not endorsed personally by Mao.

In June the provincial and municipal authorities made a concerted
effort to restore order. They convened numerous meetings emphasizing
the importance of production, unity, discipline, and order. The local official newspapers devoted a series of editorials to appealing for the faithful implementation of Beijing's directives.[62] However, factionalism did
not wither away. In mid-June the fanatical atmosphere revived somewhat in Wuhan, and by the end of the month the city was once again in
turmoil. Propaganda stations were re-established in the downtown area
and propaganda cars reappeared on the streets. The contending factions
once again put up posters attacking each another. And mass rallies and
demonstrations were held almost daily. Worst of all, the Revolutionary
Masses and the Workers–Peasants–Soldiers began to resort to violence.
On the last day of June, for instance, at least two sanguinary events were
reported.[63] It seemed that the situation could worsen unless some
resolute measures were to be taken.

While the Wuhan authorities were fighting in vain against the seemingly unstoppable factionalism, the central leadership was alarmed by
the steadily deteriorating state of the national economy. According to a
report submitted by the National Planning Commission to the Politburo
on 18 June, in eleven of the twenty-nine provinces, industrial output in
the first five months of 1974 had declined substantially compared with
the same period in 1973.

On 1 July, sanctioned by Mao, the Party's Central Committee issued
a Circular Concerning Grasping Revolution and Promoting Production,
calling for an end to factional disturbances and a greater commitment to
production and a strict observance of discipline. It specifically warned
that whoever disobeyed Beijing's directives would be punished. Wuhan
was singled out as one of the nation's worst trouble-spots, which gave
the local authorities an impetus to restore order as quickly as they
could.[64]

On the same day as Beijing issued the circular, about thirty rebels led
by Xie Miaofu raided an office building of the HPPC in Wuhan. The
intruders were detained. In protest, a group of Xie's cohorts stormed
another office building of the committee on 3 July. The two events
served as negative examples when Beijing's circular of 1 July was
communicated to Wuhan residents.[65] The implementation of the circular was much smoother than that of the May resolution on the problems
of Wuhan, for few dared to challenge the authority of a central directive that had been personally endorsed by Mao.

On 13 July the Workers–Peasants–Soldiers held a grand mass rally to
declare its dissolution. This was both a political gesture to show that the
Workers–Peasants–Soldiers was responding to Beijing's call and a cere-
mony to celebrate the group's victory over the Revolutionary Masses.
Almost all the former leaders of the Million Heroes at the municipal,
district, and sector levels were included in the presidium of the rally.
The message was clear: although the Workers–Peasants–Soldiers was
disbanding itself now, it could rise again whenever necessary. In fact,
after the rally, informal networks between the conservative forces
remained.[66]

The Revolutionary Masses never officially declared its dissolution,
because, as a loose coalition, it had no unified leadership. Nevertheless,
by the end of July, factionalism had been largely contained in Wuhan.

In August and September, 'unity' became the central theme of a series
of editorials in the *People's Daily* and the *Red Flag*.[67] In October, recommended by Mao, Deng Xiaoping, the man who had been previously
labelled as 'the second biggest capitalist roader in China', was appointed
as the First Vice Prime Minister. Deng's mission was to clean up the
mess that had resulted from the Campaign to Criticize Lin Biao and
Confucius, as Zhou Enlai had been hospitalized since June. To make
Deng's job easier, Mao issued a further instruction: 'The Cultural Revolution has been going on for eight years. It is time to stabilize. The entire
Party and army should unite.'[68] This remark gave voice to the innermost
feelings of the majority of the Chinese people. Tired of anarchy and

chaos, they longed for stability and unity. Thereafter, the theme of stability and unity dominated the mass media.

The stabilization produced a marked effect in Wuhan. The city's industrial output soared in the second half of 1974: the monthly outputs registered growth rates of 2.1, 10.4, 21.1, 11.9, 14.9, and 5.9 per cent from July to December.[69] But because industrial production had been affected so severely in the first six months, the total output for the whole year declined 24.3 per cent compared with the previous year, a drop worse than that in 1967 and only slightly better than that in 1968. Nevertheless, the success resulting from the policies of stabilization could not be denied. Except for a few minor incidents of factional strife, the city was returning to normal. Rebel celebrities who had been appointed to official posts retained their positions. However, now they not only had no real influence in decision making but also had to behave themselves so as not to lose their largely nominal posts.[70] As 1974 was drawing to a close, the Campaign to Criticize Lin Biao and Confucius quietly came to an end in Wuhan.

New Features of the Old Factionalism

The factionalism of 1973–4 had its roots in the events of 1966–9. But the old factionalism demonstrated some new features.

The most striking difference was that far fewer people threw themselves into factional conflicts. The rebel camp is an example. Whereas in 1966 students had played a pioneering role in advancing the rebels' cause, college as well as high school students in 1974 were generally indifferent to politics. At the peak of the new radicalism of March and April 1974, many former rebel students returned to their old schools, trying to enlist their juniors to fight for the rebels' cause. To their great disappointment, those juniors turned a deaf ear to their appeal.[71] The reason for the political apathy was simple: the issues that had divided students in the mid-1960s no longer existed and the issues that were currently in dispute were not relevant to the students.

During 1966–9, units with a large percentage of intellectuals as their employees, such as schools, hospitals, scientific research institutes, and cultural establishments, were generally bastions of the rebels. In 1974, however, such units were fairly quiet, not because the rebel intellectuals had converted but because they were fearful of expressing their sympathy for the Revolutionary Masses. Intellectuals were politically more sophisticated than others. They therefore tended to be more calculating and cautious in political games. After having experienced the ups and downs of the years from 1966 to 1968 and the hardships since then, they did not want to be trapped again.

Moreover, intellectuals mostly came from middle and bad class backgrounds. If they had learned anything from the Cultural Revolution, it must have been that any attempt by people like them to give vent to their grievances would eventually backfire. The campaign to purify the class ranks remained fresh in their memories. It was therefore better for them to play it safe in politics. More important, the rebel intellectuals were becoming increasingly ambivalent about the Cultural Revolution and the phenomena it had spurred (for example, workers' propaganda teams, 7 May cadre schools, education reform, barefoot doctors, revolutionary model operas, and so on). On the one hand, they had an interest in fighting together with other rebels against the 'restorationist adverse current' that emerged after 1969, from which they as rebels had suffered a great deal. On the other hand, however, they realized that the reversal of the restorationist adverse current would also reinforce the new phenomena, which they saw as running counter to their interests.[72]

In other sectors, the activism that characterized the early stage of the Cultural Revolution, especially 1966–7, was also found wanting. Rebels who had withdrawn from politics in late 1967 or early 1968 tended to remain aloof from the current campaign. Those who had not suffered much or had turned against their leaders during the Double-checkup Campaign, were also likely to keep the insurgent Revolutionary Masses at a distance, since they could not see how the new uprising could benefit them.[73]

Only those rebels who considered the Campaign to Criticize Lin Biao and Confucius as an opportunity for upward mobility tended to be active and outspoken. As shown previously, those quick to revolt were almost without exception desperate persons. Already at the bottom of society, they had nothing more to lose. It was for this reason that people like Wang Huazhen were quick to jump on the bandwagon of 'going against the tide'. Later, more rebels threw themselves into the battle. For the most part, they were former leaders of rebel organizations at various levels who had savoured the sweetness of power during the period from 1967 to 1968. They were striving for 'leadership replenishment', or appointment to official positions. Together, the 'complainants' and the 'climbers' accounted for only a small percentage of former rebels, let alone the general population of the city. For instance, in the Wuhan Beef and Mutton Processing Plant, a factory with more than 500 employees, only about 20 people took part in 'going against the tide'.[74] A similar distribution pattern was observed in most units.[75]

The camp of the Workers–Peasants–Soldiers was also composed mainly of former leaders of the Million Heroes at different levels.[76] It does not follow that those who were not actively involved in factional politics did not care about factional conflicts. In their hearts, many did take sides. Generally, former rebels felt sympathy for the Revolutionary Masses, while former conservatives identified with the Workers–Peasants–Soldiers. But they no longer thought it worthwhile to make a personal contribution to the factional fight.[77]

Despite their much thinner mass base, the factional warriors, by means of their high spirits, forceful personalities, and tactical skills, exercised a considerable influence over city politics that was disproportionate to their numbers. For about four months, they generated such a tense and volatile atmosphere that the leadership of the city was rendered virtually impotent.

Although rebellious Revolutionary Masses echoed many of the radical slogans put forward by radical central leaders during this period, the former were by no means blind followers of the latter. Except for a few rebel leaders such as Hu Houmin, most of the Revolutionary Masses either did not realize that moderate central leaders were the real targets against whom the radical central leaders meant to strike a blow in the campaign, or realized it but had no interest.[78] They were concerned with their own immediate interests. An activist of the Revolutionary Masses later testified: 'If in the first two years of the Cultural Revolution we rebels had subconsciously used the slogans put forward by radical central leaders for our own interests, in 1974 we were fully aware that the radical slogans we were chanting and shouting were simply ritualistic clichés, the only function of which was to disguise our self-interest.'[79]

The pursuit of self-interest not only spoiled the seemingly clientelist relationship between the rebels in Wuhan and their patrons in Beijing, but also split the rebel ranks. The Revolutionary Masses were divided into eight cliques, which fell into two large categories: the mainstream wing and the non-mainstream wing. Led by former rebel leaders such as Xia Bangyin, Zhu Hongxia, and Hu Houmin, the mainstream wing focused its attention on leadership replenishment, that is, on pressing the local authorities to appoint some outstanding rebels to official positions, or if they already had official positions, to grant them real power. The non-mainstream wing was made up of rebels who were not in a position to demand promotion and who therefore were more concerned about material compensation for individual losses than about leadership replenishment.[80]

The mainstream and non-mainstream wings were internally divided along two other dimensions: preferred strategies and former factional affiliations. In both wings, there were people who preferred to deal with the local leadership tactfully and those who favoured direct action on the streets. The former were called 'the diplomatic ring' and the latter 'the street ring'. Moreover, the old distinction between the Strong Faction and the New Faction was still a hindrance to the unity of the rebels. For instance, Wu Yanjin, the former leader of the Workers' Rebel Headquarters, created a writing group under the name of *Duzhejin* (in Wuhan dialect, the name sounds like a slogan prevalent at the time: 'Moving forward through fighting') as the mouthpiece of the former New Faction rebels. Another influential writing group called *Shaozheng-mao* (a homonym of the name of a political opponent of Confucius, who was used as a symbol of the rebel), however, was controlled by Zhu Hongxia, Hu Houmin, and other former leaders of the Workers' Head-quarters.[81]

All eight cliques shared some common interests. The differences in their interests, strategies, and former factional affiliations, however, led them always to view each other with suspicion.[82] Without a unified lead-ership, the Revolutionary Masses thus made up at best a loose coalition, which might appear strong in a favourable situation but would have diffi-culty in riding out the storm when the political climate changed.

The Workers–Peasants–Soldiers were not homogeneous either. The conservative camp was divided into two wings: the orthodox wing and the action wing. Led by former leaders of the Million Heroes, the ortho-dox wing built up a huge, well-organized, effective network that reached every corner of the city. According to one of its leaders, 'a large conser-vative force' could be promptly mobilized through the network at the first call for action. But the action wing was often at odds with the unified leadership. Consisting of a small group of young militants, the action wing was fond of extreme actions. In its view, the former leaders of the Million Heroes tended to be overcautious in dealing with the local authorities and the rebels. In the view of the orthodox wing, however, the action wing was too reckless and tactless. By the time the Workers–Peasants–Soldiers declared its dissolution in mid-July, the two wings had still not been able to reconcile their differences.[83]

As Marx observed, 'the repetition of historical facts and personages of great importance may occur as farce'.[84] Indeed, the factionalism of 1974 was qualitatively different from the previous pattern, although certain aspects of the so-called Second Cultural Revolution did elicit images of the period 1966–9. With the substantial mobilizational and organizational talents acquired in the tumultuous years from 1966 to 1969, the factional warriors generally manoeuvred more skilfully in 1974. But the new factionalism was more narrowly based, secularized, and fractionary than the old factionalism. Given the nature of the new factionalism, it was not surprising that even more so than in the past, Beijing's instructions tended to be either ignored or interpreted in a way contrary to its intention. This was probably one reason why Mao called for an end to radicalism only a few months after he had set it in motion.

The Repression of Factionalism in 1975

When Deng Xiaoping started a course of reconstruction in early 1974, Wuhan was not yet at peace. Although violent factional conflicts had waned in the city after July, the street ring of the Revolutionary Masses and the action wing of the Workers–Peasants–Soldiers were still in evidence. In the last four months of 1974, they still occasionally held gatherings on the streets but caused little trouble.[85] At the beginning of 1975 the rebel street ring attempted to fan new flames of disorder. On 13 January, the day that the Fourth National People's Congress began in Beijing, a group calling itself the Rebel Militia was set up in Wuhan. The Rebel Militia had no more than 100 members. Most of them were young men associated with Xie Miaofu, and two-thirds of them allegedly had either criminal records or had been disciplined. Rallying under the banner of the Rebel Militia only made them more unbridled and more destructive.

On 15 January, two days after the Rebel Militia had come into being, the group, disregarding Beijing's call for stability and unity, staged an oath-taking rally in Hankou, which caused a traffic jam for the first time in six months. On 18 January the Fourth National People's Congress was closed. If any aspect of the Congress attracted the attention of the Rebel Militia, it was not Zhou Enlai's plan for the Four Modernizations but the right of citizens to strike, which was guaranteed by the new constitution passed at the congress. The Rebel Militia wanted to exercise this right.

Around that time, however, the minutes of a conversation between certain central leaders and Zhu Hongxia, Zhang Liguo, Ma Xueli, and Yang Daoan (the latter two had been well-known 'model workers' before the Cultural Revolution and had associated with the Workers–Peasants–Soldiers the year before) were relayed through official channels to local residents. According to the minutes, the central leaders (mainly the vice premier Li Xiannian) condemned what the rebels had done in 1974 and reprehended those who were still making trouble in the city.[86] The Rebel Militia was, of course, enraged. They tried to belittle the importance of the minutes by describing the conversation as a 'casual chat' and protested that the local authorities had tried to make a big deal out of it. Their protest, however, was overwhelmed by the provincial and municipal authorities' intensive propaganda drive based around the document.

In order to make their viewpoint known to more people, the Rebel Militia decided to build a propaganda station in Hankou. On 13 February they seized the Zhongnan Hotel, which was located at an intersection of the city equivalent to Times Square in Manhattan. They drove out staff and guests and, defying warnings by the Public Security Bureau, installed eight loudspeakers and began to broadcast. Over the following three days, the local authorities tried in vain to persuade the Rebel Militia to withdraw from the hotel. In the early hours of 17 February, the police were sent in to try and force them to leave; they not only failed to drive the Rebel Militia out, but ended up in a hand-to-hand fight with the occupiers. Enraged by the intervention of the police, the Rebel Militia used a wrecked truck to block the intersection at the front of the hotel for eleven days. With one of the three main avenues in Hankou blocked, a large part of the metropolitan transit system was paralysed. Consequently, production and daily life were greatly affected. The industrial output of Wuhan in February declined 28.7 per cent compared with the previous month.

During the eleven days of the blockade, the provincial and municipal authorities repeatedly laid injunctions upon the Rebel Militia to remove the roadblock, but the latter ignored them. They insisted that they would not clear the blockade until the provincial and municipal authorities made a public apology. Moreover, they threatened to block the Hanshui Bridge, which linked Hankou, Hanyang, and Wuchang. They reckoned that once the city became immobilized, Beijing might come forward and force the local authorities to make a deal with them, as had often happened between 1966 and 1968. The diplomatic ring rebels were, of course, heartened to see the provincial and municipal authorities being put in an awkward situation, but they kept silent, even though they shared the street ring's opposition to the developments which had begun the previous July. Zhu Hongxia, for instance, told his friends in private: 'The Zhongnan Hotel incident is a good thing. Whether or not they [the Rebel Militia] succeed, we [the diplomatic ring] are definitely winners.' Zhu meant that if Beijing forced the local authorities to give in, the diplomatic ring would benefit from concessions to the rebels just as the street ring would, and if Beijing criticized the Rebel Militia, the unruliness of the street ring would contrast unfavourably with the law-abiding nature of the diplomatic ring.

The Rebel Militia miscalculated. On 26 February, Beijing issued a directive authorizing the HPPC to 'sternly deal with saboteurs who have been blocking a vital thoroughfare in Hankou'. Once the local authorities had firm backing from Beijing, they quickly rid themselves of irresolution. The next day, an order was released in the name of the HPRC, which required the Rebel Militia immediately to remove the roadblock. In the following days, almost all the active members of the Rebel Militia were arrested. In all, about 100 men and women were imprisoned.[87] This action completely wiped out the rebels' street ring. After the incident, factionalism ceased to be visible in Wuhan.

The diplomatic ring of the rebels also miscalculated. In March, Zhu Hongxia, Xia Bangyin, Zhang Liguo, and several other rebel celebrities who held positions in the HPRC and the WMRC were sent to the countryside.[88] They were told that they were there to be 'tempered', a prerequisite for their ultimate promotion. But no one knew how long the process was to take. The local authorities could keep them in the countryside forever by insisting that they had failed to pass the test. In any case, for the moment, with its leaders being uprooted and transplanted to other places, the diplomatic ring of the rebels dispersed.

Meanwhile, Deng Xiaoping's speech of 5 March and Beijing's Decision to Improve Railway Works inspired a savage attack on 'bourgeois factionalism' throughout the nation. The attack was intensified in April when several of Deng's close associates, including Wan Li and Gu Mu, made frequent speeches condemning diehard factionalists and the pernicious influence of factionalism. Beijing's increasingly firm stand against factionalism threw many factional warriors into a panic and even drove some to desperation. Many rebels feared that what had happened to them during 1969–72 would be repeated. One of Xie Miaofu's closest confederates, Wu Qihua, who was detained in prison as a result of the Zhongnan Hotel incident, took his own life on 24 April to avoid possible suffering in the future.[89]

In May, Xie Miaofu became the target of a massive criticism in Wuhan. Evidence of his 'crime' was compiled and distributed to every unit. In June, Xie was sentenced to seven years' imprisonment, and many of his Rebel Militia comrades were sentenced to punishment ranging from five years' imprisonment to one year of reform through labour. The trial was open, and every unit in the city was required to send an observer to it. The purpose of such an arrangement was obvious: the local leadership wanted its subjects to know that those who dared to defy the authorities would come to no good end.[90]

The criticism of factionalism developed into a widespread mass campaign in June and reached its height over the next three months. The HPPC and the WMPC, which had been more or less impotent since late 1973, became active, resolute, and efficient again.[91] The effective local leadership enabled the criticism of factionalism to develop in an orderly way. In the four months from June to September, all the means of propaganda were mobilized to besiege factionalism. It was declared that the purpose of the campaign was to create an environment in which there would be no soil in which factionalism could flourish again.[92]

The Anti-factionalism Campaign of 1975 was very different from that of 1969–71 in terms of scope and method. Indeed, some rebels (for example, Xie Miaofu) were imprisoned and some (such as Zhu Hongxia) transferred to other places; but the campaign did not turn into a purge against all rebel activists. While those rebels who had become active again in 1974 were apprehensive, no special investigative group was set up to incriminate Revolutionary Masses activists at the grassroots, and rarely were any public accusation meetings held to struggle against them.

By the autumn of 1975, things seemed to have been largely put in order in Wuhan. As life returned to normal, the economy began to prosper. For instance, industrial production in Wuhan increased at rates ranging from 11 to 17 per cent between March and November.[93]

The Beginning of the End of Cultural Revolution Factionalism

In November 1975, supported by Mao, a group of radical central leaders (Jiang Qing, Zhang Chunqiao, Yao Wenyuan, and Wang Hongwen), who were later known as the 'Gang of Four', launched a campaign against what they called 'a right deviationist wind', which turned into a campaign against 'Deng Xiaoping's revisionist line' in February 1976. Up to February 1976, however, the campaign provoked little excitement in Wuhan.[94] Only a very small proportion of local residents responded to Beijing's battle cry to 'strike back at the right deviationist wind'. However, most people began to feel that the political atmosphere was once again becoming depressing. The contrast between the stability brought about by Deng's pragmatic policies in 1975 and the chaos in 1966–8 and 1973–4 resulting from the radical central leaders' seditious policies was so striking that even many former rebels now looked with favour on Deng. There was widespread fear that the attack on Deng would plunge the country into chaos again. Cadres, especially, were in a state of anxiety. The phrase 'unrepentant capitalist-roaders' began to gain currency through the official media, which made them very nervous, as the label 'capitalist roader' had caused them great suffering during the first three years of the Cultural Revolution. They were afraid that the tragedy might be repeated. Some decided to apply for early retirement; others chose to keep quiet so as not to invite trouble. All paid lip service to the campaign, but did nothing beyond echoing the official press's line.[95]

Most of the former rebel rank-and-filers had by now become politically apathetic.[96] The only constituency whom the Gang of Four might count on to support the campaign in the provinces was those who believed that their political future hinged on the outcome of such a radical campaign and were prepared to gamble everything on the venture. Mostly former rebel leaders, such people at most constituted a tiny proportion of the population. This was the case, at least, in Wuhan. They were eager to throw in their lot with the radical central leaders not because they appreciated the radical policies advocated by the Gang of Four, but because they had learned from past experience that the preponderance of individuals like Jiang Qing and Zhang Chunqiao in Beijing was a precondition for them to reign in local politics. Hu Houmin, the sharpest rebel strategist in Wuhan, hit the nail on the head: 'The brand "rebel" has been stamped on our faces. Whatever we do, others will regard us as rebels and treat us accordingly anyway. We either fight to win or die; we don't have a third choice.'[97]

In order to improve their chances of success, those rebels would need to support the radical central leaders in Beijing. In 1976, it was commonly believed that the power struggle currently under way in Beijing was the final battle between the radical cultural revolutionaries and the moderates, because Zhou Enlai had passed away on 8 January and Mao's death was expected at any moment. If the radical central leaders were to fall into disgrace, the former rebel leaders in Wuhan would be wiped from the political arena without redemption. For these reasons, despite their shrunken forces, the rebels were ready to fight. Around this time, Wu Yanjin allegedly said: 'I stake my future on the outcome of this final engagement. Opportunity like this knocks but once.'[98]

In February 1976, sensing that the direction of the political wind was changing, Zhu Hongxia, Xia Bangyin, and Zhang Liguo returned to Wuhan from the countryside. The first thing they set out to do was to rally the routed rebel forces. For this purpose, a series of secret meetings was held. At one of those meetings, Xia Bangyin reportedly pledged that this time he would 'go into battle stripped to the waist'. Zhang Liguo was more direct: 'This is the final battle. We are fighting with our back to the river and all boats have been burnt. There is no possibility of retreat. If we win, we shall take over the leadership of the province; if we lose, we will all end up in gaol. The rules of the game are that simple.'[99]

After making preparations, on 23 February, seventeen rebel celebrities, all of whom held positions in the HPRC or the WMRC, published an open letter addressed to the HPPC and the WMPC. The letter criticized the Party committees in Wuhan from the provincial level down to the grassroots for failing to follow Beijing's strategic plan. Specifically, it charged that many officials had taken others' criticisms against them during the first three years of the Cultural Revolution amiss and had long nursed thoughts of revenge. The letter labelled those cadres 'unrepentant capitalist-roaders', and called for all unrepentant capitalist-roaders to be driven from power.[100]

Soon after the publication of the letter, a self-styled 'leading nucleus' was formed to act as the leadership core of all the rebel forces in Wuhan. Indeed, its seven members, Xia Bangyin, Xie Wangchun, Zhu Hongxia, Hu Houmin, Gu Jiantang, Li Xiangyu, and Wu Yanjin, were among the most influential rebel leaders in Wuhan. The first two held positions in the CCP Central Committee, the middle three in the HPRC, and the last two in the WMRC. The nucleus were supported by a writing group and six departments respectively in charge of strategic planning, propaganda, information, communication, administrative support, and security affairs. In addition, attempts were made to set up branches of the nucleus in every municipal administrative bureau and in every district of the city. The seven members had in mind a 'shadow cabinet', which, in case of crisis, could function as an alternative power centre in the city.[101]

On 2 March, Jiang Qing and Wang Hongwen met in Beijing the civilian and military leaders of twelve provinces, including Hubei. When Jiang asked Dong Minghui, a secretary of the WMPC, if he as a former rebel had felt repressed in Wuhan, Dong replied in the positive. Making use of Dong's testimony, Jiang reprimanded Zhao Xingchu, the First Secretary of the HPPC, and Yang Dezhi, the commander of the WMR, for having tyrannized the rebels. Wang Hongwen then questioned Zhao and Yang as to why the Hubei authorities had sent Xia Bangyin, Zhu Hongxia, and Zhang Liguo to the countryside in 1975 without Beijing's permission. He concluded that such evil things had happened because 'the composition of the leading body in Hubei does not manifest the great achievements of the Cultural Revolution'. Zhao and Yang were enjoined to offer apologies to the rebels after they returned to Wuhan.[102]

The news that Jiang and Wang had criticized the provincial leaders spread quickly in Wuhan. On the very next day, rebel celebrities in the city published another open letter, urging the authorities at both the provincial and municipal levels to reverse their position.[103] A few days later, when the HPPC held an enlarged conference of its standing committee, a group of rebels, under the command of Zhu Hongxia and Wu Yanjin, twice harried the meeting. Xia Bangyin, who was attending the meeting, co-ordinated with forces attacking from the outside. On 19 March the same group raided the General Office and Organization Department of the HPPC, during which several officials were physically assaulted. The next day, the group forcibly occupied the First Guest House of the HPRC and issued an ultimatum threatening to conduct more violent actions unless the provincial and municipal authorities made concessions.[104]

The principal issue at stake was, in Hu Houmin's words, power. 'Politically speaking,' he declared, 'the Cultural Revolution has won tremendous successes; but in terms of power distribution, the movement has fallen far short of our expectations. Now it is time to solve the problem of power distribution.'[105] Xia Bangyin was more frank. He said: 'Yes, we are scrambling for power. Tell me who is not? If we have power in our hands, who on earth will dare to say "no" to us.'[106] The 'leading nucleus' even drew up a plan to revolutionize the existing pattern of power distribution from the provincial level down to the grass-roots, with the emphasis on the top. According to the plan, eight rebels should be placed on the standing committee of the HPPC, four of them as secretaries. Though the provincial trade union council already had 111 members, the 'leading nucleus' suggested that 120 more rebels be added to it. Attempts were also made to appoint nine rebels as deputy heads of various departments under the council. The Hubei Provincial Committee of the Youth League was another apparatus the rebels wanted to control. It was proposed that in addition to the positions of one secretary and six deputy secretaries that were already occupied by rebels, seven more rebels should be made deputy secretaries. The proposition was ridiculous, as four of the seven candidates recommended by the rebels were neither CCP members nor Youth League members and were too old to be eligible for recruitment into the League. Similar demands were made at the municipal level.[107]

In addition, rebel celebrities made individual claims. Each time the standing committee of the HPPC met, for instance, Xia Bangyin urged the old guards to appoint him as a secretary of the committee.[108] Dong Minghui, though already a secretary of the WMPC, aspired to be a secretary of the HPPC.[109] Zhang Liguo regarded himself as a 'tactful man'. On the surface, he kept other rebel personages at a distance, but he had as strong a thirst for power as his more imprudent comrades and wanted also to be a secretary of the HPPC. What distinguished him from the other rebel celebrities was that he preferred to bargain with the old guards at the conference table rather than to put pressure on the authorities through direct actions. Zhu Hongxia's case was more interesting. He was not a Party member but desired to be a Party secretary of the HPPC. In accordance with the CCP Constitution, to join the Party, he had to get approval from the Party branch of his work unit. Zhu, certain that such approval would not be forthcoming, bypassed that procedural hurdle by writing directly to Wang Hongwen and asking the vice chairman of the CCP to grant him Party membership.[110]

Following the examples of their leaders, less-well-known rebel leaders clamoured for official posts at lower levels.[111] If all the demands made by the rebels were to be met, not only would the veteran officials be put in the shade but the whole establishment would be shaken to its foundations.

Aggressive as they were, however, the rebels were not a puissant force. In the spring of 1976, at most only a few thousand rebels were still active in Wuhan. The most violent elements in the rebel ranks, such as Xie Miaofu and his associates, were still in gaol. Although there were calls for their release from prison, no action was taken. And it was doubtful whether they would have become involved in the new uprising even if they had been set free, for most of their comrades outside of prison were now weary of politics. Such apathy was understandable. The politics of 1976 was not about the fate of those who had suffered before the Cultural Revolution, at the beginning of the movement, during the process of the Double-checkup Campaign, or in the Anti-factionalist Campaign of 1975. People of bad class backgrounds had realized that it was an unattainable goal for them to acquire socio-political status equal to that of people of good class backgrounds. For former backward elements, recusancy had allowed them to enjoy some gratification only for short periods of time, but could not change the structure of authority that kept reproducing the gulf between the activist and the backward element.[112] Moreover, it had become apparent to people of both categories that whenever they pushed their agendas forcefully, their activities tended to give rise to a strong backlash. Since 'voice' had proved to be ineffective and costly, 'exit' had become an increasingly attractive option.[113] Thus, by 1976, probably over 90 per cent of former rebels had lost their will to fight, which explains why the radicalist atmosphere of 1976 could not generate much real political activism in Wuhan or, for that matter, in other parts of China. While there were posters on the walls along the main streets and occasional rallies were held, few paid attention to them. This was a striking contrast to what had occurred in 1974, and in the period from 1966 to 1968.[114] In many units, including some of those that had long been known as rebel strongholds, rebel activity was not resumed at all. Most former rebel activists were now inclined to retreat from factional politics.[115]

In early April a popular uprising suddenly broke out and soon swept China, including Wuhan,[116] before reaching a climax in Beijing's Tiananmen Square. The target of the uprising, however, was not Deng Xiaoping but the Gang of Four and, to a less extent, Mao himself.[117] Since the foundation of the People's Republic, Mao's regime had never faced such a direct challenge. Although the revolt was promptly put down, for the Gang of Four the handwriting was on the wall. This episode marked the beginning of the end of Mao's era.

The suppression of the Tiananmen Incident, while depressing most of the people, cheered up the rebel factional warriors in Wuhan. That the local authorities had failed to stop anti-Gang of Four activities in the city provided them with a golden opportunity to compel the authorities to make more concessions.

On 8 April the HPPC reluctantly held a mass rally to make a show of condemning the Tiananmen Incident. Before the rally closed, a group of rebels led by Zhu Hongxia and Wu Yanjin rushed in and kidnapped several provincial leaders. These leaders were then paraded at another mass rally staged by the rebels. They were forced to make a public pledge that they would make an about-face and side with the 'new forces' rising from the Cultural Revolution.[118]

To the rebels' surprise, Beijing condemned this action the next day. The rebel leaders soon learned through their information channels that they had been criticized not because their demands were improper but because the form of their conduct was not compatible with the strategy currently preferred by the Gang of Four. The Gang of Four preferred a strategy of 'tense inside and relaxed outside', that is, to create a situation that allowed their constituents in the provinces to bring increasing pressure on conservative local leaderships while avoiding disturbing the public order. The new strategy was adopted because those radical central leaders had come to realize from past experience that whenever the country was thrown into chaos by a radical drive, the moderate leaders had to be brought in to clear up the mess. The new strategy was expected to bring about what they viewed as positive results without bad side-effects.[119]

In mid-April 1976 the rebel leaders in Wuhan began to adopt this strategy. Accordingly, some readjustments were made. First, the two members of the CCP Central Committee, Xia Bangyin and Xie Wangchun, retired backstage, while Zhu Hongxia and the other members of the 'leading nucleus' were made commanders of the rebel forces. Second, it was decided that the rebels should try to avoid the image of factionalist warriors. In Wu Yanjin's words, 'we now need neither banner nor signboard for our forces'. Third, the wall journal directly controlled by the 'leading nucleus', which had appeared periodically in Hankou since February 1976, would cease to publish. The members of the writing group supporting the wall journal were advised to contribute articles to the *Yangtze Daily*. Xia Bangyin told the group, 'As the situation changes, our tactic needs to be changed. That is why we decided to stop publication of the wall journal and turn to the *Yangtze Daily*. After all, the *Yangtze Daily* has a much broader audience.'[120]

Thereafter, street actions were substantially reduced. But behind the scenes, the rebels intensified their efforts to press the local authorities for more power.

Under growing pressure from both Beijing and Wuhan, the provincial and municipal authorities made a concession to the rebels in late May: Hu Houmin and four other rebels became full-time officials of the HPRC or the WMRC. They need no longer work in their factories. For the authorities, this was a big concession. Allowing the five rebels to work full-time in these two powerful organizations not only changed their personal social status from manual workers to high-ranking cadres, a meteoric rise by any measure, but also greatly enhanced the rebels' chance of influencing decision making at the provincial and municipal levels. For the rebels, however, this was merely the first victory. Hu Houmin told his comrades that their next objective was to obtain full-time positions in the HPPC and the WMPC, the real nucleus of power. He remarked, 'Starting with the five, we would put fifty, then five hundred, then five thousand, and eventually fifty thousand of our rebel comrades into official posts.'[121]

Significantly, around that time, the rebels in Wuhan were given a new impetus by Wang Hongwen. In early June, during a meeting with the chief leaders of Hubei Province, Wang asserted that Hubei ranked last among China's twenty-nine provinces in terms of the number of rebels placed in leading positions at various levels. He again urged the provincial chiefs to make a thorough self-criticism and to reverse their attitudes towards the rebels. On 19 June, Zhao Xingchu reluctantly made a self-criticism on behalf of the HPPC. But the rebels were not impressed, condemning it as insincere. Encouraged by Wang Hongwen's personal intervention in Wuhan affairs, the rebels decided that it was time to press the authorities for more and bigger concessions. The 'leading nucleus' then formulated a four-phrase strategy statement, 'attacking from both above and below', 'using both hard and soft tactics', 'having our feet firmly planted at the grassroots', and 'being independent and self-reliant'. Thereafter, this strategy became the rebels' guide to action.

At the provincial and municipal levels, the rebels staked out four claims:

(1) All the members of the CCP Central Committee from Wuhan must be appointed as secretaries of the HPPC, which referred to Xia Bangyin, Dong Minghui, and Xie Wangchun.

(2) A certain number of additional rebels must be placed in the HPPC and the WMPC either as secretaries or as members of the standing committees.

(3) The organizational departments, propaganda departments, and general offices of both the HPPC and the WMPC must be headed by rebels.

(4) A large percentage of the functionaries of the HPPC and the WMPC must be staffed by rebels.

In order to fulfil those demands, the rebels coupled threats with promises in dealing with the provincial and municipal chiefs. On the one hand, in trying to intimidate the incumbents into accepting them as 'new blood' within the power organs, they repeatedly warned that anyone who discriminated against the 'new forces rising from the Cultural Revolution' would come to no good end. On the other hand, enormous publicity was given to the experience of Shanghai. It was said that in Shanghai a large number of veteran cadres had voluntarily taken early retirement and were now living in ease and comfort. Local veteran cadres were encouraged to do the same. They were assured that as soon as they gave up their seats to 'new cadres', the rebels would cease to bother them.

At lower levels, the rebels acted much more relentlessly than their counterparts at the provincial and municipal levels. The 'leading nucleus' believed that if the provincial and municipal authorities were to be forced to come to terms, the existing power structure must be subverted from the bottom up. In units where enough rebel forces could be rallied, they were encouraged to seize rather than merely to share power with the old guard. From June on, in thirty-one large or medium-sized enterprises and fourteen administrative bureaux, the rebels declared the restoration of 'real revolutionary committees', by which they meant committees that had existed for a very short period in 1967 and 1968. The present revolutionary committees were then declared illegitimate. In each of those units, there thus appeared two revolutionary committees, both of which claimed sole authority over the unit. As a result, production in those units was severely disturbed, if not completely stopped. In some other units, although the rebels were not powerful enough to restore the so-called real revolutionary committees, they acted defiantly, which in varying degrees weakened the existing authorities.[122]

Without exception, wherever the rebels attempted to grab power, their actions were resisted. The overwhelming majority of the people were hostile to them. Not only the provincial and municipal leaders had grudges against them, but cadres at lower levels also bore them malice. Among the people generally, a large proportion of the rebels' former comrades-in-arms now took a hostile attitude to their activities, not to mention former conservatives.[123] One rebel reportedly bemoaned, 'It seems that nowadays at least 80 per cent of the people are the social bases of Deng Xiaoping's revisionist line.'[124]

Given the shrinking popular support for the rebels, they chose to stake their future on the ascendancy of the Gang of Four in Beijing. They tended to regard all those who refused to collaborate with them as obstacles in their way to power. At that time, Deng Xiaoping was condemned by central propaganda as the ringleader of a so-called bourgeois restitution corps (*huanxiangtuan*). Using this derogatory metaphor, rebel activists in Wuhan elaborated that the 'restitution corps' had, in addition to its 'ringleader', 'junior officers' and 'rank-and-filers'. It was a way to justify their attacks against virtually anyone they wanted to attack. In some units, the rebels set out to punish what they called 'junior officers and rank-and-filers of Deng Xiaoping's restitution corps'. They warned their personal rivals that once they were in power, they would execute some, imprison some, purge some, send some to the countryside, and label some as 'capitalist-roaders' or 'newborn bourgeois elements'.[125] Even former rebel activists who had withdrawn from politics were blackmailed. They were told that they would be punished as 'capitulationists' after the rebels' final victory unless they threw themselves into the battle once again.[126]

The rebels' threats against non-collaborators intimidated some people, but also made many angry. In mid-June the conservative forces rallied again, this time under the banner of 'Revolutionary Workers', which were essentially made up of the same elements who had been active in 1974–5 under the name of the Workers–Peasants–Soldiers. Ironically, the Revolutionary Workers were no less critical of the provincial and municipal authorities than were the rebels. The rebels complained that the authorities at both levels were too stubborn in keeping the rebels from taking up powerful positions, but the Revolutionary Workers condemned them for being too obsequious to the rebels. The goal of the Revolutionary Workers was to prevent the authorities from making more concessions to their rivals. In order to show the influence they wielded over the affairs of the city and to put pressure on the provincial and municipal authorities, the Revolutionary Workers staged slow-downs in many factories, especially in those where the rebels were making claims for leadership.[127] As a result, production in the city came to a standstill in the summer.[128]

Another target of the Revolutionary Workers was the *Yangtze Daily*. They condemned the paper as 'nothing less than a factional leaflet'. Indeed, since mid-April, the *Yangtze Daily*, the professedly official mouthpiece of the WMPC, had become an important means for the rebels to present their views. A number of rebel celebrities, such as Xia Bangyin and Zhu Hongxia, had published articles in the paper; more articles were in the process of being written. But the conservatives were denied such a privilege. In protest, on 26 June the Revolutionary Workers broke into the office of the paper and demanded that the WMPC reshuffle its editorial board at once. The WMPC, which had largely lost control over its mouthpiece, had no objection. On the contrary, it secretly hoped that the incident would put sufficient pressure on the radical editors to restrain their radicalism. Afterwards, the WMPC assumed a detached air, commenting, 'It is a new thing for workers, peasants, and soldiers to monitor our paper'.

The rebels, who seemed more skilful at political struggle, found that the incident could be turned against both the conservative Revolutionary Workers and the authorities. In the early morning of 27 June, Xia Bangyin reported this occurrence to Wang Hongwen by telephone. He charged that 'a handful of capitalist-roaders' within the HPPC and the WMPC had masterminded the event. Meanwhile, a secret meeting of rebel leaders was held, which came to a decision that the paper should stop publication for a while so as to bring the incident to Beijing's attention. From 27 to 30 June, no paper was printed, despite the provincial and municipal authorities' efforts to prevent this from happening. As the rebels expected, Beijing intervened in favour of the rebels. On charges of committing of misdemeanour, five activists from the Revolutionary Workers were detained and locked up for fifteen days. More important, the credibility of the administration at the provincial and municipal levels was further undermined. The incident thus produced a great gain for the rebels.[129]

In July and August 1976 the rebels in Wuhan became active and over-bearing. The *Yangtze Daily* no longer bothered to pretend to be neutral in the factional conflict. On 22 July, to celebrate the ninth anniversary of the Wuhan Incident of 1967, the paper devoted one-fourth of its space to reprinting a dozen of the rebels' 'combat poems' written and circu-lated in 1967. Those provocative poems once again stirred the conserv-ative masses' wrath against the paper and against the rebels in general. Before long, posters protesting the paper's factionalism appeared all over the city. The *Yangtze Daily*, however, set the popular indignation at naught. In August it carried scores of even more provocative articles written by rebel leaders such as Hu Houmin.[130]

Meanwhile, the rebels stepped up their pressure on the provincial and municipal authorities to give them more power. Rebel leaders twice secretly met in July to discuss the possibility of taking over power in the city. At the meetings, Hu Houmin, the most resourceful rebel strate-gist, put forward a preliminary plan, which was accepted as the rebels' programme of action by the other participants. Efforts then were made to put the programme into practice. In July and August the HPPC held two conferences in two remote counties of north-west Hubei to avoid being harassed by Wuhan rebels. The conferences were originally designed to deal with issues concerning industrial production, but Xia Bangyin, Dong Minghui, Zhu Hongxia, and other rebel participants kept raising the issue of power redistribution. They protested that the rebels were not adequately represented at the conferences. Furthermore, they complained that the rebels' representation in all power organs was still far short of what it should be. The HPPC was urged to take the lead in promoting more rebels to positions of leadership, thus setting an exam-ple for veteran cadres at lower levels to follow. By early autumn of 1976, it appeared that the rebels in Wuhan were at last on their way to power.[131]

In an atmosphere of national unrest and uncertainty, Mao died on 9 September 1976 at the age of eighty-three. Less than a month later, a coup took place in Beijing, in which the Gang of Four were arrested. The radical group that had run wild on the Chinese political scene for ten years finally met its doom.

It did not take long for the news to reach Wuhan. Immediately, tens of thousands of wall posters appeared in the city denouncing the Gang of Four. The pent-up feelings, emotions, and frustrations of the people erupted in a volcanic fury. Throughout October, Wuhan, like other parts of the country, was permeated with a festive atmosphere. Many people had not felt so happy in years.[132]

But there were a few people who were dejected by the fall of the Gang of Four. Until 8 October, the rebels in Wuhan, though small in number, were still on the crest of a wave.[133] Now, with the collapse of their patrons, their hopes for wielding power in the city vanished. Although there were a few who planned to retreat to the mountains and to wage guerrilla warfare from there, most thought it impractical. Hu Houmin's suggestion was to pretend to support the new regime. In his view, the rebels had an age advantage over the old guard of the authorities. 'Let's vie with those old fogies to see who will eventually win in twenty years.'[134]

For the moment, however, they had to prepare for hardship. In early November, Zhu Hongxia, Xia Bangyin, Hu Houmin, and other rebel leaders were ordered to participate in a study programme.[135] From December on, as part of a national campaign against the 'Gang of Four's factionalist set-up in the provinces', they became subjects of mass criticism. The mass criticism lasted a full year, during which numerous public accusation meetings were held to denounce them. The local newspapers published scores of articles condemning 'crimes' allegedly committed by them in the past ten years. At the end of 1977, Xia Bangyin, Zhu Hongxia, Hu Houmin, Zhang Liguo, Dong Minghui, Li Xiangyu, Wu Yanjin, and several dozen rebel leaders were formally arrested and sentenced to between two and fifteen years' imprisonment.[136]

On 12 August 1977, Hua Guofeng, Mao's successor as chairman of the Party, in his report to the Eleventh Party Congress, announced, 'The downfall of the Gang of Four marked the end of the first Great Proletarian Cultural Revolution.' On 26 November 1978 the CCP Central Committee reversed the 'unjust verdict' on the Wuhan Incident of July 1967.[137] For veteran cadres and former conservatives in Wuhan, the curtain of the Cultural Revolution had finally fallen.[138] But for those who had been sentenced to spend several years behind bars for their activities during the last ten years, the movement was far from over.

12
Failure of Charisma

The Failure of the Cultural Revolution

W H E N Mao told the participants of a meeting held in Hangzhou on 8 June 1966 that the Cultural Revolution he had just launched would last about three months, he could not have foreseen that the movement would drag on for ten years and end in failure.

In fact, by the end of July 1966, it had already become apparent that three months were not sufficient. The state of the movement at that time, as viewed by Mao, was extremely unsatisfactory (see Chapter 3). Hence, he decided that three more months were necessary.[1] Accordingly, students at middle schools and colleges were told that classes would be suspended for half a year so that they could devote themselves to the movement. Until early October, Zhou Enlai was still insisting that, according to Mao's plan, school would be resumed by the next February. At a work conference of the central committee in October, however, Mao found that most Party leaders still didn't understand his purpose in initiating the Cultural Revolution. Therefore, he proposed to extend the movement for a few months. Nevertheless, his tentative plan then was to end 'the first phase of the movement' by February 1967.[2] The last two months of 1966 witnessed the collapse of public authority and the rise of factionalism. The situation was in such a state of flux that it was unlikely that the movement would achieve a decisive victory within two months (see Chapters 4 and 5). Mao thus was led to the conclusion at the end of 1966 that it would probably take another year to bring about what he had expected the movement to achieve.[3]

In early February 1967 when Mao met a group of Albanian visitors, he told them that the decisive battle had not yet finished, but it would become clear which side would win by the coming May. The movement, however, underwent two abrupt twists in the next three months. First, in the wake of the ill-planned January power seizure, Mao's attempt to use the army to stabilize the chaotic situation resulted in a wave of indiscriminate suppression of rebels in the provinces. Second, when he tried to restore revolutionary momentum by circumscribing the PLA's power, the last pillar of social order began to crack. In the summer of 1967, China was almost on the edge of total anarchy (see Chapters 6 and 7).

Even after intensive efforts to moderate the movement in the autumn of 1967, what ensued was far from satisfactory. For one thing, the establishment of a new power structure was much slower than Mao had planned. In October, Mao set the next February as the deadline for completing the construction of revolutionary committees in all the twenty-nine provinces. But by the end of 1967, only eleven provinces had set up revolutionary committees (see Chapter 8).[4] Such a disappointingly slow pace of development forced Mao to revise his timetable again. The 1968 New Year joint editorial of the *People's Daily*, the *Red Flag*, and the *PLA Daily* thus predicted that it would take the whole of 1968 for the Cultural Revolution to achieve a complete victory. More revolutionary committees were established in 1968, but they were not what Mao originally had in mind when he promoted the power seizure. Dominated by military men, they were instruments for maintaining social order but hardly vehicles for revolutionary changes. Mao tried to give an impulse to the radicalization of the new power authorities by initiating a renewed attack on 'rightist trends' in the spring of 1968. The result, however, was widespread armed conflict between the factions, which disrupted social order and paralysed production. In the summer of 1968, China was once again thrown into an almost total civil war. Alarmed by the devastating effects of his radicalization programme, Mao had to back down. Only after he imposed military control over the whole of China did the situation start to stabilize (see Chapter 9).

At the Twelfth Plenum of the CCP's Eighth Congress held in October 1968, Mao assured the participants that the Cultural Revolution would finish in victory by the summer of 1969. But when the Party's Ninth Congress was convened in April 1969, he adjusted his plan, asserting that one more year was needed to reach a total victory. The year of 1970, however, saw intensified power struggles between the Lin Biao and Jiang Qing cliques, which eventually resulted in the fall of Lin Biao in September 1971. By that time, it must have become apparent to Mao that there was no way for him to predict precisely when the movement he had launched would end. He stopped making any estimates about the end date of the Cultural Revolution in 1970.

Between 1969 and 1973 the pre-Cultural Revolution pattern of power distribution was largely restored. What had changed since the start of the movement were merely forms and rhetoric rather than the substance of politics. And there was a tendency to discredit everything associated with the period of 1966–8 (see Chapter 10). Mao had reason to doubt that his radical policies would continue after his death. In order to save the Cultural Revolution from falling apart, Mao began in late 1973 to introduce waves of radical initiatives in an attempt to reverse the trend. Those attempts, however, ended in disorder in the spring of 1974. Mao was forced to accept a new line: 'The Cultural Revolution has gone on for eight years. It is better to keep the people united and society in order.' In early 1976 when Mao was on his deathbed, he made renewed attempts to push ahead with his radical line (see Chapter 11). But he was becoming increasingly uncertain about whether the movement would end in victory or in failure. In his final moments, he was heard to sigh: 'Only God knows what may happen after my death.'[5] He left the question of how the Cultural Revolution would end to his successor.

Rational Behaviour of the Participants

The fact that a movement originally planned to last three months endured for more than ten years forcefully demonstrates the impotence of Mao's role as a charismatic leader. This study suggests that what most effectively limited Mao's power was the behaviour of the masses. Despite Mao's charisma and the loyalty of the Chinese to him, the participants in the movement were by no means his blind followers. Rather, they were rational political actors. Evidence for this generalization is abundant in the preceding chapters.

Entry

Contrary to the conventional impression that all Chinese enthusiastically threw themselves into the Cultural Revolution as soon as they were called by Mao to do so, adult Chinese were in fact extremely cautious. Politically naive students first took action, because, on the one hand, they were unable to assess the potential risks of their action; and on the other hand, in a revolutionary atmosphere, their expectation of the benefits they would reap was so high that they often overlooked the potential costs of collective action. Adults, however, tended to stand aside and to let others act when they faced a great likelihood of suppression or vengeance. For this reason, spontaneous mass organizations did not really emerge in Wuhan until Mao's cohorts had largely disabled the local authorities' social control function. Moreover, the point at which many people with little commitment to the movement finally found incentives to participate in collective action was reached only after political entrepreneurs had helped them to overcome the temptation to take a free ride (see Chapters 3 and 4). The enthusiastic involvement of Chinese in the Cultural Revolution thus was not the manifestation of a blind faith in Mao, but rather the results of a careful weighing of the risks and costs by millions of participants.

The Formation of Conflict Groups

When the spontaneous mass organizations were forming, members of the rebel organizations were recruited mainly from social groups which had grievances against the establishment, whereas the conservatives were principally those who had much to gain from preserving the *status quo*. Accordingly, their targets of attack were distinctively different. The rebels generally ignored non-Party administrators and experts and moved directly against the core Party leadership hierarchy of the units and localities in which they worked and lived. The conservatives, on the other hand, tended to attack cadres in functional fields, especially those with questionable class backgrounds and personal histories. If they criticized at all the Party officials who had been their patrons, their criticisms were generally mild and politely stated. This divergence was a direct outgrowth of the pre-Cultural Revolution structure of social conflicts (see Chapters 2 and 5).

Even bystanders (*xiaoyaopai*) sat on the sidelines for good reasons. For some, such as people with extremely bad class designations, it was too risky to take a decided stand in factional conflicts; while for others, such as middle-of-the-road workers, there was little to be gained from participating in the seemingly unprincipled factional strife (see Chapters 3 to 5).

The distribution of the participants in the movement in different factions was an indication that they were clearly aware of their distinctive interests.

Behavioural Pattern

Because of the relative power position of the rebels *vis-à-vis* the conservatives, the two sides behaved quite differently. Being minorities in most cases, the rebels preferred to operate outside their own work units. City-wide organizations could make them appear stronger than they really were in the daily tussle with the conservatives in their units. The conservatives, however, preferred to engage the rebels within the boundaries of individual units because there they were not only likely to constitute the majority but also possessed ready leverages (for example, bad class labels) with which to subdue their enemies. Rational calculation best explains such behavioural divergence.

The Degree of Group Solidarity

Mancur Olson's argument that people act collectively only when there are selective incentives for them to do so is helpful in accounting for the varying degrees of solidarity in different conflict groups in the Cultural Revolution.

Rebel organizations generally had greater solidarity than their conservative counterparts, for a simple reason. In their efforts to overturn the establishment (a binary public bad), the rebels strove for social acceptance and a higher social status. There was little hope of them changing the negative political labels imposed on them merely through individual efforts. However, it was also impossible for them to better their political positions without making a personal effort. The distinction between individual and collective benefits was blurred, which gave the rebels selective incentives to participate in collective action.

Despite their relatively large size, the conservative organizations often appeared to be rather inert and feeble. This was due largely to the fact that they were attempting to defend a public good—the existing pattern of power distribution.[6] As long as this public good was available, every conservative could benefit whether or not he had contributed to its provision. Therefore, the conservatives tended to expect others to make contributions. As a result, their organizations were usually much less combative than the rebel organizations. However, whenever the rebels' challenge became so serious as to threat to destroy the existing power equilibrium, the conservative masses were always able to overcome the temptation to take a free ride. The more pressing the rebels' challenge was, the more solid their ranks became. For now what was at stake was no longer merely the survival of the present power structure but also the vested interests they had individually enjoyed under such a system (see Chapters 6 and 7).

It would thus appear that individual calculation of the value of collective action was the determinant of the degree of group solidarity.

The Cohesiveness of Coalition

Whereas individual conservatives were less inclined to take part in collective action than their rebel counterparts, a coalition of conservative organizations tended to be more cohesive than a rebel coalition. As

Chapters 6 to 9 demonstrated, the cohesiveness of a coalition depended to a large extent upon the goal the coalition partners were pursuing. The conservatives were able to form a relatively cohesive coalition because their common goal was merely to defend the *status quo*. Since there were no spoils for them to divide up in the case of victory, they did not have to worry about their coalition becaming too big. Their interests thus could be served by a maximal winning coalition.[7]

The rebels' coalition did not come about as easily as the conservatives', because in addition to the destruction of the establishment, the rebels expected some palpable personal benefits from the Cultural Revolution, ranging from material gains and a higher socio-political status to power positions. Since the scarcity of resources did not allow them to profit equally, they were forced to compete with each other over the distribution of whatever might come to them if they were to gain the ascendancy. Thus, while perfectly understanding the necessity of forming an effective winning coalition, they nevertheless had an incentive to keep its size to a minimum. This explains why the rebel organizations kept a constant eye on each other (as potential competitors) even when fighting shoulder to shoulder against the conservatives, which impaired the cohesiveness of the rebel coalition (see Chapters 6 to 9).

Strategy

Chapters 3 to 11 illustrate that individuals and organizations acted strategically in order to maximize the achievement of their presumed goals. The best example of this is political manoeuvres carried out by the various organizations during two crucial periods—January to February 1967 and September 1967 to January 1968. In both periods, the central issue in Wuhan was how to distribute the seats of future power organs between the two main rebel factions. Both wanted to dominate the future power structure. Accordingly, they tried to outsmart each other at every step of the bargaining. As Chapters 6, 8, and 9 described, almost every move and counter-move of the two factions was calculated. Those manoeuvres would become unintelligible if we assume that those actors' behaviours were not goal-oriented or instrumental.

Since what the two Wuhan factions were playing during the two periods was a prisoners' dilemma game, as would be expected from rational actors, non-cooperation was chosen as a dominant strategy by both sides (see Chapters 8 and 9). Maoist leaders made painstaking efforts to patch things up between them. However, despite their loyalty to Mao, they always let the 'great helmsman' down. Here, people's rational calculations seem to have eclipsed their affective attachment to their charismatic leader.

Violence

Given that collective violence is costly whether one faction wins or loses, human irrationality has often been used to explain why the participants in the movement sometimes resorted to violence. Chapters 7 to 9, however, showed that violence occurred only when the public authority was absent or existent but too weak to maintain social order (for example, during the periods May to July 1967 and May to June 1968). This was not accidental. Among political actors, there is no automatic adjustment of their interests. In normal times, organized violence is generally ruled out as a strategy, because the state that monopolizes the use of force threatens to punish groups or individuals who use force against others without authorization. Under anarchy, however, there is no law, and no law enforcer, to mitigate conflicts. Consequently, there is the constant possibility that conflicts will be settled by force. In other words, whether people resort to violence in social conflicts depends to a large extent on their calculation of the marginal gains from such a strategy as compared with those from other options. Violence thus should be understood as a deplorable yet rational form of action.

Exit

People's commitment to the causes of their groups varied in accordance with the benefits they expected to derive from further collective action. The successful achievement of group goals could weaken such a commitment. Since the demands of the group were largely met, the residual demands took on less importance. As a result, many activists might lose enthusiasm and drop out, becoming new *xiaoyaopai*.[8] In the case of factional leaders of various levels, however, positive selective incentives such as opportunities for personal career advancement (for example leadership positions in revolutionary committees) should they be successful, entered into their calculations. They thus had a stake in continued collective action (see Chapters 8 and 9).

Conversely, a backlash could also halt political activism. Failure tended to reduce the value of collective action, because it caused many to believe that their goals were either unattainable or attainable only at a high cost. Since voicing their concerns could not bring about the expected results, many chose to exit instead. However, due to their

previous heavy investment in the causes of their groups, factional leaders were in a sense locked into a part of the social fabric from which
escape was not only undesirable but also almost impossible. Even if they
became disillusioned with the causes they had committed themselves to,
those factional leaders often found that the costs and rewards were
balanced in such a way that made the decision to end their commitment
traumatic (see Chapters 6, 7, 10, and 11).[9]

In any event, people tended to exit from factional activities when the
marginal utility of further collaboration and collective action began to
dwindle. This observation can be used to explain the gradual degenera-
tion of factionalist activism during the Cultural Revolution.

The Cultural Revolution was a movement that proceeded in waves.
An upsurge of radicalism was often followed by a conservative interval.
Since both success and failure could reduce the value of further collective action, the ebb and flow of the movement tended to halt the political activism of the participants. Thus, a recurrent challenge for factional
leaders was how to rally routed former activists into collective action at
each turn of the movement. As Chapters 6 to 11 showed, this was a
formidable task. Those political entrepreneurs might be able to revital-
ize some former activists, but most were incorrigible in the sense that
they never resumed their factional activism after they had chosen to exit.
Having experienced disillusionment, such people tended to greatly
depreciate the possible payoffs from collective action and were difficult
to convince of the benefits of further participation. As a result, more and
more people made their exit as the movement ran its course. By the time
the Cultural Revolution was drawing to a close, the number of active
participants accounted for only a tiny minority of the population in
Wuhan (see Chapter 11).

Relations between Rebels at the Grassroots and Radical Leaders in Beijing

Unlike many social movements in which the élite and the masses
confront each other, the Cultural Revolution had a distinctive character:
both the élite and the masses were divided among themselves, and the
division between the radicals and the conservatives cut through the élite
as well as the masses. But it would be a gross oversimplification to
present the rebels and the conservatives at the grassroots as homogeneous social groups ever ready to spring into action at the behest of
their élite counterparts in Beijing. Take the rebels as an example.
Although the rebellious masses were permeated with slogans coined by

the radical central leaders, their aims were qualitatively different from those of their leaders. Mao's basic objectives were to revolutionize the superstructure, to transform the Chinese people into 'new men' and 'new women', and above all to eliminate his opponents; and the motive of his radical retinue was to defeat their rivals and to improve their own power positions within the central leadership. But most rebels threw themselves into the movement for catharsis and with a desire to change their own socio-political status. They all attacked the establishment, but for different reasons. Moreover, what they were actually attacking were different parts of the establishment. In a sense, both the radical central leaders and the rebels at lower levels were fighting for a redistribution of power. But even in this sense, their goals differed: the former were preoccupied with issues concerning power redistribution at the very top, whereas the latter were immersed in the redistribution of local power. To a large extent, the central radicals cared about politics in the provinces only to enlist support from below in order to bring pressure to bear on their rivals within the central leadership. The rebels, for their part, had little real interest in the issues causing the central cleavages. This was why the criticisms of Liu Shaoqi, Deng Xiaoping, and Lin Biao rarely aroused the rebels' enthusiasm.

Georges Lefebvre, in his famous study of the French Revolution, puts forth a concept of 'parallel revolutions'. By the same token, we may argue that the Cultural Revolution was not a single movement but rather a series of parallel movements. The interests of the central and local radicals were parallel, this is, pointing in the same direction but not able to intersect.

By now, it should be clear that the participants in the Cultural Revolution were rational political actors. It was their pursuit of their independent agendas in both individual and collective actions that ultimately led to the failure of Mao's Cultural Revolution.

This rationalistic explanation of the 'failure of charisma', however, would not be complete without a solution being found to two remaining minor puzzles: How is it possible for true believers of a charismatic leader to act rationally, and why do rational participants in the events described insist even today that they were irrational at the time of the Cultural Revolution?[10] The previous chapters have shown that Mao's true believers did act rationally in the course of the Cultural Revolution in Wuhan. The following paragraphs attempt to explain why the charismatic relationship could not prevent Mao's followers from acting rationally. I will first discuss the rational aspect of the charismatic relationship ignored by Max Weber, and then try to explore why rational actors are often not able to understand their own behaviour and motivations.

Charisma and Rational True Believers

A charismatic relationship should be examined along two dimensions: the emotional and the cognitive. No doubt, a charismatic leader can elicit emotions such as devotion, awe, and reverence among his followers. In a charismatic relationship, by definition, followers lose in varying degrees the capacity for rational decision making because their commitment to the leader is rooted in strong affective states. However, a charismatic relationship is much more than an affective devotion. The emotional aspect, important as it may be, would never be able to displace or override the cognitive aspect. The cognitive dimension involves followers' efforts to understand and to concretize messages they receive from the leader. Here, the leader is a subject to be perceived by his followers. The Weberian concept of charismatic relationship probably overemphasizes the emotional aspect, and thus fails to appreciate the weight of the cognitive aspect, which is just as fundamental in such a relationship.

The two dimensions of charismatic relationship have different impacts on followers' behaviour: the emotional aspect is more likely to be reflected in the relationship between the leader and his followers, and the cognitive aspect in the followers' relations with one another and with the outside world. Although followers may have the same nature of emotional attachment to the common leader, they do not necessarily share the same view of the world, and therefore may behave very differently. Moreover, the followers' affective commitment towards the adored leader does not necessarily lead to an accurate understanding of the messages received from their idol. Therefore, it is conceivable for misunderstandings to occur between the leader and his followers.

In a charismatic relationship, the followers constantly look for messages relevant to their own lives from their leader. A message, however, is not an object that stands by itself and offers the same face to every message receiver. Rather, it is an event, something that happens to, and with the participation of, the receivers. In other words, messages need to be interpreted.

Interpretation is imperative in a charismatic relationship, because, unlike in normal dyadic interactions where the partners can ask each other questions to ascertain how far their perceptions have deviated from one another's original meaning, a charismatic leader cannot adapt himself to each and every follower. During the Cultural Revolution, for instance, although Mao received eleven million Red Guards at Tiananmen Square in the first half-year of the movement, he rarely made public appearances afterwards, never made a public speech, and talked face to face with individual Red Guards only once, in the summer of 1968, that is, after he had decided to disband all Red Guard organizations.[11] The great distance between Mao and his followers made it impossible for his followers to ask him to clarify his messages. Nor did he make any effort to do so. James Davies has rightly pointed out, 'It is the distance itself which leads to enchantment,' because 'no man can be great in the eyes of his intimates.'[12] But the distance makes interpretation essential.

Since in a charismatic relationship all options open to the followers have to be based on plausible interpretations of messages from the leader, people have to rule out a certain portion of the possible strategies as beyond the pale. To the extent that a rejection of the leader's charisma would permit them to pursue their interests more efficiently, they are not quite rational. Moreover, there are limitations on the degree to which followers may stretch their leader's messages when they interpret them. However, messages from a charismatic leader are often ambiguous, for two reasons. First, the validity of a message can be proved or disproved by and through events. Obviously, the more precise a message is, the more vulnerable it is to disconfirmation. Therefore, a charismatic leader may deliberately send out equivocal messages. Second, the heterogeneous nature of followers makes it difficult for a charismatic leader to issue messages that are equally relevant to all people. Thus, messages from a leader who stands high above his followers are inherently nebulous. The ambiguous nature of a charismatic leader's messages offers considerable room for interpretation despite the above-mentioned limitations, which allows his followers to make a broad range of rational choices.

The so-called highest directives of Mao during the period of the Cultural Revolution, for instance, were extremely fragmented and vague. Mao defined the movement as a 'class struggle', but he did not define the concept of 'class'.[13] Similarly, the 'power holder taking the capitalist road' was the officially sanctioned target of the Cultural Revolution, but no one rendered a precise definition of that concept either. The vagueness of the two key concepts created a situation in which one interpretation could be diametrically opposed to another, causing a great deal of confusion during the course of the movement.

Interpretation is a constructive act. When people interpret messages from a charismatic leader, what they do in effect is not to discover the core of determinate meanings of those messages but to create them.[14] Their interpretations are influenced and structured by everything they bring with them and by their varied competencies. Consequently, we should expect that followers will find ways of adapting given messages comfortably to the pursuit of self-interest. The leader–follower relationship therefore is not a one-way process in which passive followers merely internalize messages sent out by their leader; rather, it is a dynamic relationship in which followers always actively interact with their leader by interpreting the messages they receive in ways that make sense to them.

When one interprets messages from a leader in a consistent way, one creates an image of the leader. The image of an object should not be regarded as identical with the object itself, though image-holders may not be able to distinguish what is given to them from what they produce in the process of interaction with the object. Thus, when followers think that they are following a leader, they may actually be following their images of the leader, which are their own products containing their own expectations.

The image of a charismatic leader is both an individual and a social product, because one's image of the leader is shaped within the context in which he, as a member of a particular social group, lives. Therefore, if a charismatic leader has followers from various social groups, each group may have a relatively unified image of the leader, and different social groups may have different images.

When people from different social groups became Mao's followers during the Cultural Revolution, their conflicting interests and expectations did not disappear. Instead, they subconsciously built their expectations into their respective images of Mao. In other words, a follower's willingness to accept Mao's initiative was not merely a result of blind faith in Mao; it was also a product of his perception that Mao's initiative would provide solutions to his personal problems, although the follower might not realize this fact.

An image-holder tends to frame the situation in such a way that the image tells him to do what he would like to do anyway. During the Cultural Revolution, as the previous chapters have shown, Mao was seen as the symbol of the establishment by some Chinese, but as the supreme commander of rebellious forces fighting against the establishment by others. One's position in pre-Cultural Revolution society to a great extent determined which image of Mao one took during the movement. The existence of conflicting images clearly suggests that ultimately Mao's followers found in their idol solely what they themselves imported into their images of Mao. They followed Mao because they believed that Mao was articulating their resentments, hopes, and conceptions of society. More precisely, they thought that they were following Mao, but they were actually following their own images of Mao. It is difficult to imagine that people from different backgrounds and who joined opposing factions would embrace the same Mao. What they embraced could only be their own images of Mao. In this sense, the participants in the Cultural Revolution were not true believers of Mao but true believers of their own images of Mao. Although they all adopted Mao's words, and shouted the same prevailing slogans, they were in fact expressing different and sometimes opposing feelings. Such behaviour may be called consciously irrational and subconsciously rational. That is, at the conscious level, the participants had a blind faith in Mao; but at the subconscious level, they were pursuing their self-interests. As such, the true believers of Mao could behave very rationally in factional conflicts.

Once images are developed, they become somewhat independent of the given leader, receiving their own 'lives'. It is possible, therefore, for a group of followers to find that some of their beloved leader's messages diverge from their established image of the leader. Occasional divergence may make them perplexed and uneasy. If such divergence persists, however, the followers may be led to question their image of the leader. Consequently, their support of the leader may recede, and their enthusiasm may become merely ritual. During the Cultural Revolution, the Wuhan conservatives were greatly baffled on four occasions—the winter of 1966–7, after the 20 July Incident of 1967, the spring of 1974, and the first three-quarters of 1976—because they could not understand why Mao, 'the leader of labouring people', was then supporting 'monsters and ghosts'. The rebels, on the other hand, found themselves at a loss on three different occasions—the February Adverse Current of 1967, from late 1968 to 1973, and in 1975—when Mao, 'the red commander of the rebels', seemed to be leaning towards the establishment. In all those cases, in the eyes of Mao's followers, the official line of the moment ran counter to their perceptions of Mao's line. The constant changes in the official line gradually diluted the sacredness of Mao's leadership, contributing to a gradual demystification of Mao's charisma in the later years of the Cultural Revolution.

If the above analyses of the charismatic relationship are sound, we should probably call the participants in the Cultural Revolution 'rational true believers'. They were 'true believers' in that, treating Mao as 'endowed with supernatural, superhuman, or at least specifically exceptional power or qualities',[15] they were willing to devote themselves to Mao's cause, whatever that cause might be, at least in the early years of the movement. They were 'rational' in that they consistently pursued their own objectives throughout the course of the Cultural Revolution, by taking up slogans propagated by Mao and changing their content so that they corresponded more closely with their own interests than with Mao's. It was this rational element in the participants' behaviour that often caused Mao to be taken aback by the torrent he had unleashed and to feel powerless to control it. At the beginning of the Cultural Revolution, Mao might have hoped that the cult of personality around him would work as an effective tool in orchestrating the movement. But despite his charisma, he was often stymied in his objectives by the rampant pursuit of self-interests. Apparently, Mao misread the ebullience of the masses.

If the participants in the Cultural Revolution were indeed 'rational true believers' rather than merely passive instruments of the supreme leader, there must be something wrong with Weber's concept of charisma. The closer examination of the charismatic relationship presented above suggests that the fatal deficiency of Weber's theory of charisma lies in its neglect of the cognitive dimension in the relationship between a charismatic leader and his followers.

Rational Actors and Rationalization

The question remains as to why the majority of participants in the Cultural Revolution still insist that they were fooled by Mao into taking part in the movement, implying that they were fighting for Mao, not for themselves.

One explanation is that those people are not willing to shoulder responsibility for their own actions. Today there is a consensus among the Chinese that the Cultural Revolution was a catastrophe. Every former participant, whether a cadre, a conservative, a rebel, or a bystander, claims that he or she was a victim of the protracted movement. It is true that the Cultural Revolution was a game with no winner. People feel that they were betrayed because they all suffered in some way during the ten-year movement. What is also true, however, is that most of those who were wronged also wronged others at some time. It is convenient for them to shift the blame on to their superiors, and ultimately on to Mao.

This explanation, however, is not convincing, for most of those who insist that they were misled sincerely believe this to have been the case. Why did rational actors claim that they were not rational?

The reason is that the participants were not aware of all the stimuli that contributed to their behaviour. Given the circumstances of the Cultural Revolution, they had to attach an ideological cliché to their actions and to moralize about the means they took to achieve the end they valued. It is common in social conflict situations for both established and discontented groups to make claims about their goals, programmes, and actions in terms of ideals and values that have some legitimacy.[16] This is especially true when their desires strongly contradict socially acceptable norms. In such a situation, only through some form of rationalization can they make it appear that unworthy desires are motivated by reasonable and noble motives.[17] In traditional China, the public interest had occupied a position of sacrosanct priority; group and individual interests could be tolerated only within the latitude of some plausible interpretation of the public interest. The Cultural Revolution reinforced the indigenous corporate concept of interest. Self-interest and group interest were condemned as a bourgeois mode of thinking that should make way for general dedication to the public interest and to universal values. The slogan 'fight self, champion the public' was typical of this view. Private interests, of course, did not disappear during those years. They were pursued through subtle modification of consensually acceptable themes. The open-textured quality of Mao's vague directives permitted the participants in the Cultural Revolution to validate their private interests in altruistic rhetoric.[18] As the previous chapters have shown, the participants in the movement pursued their own interests in this manner. But they unconsciously confused their real motives with the rationalization of those motives, arriving at a belief that they were fighting for a charismatic leader with no ulterior motives.

That the participants were not aware of their real motives does not imply that they did not have such motives. Even if they are sincere with regard to what they know, they may still be dissembling or misrepresenting the 'truth' because their consciousness does not represent their own underlying experience. Here rationality exists at an unconscious or barely conscious level. The participants might deny the relevance of this account of events to their own behaviour and motivations. They might even feel falsely accused and indignant. There is nothing unusual about such a reaction. As Russell Hardin rightly pointed out, 'Plausibly every theory worth thinking about violates agents' understandings of their behaviour and motivations.'[19] It should not be surprising that those who have given no serious thought to their own actions might reject or fail to comprehend the explanation of their behaviour provided here. Whether or not they were conscious of their real motives, the participants in the Cultural Revolution were rational fighters rather than pawns or robotic devotees. Throughout the ten years from 1966 to 1976, they scrambled with each other for scarce political influence and resources. It was their pursuit of self-interests that stymied Mao's plan for the movement, thus resulting in the ultimate failure of the Great Helmsmen's last experiment of social change.

Descriptive List of Interviewees

(Sex, year of birth, family background, membership in political organization, occupation, education level, monthly salary if any, and political affiliation during the Cultural Revolution. State employees received no pay raise between 1964 and 1971; figures given reflect the level of income throughout those years.)

1. Male, born in 1930, 'good' class designation, Party member, cadre (rank 22) in a state-owned factory, elementary education, 51.26 yuan, 'conservative'.

2. Male, born in 1923, 'good' class designation, Party member, cadre (rank 17) in a state-owned factory, elementary education, 92 yuan, 'conservative'.

3. Female, born in 1932, 'good' class designation, Party member, worker in a state-owned factory, junior high education, 37.44 yuan, 'conservative'.

4. Male, born in 1937, 'good' class designation, Youth League member, cadre (rank 27) in a government agency, senior high education, 28 yuan, 'conservative'.

5. Male, born in 1939, 'middle' class designation, Youth League member, cadre (rank 24) in a government agency, senior high education, 41 yuan, 'rebel'.

6. Male, born in 1926, 'middle' class designation, Party member, cadre (rank 20) in a government agency, junior high education, 66.5 yuan, 'rebel'.

7. Female, born in 1938, 'bad' class designation, worker in a state-owned factory, junior high education, 46 yuan, 'conservative'.

8. Male, born in 1940, 'good' class designation, Youth League member, technician in a state-owned factory, college education, 53 yuan, 'rebel'.

9. Male, born in 1936, 'good' class designation, Party member, cadre (rank 20) in a college, college education, 66.5 yuan, 'conservative'.

10. Male, born in 1944, 'good' class designation, Youth League member, teacher in a middle school, polytechnic school education, 36 yuan, 'conservative'.

11. Male, born in 1942, 'bad' class designation, teacher in a middle school, college education, 51 yuan, 'conservative'.

12. Male, born in 1944, 'good' class designation, Youth League member, worker in a state-owned factory, elementary education, 43.81 yuan, 'rebel'.

13. Male, born in 1946, 'bad' class designation, Youth League member, teacher in a middle school run by the

community, senior high education, 36 yuan, 'rebel'.

14. Male, born in 1946, 'bad' class designation, teacher in a middle school run by the community, senior high education, 36 yuan, 'rebel'.

15. Male, born in 1943, 'middle' class designation, Youth League member, teacher in a middle school, college education, 51 yuan, 'rebel'.

16. Male, born in 1928, 'good' class designation, Party member, cadre (rank 17) in a post office, senior high education, 96 yuan, 'conservative'.

17. Male, born in 1922, 'good' class designation, Party member, cadre (rank 16) in a state-owned factory, elementary education, 110 yuan, 'conservative'.

18. Male, born in 1948, 'good' class designation, Youth League member, student in a polytechnic school, 17 yuan, 'conservative'.

19. Male, born in 1923, 'good' class designation, worker in a state-owned factory, junior high education, 64.6 yuan, 'rebel'.

20. Male, born in 1935, 'good' class designation, technical cadre (rank 24) in a state-owned factory, junior high education, 41 yuan, 'rebel'.

21. Male, born in 1928, 'middle' class designation, Party member, cadre (rank 19) in a government agency, senior high education, 74 yuan, 'conservative'.

22. Female, born in 1931, 'bad' class designation, teacher in a middle school, senior high education, 59 yuan, 'conservative'.

23. Male, born in 1949, 'good' class designation, worker in a collective factory, junior high education, 27 yuan, 'rebel'.

24. Male, born in 1942, 'bad' class designation, worker in a state-owned factory, junior high education, 38.4 yuan, 'rebel'.

25. Female, born in 1942, 'good' class designation, worker in a state-owned factory, junior high education, 32.5 yuan, 'conservative'.

26. Male, born in 1935, 'bad' class designation, Party member, cadre (rank 23) in a hospital, junior high education, 47 yuan, 'conservative'.

27. Male, born in 1936, 'middle' class designation, Party member, cadre (rank 21) in a government agency, junior high education, 59 yuan, 'rebel'.

28. Male, born in 1924, 'good' class designation, Party member, cadre (rank 17) in a state-owned factory, elementary education, 92.6 yuan, 'conservative'.

29. Male, born in 1939, 'bad'

class designation, Youth League member, teacher in a middle school, college education, 59 yuan, 'rebel'.

30. Female, born in 1943, 'middle' class designation, Youth League member, teacher in a middle school, college education, 51 yuan, 'rebel'.

31. Male, born in 1927, 'middle' class designation, Party member, cadre (rank 16) in a government agency, senior high education, 104.5 yuan, 'conservative'.

32. Male, born in 1926, 'good' class designation, Party member, artist in a state-owned troupe, senior high education, 79.5 yuan, 'rebel'.

33. Male, born in 1928, 'good' class designation, Party member, cadre (rank 17) in a polytechnic school, elementary education, 93.5 yuan, 'conservative'.

34. Female, born in 1932, 'good' class designation, Party member, cadre (rank 24) in a polytechnic school, elementary education, 41 yuan, 'conservative'.

35. Male, born in 1942, 'good' class designation, Youth League member, worker in a post office, junior high education, 46 yuan, 'rebel'.

36. Male, born in 1948, 'middle' class designation, Youth League member, student in a senior high school, 'conservative'.

37. Male, born in 1948, 'good' class designation, Youth League member, student in a senior high school, 'conservative'.

38. Male, born in 1951, 'good' class designation, student in a junior high school, 'conservative'.

39. Male, born in 1936, 'bad' class designation, technician in a scientific research institute, college education, 59 yuan, 'rebel'.

40. Female, born in 1940, 'middle' class designation, Youth League member, technician in a scientific research institute, college education, 51 yuan, 'rebel'.

41. Male, born in 1934, 'good' class designation, Party member, worker in a state-owned factory, junior high education, 45.3 yuan, 'conservative'.

42. Male, born in 1931, 'good' class designation, Party member, cadre (rank 19) in a government agency, junior high education, 74 yuan, 'conservative'.

43. Male, born in 1950, 'good' class designation, student in a polytechnic school, 'rebel'.

44. Male, born in 1947, 'bad' class designation, Youth League member, student in a college, 'rebel'.

45. Male, born in 1936, 'good' class designation, Party member, cadre (rank 21) in a government agency, junior high education, 59 yuan, 'conservative'.

46. Female, born in 1950, 'bad' class designation, student in a senior high school, 'rebel'.

47. Male, born in 1947, 'bad' class designation, student in a polytechnic school, 'rebel'.

48. Male, born in 1948, 'bad' class designation, student in a polytechnic school, 'rebel'.

49. Male, born in 1949, 'middle' class designation, student in a senior high school, 'rebel'.

50. Male, born in 1943, 'good' class designation, Youth League member, student in a college, 'rebel'.

51. Male, born in 1947, 'good' class designation, Youth League member, student in a senior high school, 'rebel'.

52. Male, born in 1938, 'good' class designation, Youth League member, worker in a state-owned factory, junior high education, 45.3 yuan, 'conservative'.

53. Male, born in 1946, 'good' class designation, student in a college, 'rebel'.

54. Male, born in 1934, 'good' class designation, Party member, teacher in a college, college education, 59 yuan, 'rebel'.

55. Male, born in 1919, 'bad' class designation, Party member, cadre (rank 10) in a government agency, senior high education, 199 yuan, 'rebel sympathizer'.

56. Male, born in 1947, 'good' class designation, Youth League member, student in a senior high school, 'conservative'.

57. Male, born in 1949, 'bad' class designation, student in a senior high school, 'rebel'.

58. Male, born in 1950, 'good' class designation, student in a junior high school in a Wuhan suburb, no affiliation.

59. Male, born in 1947, 'good' class designation, worker in a state-owned factory, elementary education, 32.5 yuan, 'rebel'.

60. Male, born in 1940, 'bad' class designation, teacher in a spare time school, senior high education, 45.5 yuan, 'rebel'.

61. Male, born in 1948, 'middle' class designation, student in a senior high school, 'rebel'.

62. Male, born in 1949, 'middle' class designation, Youth League member, student in a senior high school, 'rebel sympathizer'.

63. Male, born in 1946, 'bad' class designation, Youth League member, student in a senior high school, 'rebel'.

64. Female, born in 1947, 'middle' class designation, Youth League member,

student in a senior high school, 'rebel'.

65. Male, born in 1930, 'good' class designation, Party member, cadre (rank 19) in a hospital, junior high education, 74 yuan, 'conservative'.

66. Male, born in 1934, 'good' class designation, Party member, cadre (rank 22) in a hospital, junior high education, 53 yuan, 'conservative.

67. Male, born in 1942, 'bad' class designation, Youth League member, teacher in a secondary tectonic school, college education, 51 yuan, 'rebel'.

68. Male, born in 1940, 'good' class designation, teacher in a middle school run by the community, senior high education, 36 yuan, 'rebel'.

69. Male, born in 1948, 'bad' class designation, student in a senior high school, 'rebel'.

70. Male, born in 1930, 'good' class designation, Party member, cadre (rank 21) in a collective factory, no formal education, 59 yuan, 'conservative'.

71. Female, born in 1945, 'good' class designation, Youth League member, student in a college, 'rebel'.

72. Male, born in 1933, 'good' class designation, Party member, cadre (rank 22) in a collective factory, elementary education, 53 yuan, 'conserv-

ative'.

73. Male, born in 1933, 'good' class designation, Party member, worker in a state-owned factory, no formal education, 53.5 yuan, 'conservative'.

74. Male, born in 1936, 'good' class designation, Party member, cadre (rank 18) in a government agency, junior high education, 83 yuan, 'rebel'.

75. Female, born in 1938, 'good' class designation, nurse in a factory clinic, junior high education, 32.5 yuan, 'rebel'.

76. Female, born in 1948, 'middle' class designation, student in a senior high school, 'rebel'.

77. Male, born in 1943, 'good' class designation, student in a college, 'rebel'.

78. Male, born in 1942, 'middle' class designation, Youth League member, student in a college, 'rebel'.

79. Male, born in 1949, 'good' class designation, Youth League member, student in a senior high school, 'conservative'.

80. Female, born in 1930, 'middle' class designation, Party member, worker in a government agency, elementary education, 53 yuan, 'conservative'.

81. Male, born in 1927, 'good' class designation, Party

member, cadre (rank 17) in a government agency, elementary education, 92.6 yuan, 'conservative'.

82. Female, born in 1932, 'bad' class designation, Party member, cadre (rank 21) in a government agency, junior high education, 59 yuan, 'conservative'.

83. Male, born in 1928, 'good' class designation, Party member, cadre (rank 13) in a government agency, elementary education, 145.5 yuan, 'conservative'.

84. Female, born in 1931, 'good' class designation, Party member, cadre (rank 23), in a state-owned factory, elementary education, 47 yuan, 'conservative'.

85. Male, born in 1944, 'good' class designation, Youth League member, student in a college, 'rebel'.

Notes

Notes to Chapter 1

1. Roderick MacFarquhar, *The Origins of the Cultural Revolution*, 3 vols., New York: Columbia University Press, 1974 and 1983, Vols. 1 and 2; Paul L. Hiniker, *Revolutionary Ideology and Chinese Reality*, London: Sage Publications, 1977; K. S. Karol, *The Second Chinese Revolution*, New York: Hill and Wang, 1974; Lowell Dittmer, *Liu Shao-ch'i and the Chinese Cultural Revolution: The Politics of Mass Criticism*, Berkeley: University of California Press, 1974; Jean Daubier, *A History of the Chinese Cultural Revolution*, New York: Vintage Books, 1974; William Hinton, *Turning Point in China: An Essay on the Cultural Revolution*, New York: Monthly Review Press, 1972; Committee of Concerned Asian Scholars, *China! Inside the People's Republic*, New York: Bantam Books, 1972; Stanley Karnow, *Mao and China: From Revolution to Revolution*, New York: Viking, 1972; Edward E. Rice, *Mao's Way*, Berkeley: University of California Press, 1972; Robert Jay Lifton, *Revolutionary Immortality: Mao Tse-tung and the Chinese Cultural Revolution*, New York: Vintage Books, 1968; and Byung-joon Ahn, *Chinese Politics and the Cultural Revolution: The Dynamics of Policy Process*, Seattle: University of Washington Press, 1966.

2. Eric Hoffer, *The True Believer*, New York: Harper & Row, 1966.

3. Max Weber, *The Theory of Social and Economic Organization*, New York: Oxford University Press, 1949, p. 359. Also see Ann Ruth Willner, *Charismatic Political Leadership: A Theory*, Princeton, NJ: Princeton University Press, 1968, pp. 4–6; and James V. Downton, Jun., *Rebel Leadership: Commitment and Charisma in the Revolutionary Process*, New York: The Free Press, 1973, pp. 209–10.

4. That the early works largely neglected the emotions, activities, and experiences of the great mass of ordinary Chinese was, in a sense, inevitable, for at the time scholars had only very limited access to the People's Republic of China (PRC). They had to concentrate on what were available to them in plentiful supply: open publications.

5. Anita Chan, *Children of Mao: Personality Development and Political Activism in the Red Guard Generation*, Seattle: University of Washington Press, 1985; Jonathan Unger, *Education under Mao: Class and Competition in Canton Schools, 1960–1980*, Seattle: University of Washington Press, 1985; Stanley Rosen, *Red Guard Factionalism and the Cultural Revolution in Guangzhou (Canton)*, Boulder, CO: Westview Press, 1982; and Marc J. Blecher and Gordon White, *Micropolitics in Contemporary China*, White Plains, NY: M. E. Sharpe, 1979; Hong Yung Lee, *The Politics of the Chinese Cultural Revolution: A Case Study*, Berkeley: University of California Press, 1978; David M. Raddock, *Political Behavior of Adolescents in China: The Cultural Revolution in Kwangchow*, Tucson: The University of Arizona Press, 1977; and Gordon White, *The Politics of Class and Class Origin: The Case of the Cultural Revolution*, Canberra:

Australian National University Contemporary China Centre, 1976.

6. Keith Forster, *Rebellion and Factionalism in a Chinese Province: Zhejiang, 1966–1976*, Armonk, NY: M. E. Sharpe, 1990. Exceptions, in addition to Forster's book, are Sherry Gray, *Bombard the Headquarters: Local Politics and Citizen Participation in the Great Proletarian Cultural Revolution and the 1989 Movement in Shenyang*, Ph.D. dissertation, University of Denver, 1992; Lynn T. White, III, *Policies of Chaos*, Princeton, NJ: Princeton University Press, 1989; and Constance Squires Meaney, *Stability and the Industrial Elite in China and the Soviet Union*, Berkeley: Berkeley Center for Chinese Studies, 1988.

7. Mancur Olson, Jun., *The Logic of Collective Action*, Cambridge, MA: Harvard University Press, 1965.

8. Russell Hardin, 'Theory on the Prowl', Unpublished paper, 1992.

9. In fact, none of those works makes reference to Olson's book.

10. An early attempt was Deborah Davis's 'The Cultural Revolution in Wuhan'. See *Cultural Revolution in the Provinces*, Cambridge, MA: Harvard East Asian Monograph, No. 42, 1971.

11. Anita Chen argues that the Cultural Revolution ended with the Ninth Party Congress in 1969, because the war between factions was over. See her 'Dispelling Misconceptions about the Red Guard Movement: The Necessity to Re-Examine Cultural Revolution Factionalism and Periodization', *The Journal of Contemporary China*, 1, 1 (1992). I disagree with Chen in that the factional war did not end in 1969. As I will show in Chapters 10 and 11 of this book, the factional war revived in Wuhan at the time when the Ninth Party Congress was in progress, and again between 1973 and 1976. In fact, Wuhan was not unique in this aspect. Many provinces, such as Henan, Shanxi, Hebei, and Zhejiang, witnessed the resurgence of factionalism in the early 1970s. For the case of Zhejiang, see Forster, *Rebellion and Factionalism in a Chinese Province*.

12. Anne F. Thurston, *Enemies of the People: The Ordeal of the Intellectuals in China's Great Cultural Revolution*, New York: Knopf, 1987, pp. 284–5.

13. Ann Ruth Willner, *Charismatic Political Leadership: A Theory*, Princeton, NJ: Princeton University Press, 1968, pp. 4–6; and James V. Downton, Jun., *Rebel Leadership: Commitment and Charisma in the Revolutionary Process*, New York: The Free Press, 1973, pp. 209–10.

14. Thomas C. Schelling, *Micromotives and Macrobehavior*, New York: Norton, 1978.

15. Michael Taylor, 'Rationality and Revolutionary Collective Action', in Michael Taylor (ed.), *Rationality and Revolution*, Cambridge: Cambridge University Press, 1988, pp. 63–97.

16. Karl-Dieter Opp, *The Rationality of Political Protest: A Comparative Analysis of Rational Choice Theory*, Boulder, CO: Westview Press, 1989, pp. 19–20.

17. Herbert Simon, 'From Substantive to Procedural Rationality', in Frank Hahn and Martin Hollis (eds.), *Philosophy and Economic Theory*, Oxford: Oxford University Press, 1979.

18. Neil J. Smelser, 'The Rational Choice Perspective: A Theoretical Assessment', *Rationality and Society*, 4, 4 (1992): 399.

19. Russell Hardin, 'The Normative Core of Rational Choice Theory', Unpublished paper, 1992.

20. Hardin, 'Theory on the Prowl', pp. 16–20.

21. Kristen Renwick Monroe, 'The Theory of Rational Action: Its Origins and Usefulness for Political Science', in Kristen Renwick Monroe (ed.), *The Economic Approach to Politics: A Critical Reassessment of the Theory of Rational Action*, New York: Harper Collins, 1991, pp. 14–15.

22. Steven J. Brams, 'The Study of Rational Politics', in Bernard Susser (ed.), *Approaches to the Study of Politics*, New York: Macmillan, 1992, p. 315.

23. Daniel Little, 'Rational-Choice Models and Asian Studies', *The Journal of Asian Studies*, 50, 1 (1991).

24. Stanley I. Benn, 'Rationality and Political Behaviour', in S. I. Benn and G. W. Mortimore (eds.), *Rationality and the Social Science: Contributions to the Philosophy and Methodology of the Social Sciences*, London: Routledge and Kegan Paul, 1976, p. 247.

25. Jon Elster designates norms as unconcerned with outcomes, generally simple, socially shared, and backed by sanctions. See his *The Cement of Society: A Study of Social Order*, Cambridge: Cambridge University Press, 1989.

26. Albert O. Hirschman, 'Against Parsimony: Three Easy Ways of Complicating Some Categories of Economic Discourse', *Economics and Philosophy*, 1 (1985): 7–21.

27. Tibor Scitovsky, *The Joyless Economy*, New York: Oxford University Press, 1976.

28. Russell Hardin, *Collective Action*, Baltimore: The Johns Hopkins University Press, 1982, pp. 101–24; and Hardin, 'Acting Together, Contributing Together', *Rationality and Society*, 3, 3 (1991): 365–80.

29. Dennis Chong, *Collective Action and the Civil Rights Movement*, Chicago: University of Chicago Press, 1991, pp. 75–6.

30. Smelser, 'The Rational Choice Perspective', pp. 381–410.

31. Jon Elster, *Sour Grapes: Studies in the Subversion of Rationality*, Cambridge: Cambridge University Press, 1983.

32. Elster, *The Cement of Society*, pp. 35–6.

33. George Tsebelis, *Nested Game: Rational Choice in Comparative Politics*, Berkeley: University of California Press, 1990, pp. 92–6.

34. Chong, *Collective Action and the Civil Rights Movement*, p. 11.

35. Sidney Tarrow, 'National Politics and Collective Action: Recent Theory and Research in Western Europe and the United States', in *Annual Review of Sociology 1988*, pp. 429–30; and Tarrow, *Struggling to Reform: Social Movements and Policy Change during Cycles of Protest*, Western Societies Program Occasional Paper No. 15, Center for International Studies, Ithaca, NY: Cornell University, 1983, pp. 3 and 28.

36. Theda Skocpol, *States and Social Revolutions*, Cambridge: Cambridge University Press, 1979; Barrington Moore, *Social Origins of Dictatorship and Democracy: Land and Peasant in the Making of the Modern World*, Boston, MA: Beacon Press, 1966; and Crane Brinton, *The Anatomy of Revolution*, New York: Vintage Books, 1965.

37. Hardin, *Collective Action*, pp. 50–1.

38. Ibid., p. 121.

39. Ibid., p. 67.

40. Chong, *Collective Action and the Civil Rights Movement*, p. 148.

41. Ibid., p. 132.

42. Hardin, *Collective Action*, pp. 31–5.

43. Olson, *The Logic of Collective Action*, pp. 43–65.

44. Taylor, 'Rationality and Revolutionary Collective Action', p. 84.

45. Chong, *Collective Action and the Civil Rights Movement*, p. 129.

46. Michael Taylor, *The Possibility of Cooperation*, Cambridge: Cambridge University Press, 1987, p. 25.

47. Michael Taylor, *Community, Anarchy and Liberty*, Cambridge: Cambridge University Press, 1982, p. 20.

48. Samuel L. Popkin, 'Political Entrepreneurs and Peasant Movements in Vietnam', in Taylor, *Rationality and Revolution*, pp. 20–1.

49. Hardin, *Collective Action*, pp. 35–7.

50. Taylor, *Community, Anarchy and Liberty*, pp. 12–13; Taylos, *The Possibility of Cooperation*, pp. 17–18; and Hardin, *Collective Action*, pp. 101–24.

51. Elster, *The Cement of Society*, p. 37.

52. Chong, *Collective Action and the Civil Rights Movement*, p. 197.

53. Gustav LeBon, *The Crowd: A Study of the Popular Mind*, New York: Viking, 1960 [1909].

54. Anthony Downs, *An Economic Theory of Democracy*, New York: Harper and Brothers, 1957.

55. Gudmund Hernes, 'We Are Smarter Than We Think', *Rationality and Society*, 4, 4 (1992): 421–36.

56. Elster, *The Cement of Society*, p. 250.

57. Smelser, 'The Rational Choice Perspective', p. 387.

58. Brian Barry, *Sociologists, Economists and Democracy*, Chicago: University of Chicago Press, 1978, p. 16.

59. Debra Friedman and Michael Hechter, 'The Contribution of Rational Choice Theory to Macrosociological Reseach', *Sociological Theory*, 8 (1988): 202.

60. James B. Rule, 'Rational Choice and the Limits of Theoretical Generality', *Rationality and Society*, 4, 4 (1992): 451–69.

61. Hardin, 'Theory on the Prowl', pp. 21–2.

62. Tang Tsou, *The Cultural Revolution and Post-Mao Reforms: A Historical Perspective*, Chicago: University of Chicago Press, 1986, pp. xx–xxi.

63. Hardin, *Collective Action*, pp. 229–30.

64. Clifford Geertz, 'Deep Play: Notes on the Balinese Cockfight', in Chandra Mukerji and Michael Schudson (eds.), *Rethinking Popular Culture: Contemporary Perspectives in Cultural Studies*, Berkeley: University of California Press, 1991, pp. 239–77.

65. Richard J. Ellis, 'Explaining the Occurrence of Charismatic Leadership in Organizations', *Journal of Theoretical Politics*, 3, 3 (1991): 305–19.

Notes to Chapter 2

1. The population living in the four suburban districts were excluded here. Wuhan Statistics Bureau (ed.), *Wuhan Sishinian: 1949–1989* [Forty Years of Wuhan: 1949–1989], Wuhan: Wuhan University Press, 1989, p. 249.

2. Milovan Djilas, *The New Class: An Analysis of the Communist System*, New York: Praeger, 1957.

3. *Zhongguo Gongren* [Chinese Workers], 17 (1957): 4.

4. Ministry of Labour, 'Guanyu 1963 Nian Gongzi Gongzuo Anpai' [Wage Plan of 1963], 21 July 1963.

5. Richard Lowenthal, 'Development vs. Utopia in Communist Policy', in

Chalmers Johnson (ed.), *Change in Communist Systems*, Stanford, CA: Stanford University Press, 1970, pp. 33–117.

6. Wuhan Party History Office, *Zhonggong Wuhan Difang Dangshi* [The Local Party History of Wuhan] (hereafter *DFDS*), p. 3.

7. Ibid., p. 13.

8. *Changjiang Ribao* [Yangtze Daily] (hereafter *CJRB*), 22 November 1957.

9. *Renmin Jiaoyu* [People's Education], 10 (1957): 14–21.

10. *Xinghua Yuekan* [New China Monthly] (hereafter *XHYK*), 7 (1955): 175; and *Renmin Jiaoyu*, 5 (1958): 3–4.

11. Constance Squires Meaney, *Stability and the Industrial Élite in China and the Soviet Union*, Berkeley: Institute of East Asian Studies, University of California, 1988, pp. 9–16.

12. *XHYK*, 6 (1950): 1350.

13. *DFDS*, pp. 3 and 80–9.

14. The Central Administrative Bureau of Industry and Commerce, *Siying Gongshangye Shehuizhuyi Gaizao Dashiji* [Chronicle of the Socialist Reform of Private Industry and Commerce], 1957, p. 88.

15. *CJRB*, 16 November 1957.

16. Wuhan Education Bureau, 'Putong Zhongxue Zonghe Baobiao 1965–1966 [Wuhan Middle School Statistics]', 'Quanrizhi Xiaoxue Zonghe Baobiao 1965–1966 [Wuhan Elementary School Statistics]', and 'Quanrizhi Jigong Zhiye Xuexiao Zonghe Baobiao 1965–1966 [Wuhan Technical Training School Statistics]'.

17. Central Party School, *Zhonggong Dangshi Cankao Ziliao* [Reference Materials of Party History], Beijing: People's Press, 1980, Vol. 8, pp. 204–31.

18. Ibid., p. 639.

19. *Dangshi Tongxun* [Newsletter on Party History], 18 (1983).

20. Frank Parkin, 'Strategies of Social Closure in Class Formation', in Frank Parkin (ed.), *The Social Analysis of Class Structure*, London: Tavistock, 1974; and *The Marxist Theory of Class: A Bourgeois Critique*, London: Tavistock, 1979.

21. Parkin, *The Social Analysis of Class Structure*, p. 3.

22. Richard Kraus, *Class Conflict in Chinese Socialism*, New York: Columbia University Press, 1981, p. 139.

23. *Hubei Ribao* [Hubei Daily] (hereafter *HBRB*), 3 June 1957; and *Shanghai Gongshang* [Shanghai Industry and Commerce], 1 (1958): 6.

24. *CJRB*, 9 October 1957.

25. Ibid., 28 August 1957.

26. *HBRB*, 4 June 1957.

27. *DFDS*, pp. 106–8.

28. During the Elimination of Counter-revolutionaries Campaign, 1.3 million people were identified as having 'historical problems' and 81,000 were labelled 'counter-revolutionaries', *HBRB*, 19 July 1957.

29. The Socialist Transformation Campaign in 1956 labelled about 800,000 as capitalists. *Dangshi Yanjiu* [Researches in Party History], 3 (1981): 11.

30. A total of 552,877 were labelled 'rightists' in 1957 and 1958; half of these were intellectuals and 24,500 were capitalists. See He Mengbi and Duan Haoran, *Zhongguo Gongchandang Liushinian* [The Sixty Years of the Chinese Communist Party] (hereafter *LSN*), Beijing: PLA Press, 1984, Vol. 2, p. 491. Although

the Anti-Rightist Campaign was not applied to factories, it did not ignore workers. Many workers received the label 'antisocialist element' or 'bad element'. See *Renmin Ribao* [People's Daily] (hereafter *RMRB*) editorial, 'Bad Elements Must be Punished', 19 August 1957.

31. The Central Group of Ten Persons: 'Guanyu Fangeming Fenzi He Qita Huaifenzi De Jieshi Ji Chuli De Zhengce Jiexian Di Zanxing Guiding [How to Define Counter-revolutionary and Bad Elements, and How to Deal with Them]', 10 March 1956.

32. *XHYK*, 21 (1956): 112.

33. Wuhan Municipal Party Committee: *Zhibu Shenghuo* [Life in Party Branches], 23 (1956).

34. *HBRB*, 3–8 June 1957.

35. Deng Xiaoping concluded in his report on rectification: 'In general, rightists came from exploitative families.' Central Party School, *Zhonggong Dangshi Cankao Ziliao*, Vol. 8, p. 640. In a scientific research institute in Wuhan, more than 80 per cent of rightists came from bad family backgrounds. See *CJRB*, 2 December 1957.

36. *XHYK*, 2 (1958): 41–2.

37. Frank Parkin, *Class Inequality and Political Order*, New York: Praeger, 1975.

38. Mao Zedong, *Selected Works*, 4 vols., New York: International Publishers, 1956, Vol. 4, p. 112.

39. *XHYK*, 8 (1956).

40. *Zhongguo Qingnian Bao* [Chinese Youth Daily], 25 May 1963.

41. *Zhibu Shenghuo*, 22 (1958).

42. *Gongren Ribao* [Workers Daily], 15 September 1962.

43. *RMRB*, 15 May 1956.

44. Ibid.

45. *Gongren Ribao*, 23 March 1962, and 1 July, 6 August, 23 September, and 14 October 1964.

46. *Gongren Ribao*, 1 March–12 April and 14 November 1964; and *Zhongguo Qingnian Bao*, 10 September 1964.

47. *Gongren Ribao*, 20 June and 14 October 1964; and 9 January and 14 April 1965.

48. *RMRB*, 15 May 1956.

49. David Lane, *Soviet Economy and Society*, London: Oxford University Press, 1985, p. 162.

50. *RMRB*, 19 December 1955; and *Zhongguo Gongren*, 18 (1956): 3–4.

51. *CJRB*, 9 October 1957; and *Zhongguo Gongren*, 15 (1957).

52. *CJRB* editorials: 'Protect Activists', 5 August 1957; and 'Report System and Its Functions', *Zhongguo Gongren*, 15 (1957): 7.

53. *Gongren Ribao*, 5 July 1964.

54. *RMRB* editorials: 'The Party Organizations of Enterprises must be Close to the Masses', 19 December 1955; 'Correctly Treat Backward Workers', 15 May 1956; and 'Bring the Initiative of the Young into Full Play', 4 May 1965. *Gongren Ribao* editorials: 'Help Backward Workers Enthusiastically', 8 February 1964; 'The Significance of Helping Backward Elements', 26 June 1964; 'Correctly Treat Backward Colleagues', 3 July 1964; 'What is the Correct Attitude towards Backward Workers?', 24 July 1964; 'What Should be Done if

Your Effort to Help Backward Workers Turns out to Have No Effect', 12 August 1964; 'How to Treat Your Backward Friends', 9 April 1965; and 'It is Advanced Workers' Responsibility to Help Backward Colleagues', 20 November 1965. *Zhongguo Qingnian Bao* editorials: 'How to Treat the Minority and Backward Elements', 19 April 1962; and 'Look at a Person with an Eye on the Course of His Development', 3 July 1965.

55. *Wenhuibao* [Wenhui Daily], 20 May 1957; and *Gongren Ribao*, 26 May 1962, and 26 February, 11 March, and 22 April 1965.

56. *Gongren Ribao*, 16 November 1963; and *Zhongguo Qingnian Bao*, 10 September 1964.

57. Tang Tsou, *The Cultural Revolution and Post-Mao Reforms: A Historical Perspective*, Chicago: University of Chicago Press, 1986, p. 63.

58. William L. Parish, 'Destratification in China', in James L. Watson (ed.), *Class and Social Stratification in Post-Revolution China*, Cambridge: Cambridge University Press, 1984, pp. 89, 99.

59. Cao Zhi, *Zhonghua Renmin Gongheguo Renshi Zhidu Gaiyao* [The Personnel System of the People's Republic of China], Beijing: Beijing University Press, 1985, p. 267.

60. The State Council, 'Guanyu Jiangdi Guojia Jiguan 10 Ji Yisheng Ganbu De Gongzi Biaozhun De Jueding [Resolution Concerning Cutting the Salaries of Party Cadres at Level Ten and Above]', 18 December 1956; the Central Party Committee, 'Guanyu Jiangdi Guojia Jiguan 3 Ji Yishang Dangyuan Ganbu Gongzi Biaozhun De Jueding [Resolution Concerning Cutting the Salaries of Party Cadres at Level Three and Above]', 7 February 1959; the National Planning Commission and Ministry of Labour, 'Guanyu Dangqian Laodongli Anpai He Zhigong Gongzi Weiti De Baogao [Report Concerning the Arrangement of Labour Forces and the Distribution of Wages]', 26 September 1960; and Ministry of Labour, 'Guanyu 1963 Nian Gongzi Gongzuo Anpai [Wage Plan of 1963]', 21 July 1963.

61. Center for Chinese Research Materials, *Red Guard Publications: Supplement I* (hereafter RGPS), 20 vols. Washington, DC, 1980, Vol. 4, p. 334.

62. Kraus, *Class Conflict in Chinese Socialism*, p. 149.

63. *Zhengzhi Pashou—Wang Renzhong* [Political Thief—Wang Renzhong], October 1967.

64. *Dadao Song Kanfu* [Down with Song Kanfu], Vol. 1, October 1967.

65. Wuhan Party History Office, *Zhonggong Wuhan Dangshi Dashiji* [Chronicle of Wuhan Party History], Wuhan: Wuhan University Press, 1989, pp. 355–6.

66. All my interviewees acknowledged that in their units, income inequality was insignificant.

67. Wang Renzhong and his wife together earned 507.3 yuan a month, and there were seven family members. Song Kanfu's family also had seven members, but he and his wife made 420.50 yuan. See *Zhengzhi Pashou—Wang Renzhong; Dadao Song Kanfu*, Vol. 1.

68. By comparison, the very rich in the United States had an income ratio of 7,000:1 between the highest and the average in the 1960s. See David Lane, *End of Social Inequality*, Middlesex: Penguin Books, 1971, p. 59.

69. Interviewees 2, 9, 16, 17, 31, 65, and 67.

70. Li Zhongying, 'Shehui Zhuyi Gemingshi Shang De Weida Chuangju [A Great Achievement in Socialist Revolution], in *Dangshi Yanjiu*, 3 (1981).

71. Ibid.

72. In 1956, Liu Shaoqi visited the Fourth Textile Factory in Wuhan. The former owner of the factory received 10,000 yuan a year in dividends and a salary of 130 yuan a month. But he was not satisfied because the Party secretary, as a veteran revolutionary cadre, earned 160 yuan a month, a little more than he did. He complained about this to Liu. Soon after, his salary was increased to 160 yuan. Hubei Radio, 21 September 1967.

73. *RGPS*, 4: 1865.

74. *CJRB*, 9 June 1958.

75. *Liu Huilong Sanfan Yanxing* [Liu Huilong's Anti-Mao Speeches], 10 March 1968.

76. Feng Jicai, *Voices from the Whirlwind: An Oral History of the Chinese Cultural Revolution*, New York: Pantheon Books, 1991, p. 160.

77. *RGPS*, 4: 1882.

78. Hubei Labour Bureau, *Gongzi Biaozhun Xuanbian* [Selected Documents on Wage Policy], Wuhan, 1973, pp. 1–60.

79. *RGPS*, 1: 36; and 4: 1871.

80. *Dadao Chen Bohua* [Down with Chen Bohua], February 1968.

81. *Fangeming Xiuzheng Zhuyi Fenzi Wang Renzhong Ducao Xuanbian* [Selected Harmful Writings of Counter-revolutionary Revisionist Wang Renzhong], Vol. 1, December 1967, p. 70.

82. *Jianjue Ba Liu Shaoqi Jiuhui Beijing Jiangong Xueyuan Doudao Douchou* [Take Liu Shaoqi Back to Beijing Construction Institute to Struggle against Him], 20 May 1967.

83. *Laodong* [Labour], 10 (1964): 14–15.

84. Christopher Howe, *Wage Patterns and Wage Policy in Modern China, 1919–1972*, London: Cambridge University Press, 1973.

85. Interviewee 8.

86. Lane, *Soviet Economy and Society*, p. 193.

87. Despite tremendous efforts to eliminate illiteracy in the early 1950s, 78 per cent of the population was illiterate in 1956. See *XHYK*, 14 (1956): 11–19.

88. *Wenjiao Cankao Zhiliao* [Reference Materials Concerning Culture and Education], 10 (1951): 343.

89. *Renmin Jiaoyu*, 8 (1957): 13; and 10 (1957): 14–15; and *XHYK*, 1 (1958): 139.

90. *XHYK*, 21 (1957); and *CJRB*, 6 January 1958.

91. *XHYK*, 1 (1958); and *RMRB*, 3 July 1958.

92. *XHYK*, 20 (1959).

93. Archives of the Wuhan Education Bureau.

94. *Mao Zedong Sixiang Shengli Wansui* [Long Live Mao Zedong Thought], version 2 (of three different versions extant), pp. 270–7.

95. The Ministry of Education, *Zhongguo Jiaoyu Nianjian 1949–1985* [Yearbook of Chinese Education, 1949–1985], p. 338.

96. The Central Party Committee, 'Guangu Gaodeng Xuexiao Luqu Xinsheng De Zhengzhi Shencha Biaozhun [Political Criteria for Admitting New College Students]', 1962 edition.

97. The Central Party Committee, 'Dui 1962 Nian "Gaodeng Xuexiao Luqu Xinsheng De Zhengzhi Shencha Biaozhun" De Jidian Jieshi Yijian [Interpretations of the 1962 Edition of Political Criteria for Admitting New College

Students]', 1964.

98. Wuhan Education Bureau and Wuhan Public Security Bureau, 'Guanyu Jiyibu Miqie Peihe Zuohao Gaodeng Zhongdeng Xuexiao Zhaosheng De Zhengzhi Shencha Gongzuo De Jidian Yijian [Suggestions on How to Implement the Political Criteria for Admitting New College Students and Senior High Students]', 27 April 1964.

99. Archives of Wuhan Education Bureau, July 1964.

100. Beijing Education Bureau, 'Guanyu Dui Chuzhong Biyesheng Jiating Qingkuang Jinxing Diaocha De Qingshi [Request for Starting Family Background Investigation of Junior High Graduates]', 14 January 1964.

101. Wuhan Education Bureau, 'Guanyu Shixing Zhongdian Zhongxue Xishou Baosongsheng Mianshi Ruxue Banfa De Tongzhi [Circular Concerning the Admission of Recommended Students to Key Schools]', 26 July 1964.

102. Wuhan Education Bureau, 'Gaodeng Xuexiao Nianchu Baobiao 1964–5 [Early Report on the Situation of Higher Education Institutions, 1964–5]'.

103. Wuhan Education Bureau, 'Wuhan Shi Zhongxiaoxue Xuesheng Jiating Chusheng Dianxing Diaocha 1965–6 [Wuhan Elementary and Middle School Student Family Background Survey, 1965–6]'.

104. Parish, 'Destratification in China', pp. 100–1.

105. *Renmin Jiaoyu*, 9 (1957).

106. Interviewees 37 and 38.

107. Wang Renzhong's son, for instance, was still in junior high in 1966. Interviewees 37 and 51.

108. Many students from middle or bad class backgrounds believed that despite their academic accomplishments, class sponsorship rigged the mobility game against them. Students from good family backgrounds also viewed the contest for advancement as inherently unfair. See Wuhan Education Bureau, 'Guanyu 1961 Nian Weiluqu Zhongxiaoxue Biyesheng De Anpai [Arrangements for Elementary and Middle School Graduates Who were not Accepted by Higher Education Institutions]' and 'Guanyu Biyesheng Sixiang Qingkuang De Fanying [Report on the Thinking of High School Graduates]', May 1965.

109. Cited from Hong Yung Lee, 'Radical Students in Kwangtung during the Cultural Revolution', *China Quarterly*, 64 (1975): 654.

110. *Zhongguo Gongren*, 12 (1957): 8; and *XHYK*, 15 (1956): 34.

111. *Zhongguo Gongren*, 19 (1956): 3–4.

112. *RGPS*, 4: 1868 and 1874–5.

113. *Zhongguo Gongren*, 13 (1957): 13.

114. *DFDS*, pp. 2–3, 72, 80–81, 98–103, and 113; *CJRB*, 17 November 1957; and Wuhan Statistics Bureau, *Wuhan 1949–1984*, Wuhan, 1985, p. 38.

115. *Qiyue Fengbao* [July Storm], 25 June 1968.

116. Wuhan Party History Office, *Zhonggong Wuhan Dangshi Dashiji*, p. 215.

117. Ibid. p. 219.

118. Ibid. pp. 246, 281.

119. Ibid. pp. 260, 392–3.

120. Ibid. pp. 280, 297; and *Dadao Song Kanfu*, Vol. 11, July 1968.

121. Wuhan Party History Office, *Zhonggong Wuhan Dangshi Dashiji*, pp. 309–15.

122. Wuhan Intermediate People's Court, *Wuhan Fayuan Zhi* [The History

of Wuhan Court], Unpublished draft, 1992.

Notes to Chapter 3

1. *Zhongyang Fuzhe Tongzhi Jianghua Chaolu* [Selected Speeches of Central Leaders] (hereafter *JHCL*), 3 vols., Wuhan, 1967, Vol. 1, pp. 2 and 193.

2. *People's Daily* declared that if party leaders were judged to have behaved against Mao's Thought, it was legitimate to challenge them, no matter how high their positions might be and how long they had been Party members. *Renmin Ribao* [People's Daily] (hereafter *RMRB*), 2 June 1966.

3. Kurt Lewin, 'Group Decision and Social Change', in Guy E. Swanson, Theodore Newcomb, and Eugene L. Hartley (eds.), *Readings in Social Psychology*, New York: Henry Holt, 1952.

4. At a meeting held in early June, Liu Shaoqi said, 'The current movement is very much like the one of 1957.' See *Fangeming Xiuzhengzhuyi Fenzi Wang Renzhong Zuixinglu* [Crimes Committed by Counter-revolutionary Revisionist Wang Renzhong], September 1967.

5. *Changjiang Ribao* [Yangtze Daily] (hereafter *CJRB*), 24 April 1968.

6. *Wuda Sanjiacun An* [The Case of the Three-Family Village at Wuhan University], September 1967.

7. Jin Chunming, *Chedi Fouding Wenhua Dageming Shijiang* [Ten Talks on the Cultural Revolution], Beijing: PLA Press, 1985, pp. 8–9.

8. *Hubei Ribao* [Hubei Daily] (hereafter *HBRB*), and *Wuhan Wanbao* [Wuhan Evening News], May 1966.

9. *Fangeming Xiuzhengzhuyi Fenzi Wang Renzhong Zuixinglu; Chedi Pipan Hubei Shengwei Ziliao Huibian* [Selected Materials on Thoroughly Criticizing the HPPC], 29 October 1966; and interviewees 29, 30, 31, 42, and 57.

10. *Wuhan Dichu Wuchan Jieji Wenhua Dageming Dashiji* [Chronicle of the Great Proletarian Cultural Revolution in Wuhan] (hereafter *WWDJ*), August 1967.

11. *WWDJ*.

12. *Wuhan Heluxiaofu* [A Khrushchev of Wuhan], October 1967.

13. Interviewee 63.

14. *Hubei Shengwei Shujichu Changwei Huiyi Jilu* [The Minutes of Meetings of the Hubei Provincial Party Committee Secretariat], February 1967.

15. *Fangeming Xiuzhengzhuyi Fenzi Song Kanfu Zuixinglu* [Crimes Committed by Counter-revolutionary Revisionist Song Kanfu], 10 February 1967; and *Chedi Pipan Hubei Shengwui Ziliao Huibian*.

16. *WWDJ*.

17. *JHCL*, Vol. 3, p. 3.

18. *Fangeming Xiuzhengzhuyi Fenzi Wang Renzhong Zuixinglu*.

19. *Wang Renzhong Zuixinglu* [Crimes Committed by Wang Renzhong], 1 February 1967.

20. *Wang Renzhong Sanfan Yanlunlu* [Wang Renzhong's Anti-Mao Speeches], September 1967; and *Pitao Zhanbao* [Battlefield Report on Criticizing Tao Zhu], 14 March 1967.

21. *WWDJ*.

22. *Dadao Wuhan De Heluxiaofu* [Down with the Khrushchev of Wuhan], October 1967.

23. *CJRB*, 26 April 1968. Five days later, in his letter to Jiang Qing, Mao used the phrases 'monsters and ghosts have come out themselves' and 'our central task at present is to wipe out the rightists', which in many ways resembled the terms used by Wang. See Institute of International Relations (ed.), *Classified Chinese Communist Documents: A Selection*, Taipei: National Chengchi University, 1978, pp. 54–7.

24. *Xinshuiyun* [New Water Transport Institute], October 1967.

25. *WWDJ*.

26. *Wang Renzhong Sanfan Yanlunlu*, September 1967. The slogan 'look for targets in all directions' also prevailed in Beijing. Until December 1966, Lin Biao still used the phrase. See *Lin Biao Wenxuan* [Selected Works of Lin Biao], Wuhan, 1968, p. 276.

27. *Zhibu Shenghuo* [Life in Party Branches], 12–13 (1966); and interviewee 51.

28. Liu Guokai, *A Brief Analysis of the Cultural Revolution*, Armonk, NY: M. E. Sharpe, 1987, p. 20.

29. *RMRB* and *Jiefang Junbao* [PLA Daily], 1–10 June 1966.

30. Interviewee 60.

31. Wuhan Education Bureau, 'Putong Zhongxue Zhonghe Baobiao 1965–6 [Wuhan Middle Schools Statistics]'; 'Quanrizhi Xiaoxue Zhonghe Baobiao 1965–6 [Wuhan Elementary Schools Statistics]'; and 'Quanrizhi Jigong Zhiye Xuexiao Zhonghe Baobiao 1965–6 [Wuhan Technical Training Schools Statistics]'.

32. Interviewee 14.

33. Interviewees 10, 13, 15, 30, 31, 46, and 51.

34. Interviewee 13.

35. Interviewees 10, 13, and 15.

36. Interviewee 13.

37. Interviewees 10, and 69.

38. Interviewee 10.

39. Interviewee 53.

40. The Ministry of Education, *Zhongguo Jiaoyu Dashiji* [Chronicle of Chinese Education], Beijing: People's Education Press, 1986, p. 401.

41. *HBRB*, 20 June 1966; and *Wuhan Wanbao*, 20 June 1966.

42. *Deng Ken Zai Wuhan Shi Zhongxue Biyesheng Daibiao Huiyi Shang Di Jianghua* [Deng Ken's Speech at the Meeting of Middle School Graduates], 19 July 1966.

43. Interviewee 51.

44. In many key schools, the students from intellectual families were treated as if they were from exploitative classes. For instance, a girl did not get a recommendation for senior high from her good origin classmates because her father was a chief engineer and her mother a chief accountant. Her classmates reasoned: 'Before the Liberation, her family had a good life. Now her family still has a housekeeper. So it is better to send her to the countryside.' See Wuhan Senior High Admission Committee, 'Chuzhong Biyesheng Tuijian Gongzuo De Qingkuang Fanyin [Report on Recommendation of Junior High Graduates for Senior Highs]', September 1966.

45. Interviewees 52, 77, and 78.

46. *Wang Renzhong Hexurenye* [The Kind of Person Wang Renzhong Really

Is], December 1966.

47. *Chiweijun* [Red Guard Army], 14 April 1967.

48. For instance, the work team of the Wuhan Institute of Hydroelectric Engineering criticized only four students by name, but more than 200 students were criticized on the students' initiative: *Wang Renzhong Hexurenye*.

49. The Chinese Department of the Central China Teachers College provided a good example. The 1962 and 1964 classes of the department had 150 students. Although only eleven (7.3 per cent) in the former were criticized, forty-three (28.7 per cent) in the latter were attacked. In the Central China Institute of Technology as a whole, less than 5 per cent of the students were criticized. In a class of the Dynamics Engineering Department of the same institute, however, twenty-four out of thirty-one students were criticized, which made the range as high as 77 per cent.

In the 1964 class of the Chinese Department of the Central China Teachers College, nearly half of those attacked were good origin students who had been considered as backward elements. See *Chedi Pipan Hubei Shengwei Ziliao Huibian*.

50. *Wang Renzhong Sanfan Yanlunlu*.

51. The Socialist Education Movement work team was called *gongzuodui*, while the Cultural Revolution work team was called *gongzuozu*.

52. Interviewees 8, 12, 17, and 19.

53. Interviewees 26, 32, 65, and 66; and *Xinhuagong*, 1 June 1967.

54. Interviewees 2 and 70.

55. *Fangeming Xiuzhengzhuyi Fenzi Li Pingqing Fandong Yanlun Huibian* [Selected Reactionary Speeches of Counter-revolutionary Revisionist Li Pingqing], 26 October 1967; *Dadao Wuhan Touhao Zouzipai Song Kanfu* [Down with the Number One Capitalist Roader Song Kanfu], Vol. 2, July 1968; and interviewees 20, 24, 31, and 35.

56. Interviewees 31 and 72. On 18 June the WMPC issued an instruction requiring such a classification in all units. *Wang Renzhong Fandong Yanlunji* [Selected Reactionary Speeches of Wang Renzhong], *Fangeming Xiuzhengzhuyi Fenzi Song Kanfu De Zuixinglu*; and *Dadao Wuhan Touhao Zuozipai Song Kanfu*, Vol. 3.

57. *Xinhuagong* [New Central China Institute of Technology], 1 March and 24 March 1967; and interviewee 35.

58. Interviewees 26, 27, and 31.

59. Interviewees 12, 17, and 19.

60. Interviewee 31.

61. Interviewees 8, 12, and 19.

62. The Hubei Provincial Revolutionary Committee, *Wuchanjieji Wenhuadageming Wenjian Huibian* [Selected Documents of the Great Proletarian Cultural Revolution], 3 vols., Wuhan, 1968, Vol. 1, p. 142.

63. Interviewees 1, 6, 23, 25, 27, 70, 80, 81, and 84.

64. Interviewee 11.

Notes to Chapter 4

1. *Hubei Shengwei Shujichu Changwei Huiyi Jilu* [The Minutes of Meetings of the Hubei Provincial Party Committee Secretariat] (hereafter *HYJL*),

February 1967.

2. Hong Yung Lee, *The Politics of the Chinese Cultural Revolution: A Case Study*, Berkeley: University of California Press, 1978, pp. 26–63.

3. *Hubei Ribao* [Hubei Daily] (hereafter *HBRB*), 3 August 1966.

4. *HBRB*, 21 August 1966.

5. Interviewees 3, 16, 28, 80 and 81.

6. *Renmin Ribao* [People's Daily] (hereafter *RMRB*), 19 August 1966.

7. *Wuhan Dichu Wuchan Jieji Wenhua Dageming Dashiji* [Chronicle of the Great Proletarian Cultural Revolution in Wuhan] (hereafter *WWDJ*), August 1967.

8. *HBRB*, 20–30 August 1966.

9. *HYJL*.

10. Crane Brinton, *The Anatomy of Revolution*, New York: Vintage Books, 1965, pp. 178–80.

11. *HBRB*, 24–30 August 1966.

12. Interviewees 13, 14, 63 and 64.

13. Wuhan Party History Office, *Zhonggong Wuhan Dangshi Dashiji* [Chronicle of Wuhan Party History], Wuhan: Wuhan University Press, 1989, p. 324.

14. Wuhan Party History Office, *Zhonggong Wuhan Dangshi Dashiji*, p. 324.

15. *RMRB*, 23 August 1966.

16. *HYJL*.

17. Interviewee 49.

18. *People's Daily* published several editorials to persuade teenagers to observe discipline by 'learning from the PLA' and to use only verbal means of struggle rather than violence. See *RMRB*, 28 August and 5 September 1966.

19. *RMRB*, 26 August 1966.

20. Interviewees 36, 37 and 51.

21. Interviewee 69.

22. *Bingtuan Zhanbao* [Corps Battlefield Report], 25 March 1967.

23. *Zhongyang Fuzhe Tongzhi Jianghua Chaolu* [Selected Speeches of Central Leaders] (hereafter *JHCL*), 3 vols., Wuhan, 1967, Vol. 1, pp. 127, 164, 167 and 202.

24. *Hongqi* [Red Flag], 10 (1966).

25. *Chedi Pipan Hubei Shengwui Ziliao Huibian* [Selected Materials on Thoroughly Criticizing the HPPC], 29 October 1966.

26. *WWDJ* and *HYJL*.

27. *WWDJ*.

28. *HYJL* and *WWDJ*.

29. *HYJL*; and *Chedi Pipan Hubei Shengwei Ziliao Huibian*.

30. *Chedi Pipan Hubei Shengwei Ziliao Huibian*; *WWDJ*; and *HYJL*.

31. Pu was the initiator of the first Red Guard organization in Beijing; Song became famous as one of the people who had put on a Red Guard armband for Mao when he received Red Guards for the first time on 18 August.

32. Liang Liang, 'Yige Hongweibing Faqizhe De Zhishu [The Story of a Red Guard Initiator]', *Zhongguo Qingnian* [Chinese Youth], 8 (1986); and *JHCL*, 3: 119.

33. *Chedi Pipan Hubei Shengwei Ziliao Huibian*.

34. *Zhang Tixue Tongzhi Di Jianghua* [Comrade Zhang Tixue's Speech], 5 September 1966.

35. *Chedi Pipan Hubei Shengwei Ziliao Huibian.*

36. *HYJL.*

37. Zhao Cong, *Wenge Yundong Licheng Shulue* [A Concise History of the Cultural Revolution], 4 vols., Hong Kong: Union Research Institute, 1971–8, Vol. 1, pp. 309–11.

38. *Fangeming Xiuzheng Zhuyi Fenzi Wang Renzhong Zuixinglu* [Crimes Committed by Counter-revolutionary Revisionist Wang Renzhong], September 1967.

39. For instance, 'Zhang Tixue is a good student of Chairman Mao, and a close friend of poor and lower-middle peasants', and 'Attacking Zhang Tixue amounts to an attack on us—poor and lower-middle peasants.' Zhang was a popular leader among the peasants of the province. See *WWDJ.*

40. *HYJL.*

41. *Chedi Pipan Hubei Shengwei Ziliao Huibian.*

42. Ibid.

43. *WWDJ.*

44. *Chedi Pipan Hubei Shengwei Ziliao Huibian.*

45. *Pitao Zhanbao* [Battlefield Report on Criticizing Tao Zhu], 14 March 1967.

46. *JHCL*, Vol. 1, pp. 118 and 129.

47. *Chedi Pipan Hubei Shengwei Ziliao Huibian*; and interviewees 69 and 77.

48. *JHCL*, Vol. 1, pp. 225 and 268.

49. Some of the students from Beijing were natives of Wuhan. They led others to their *alma maters* to mobilize the local students. Interviewee 51.

50. Interviewees 50 and 51.

51. For instance, 2,000 out of 2,800 students of the Wuhan Water Transport Institute were organized by the Cultural Revolution committee of the institute to visit Beijing in late September. Interviewee 50.

52. For instance, Mao Zedong Thought Red Guards was established at the Central China Institute of Technology on 27 September, which then had only 700 members in a school of more than 10,000 students and faculty members. *Xinhuagong* [New Central China Institute of Technology], 10 August 1967.

53. The first local rebellious students tended to be from good and middle-origin backgrounds. It was still out of the question to recruit students from bad class backgrounds at that time.

54. As one of my interviewees put it: 'In Wuhan, I was a son of 'monsters and ghosts'. But in Beijing I was treated as a guest of Chairman Mao. I therefore rediscovered my own value.' Interviewee 49.

55. *JHCL*, Vol. 1, pp. 193 and 197.

56. *Lin Biao Wenxuan* [Selected Works of Lin Biao], Wuhan, 1968, pp. 256–8.

57. *JHCL*, Vol. 3, p. 263; and *Qiyue Fengbao* [July Storm], 13 February 1968.

58. *JHCL*, 3: 139; and *Pitao Zhanbao*, 14 March 1967.

59. *HYJL.*

60. *HBRB*, 11 October 1966.

61. On 19 October the HPPC made its collective self-criticism. Two days later, Zhang Tixue and Wang Shucheng made their personal self-criticisms.

During the following days, the local officials even held self-criticism sessions in various colleges. *Chedi Pipan Hubei Shengwei Ziliao Huibian.*

62. *WWDJ.*

63. *HBRB*, 13 September 1966.

64. *WWDJ.*

65. Interviewees 36, 37, 46, 49, 50, 51 and 69.

66. Interviewees 24, 27 and 50.

67. *WWJD.*

68. *Zaixianfeng* [On a Perilous Peak], 30 October 1967; and interviewees 50 and 77.

69. *JHCL*, Vol. 1, p. 261; and Vol. 2, pp. 86, 89, 225, 289.

70. Mario Von Cranach, 'Leadership as a Function of Group Action', in Carl F. Graumann and Serge Moscovici (eds.), *Changing Conception of Leadership*, New York: Springer-Verlag, 1986, pp. 117–18.

71. *JHCL*, Vol. 2, p. 96.

72. Interviewees 1, 2, 3, 7, 9, 16, 25, 26, 28, 65, 70, 72, 73, 80, 81, and 84.

73. Interviewees 8, 12, and 19.

74. Among them were Zhu Hongxia of Wuhan Heavy-Duty Machine Tool Factory and Hu Houming of Wuchang Shipyard. Interviewee 19.

75. Interviewees 12, 19 and 77.

76. *Guanyu Ganggongzong Wenti Diaocha Baogao* [Report on the Case of the Workers' Headquarters], July 1967.

77. Ibid.; and Jin Chunming, 'Shanghai Yiyue Fengbao Di Qianqian Houhou [The January Storm in Shanghai]', *Dangshi Tongxun* [Newsletter on Party History], 18 (1983).

78. *JHCL*, Vol. 2, p. 63.

79. Interviewees 19 and 77.

80. *Xinhuda* [New Hubei University], 16 September 1967.

81. *WWDJ.*

82. Interviewee 24.

83. Lin Biao characterized the situation in late 1966 as one in which the minority felt avenged while the majority was bullied. *Lin Biao Wenxuan*, p. 269.

84. Interviewees 2, 3, 25, 26, 33, 34, 52, 72, 73, 80, 81 and 84.

85. *Liangtiao Luxian De Dabodou* [Struggle between Two Lines], November 1966.

86. *Jiefang Ribao* [Liberation Daily] of Shanghai was closed on 31 November; *Hunan Ribao* [Hunan Daily] was closed on 3 December; and *Hongweibao* [Red Guard Daily] of Guangzhou, which had changed its name from *Nanfang Ribao* [South Daily] to *Hongweibao* in September, was closed on 13 December.

87. *WWDJ.*

88. Interviewee 52. The conservative worker organization of Beijing, the Guard Regiment, was established with 300,000 members on 19 November. Its counterpart in Shanghai, the Red Escort, was set up with 400,000 members on 26 November. See *Jinggangshan* [Jinggang Mountain], 22 December 1966; and *JHCL*, Vol. 2, p. 210.

89. *WWDJ.*

90. *JHCL*, Vol. 1, p. 254.

91. Zhou Enlai instructed that the evidence against 'real counter-revolutionary activities' should not be given out, regardless of whether it was collected

before or after 16 May 1966. *JHCL*, Vol. 2, p. 254.

92. Zhou Enlai later admitted, 'The problem of so-called "black materials" is a real headache for us.' *JHCL*, Vol. 3, p. 291.

93. *WWDJ*; and interviewees 80 and 81.

94. Interviewees 7, 25 and 52.

95. Interviewee 52.

96. *Xinhuda I* [New Hubei University], 2 March 1967; and *Xinhuagong* [New Central China Institute of Technology], 24 March 1967.

Notes to Chapter 5

1. *Zhongyang Fuzhe Tongzhi Jianghua Chaolu* [Selected Speeches of Central Leaders], Vol. 1, p. 102.

2. *Mao Zedong Sixiang Shengli Wansui* [Long Live Mao Zedong Thought], version 2, p. 346.

3. Anita Chan, *Children of Mao: Personality Development and Political Activism in the Red Guard Generation*, Seattle: University of Washington Press, 1985, p. 139.

4. Interviewee 69.

5. Interviewees 13, 14, 57, and 69. Also see Liu Guokai, *A Brief Analysis of the Cultural Revolution*, Armonk, NY: M. E. Sharpe, 1987; Hong Yung Lee, *The Politics of the Chinese Cultural Revolution: A Case Study*, Berkeley: University of California Press, 1978; Marc J. Blecher and Gordon White, *Macropolitics in Contemporary China: A Technical Unit during and after the Cultural Revolution*, White Plains, NY: M. E. Sharpe, 1979; and Stanley Rosen, *Red Guard Factionalism and the Cultural Revolution in Guangzhou (Canton)*, Boulder, CO: Westview Press, 1982.

6. *Yangzijiang Pinglun* [Yangtze Review], 20 June 1968; and interviewees 61 and 62.

7. *Wenge Pinglun* [The Cultural Revolution Review], January 1968.

8. *Guanyu Ganggongzong Wenti Diaocha Baogao* [Report on the Case of Workers' Headquarters], July 1967; *Xinhuagong* [New Central China Institute of Technology], 24 March 1967; *Hou Lianzheng Hezuizhiyou* [Who is Hou Liangzheng?], March 1968; *Changjiang Ribao* [Yangtze Daily], 1–2 December 1977; and interviewees 35 and 59.

9. *Wuhan Gongren* [Wuhan Workers], 10 May 1969; and interviewees 19 and 23.

10. Interviewees 16, 20, 24, 35, 51, 71, and 78.

11. Interviewee 24.

12. Interviewees 6, 8, 12, 15, 19, 20, and 35. Liu Guokai also notes that 'one cannot equate the "rebels" or "conservatives" who were active within their own units with those "rebels" or "conservatives" who operated on a much wider scope in society at large.' Liu Guokai, *A Brief Analysis of the Cultural Revolution*, pp. 81–2.

13. Interviewees 10 and 24.

14. *Wang Renzhong Zuixingji* [Crimes Committed by Wang Renzhong], March 1967.

15. *Wuhan Dichu Wuchan Jieji Wenhua Dageming Dashiji* [Chronicle of the Great Proletarian Cultural Revolution in Wuhan], August 1967.

16. *Yangzijiang Pinglun*, 20 June 1968.

17. Interviewees 2, 6, 35, 58, 60, and 62.

18. Feng Jicai, *Voices from the Whirlwind: An Oral History of the Chinese Cultural Revolution*, New York: Pantheon Books, 1991, pp. 149–50.

19. Interviewees 15 and 49.

20. Dennis Chong, *Collective Action and the Civil Rights Movement*, Chicago: University of Chicago Press, 1991, p. 147.

21. Hardin, 'Acting Together, Contributing Together', *Rationality and Society*, 3, 3, (1991): 366–8.

22. Interviewees 25, 70, 73, 74, 80, 81, and 84.

23. Interviewees 9, 10, 11, 13, 14, 15, 26, 29, 30, 32, 33, 34, 49, 50, 60, 65, and 67.

24. Interviewees 1, 2, 3, 5, 6, 7, 8, 12, 16, 17, 18, 19, 20, 21, 23, 24, 27, 28, 31, 35, 42, 52, 59, 67, 72, and 75.

25. Interviewee 51.

26. Interviewees 15, 29, and 30.

27. Interviewees 65 and 66.

28. Interviewee 31.

29. Two of my interviewees who at one time were involved in the leadership of the Second Headquarters observed: 'Mass organizations did not have any internal binding force at all. Every group wanted to recruit as many members as possible so that they could not take any disciplinary action against its members. The Second Headquarters was no more than a loose coalition. Since its branches did not have to follow the guidelines set by the headquarters, the headquarters had little control over the actions of its branches. Within the headquarters there were no commonly accepted procedure for making decisions. The process of decision formation was therefore always one of fierce wrangling. Even when a decision had been reached, there was no guarantee that the branches would follow it. And what is worse, the branches would flaunt the banner of the Second Headquarters while pursuing their narrow group interests.' Interviewees 50 and 51.

30. Andrew G. Walker, 'Communist Social Structure and Workers' Politics in China', in Victor C. Falkenhein (ed.), *Citizens and Groups in Contemporary China*, Ann Arbor: Center for Chinese Studies, University of Michigan, 1987, p. 84.

31. Interviewees 24, 49, and 57.

32. Interviewees 1, 26, 41, 45, 52, 72, and 73.

33. James G. March and Herbert A. Simon, *Organizations*, New York: John Wiley & Sons, 1958, pp. 2–4.

34. For instance, in October and November there was a widely circulated article which was said to be 'Chairman Mao's second *dazibao*'. See *Hongweibing* [The Red Guard], 16 November 1966.

Notes to Chapter 6

1. Michael Taylor, *Community, Anarchy and Liberty*, Cambridge: Cambridge University Press, 1982, pp. 39–58.

2. For a good analysis of the phenomenon of economism, see Evelyn Anderson, 'Shanghai: The Masses Unleashed', *Problems of Communism*, 17 (1968).

3. *Wuhan Dichu Wuchan Jieji Wenhua Dageming Dashiji* [Chronicle of the Great Proletarian Cultural Revolution in Wuhan] (hereafter *WWDJ*). Some authors have exaggerated the role of contract and temporary workers in the rebel faction. See Hong Yung Lee, *The Politics of the Chinese Cultural Revolution: A Case Study*, Berkeley: University of California Press, 1978. In fact, occupational cleavage was not an important factor in the factional strife of the Cultural Revolution. Contract and temporary workers never represented the mainstream of the rebel movement. Most rebels were politically motivated rather than inspired merely by short-term economic gains.

4. The Hubei Provincial Revolutionary Committee, *Wuchanjieji Wenhuadageming Wenjian Huibian* [Selected Documents of the Great Proletarian Cultural Revolution] (hereafter *WJHB*), Vol. 1, pp. 178, 233–5, 241–3; *Changjiang Ribao* [Yangtze Daily] (hereafter *CJRB*), 21 February 1967; and *82 zhanbao* [2 August Battlefield Report], 28 April 1968.

5. Interviewee 14; and *CJRB*, 22, 24, and 30 January, and 1 February 1967.

6. This section mainly draws on four sources: *WWDJ*; *Xinhuda* [New Hubei University], 2 March 1967; *CJRB*, 22 February 1967; and *Chedi Maizang Wuhan Dichu Fangeming Xiuzhen Zhuyi Jituan* [Bury the Counter-revolutionary Revisionist Group of Wuhan], Vol. 2, December 1967. For a secondary account about the power seizure in Wuhan, see Deborah S. Davis, 'The Cultural Revolution in Wuhan', in *The Cultural Revolution in the Provinces*, Cambridge, MA: Harvard East Asian Monographs, No. 42, pp. 147–70.

7. Zhang Chunqiao once laid bare this secret with one remark: 'The primary purpose of the power seizure was to keep our economy functioning and to arrest the spread of economism'. *Guangyin Hongqi* [Guangzhou Printing House Red Flag], 23 November 1967.

8. *WWDJ*; *Xinhuda*, 2 March 1967; *CJRB*, 5 February 1967; and Hubei Ribao [Hubei Daily] (hereafter *HBRB*), 6 February 1967. The *Yangtze Daily* was the former *Wuhan Evening News*, which then was controlled by the Red Building coalition of rebel organizations. The *Hubei Daily* was under the control of a non-Red Building coalition of rebel organizations.

9. *CJRB*, 8, 9, and 12 February 1967; and interviewees 8, 11, 49, 50, and 51.

10. Interviewees 46, 47, 49, 50, and 67; *CJRB*, 10 February 1967; and *Hongbayue Zaofanbao* [Red August Rebels], 27 February 1967.

11. *CJRB*, 21 February 1967; and *Xinhuagong* [New Central China Institute of Technology], 23 February 1967.

12. At the Wuhan Heavy Machinery factory, for instance, twenty party members were expelled in January. See *Guanyu Ganggongzong Wenti Diaocha Baogao* [Report on the Case of Workers' Headquarters], July 1967. Later the Central Committee of the CCP issued a circular to prohibit non-Party people from deciding the affairs of Party organizations. See *WJHB*, Vol. 1, pp. 222–3.

13. *Dongfanghong* [East is Red], 22 March 1967; *Jinjunbao* [March Daily], 5 March 1967; and *Jinggangshan* [Jinggan Mountain], 8 February 1967.

14. On 20 January alone, more than 6,000 people wearing dunce caps were paraded through the streets by the rebels in Wuhan. *Xinhuagong*, 8, 23, and 24 February 1967.

15. *Duoquan Zhanbao* [Power Seizure Battlefield Report], 12 February 1967.

16. *Xinhuagong*, 4 February 1967.

17. *Mao Zedong Sixiang Shengli Wansui* [Long Live Mao Zedong Thought]

(hereafter *Wansui*), version 2, p. 341; and *Zhongyang Fuzhe Tongzhi Jianghua Chaolu* [Selected Speeches of Central Leaders] (hereafter *JHCL*), Vol. 3, pp. 139, 166, 168.

18. *WJHB*, Vol. 1, pp. 256–9.

19. *WJHB*, Vol. 1, pp. 219–21, 264, 282.

20. *Renmin Ribao* [People's Daily] (hereafter *RMRB*), 31 January 1967.

21. *JHCL*, Vol. 3, p. 283; and *Zhang Chunqiao Yao Wenyuan Tongzhi Zai Shanghai Shi Geming Weiyuanhui Baogaohui Shang De Jianghua* [The Speeches of Zhang Chunqiao and Yao Wenyuan at a Meeting of the Shanghai Municipal Revolutionary Committee], 3 June 1967.

22. *Wansui*, version 3, p. 667.

23. Chen Zaidao, '720 Shijian Shimo [The Whole Story of the July 20 Incident]', in *Gemingshi Ziliao* [Materials on Revolutionary History], Beijing: Historical Material Publishing House, 1981, Vol. 12.

24. *WWDJ*; and *Chen Zaidao Yu Zhibao* [Chen Zaidao and His Support of the Conservatives], August 1967.

25. Zhao Cong, *Wenge Yundong Licheng Shulue* [A Concise History of the Cultural Revolution], Vol. 2, pp. 640, 686–9, 700–1, and 904.

26. Chen Zaidao, '720 shijian shimo'.

27. *Chen Zaidao Yu Zhibao*.

28. *Xinhuagong*, 11 and 23 February 1967; and *Hongbayue Zaofanbao*, 2 and 21 February 1967.

29. *WWDJ*.

30. Chen Zaidao, '720 shijian shimo'; and *WWDJ*.

31. *WWDJ*; and *Jiangcheng Fengbao* [Wuhan Storm], August 1967.

32. *WWDJ*; and *Chen Zaidao Zhibao Zuixinglu* [Chen Zaidao Crimes in Supporting the Conservatives], May 1967.

33. *Chen Zaidao Zhong Hanhua Zhiliu Fangeming Zuixing* [Crimes Committed by Chen Zaidao, Zhong Hanhua, and the Like], November 1967; Chen Zaidao, '720 Shijian Shimo'; and interviewees 19 and 53.

34. *Qiandaowangua Chen Zaidao* [Slash Chen Zaidao], August 1967; and interviewee 51.

35. Interviewees 46, 47, 49, 50, and 51.

36. *Qiandaowangua Chen Zaidao*, August 1967.

37. Interviewees 51, 54, and 77.

38. *HBRB*, 4 March 1967; *WWDJ*; *Chen Zaidao Zhibao Zuixinglu*; and *Chedi Jiekai Shengwei Zhuaban Di Heimu* [The Inside Story of the Provincial Office of Grasping Revolution and Promoting Production], 14 September 1967.

39. *WWDJ*; and interviewees 54 and 77.

40. *Qiandaowangua Chen Zaidao*.

41. Ibid.

42. *Chen Zaidao Zhong Hanhua De Zuizheng* [Evidence against Chen Zaidao and Zhong Hanhua], 1 September 1967; *Zhanduan Chen Zaidao Zhiliu Shengxiang Jiedao Zhong De Mozhao* [Cut off Chen Zaidao's Hands in Neighbourhood Committees], 28 November 1967; and interviewees 26, 42, 52, 72, and 73.

43. *Chen Zaidao Yu Zhibao*; and interviewees 24, 47, 48, and 52.

44. *913 Zhanbao* [13 September Corps' Battlefield Report], 21 July 1967.

45. *Chen Zaidao Zhong Hanhua Zhiliu Fangeming Zuixing; Qiandaowangua Chen Zaidao*; *Hubei Xinhua Yinshuachang Geweihui* [The Revolutionary

Committee of Hubei Xinhua Printing House], 26 December 1967; and interviewees 35 and 67.

46. Radio Hubei, 28 February, and 8 and 11 March 1967.

47. *Chedi Jiekai Shengwei Zhuaban Di Heimu.*

48. Radio Hubei, 15 March 1967.

49. *Qiyue fangbao* [July Storm], September 1967; *Chen Zaidao Yu Zhibao*; and *Chen Zaidao Zhibao Zuixinglu,* May 1967.

50. *Chedi Jiekai Shengwei Zhuaban Di Heimu.*

51. Radio Hubei, 2, 5, 11, 13, 15, and 19 March 1967; and interviewees 26, 35, and 67.

52. Radio Hubei, 15 and 30 March 1967.

53. *Fangeming Xiuzhengzhuyi Fenzi Liu Huilong Zuixing Dashiji* [Major Crimes Committed by Counter-revolutionary Revisionist Liu Huilong], 10 March 1968.

54. Centre for Chinese Research Materials, *Red Guard Publications: Supplement I,* Vol. 4, pp. 1721–2.

55. *Zhengfa Gongse* [Legal Commune], 22 March 1967; *Jinggangshan,* 15 March 1967; *Jinjunbao,* 15 March 1967; and *Xinbeida* [New Beijing University], 16 March 1967.

56. *WWDJ*; *Xinhuda,* 11 April 1967; *Yangzijiang Pinglun* [Yangtze Review], 7 September 1967; and *Chen Zaidao Zuixinglu.*

57. Xiang Jinhong: 'Han Aijing De Longpaomeng [Han Aijing's Wild Dream]', in *Zhongguo Qingnian* [Chinese Youth], 8 (1986); and *RMRB,* 2 April 1967.

58. *WJHB,* Vol. 1, pp. 314–21, 326–30, 332–43, 354–63, and 413–14.

59. *Guanyu Ganggongzong Weiti De Diaocha Baogao*; and interviewees 24 and 35.

60. *WWDJ*; *Xinhuagong,* 15 June 1968; and *Chen Zaidao Zhibao Zuixinglu.*

61. *Yangzijiang Pinglun,* 7 September 1967.

62. Radio Hubei, 1 April 1967.

63. *WWDJ*; and *Guanyu Ganggongzong Weiti Diaocha Baogao.*

64. Chen Zaidao, '720 Shijian Shimo'.

65. *Dadao Fangeming Xiuzheng Zhuyi Fenzi Chen Zaidao* [Down with Counter-revolutionary Revisionist Chen Zaidao], September 1967.

66. Chen Zaidao, '720 Shijian Shimo'.

Notes to Chapter 7

1. Chen Zaidao, '720 Shijian Shimo [The Whole Story of the 20 July Incident]'.

2. *Dadao Fangeming Fenzi Chen Zaidao* [Down with Counter-revolutionary Chen Zaidao], August 1967; and *Chen Zaidao Zhong Hanhua De Zuizheng* [Evidence against Chen Zaidao and Zhong Hanhua], 1 September 1967.

3. *Chen Zaidao Zhibao Zuixinglu* [Chen Zaidao's Crimes in Supporting the Conservatives], May 1967; *Chen Zaidao Yu Zhibao* [Chen Zaidao and the Support of the Conservatives], August 1967; and interviewees 24 and 48.

4. Interviewees 26 and 37.

5. *Xinhuagong* [New Central China Institute of Technology], 8 September 1967.

6. *Lun Ge Yu Bao* [On Revolution and Conservatism], 10 May 1967.

7. The number included members in suburban districts. Interviewees 26 and 52.

8. *Qiyue Fengbao* [July Storm], 25 September 1967; and interviewees 26, 52, and 72.

9. *Wuhan Gongan Zhengya Geming Qunzhong Yundong De Taotian Zuixing* [The Wuhan Public Security's Crime in Suppressing Revolutionary Mass Movement], no date; and interviewees 26 and 52. Do not confuse the Wuhan Public Security with the Wuhan Public Security Bureau. The former was a mass organization made up of policemen, which was an intimate ally of the Million Heroes but technically not a participant.

10. *Qiyue Fengbao*, 28 August and 28 October 1967; and *Wuhan Baiwanxiongshi 754 Bingtuan Zuixinglu* [The Crimes of the 754 Corps of the Million Heroes], July 1968.

11. William H. Riker, *The Theory of Political Coalitions*, New Haven, CT: Yale University Press, 1962.

12. Ibid.

13. *Xinhuagong*, 18 May 1967; *Yangzijiang Pinglun* [Yangtze Review], 7 September 1967; and interviewees 48, 50, and 67.

14. *Xinhuda*, 1 August 1967; and interviewees 53 and 74.

15. *Xinhuda* [New Hubei University], 25 April 1967; *Gongjianfa Yixiaocuo Huaitoutou Fandong Zuixinglu* [The Reactionary Crimes Committed by a Handful of Evil Leaders of the Wuhan Law Enforcement], 20 September 1967; and interviewee 53.

16. *Yangzijiang Pinglun*, 7 September 1967; and interviewee 53.

17. *Xinhuda*, 16 September 1967.

18. *Dadao Fangeming Xiuzheng Zhuyi Fenzi Chen Zaidao* [Down with Counter-revolutionary Revisionist Chen Zaidao], September 1967.

19. Interviewees 2, 3, 16, 25, 33, 52, and 80.

20. *Yangzijiang Pinglun*, 7 September 1967; and interviewees 24 and 77.

21. *Wuhan Dichu Wuchan Jieji Wenhua Dageming Dashiji* [Chronicle of the Great Proletarian Cultural Revolution in Wuhan] (hereafter *WWDJ*).

22. *Dadao Fangeming Xiuzhengzhuyi Fenzi Chen Zaidao*.

23. James D. Fearon, 'War, Relative Power, and Private Information', Paper presented at the 50th Annual Meeting of the Midwest Political Science Association, 9–11 April 1992, Palmer House Hilton, Chicago.

24. The concept is borrowed from a theory of international relations. See Robert Jervis, 'Cooperation under the Security Dilemma', *World Politics* (1978): 167–214.

25. Kenneth Waltz, *Man, the State, and War*, New York: Columbia University Press, 1959.

26. *Dadao Fangeming Fenzi Chen Zaidao*; and *WWDJ*.

27. Interviewees 23, 26, and 72.

28. The Hubei Provincial Revolutionary Committee, *Wuchanjieji Wenhuadageming Wenjian Huibian* [Selected Documents of the Great Proletarian Cultural Revolution], Vol. 1, p. 387.

29. Interviewees 26, 37, and 52.

30. *WWDJ*.

31. *Qiyue Jiangcheng Zhanqihong* [Red Flag of July in Wuhan], August

1967.

32. *WWDJ*.

33. Interviewee 26.

34. Interviewee 23.

35. *Kangbao* [Resist Suppression], no date; and interviewees 26 and 52.

36. *Qiyue Jiangcheng Zhangihong*; and interviewees 26, 50, and 52.

37. *Buwang 624* [Never Forget 24 June], 24 June 1968.

38. Interviewee 72.

39. *Gongzao Zongshi* [Workers' Rebel Headquarters], 24 August 1967; *Wuhan Gangershi* [Wuhan Second Headquarters], 30 August 1967; and interviewees 8, 23, 43, 46, and 51.

40. *Jiangcheng Fengbao* [Wuhan Storm], August 1967.

41. *Wuhan Gongjianfa Fujing Huibaotuan Zuiezhixing* [The Trip to Beijing by Wuhan Law Enforcement's Delegation], December 1967.

42. Chen Zaidao, '720 Shijian shimo'; and *WWDJ*.

43. *Xinhuagong*, 12 July 1967; and interviewees 43, 46, and 50.

44. *Chen Zaidao Yu Zhibao*, August 1967.

45. *Qiyue Fengbao*, September 1967; and Chen Zaidao, '720 Shijian Shimo'.

46. *Dadao Fangeming Xiuzhengzhuyi Fenzi Chen Zaidao*; and *Jiangcheng Zhuangge* [A Glorious Epic in Wuhan], October 1967.

47. *Wuhan Dongjianfa Fujing Huibaotuan Zuiezhixing*.

48. *WWDJ*.

49. *Chen Zaidao Zhibao Zuixinglu*; and *Chedi Jiekai Shengwei Zhuaban De Heimu* [The Inside Story of the Provincial Office of Grasping Revolution and Promoting Production], 4 September 1967.

50. Interviewees 1, 8, 16, 20, 25, 26, 41, 52, 67, and 70.

51. For secondary accounts on the Wuhan Incident, see Thomas W. Robinson, 'The Wuhan Incident', *China Quarterly*, 47 (1971): 413–38; and Yu-shen Chien, *China's Fading Revolution: Army Dissent and Military Divisions, 1967–1968*, Hong Kong: Centre of Contemporary Chinese Studies, 1969.

52. Chen Zaidao, '720 Shijian Shimo'.

53. *Xinhuagong*, 16 September 1967; and interviewees 26 and 52.

54. Chen Zaidao, '720 Shijian Shimo'.

55. *Wuhan Dichu Wuchanjieji Gemingpai Zaijing Douzheng Fangeming Xiuzhengzhuyi Fenzi Chen Zaidao Dahui Jishi* [Report on a Denouncement Session against Counter-revolutionary Revisionist Chen Zaidao in Beijing], December 1967.

56. Chen Zaidao, '720 Shijian Shimo'.

57. *Qiyue Fengbao*, September 1967.

58. *Chedi Maizang Wuhan Dichu Fangeming Xiuzhengzhuyi Jituan* [Bury the Counter-revolutionary Revisionist Group of Wuhan], Vol. 2, December 1967; and interviewees 26 and 37.

59. Chen Zaidao, '720 Shijian Shimo'; and interviewees 26 and 37.

60. *Wuhan Gongan Jianghan Fenbu Zuixing Cailiao* [Materials on the Crimes Committed by the Jianghan Branch of the Wuhan Public Security], Vol. 4, December 1967.

61. Chen Zaidao, '720 Shijian Shimo'; and interviewees 26, 37, and 53.

62. *Wuhan Gangershi*, 8 September 1967; and Chen Zaidao, '720 Shijian Shimo'.

63. *Chen Zaidao Zhong Hanhua Zhiliu Fangeming Zuixing* [Crimes Committed by Chen Zaidao, Zhong Hanhua, and the Like].

64. *Qiyue Bingbian De Pochan* [The Failure of the July Mutiny], August 1967; and *Chen Zaidao Yu Zhibao.*

65. *Wuhan Gangershi*, 8 September 1967.

66. *Changjiang Ribao* [Yangtze Daily], 7 September 1967.

67. *Qiyue Bingbian De Pochan.*

68. *Chen Zaidao Yu Zhibao*; and *WWDJ.*

69. Chen Zaidao, '720 Shijian Shimo'.

70. *Xinhuda*, 28 July 1967; and interviewees 46, 54, 57, and 78.

71. *Wuhan Gongan Zhengya Geming Qunzhong Yundong De Taotian Zuixing.*

72. *Renmin Ribao* [People's Daily], 23 July 1967.

73. *Wenhua Dageming Xuexi Wenxuan* [Study Materials of the Cultural Revolution], Vol. 12 (1967), pp. 35–40.

74. *Liehuo* [Raging Flames], September 1967.

75. Interviewee 37.

76. *Gongjianfa Yixiaocuo Huai Toutou Fandong Zuixinglu.*

77. *Zhengjing Quanguo De 720 Fangeming Baoluan* [The July 20 Counter-revolutionary Revolt that Shocked the Whole Country], August 1967.

78. Interviewees 2, 3, 33, 37, and 73.

Notes to Chapter 8

1. William Hinton, *Hundred Day War: The Cultural Revolution at Tsinghua University*, New York: Monthly Review Press, 1972, p. 123.

2. *Xinhuda* [New Hubei University], 11 August 1967.

3. Hai Feng, *An Account of the Cultural Revolution in the Canton Area*, Hong Kong: Union Research Institute, 1971, pp. 176 and 213.

4. The Hubei Provincial Revolutionary Committee, *Wuchanjieji Wenhuadageming Wenjian Huibian* [Selected Documents of the Great Proletarian Cultural Revolution] (hereafter *WJHB*), Vol. 2, pp. 426–33.

5. Wuhan Party History Office, *Zhonggong Wuhan Dangshi Dashiji* [Chronicle of Wuhan Party History], p. 331.

6. Interviewees 46, 48, 51, 54, 69, and 72; and *Xinhuda Tongxun* [Newsletter of New Hubei University], 24 August 1967.

7. *Hongwuce* [Red Wuhan Institute of Topography], 5 September 1967.

8. Zhao Cong, *Wenge Yundong Licheng Shulue* [A Concise History of the Cultural Revolution] (hereafter WGSL), Vol. 3, pp. 214–18 and 411.

9. *Hongwuce*, 5 and 18 September 1967; and *WGSL*, Vol. 3, pp. 288–308.

10. *Renmin Ribao* [People's Daily] (hereafter *RMRB*), 24–31 July 1967.

11. Interviewees 1, 2, 16, 33, 34, 65, and 66.

12. Interviewees 1, 2, 10, 11, 26, 37, 42, 52, 53, 67, and 70.

13. Interviewees 10, 52, and 72.

14. *Xinhuagong* [New Central China Institute of Technology], 12 February 1968; and *Changjiang Ribao* [Yangtze Daily] (hereafter *CJRB*), 14 August and 3 September 1967.

15. *Xinzhongyuan* [New Zhongyuan Machine], 17 October 1967; and interviewees 7, 8, 25, and 84.

16. *Xin Shierzhong* [New No. 12 Middle School], 24 August 1967.

17. Interviewees 31, 55, 65, 66, and 74.

18. *Xinhuagong*, 5 August 1967.

19. *Xinhuagong*, 5 and 10 August 1967; and interviewees 1, 6, 20, 23, 25, 50, and 52.

20. Chen Zaidao, '720 Shijian Shimo [The Whole Story of the 20 July Incident]', p. 42.

21. *Xinhuagong*, 5 August 1967; and interviewees 46 and 50.

22. Interviewees 1, 2, 3, 4, 9, 18, 33, 34, 43, 52, 67 and 72.

23. Interviewees 12, 24, 60, and 69; and *CJRB*, 20 November 1967.

24. *CJRB*, 19 September 1967, and 26 February 1968; *Xinhuagong*, 20 August, 2 September, and 13 November 1967; *Xinshuiyuan* [New Water Transport Institute], October 1967; *Wuhan Gangersi* [Wuhan Second Headquarters], 30 August 1967; *Qiyue Fengbao* [July Storm], 25 September 1967; and interviewees 46, 61, and 62.

25. *CJRB*, 4 January 1968; *Yangzijiang Pinglun* [Yangtze Review], 16 July 1968; and *Wuhan Gongren* [Wuhan Workers], 24 February 1968.

26. *WJHB*, Vol. 2, pp. 692–4, 868–9.

27. *CJRB*, 21 September and 21 December 1967, 10 and 11 January, 6 and 22 March 1968; *WJHB*, Vol. 2, pp. 787–8; and interviewee 14.

28. *Wuhan Hongdaihui* [Wuhan Congress of Red Guards], 18 May 1968; and *CJRB*, 22 December 1967, and 21 and 27 March and 13 April 1968.

29. *Wuhan Sanjiancun An* [The Case of the Three-family Village at Wuhan University], September 1967; and interviewee 49.

30. *Fangeming Xiuzheng Zhuyi Fenzi Cheng Yun Fandong Yanlun Huiban* [Selected Reactionary Speeches of Counter-revolutionary Revisionist Cheng Yun], Vol. 3, January 1968; and interviewee 32.

31. *CJRB*, 27 March 1968; and interviewees 55 and 74.

32. *Xinhuagong*, August 1968; and *CJRB*, 22 December 1967, 21 and 27 March, and 13 April 1968.

33. Interviewees 51, 60, and 69.

34. William H. Riker, *The Theory of Political Coalitions*, New Haven, CT: Yale University Press, 1962.

35. It was so because the Workers' Headquarters, the Second Headquarters, and the 13 September Corps often affixed the adjective *gang* (literally meaning 'steel' but in the context meaning 'strong') to the names of their organizations; and the names of several major organizations in the Poisonous Weed Faction contained the character *xin* ('new').

36. *Wuhan Shijian* [The Wuhan Incident], August 1967.

37. *Yangzijiang Pinglun*, 7 September 1967; *Xinhuagong*, 28 September 1967; *Wuhan Gangersi*, 31 October 1967; and *CJRB*, 18 August 1967.

38. Interviewees 8 and 35.

39. *Xinhuagong*, 5 and 20 August 1967; and *Xinhuda*, 16 September 1967.

40. *RMRB*, 19 August 1967.

41. *Wuhan Gangersi*, 20 August 1967; and *Yangzijiang Pinglun*, 7 September 1967.

42. *Xinhuagong*, 14 September 1967.

43. *Renda Sanhong* [The Three Reds at People's University], 31 August 1967; and *Xin Shierzhong*, 24 August 1967.

44. *Wuhan Gangersi*, 31 August 1967.
45. *Wuhanshi Geming Gongdaihui Choubei Xiaozhu Huitai Jiyao* [The Summary of Negotiation on the Formation of Wuhan Revolutionary Workers' Congress], 5 November 1967.
46. Interviewee 24.
47. *Xinhuagong*, August 1968.
48. *RMRB*, 18 and 22 September 1967.
49. *CJRB*, 24 September 1967.
50. *Wuhan Gangersi*, 1 October 1967; and *Gongzao Zongsi* [Wuhan Workers' Rebel Headquarters], 27 September and 20 October 1967.
51. *Xinhuagong*, 28 September 1967.
52. *Wuhanshi Geming Gongdaihui Choubei Xiaozhu Huitan Jiyao*.
53. *CJRB*, 8–13 October 1967.
54. *Xindongzhong* [New East Lake Middle School], 15 October 1967.
55. *CJRB*, 12–23 October 1967.
56. The six organizations were the Second Headquarters, the New Central China Institute of Technology, the New Hubei University, the New Central China Agricultural College, the Revolutionary Committee of the Third Headquarters, and the United Headquarters of Mao Zedong Thought Red Guard of Secondary Schools. *Xinhuagong*, 17 November 1967; and *Wuhan Gangersi*, 14 October 1967.
57. *Wuhanshi Geming Gongdaihui Choubei Xiaozhu Huitan Jiyao*.
58. *WJHB*, Vol. 2, pp. 565–6.
59. *Wuhanshi Geming Gongdaihui Choubei Xiaozhu Huitan Jiyao*.
60. *Xinhuagong*, 17 November 1967; and *Xinhuda*, 26 June 1968.
61. *Wuhan Gangersi*, 15 November 1967.
62. *Wuhan Gangersi*, 23 October, 5 November, and 14 December 1967; *Hongbayue Gongshe* [Red August Commune], 26 October, and 14 and 20 November 1967; and interviewee 50.
63. *Xinhuda*, 2 November 1967.
64. *Hongbayue Gongshe*, 14 and 20 November 1967.
65. Jean Esmein, *Chinese Cultural Revolution*, New York: Anchor Books, 1973, p. 221; K. S. Karol, *Second Chinese Revolution*, New York: Hill & Wang, 1968, p. 314.
66. *Wuhan Gangersi*, 6 and 10 November 1967.
67. *Hongbayue Gongshe*, 14 November 1967.
68. *Wuhan Gangersi*, 10 November 1967; and *Buwang 624* [Never Forget 24 June], 24 November 1967.
69. *Xinhuagong*, 17 November 1967; *Wuhan Gangersi*, 31 October 1967; and *Hongbayue Gongshe*, 14 November 1967.

Notes to Chapter 9

1. *Zhongyang Shouzhang Jianqhua* [Speeches of Central Leaders], October 1967, p. 14.
2. Robert Axelrod, 'The Emergence of Cooperation Among Egoists', *American Political Science Review*, 75 (1981): 306–18.
3. 'Beijing Fijianban Neimu [The Inside Story of the Fujian Class]', *Guanchajia* [Observers], 1 (1979).

4. *Xinroulian* [New Slaughterhouse], 8 December 1967; and interviewees 24 and 69.

5. *Wuhan Hongdaihui* [Wuhan Congress of Red Guards], 23 December 1967; and *Wuhan Gongren* [Wuhan Workers], 1 January 1968.

6. *Changjiang Ribao* [Yangtze Daily] (hereafter *CJRB*), 17 December 1967.

7. *Wuhan Gongren*, 22 January 1968; and *Wuhan Hongdaihui*, 23 December 1967.

8. *Zhouzongli Zhongyao Jianghua* [Speeches of Premier Zhou], February 1968.

9. *Jiefeng Junbao* [The PLA Daily] (hereafter *JFJB*), 28 January 1968.

10. *Renmin Ribao* [People's Daily] (hereafter *RMRB*), 1 January 1968.

11. The Hubei Provincial Revolutionary Committee, *Wuchanjieji Wenhuadageming Wenjian Huibian* [Selected Documents of the Great Proletarian Cultural Revolution] (hereafter *WJHB*), Vol. 2, p. 630.

12. *Wuhan Gongren*, 18 January 1968; *JFJB*, 13 February 1968; *CJRB*, 17 November 1967, and 16 January and 13 February 1968; and *WJHB*, Vol. 2, p. 661.

13. *WJHB*, Vol. 1, pp. 9–11, and Vol. 2, p. 586; and RMRB, 21 October 1967.

14. *Wuhan Gongren*, 15 and 18 January 1968; and interviewees 4, 5, 15, and 22.

15. Interviewees 2, 3, 6, 8, 9, 33, and 34; and *CJRB*, 15 September 1967.

16. Interviewees 12, 21, and 74.

17. Wang Ming was a protegé of Stalin in the CCP leadership in the 1930s. He was purged during the Yan'an Rectification Movement (1942–4).

18. *Xinhuagong* [New Central China Institute of Technology], August 1968.

19. *Wuhanshi Sanjiehe Ganbu Jianjie* [The Profiles of Cadre Candidates for the WMRC], 20 January 1968.

20. *Xinhuagong*, August 1968; and *Fangeming Fenzi Liu Zhen De Zibai* [The Confession of Counter-revolutionary Liu Zhen], June 1967.

21. *Guanyu Xue Puruo Wenti De Cailiao* [Materials on the Problems of Xue Puruo], 15 January 1968.

22. *Geganlian* [The Federation of Revolutionary Cadres], 5 January 1968.

23. *Xinhuagong*, August 1968.

24. *Xinhuagong*, 21 October 1968; *Xinhuda* [New Hubei University], 10 January and 26 June 1968; and *Xinhuda Tongxun* [Newsletter of New Hubei University], 14 January 1968.

25. *Xinhuagong*, August 1968; *Xinhuda*, 10 and 26 January 1968; *Xinhuda Tongxun*, 14 January and 26 June 1968; and interviewees 8, 24, 51, 69, and 77.

26. *Lin Biao Wenxuan* [Selected Works of Lin Biao], pp. 244–5.

27. *Guanyu Xie Puruo Wenti De Cailiao*; *Wuhanshi Sanjiehe Ganbu Jianjie*; *Guanyu Yang Chunting Tongzhi De Diaocha Baogao* [Investigation Report on Comrade Yang Chunting], September 1967; and *Shengshi Geming Sanjiehe Ganbu Jianjie* [The Profiles of Cadre Candidates for the HPRC and the WMRC], February 1968.

28. *Xinhuda*, 10 August 1968.

29. *Zhongyang Shouzhang Zuixin Zhongyao Jianghua Huiji* [Latest Speeches of Central Leaders], April 1968.

30. *WJHB*, Vol. 2, pp. 795–810.

31. *CJRB*, 20 January and 7 February 1968.

32. *Xinhuda Tongxun*, 24 January 1968; and *WJHB*, Vol. 2, p. 808.

33. *WJHB*, Vol. 2, p. 796.

34. *Xinhuda*, 26 June 1968; *Xinhuagong*, 26 June 1968; and interviewees 54 and 60.

35. *Jiangcheng Qianshao* [Wuhan Outpost], 1 and 26 June 1968.

36. Zhao Yu, 'Li Shunda Zai Wenhua Geming Zhong [Li Shunda in the Cultural Revolution]', *Huanghe* [Yellow River], 4 (1986): 185–200.

37. Interviewees 8, 20, 50, 54, 76, and 78.

38. *CJRB*, 22 and 24 February, and 17 March 1968.

39. *CJRB*, 4 February–11 March 1968; *Wuhan Gongren*, 24 February 1968; *Wuhan Hongdaihui*, 29 March 1968; and *Qiyue Fengbao* [July Storm], 17 June 1968.

40. *CJRB*, 25 and 28 March 1968; *Wuhan Hongdaihui*, 29 March, 5, 11, and 18 April, and 1 May 1968; and *Wuhan Gongren*, 29 March and 5 April 1968.

41. *Jiangcheng Qiaoshao*, 22 July 1968; and *Yangzijiang Pinglun*, 20 June 1968.

42. *CJRB*, 12 April 1968.

43. *CJRB*, 16 and 23 April 1968; and interviewees 26, 52, and 72.

44. *CJRB*, 28 March 1968.

45. *CJRB*, 29 November 1977.

46. Interviewee 51.

47. Interviewees 20, 23, 27, 57, 65, 66, and 67.

48. James V. Downton, Jun., *Rebel Leadership: Commitment and Charisma in the Revolutionary Process*, New York: Free Press, 1973, pp. 61–72.

49. *Xinhuda*, 22 June 1968.

50. *Buwang 624* [Never Forget 24 June], 7 August 1968; and interviewees 23 and 59.

51. *Jiangcheng Qianshao*, 1 June 1968; and *Xinhuagong*, 29 May 1968.

52. *Xinhuda*, 23 May and 26 June 1968; and *Xinhuda Tongxun*, 17 June 1968.

53. *Xinhuda Tongxun*, 9 and 17 June 1968; *Xinhuda*, 1 and 22 June 1968; and interviewee 69.

54. *Xinhuda*, 22 July 1968.

55. *Jiangcheng Qianshao*, 15 May and 22 July 1968.

56. *Xinzhongyuan* [New Zhongyuan Machine], 15 and 25 May 1968; *CJRB*, 29 November 1977; and interviewee 8.

57. *Xinhuagong*, 19 June 1968; and *Jiangcheng Qianshao*, 17 May and 22 July 1968.

58. *Jiangcheng Qianshao*, 1 June 1968.

59. *Jiangcheng Qianshao*, 17 May 1968; *Xinhuagong*, 29 May 1968; and *Xinzhongyuan*, 8 June 1968.

60. *Gongyi Dalou Xue'an* [Bloodshed at Gongyi Building], 23 May 1968.

61. *Yangzijiang Pinglun*, 12 June 1968; and *Jiangcheng Qianshao*, 1 June 1968.

62. *Buwang 624*, September 1968.

63. *Jiangcheng Qianshao*, 9 June 1968; *Xinzhongyuan*, 22 June 1968; *Xinhuda*, 22 June 1968; and *Xinhuagong*, 26 June, 29 July, and 25 August 1968.

64. *WJHB*, Vol. 3, p. 1008.

65. *Jiangcheng Qianshao*, 1 June 1968.

66. *Jiangcheng qianshao*, 9 June 1968; and *Xinzhongyuan*, 8 June 1968.
67. *Xinhuda*, 19 June and 22 July 1968.
68. *Jiangcheng Qiaoshao*, 1 June 1968.
69. *Xinhuda Tongxun*, 17 June 1968.
70. *Xinhuagong*, 19 June 1968.
71. Interviewee 8.
72. *Jiangcheng Qianshao*, 1 June 1968; and *Xinhuda*, 22 July 1968.
73. *Xinhuda*, 19 June 1968.
74. *Ziliao Zhuanji* [Issue of Special Materials], July 1968.
75. *Xinhuagong*, 20 June 1968; and *Xinhuda*, 19 and 22 June, and 19 July 1968.
76. *Jiangcheng Qianshao*, 8 July 1968; and *Buwang 624*, 10 July 1968.
77. William Hinton, *Hundred Day War*, New York: Monthly Review Press, p. 154; and Hai Feng, *An Account of the Cultural Revolution in the Canton Area*, Hong Kong: Union Research Institute, 1971, pp. 370–82.
78. *WJHB*, Vol. 3, pp. 1037–41 and 1054–7.
79. *Xinhuda*, 22 July and 18 September 1968.
80. *Ganggongzong* [Workers' Headquarters], 12 July 1968; and *Xinhuda*, 10 and 29 July 1968.
81. *WJHB*, Vol. 3, pp. 1044–8.
82. *Xinhuda*, 29 July, and 22 and 25 August 1968.
83. *RMRB*, 5 and 13 August 1968.
84. *Xinhuda*, 10 and 25 August 1968.
85. *WJHB*, Vol. 3, pp. 1095–8.
86. *CJRB*, 9, 12, 24, and 28 September, 19 November, and 22 December 1968.
87. *RMRB*, 22 December 1968.
88. *Xinhuda*, 16 September 1968.
89. *Wuhan Gongren*, 26 September 1968; and *CJRB*, 15 and 24 September 1968.
90. *Hongqi* [Red Flag], 2 (1968).
91. *Wuhan Gongren*, 23 April and 9–10 May 1969; and *Wuhan Hongdaihui*, 6 and 16 May 1969.
92. *WJHB*, Vol. 3, p. 1204.
93. *Wuhan Hongdaihui*, 5 November 1968; and interviewees 13, 14, and 29.
94. *Wuhan Hongdaihui*, 6 May 1969; and *Wuhan Gongren*, 9 and 19 May 1969.
95. *WJHB*, Vol. 3, pp. 1116–20.
96. *CJRB*, 11–13 and 21 October, 1 and 8 November, and 10 December 1968.
97. Interviewees 1, 11, 15, 65, 66, 67, and 72; and *CJRB*, 20 October, 8 and 14 November 1968.
98. *CJRB*, 12, 13, 22, 23, 31 October, 1, 6, 7, 12, 14, 21, 26 November, 10 and 19 December 1968; and *Wuhan Hongdaihui*, 23 April 1968 and 6 May 1969.
99. *CJRB*, 31 October, 1, 6, and 21 November, and 5, 10, and 16 December 1968; *Wuhan Gongren*, 23 April, and 9 and 25 May 1969; *Wuhan Hongdaihui*, 23 April and 6 May 1969. But the development was uneven. In some units where the rebel forces dominated, the campaign to purify the class ranks was directed against former conservatives. Interviewee 72.
100. *Wuhan Hongdaihui*, 16 May 1969; and *Wuhan Gongren*, 23 April, and

9 and 19 May 1969.

101. *Wuhan Gongren*, 23 April 1969; and interviewees 5, 24, and 27.

Notes to Chapter 10

1. *Renmin Ribao* [People's Daily] (hereafter *RMRB*), 7 September 1968.

2. *Changjiang Ribao* [Yangtze Daily] (hereafter *CJRB*), 12, 21, 22, and 23 January and 1 February 1969.

3. *CJRB*, 2, 3, 6, and 14 February 1969.

4. Mao's speeches on 5, 11, 13, 14, 23, and 29 April 1969 (my personal handwritten copy).

5. Shanxi Province was an example. Shanxi Provincial Editorial Board of Local Chronicles, *Shanxi Dashiji* [Chronicle of Shanxi Province], Taiyuan: 1986.

6. Interviewee 8.

7. Beijing Garrison Command, *8341 Budai Zhizuo Xianjin Jingyan* [Advanced Experiences in Supporting Leftists by Unit 8341], 3 vols., Beijing: 1968, Vol. 1, p. 90.

8. *Wuhan Gongren* [Wuhan Workers], 5 and 25 May 1969.

9. Interviewees 5, 8, 10, 11, 20, 27, 28, 35, 51, 69, and 73.

10. *Wuhan Gongren*, 23 April 1969.

11. *RMRB*, 1 January 1969.

12. *Wuhan Gongren*, 23 April 1969.

13. Interviewee 24.

14. *Wuhan Hongdaihui* [Wuhan Congress of Red Guards], 6 May 1969.

15. *Wuhan Gongren*, 30 April 1969.

16. Mao's speech on 13 April 1969.

17. Interviewees 51, and 69.

18. *Wuhan Hongdaihui*, 6 May 1969.

19. *Wuhan Gongren*, 10 May 1969.

20. *Wuhan Hongdaihui*, 16 May 1969; and *Wuhan Gongren*, 10 May 1969.

21. *CJRB*, 29 November 1977.

22. Interviewees 15, 29, 49, 50, and 67.

23. Interviewees 5, 21, 42, 55, 74, 80, 81, 82, and 83.

24. Interviewees 8, 12, 15, 19, 20, 23, 24, 27, 43, 66, 67, and 69.

25. *Wuhan Gongren*, 25 May 1969.

26. Interviewees 3, 5, 16, 28, and 35.

27. Mancur Olsen, *The Logic of Collective Action*, Cambridge, MA: Harvard University Press, 1971.

28. Wuhan Party History Office, *Zhonggong Wuhan Dangshi Dashiji* [Chronicle of Wuhan Party History], pp. 339–40.

29. Later it was reported that the campaign in Wuhan caused economic losses totalling at least 1.5 billion yuan. *CJRB*, 5 November 1977.

30. Interviewees 20 and 69; and *Dapipan* [Mass Criticism], 23 August 1969.

31. *CJRB*, 29 November 1977.

32. *RMRB*, 8 June 1969.

33. *RMRB*, 16 and 25 August 1969; and *Honggi* [Red Flag], 9 (1969).

34. *CJRB*, 10, 18, and 30 August, and 9–13 September 1969.

35. 'Juepai' are the first and last Chinese characters of the name of a group

called Liaison Office of the Proletarian Revolutionaries Who are Determined to Carry the Great Proletarian Cultural Revolution through to the End.

36. My personal handwritten copy.

37. Interviewees 60 and 78.

38. My personal handwritten copy.

39. Interviewees 20, 35, 69, and 75.

40. Interviewees 69 and 71.

41. Interviewees 35 and 71.

42. In addition to the campaign to purify class ranks and the campaign to ferret out 16 May elements, there were the One Struggle and Three Antis Campaign and the campaign to rectify and reconstruct the Party.

43. Beijing Garrison Command, *8341 Budai Zhizuo Xianjin jingyan*, Vol. 2, pp. 90–1.

44. Zeng Siyu's speech on 27 March 1971, my personal handwritten copy.

45. Interviewees 2, 4, 20, 23, 27, 35, 49, 52, 59, 61, 66, and 67.

46. Interviewees 16, 33, 34, 49, 51, 52, and 61.

47. Wuhan Party History Office, *Zhonggong Wuhan Dangshi Dashiji*, pp. 343, 355.

48. Interviewees 28, 30.

49. Interviewees 28, 31, and 66.

50. Interviewees 35, 51, 69, and 74; and *CJRB*, 6 and 10 June 1970.

51. Interviewees 5, 18, 20, 35, 50, 51, and 69.

52. Interviewees 24, 50, and 51.

53. Interviewees 8, and 20.

54. Interviewees 3, 5, 6, 27, and 28.

55. Interviewees 35, 46, 49, 50, 51, 57, 69, and 75.

56. *CJRB*, 1 December 1969.

57. *CJRB*, 25 February and 1 April 1971.

58. Wuhan Party History Office, *Zhonggong Wuhan Dangshi Dashiji*, pp. 355–6.

59. For more about the Lin Biao affair, see Philip Bridgham, 'The Fall of Lin Piao', *China Quarterly*, 55 (July–September 1973): 427–49.

60. Interviewees 28, 50, 80, 81, 82, and 83.

61. Interviewees 26, 52, and 88.

62. Interviewee 78.

63. Wuhan Party History Office, *Zhonggong Wuhan Dangshi Dashiji*, pp. 353–5.

64. Interviewees 50, and 75.

Notes to Chapter 11

1. He Mengbi and Duan Haoran, *Zhongguo Gongchandang Liushinian* [The Sixty Years of the Chinese Communist Party] (hereafter *LSN*), pp. 626–7.

2. Keith Forster, 'The Politics of Destabilization and Confrontation: The Campaign against Lin Biao and Confucius in Zhejiang Province, 1974', *China Quarterly*, 107 (1986): 442–3.

3. *Changjiang Ribao* [Yangtze Daily] (hereafter *CJRB*) 8 January 1973.

4. Wuhan Party History Office, *Zhonggong Wuhan Dangshi Dashiji* [Chronicle of Wuhan Party History], pp. 353–4.

5. *CJRB*, 1 May 1973.

6. *CJRB*, 11 May 1973.

7. My diary, 6 June 1973. At that time, I was twenty years old, teaching at a middle school in Wuhan. Highly interested in local politics, I never missed major events like mass rallies, marches, sit-ins, or demonstrations in the city. At the same time, about a dozen friends of mine and I formed a study group. We met at least once a week to discuss local as well as national politics. It was my habit to record everything I witnessed and learned from these friends in my diary afterward.

8. *CJRB*, 1 June 1973.

9. *CJRB*, 29 June 1973.

10. Russell Hardin, 'Acting Together, Contributing Together', *Rationality and Society*, 3, 3 (1991): 365–80.

11. Interviewees 50 and 75.

12. My diary, 7 September 1973; and interviewees 50 and 75.

13. Interviewee 75.

14. My diary, 14, 21, and 23 October, and 25 November 1973.

15. Interviewee 50.

16. *Jiefang Junbao* [PLA Daily], not used 30–31 January 1974.

17. Yan Jiaqi and Gao Gao, *Wenhua Geming Shinianshi* [The Ten-year History of the Cultural Revolution], Tianjin: Tianjin People's Press, 1986, p. 497.

18. *CJRB*, 5 September 1973.

19. *Renmin Ribao* [People's Daily] (hereafter *RMRB*), 12 January 1974.

20. My diary, 6 January 1974; and interviewee 50.

21. *CJRB*, 26 January and 24 November 1977.

22. Interviewees 50, 69, and 75.

23. *CJRB*, 11 February 1974; and my diary, 2 February 1974.

24. My diary, 8, 11, and 17 February 1974; and interviewee 26.

25. Stanley Rosen, 'Guangzhou's Democracy Movement in the Cultural Revolution Perspective', *China Quarterly*, 101 (1985); and Forster, 'Politics of Destabilization and Confrontation'.

26. My diary, 2 March 1974.

27. My diary, 9 and 12 March 1974.

28. *CJRB*, 11 and 14 December 1976.

29. *CJRB*, 2 October 1974.

30. Interviewees 50 and 75.

31. My diary, 16 March 1974; and *CJRB*, 17 March 1974.

32. My diary, 21 March 1974.

33. My diary, 6 March 1974.

34. *CJRB*, 10 July, 29 November, and 24 December 1977.

35. Interviewee 52; and my diary, 13 March 1974.

36. My diary, 22, 23, and 27 March 1974; and interviewee 52.

37. My diary, 24 March 1974; and interviewee 51.

38. My diary, 27 March and 2 May 1974.

39. My diary, 27 March and 7 April 1974; and interviewees 50, 51, and 69. The system of the 'Third Offices', established at the central and provincial levels in around 1969, was designated to be in charge of ferreting out 'class enemies' from the highest level to the grass-roots. See Tan Zongji, 'Guanyu Jige Wenhua

Dageming Di Wenti', in Zhejiang Provincial Party School, *Wenhua Dageming Shiqi Ziliao Xuanji* [Selected Materials on the Cultural Revolution], Hangzhou: 1984, p. 59.

40. *CJRB*, 21 March–2 April 1974.
41. My diary, 2–6 April 1974; and interviewees 26, 50, and 52.
42. My diary, 7 April 1974; and *CJRB*, 3 December 1977.
43. Wuhan Party History Office, *Zhonggong Wuhan Dangshi Dashiji*, p. 364.
44. My diary, 8, 11, and 17 February 1974.
45. Forster, 'Politics of Destabilization and Confrontation'; Zhao Yu, 'Li Shunda Zai Wenhua Geming Zhong [Li Shunda in the Cultural Revolution]', pp. 203–8; and *RMRB*, 5 January 1977.
46. *RMRB*, 21 February and 7 March 1974.
47. My diary, 7–8 April 1974.
48. *LSN*, pp. 636–7; and my diary, 14 April 1974.
49. *CJRB*, 12 April 1974.
50. *CJRB*, 11–20 April 1974.
51. My diary, 9–16 April 1974.
52. *CJRB*, 13, 17, 21, and 29 April 1974.
53. My diary, 23 and 30 April 1974.
54. *CJRB*, 29 November 1977.
55. My diary, 23 April and 2 May 1974; and interviewees 50, 58, and 59.
56. My diary, 30 April 1974; and interviewees 50 and 75.
57. My diary, 2, 4, 6, 11, 13, and 22 May 1974.
58. Interviewee 50.
59. My diary, 24–27 May 1974.
60. *CJRB*, 27 May 1974; and my diary, 26 May 1974.
61. My diary, 25 May and 16 June 1974.
62. *CJRB*, 12, 14, 15, 22, and 24 June 1974.
63. My diary, 12 June–3 July 1974.
64. *LSN*, p. 636.
65. My diary, 2 and 5 July 1974.
66. My diary, 13 July 1974; and interviewees 26 and 52.
67. *Hongqi* [Red Flag], 8–9 (1974).
68. *LSN*, p. 637.
69. *CJRB*, 11 and 14 October, 7 November, and 6, 13, and 21 December 1974, and 17 January 1975.
70. My diary, 25 November 1974; *CJRB*, 2 October 1974; and interviewee 24.
71. My diary, 24 March, 4 April, and 13 August 1974.
72. Interviewees 13, 14, 15, 27, 29, 30, 57, 65, and 66.
73. Interviewees 8, 12, 19, 20, 23, and 67.
74. My diary, 1 April 1974.
75. Interviewees 8, 10, 11, 20, 23, 27, 43, 57, 58, 65, 66, 69, and 74.
76. Interviewees 26 and 52.
77. Interviewees 10, 12, 19, 20, 23, 27, 42, 57, 65, and 74.
78. Interviewees 8, 20, and 50.
79. Interviewee 69.
80. Interviewees 50, 58, and 59.
81. My diary, 5 May 1974; interviewee 69; and *CJRB*, 21 December 1977.

82. Interviewees 50, 58, and 69.

83. Interviewees 26 and 52; and my diary, 25 November 1974.

84. Karl Marx, 'The Eighteenth Brumaire of Louis Bonaparte', *Selected Works of Marx and Engels*, Moscow: Foreign Language Publishing House, 1950, Vol. 1, p. 225.

85. My diary, 25 November 1974.

86. Wuhan Party History Office, *Zhonggong Wuhan Dangshi Dashiji*, p. 369.

87. *CJRB*, 17 January and 28 May 1977, and 25 October 1978; and interviewees 58 and 59.

88. *CJRB*, 29 November 1977.

89. My diary, 22 and 26 April 1975.

90. My diary, 20 May and 14 June 1975.

91. *CJRB*, 21 June 1978; and my diary, 5 June 1975.

92. *CJRB*, 28 June, 4, 10, and 24 July, and 5 August 1975; and my diary, 7 July 1975.

93. *CJRB*, 2 May, 8 July, 4 August, 4 September, 6 October, and 30 November 1975.

94. My diary, 30 November, and 6, 7, 16, 18, 20, and 24 December 1975.

95. My diary, 25 and 27 February 1976.

96. Interviewee 8.

97. *CJRB*, 2 December 1977.

98. *CJRB*, 14 February and 21 December 1977.

99. *CJRB*, 29 November and 1–2 December 1977.

100. *CJRB*, 7 February, 29 November, and 1 December 1977; and my diary, 25 February 1976.

101. *CJRB*, 8 December 1976, 7 February, 20 April, 10 July, 10 August, 31 October, 29 November, and 21 December 1977.

102. *CJRB*, 23 October, and 8 and 12 December 1976.

103. *CJRB*, 14 December 1976 and 7 February 1977.

104. *CJRB*, 29 November and 21 December 1977.

105. *CJRB*, 14 February 1977.

106. *CJRB*, 12 December 1976.

107. *CJRB*, 11 and 17 December 1976. and 29 November 1977.

108. *CJRB*, 8 and 11 December 1976. and 21 December 1977.

109. *CJRB*, 12 August 1977.

110. *CJRB*, 20 April, 29 November, and 11 December 1976.

111. *CJRB*, 8 and 19 December 1976.

112. For a discussion of the division between the activist and the backward elements in the 1970s, see Andrew Walder, *Communist Neo-Traditionalism, Work and Authority in Chinese Industry*, Berkeley: University of California Press, 1986.

113. For a theoretical discussion of these choices, see Albert O. Hirschman, *Exit, Voice, and Loyalty*, Cambridge, MA: Harvard University Press, 1970.

114. My diary, 11 March and 3 April 1976.

115. Interviewees 8, 19, 20, 43, and 67.

116. My diary, 7 and 16 April 1976; and *CJRB*, 3 January and 29 November 1977.

117. For an eyewitness account of these events, see Roger Garside, *Coming Alive! China After Mao*, New York: McGraw-Hill, 1981.

118. *CJRB*, 9 December 1976, 15 and 29 November, and 21 December 1977.
119. *CJRB*, 26 March and 4 November 1976.
120. *CJRB*, 29 November and 23 December 1977, and 12 May, 17, 21, and 26 June, and 14 July 1978.
121. *CJRB*, 29 November 1977.
122. *CJRB*, 8, 14, and 17 December 1976.
123. Interviewees 8, 50, 67, and 69.
124. *CJRB*, 3 January 1977.
125. *CJRB*, 12, 15, 17, and 19 November 1977.
126. Interviewee 50.
127. Interviewee 52.
128. *CJRB*, 31 October, 5 and 7 November, and 1, 3, and 24 December 1977.
129. *CJRB*, 26 June and 31 August 1978.
130. *CJRB*, 4, 18, and 25 August 1976, and 24 November 1978; and interviewee 50.
131. *CJRB*, 12 August 1977 and 29 November 1978; and interviewees 26 and 52.
132. My diary, 13 and 17 October 1976.
133. *CJRB*, 7 February and 29 November 1977; and my diary, 6 November 1976.
134. *CJRB*, 12 and 19 December 1976, and 20 April and 10 July 1977; and interviewees 24, 57, 69, and 75.
135. My diary, 8 November 1976; and interviewee 75.
136. *CJRB*, 31 October, 29 November, and 21 December 1977; and interviewees 20, 24, 50, 51, 69, 75, and 76.
137. *LSN*, pp. 673–4.
138. *LSN*, p. 695; and *CJRB*, 3 December 1978.

Notes to Chapter 12

1. Mao's speech at the Eleventh Plenum of the Party's Eighth Congress, 4 August 1966, see *Wansui*, version 3, p. 650.
2. Mao's speech at the conference on 25 October 1966, see *Wansui*, version 3, pp. 657–60.
3. Wang Li, 'Mao Zedong 73 Sui Shengri De Tanhua He Wode Kanfa [Mao's Remarks at the Party for His 73rd Birthday and My Comments], in Wang Li, *Zhongguo Wenge Yu Wang Li* [The Chinese Cultural Revolution and Wang Li], Hong Kong: Oxford University Press, forthcoming.
4. The last provincial revolutionary committee (Xinjiang) did not come into existence until September 1968.
5. Wang Nianyi, 'Mao Zedong Tongzhi Guanyu Wenhua Dageming Jieshu Shijian De Guji [Mao's Changing Estimations about the End Date of the Cultural Revolution]', *Dangshi Yanjiu Ziliao* [Research Materials on Party History], No. 6 (1983).
6. Hong Yung Lee, *The Politics of the Chinese Cultural Revolution: A Case Study*, Berkeley: University of California Press, 1978, chapter 10.
7. William H. Riker, *The Theory of Political Coalitions,* New Haven, CT: Yale University Press, 1962.
8. A Chinese historian of the Cultural Revolution notes: 'The people might

not have possessed mature political thought, but their intuition was often sur-
prisingly acute. After late 1967, the masses began to lose any enthusiasm for
the campaign. The mass movement became increasingly that of the factional
leaders.... People began to show more interest in making furniture, rearing
goldfish, knitting, and sewing. The red hot mass movement cooled and dissipated. The struggle for power, no less intense, went on internally among the
"upper echelons". Eventually, those among the latter who came away empty-
handed remembered their "masses". But they could no longer elicit a warm
response.' (Liu Guokai, *A Brief Analysis of the Cultural Revolution*, Armonk,
NY: M. E. Sharpe, 1987, pp. 113–14.)

9. James V. Downton, Jun., *Rebel Leadership: Commitment and Charisma
in the Revolutionary Process*, New York: Free Press, 1973, pp. 61–72.

10. Of course, it is fallacious to equate the whole population with true believers. Although most people really believed in Mao's natural talents, others
accepted his authority because they were afraid that they would be severely
punished if they showed the slightest irreverence for him. Still others were
neither mesmerized by Mao's personal mystique nor subjugated by their fear of
punishment, but followed him because they perceived his policies to be most
useful for advancing their personal interests. Nevertheless, the latter two groups
accounted for only a tiny proportion of the population.

11. It occurred on 28 July 1968.

12. James Davies, *Human Nature in Politics*, New York: John Wiley & Sons,
1963, p. 283.

13. Mao first proposed that class could be defined by one's political attitudes
as early as in 1958. But he never developed this proposition in a theoretical way,
and his use of the term was rather inconsistent. As a result, even top leaders
could not quite master Mao's class analysis method. In 1965 when a top leader
asked Mao to which class status a landlord's son should have been assigned,
Mao replied that the question needed to be discussed. See *Wansui*, version 1,
p. 161; and version 3, pp. 597 and 602.

14. In this respect, hermeneutic theories are suggestive. See H. G. Gadamer,
Truth and Method, London: Sheed & Ward Ltd., 1975; Paul Ricoeur, *The
Conflict of Interpretations: Essays in Hermeneutics*, Chicago: Northwestern
University Press, 1974; and Steven Mailloux, *Interpretive Conventions: The
Reader in the Study of American Fiction*, Ithaca, NY: Cornell University Press,
1982.

15. Max Weber, *The Theory of Social and Economic Organization*, New
York: Oxford University Press, 1949, p. 359.

16. Barrington Moore, Jun., *Injustice: The Social Bases of Obedience and
Revolt*, New York: M. E. Sharpe, 1978.

17. Erich Fromm, *Beyond the Chains of Illusions: My Encounter with Marx
and Freud*, New York: A Trident Press Book, 1962, pp. 88–133.

18. Lowell Dittmer, 'Public and Private Interests and the Participatory Ethic
in China', in David S. G. Goodman (ed.), *Groups and Politics in the People's
Republic of China*, Armonk, NY: M. E. Sharpe, 1984.

19. Russell Hardin, 'Theory on the Prowl', Unpublished paper, 1992,
pp. 16–20.

Bibliography

Newspapers and Periodicals

Changjiang Ribao [Yangtze Daily].
Dangshi Tongxun [Newsletter on Party History].
Dangshi Yanjiu [Researches in Party History].
Gongren Ribao [Workers' Daily].
Hongqi [Red Flag].
Hubei Ribao [Hubei Daily].
Jiefang Junbao [PLA Daily].
Renmin Jiaoyu [People's Education].
Renmin Ribao [People's Daily].
Wuhan Wanbao [Wuhan Evening News].
Xinhua Yuekan [New China Monthly].
Zhibu Shenghuo [Life in Party Branches].
Zhongguo Gongren [Chinese Workers].
Zhongguo Qingnian [Chinese Youth].
Zhongguo Qingnian Bao [Chinese Youth Daily].

English-language Materials

Barry, Brian, *Sociologists, Economists and Democracy*, Chicago: University of Chicago Press, 1978.

Benn, Stanley I. and Mortimore, G. W. (eds.), *Rationality and the Social Science: Contributions to the Philosophy and Methodology of the Social Sciences*, London: Routledge and Kegan Paul, 1976.

Bennett, Gordon A. and Montaperto, Ronald N., *Red Guard: The Political Biography of Dai Hsiao-ai*, Garden City, NY: Doubleday, 1972.

Blecher, Marc J. and White, Gordon, *Micropolitics in Contemporary China*, White Plains, NY: M. E. Sharpe, 1979.

Bridgham, Philip, 'The Fall of Lin Piao', *China Quarterly*, 55 (July–September, 1973): 427–49.

Brinton, Crane, *The Anatomy of Revolution*, New York: Vintage Books, 1965.

Chan, Anita, *Children of Mao: Personality Development and Political Activism in the Red Guard Generation*, Seattle: University of Washington Press, 1985.

Chong, Dennis, *Collective Action and the Civil Rights Movement*, Chicago: University of Chicago Press, 1991.

Daubier, Jean, *A History of the Chinese Cultural Revolution*, New York: Vintage Books, 1974.

Davis, Deborah, 'The Cultural Revolution in Wuhan', in *Cultural Revolution in the Provinces*, Cambridge, MA: Harvard East Asian Monographs, No. 42.

Dittmer, Lowell, *China's Continuous Revolution: The Post-Liberation Epoch, 1949–1981*, Berkeley: University of California Press, 1987.

Djilas, Milovan, *The New Class: An Analysis of the Communist System*, New York: Praeger, 1957.

Downs, Anthony, *An Economic Theory of Democracy*, New York: Harper and Brothers, 1957.

Downton, James V. Jun., *Rebel Leadership: Commitment and Charisma in the Revolutionary Process*, New York: Free Press, 1973.

Eisenstant, S. N., *Max Weber on Charisma and Institution Building*, Chicago: University of Chicago Press, 1968.

Eldridge, Albert F., *Images of Conflict*, New York: St. Martin's, 1979.

Elster, Jon, *The Cement of Society: A Study of Social Order*, Cambridge: Cambridge University Press, 1989.

——, *Sour Grapes: Studies in the Subversion of Rationality*, Cambridge: Cambridge University Press, 1983.

——, *Ulysses and Sirens: Studies in Rationality and Irrationality*, Cambridge: Cambridge University Press, 1984.

Esmein, Jean, *The Chinese Cultural Revolution*, New York: Anchor Books, 1973.

Etzioni, Amitai, *Modern Organization*, New York: Prentice-Hall, 1964.

Falkenheim, Victor C., *Citizens and Groups in Contemporary China*, Ann Arbor: University of Michigan Center for Chinese Studies, 1987.

Feng Jicai, *Voices from the Whirlwind: An Oral History of the Chinese Cultural Revolution*, New York: Pantheon Books, 1991.

Forster, Keith, *Rebellion and Factionalism in a Chinese Province: Zhejiang, 1966–1976*, Armonk, NY: M. E. Sharpe, 1990.

Friedman, Debra and Hechter, Michael, 'The Contribution of Rational Choice Theory to Macrosociological Research', *Sociological Theory*, 6 (1988): 201–18.

Fromm, Erich, *Beyond the Chains of Illusions: My Encounter with Marx and Freud*, New York: A Trident Press Book, 1962.

Gadamer, H. G., *Truth and Method*, London: Sheed & Ward, 1975.

Gao Yuan, *Born Red*, Stanford, CA: Stanford University Press, 1987.

Garside, Roger, *Coming Alive! China After Mao*, New York: McGraw-Hill, 1981.

Geertz, Clifford, 'Deep Play: Notes on the Balinese Cockfight', in Chandra Mukerji and Michael Schudson (eds.), *Rethinking Popular Culture: Contemporary Perspectives in Cultural Studies*, Berkeley: University of California Press, 1991, pp. 239–77.

Giddens, Anthony and Held, David (eds.), *Class, Power, and Conflict*, Berkeley: University of California Press, 1982.

Goodman, David S. G., *Group and Politics in the People's Republic of China*, Armonk, NY: M. E. Sharpe, 1984.

Graumann, Carl F. and Moscovici, Serge (eds.), *Changing Conceptions of Leadership*, New York: Springer-Verlag, 1986.

Gray, Sherry, *Bombard the Headquarters: Local Politics and Citizen Participation in the Great Proletarian Cultural Revolution and the 1989 Movement in Shenyang*, Ph.D. dissertation, University of Denver, 1992.

Hai Feng, *An Account of the Cultural Revolution in the Canton Area*, Hong Kong: Union Research Institute, 1971.

Hardin, Russell, 'Acting Together, Contributing Together', *Rationality and Society*, 3, 3 (1991): 365–80.

——, *Collective Action*, Baltimore: The Johns Hopkins University Press, 1982.

——, 'The Normative Core of Rational Choice Theory', Unpublished paper, 1992.

——, 'Theory on the Prowl', Unpublished paper, 1992.

Henderson, Gail E. and Cohen, Myron S., *The Chinese Hospital: A Socialist Work Unit*, New Haven, CT: Yale University Press, 1984.

Hinton, William, *Hundred Day War: The Cultural Revolution at Tsinghua University*, New York: Monthly Review Press, 1972.

Hirschman, Albert O., 'Against Parsimony: Three Easy Ways of Complicating Some Categories of Economic Discourse', *Economics and Philosophy*, 1 (1985): 7–21.

——, *Exit, Voice and Loyalty*, Cambridge, MA: Harvard University Press, 1970.

Hoffer, Eric, *The True Believer*, New York: Harper & Row, 1966.

Hunt, James G. and Larson, Lars L. (eds.), *Leadership: The Cutting Edge*, Carbondale: Southern Illinois University Press, 1977.

Institute of International Relations, *Classified Chinese Communist Documents: A Selection*, Taipei: National Chengchi University, 1978.

James, Davies, *Human Nature in Politics*, New York: John Wiley &

Sons, 1963.

Jenkins, J. Craig, 'Resource Mobilization Theory and the Study of the Social Movement', *Annual Review of Sociology, 1983*: 527–53.

Karol, K. S., *China: The Other Communism*, 2nd edn., New York: Hill & Wang, 1968.

Ken Ling, *The Revenge of Heaven: Journal of a Young Chinese*, New York: Putnam, 1972.

Konrad, George and Szelenyi, Ivan, *The Intellectual on the Road to Class Power*, New York: A Helen Wolff Book, 1978.

Kraus, Richard, *Class Conflict in Chinese Socialism*, New York: Columbia University Press, 1981.

Lane, David, *End of Social Inequality?* Middlesex: Penguin Books, 1971.

——, *Soviet Economy and Society*, London: Oxford University Press, 1985.

LeBon, Gustav, *The Crowd: A Study of the Popular Mind*, New York: Viking, 1960 [1909].

Lee, Hong Yung, *The Politics of the Chinese Cultural Revolution: A Case Study*, Berkeley: University of California Press, 1978.

Liang Heng and Judith Shapiro, *Son of the Revolution*, New York: Random House, 1983.

Little, Daniel, 'Rational-Choice Models and Asian Studies', *The Journal of Asian Studies*, 50, 1 (1991): 35–52.

Liu Guokai, *A Brief Analysis of the Cultural Revolution*, Armonk, NY: M. E. Sharpe, 1987.

Lo Fulang, *Morning Breeze: A True Story of China's Cultural Revolution*, San Francisco: China Books, 1989.

Luo Ziping, *A Generation Lost: China under the Cultural Revolution*, New York: Henry Holt and Co., 1990.

MacFarquhar, Roderick, *The Origins of the Cultural Revolution*, 3 vols., New York: Columbia University Press, 1974, 1980.

Mailoux, Steven, *Interpretive Conventions: The Reader on the Study of American Fiction*, Ithaca, NY: Cornell University Press, 1982.

March, James G. and Simon, Herbert A., *Organizations*, New York: John Wiley & Sons, 1958.

Marx, Karl, 'The Eighteenth Brumaire of Louis Bonaparte', *Karl Marx: Selected Works*, Vol. 2, New York: International Publishers, 1939.

Meaney, Constance Squires, *Stability and the Industrial Elite in China and the Soviet Union*, Berkeley: Berkeley Center for Chinese Studies, 1988.

Monroe, Kristen Renwick (ed.), *The Economic Approach to Politics: A*

Critical Reassessment of the Theory of Rational Action, New York: Harper Collins, 1991.

Moore, Barrington, Jun., *Injustice: The Social Bases of Obedience and Revolt*, New York: M. E. Sharpe, 1978.

Nien Cheng, *Life and Death in Shanghai*, London: Collins, 1986.

Olson, Mancur, *The Logic of Collective Action*, Cambridge, MA: Harvard University Press, 1971.

Opp, Karl-Dieter, *The Rationality of Political Protest: A Comparative Analysis of Rational Choice Theory*, Boulder, CO: Westview Press, 1989.

Parkin, Frank, *Class Inequality and Political Order*, New York: Praeger Publishers, 1975.

——, *The Marxist Theory of Class: A Bourgeois Critique*, London: Tavistock, 1979.

——, *The Social Analysis of Class Structure*, London: Tavistock, 1974.

Raddock, David M., *Political Behavior of Adolescents in China: The Cultural Revolution in Kwangchow*, Tucson: The University of Arizona Press, 1977.

Ricoeur, Paul, *The Conflict of Interpretations: Essays in Hermeneutics*, Chicago: Northwestern University Press, 1974.

Riker, William H., *The Theory of Political Coalitions*, New Haven, CT: Yale University Press, 1962.

Robinson, Thomas (ed.), *The Cultural Revolution in China*, Berkeley: University of California Press, 1971.

——, 'The Wuhan Incident', *China Quarterly*, 47 (1971): 413–38.

Rosen, Stanley, 'Guangzhou's Democracy Movement in the Cultural Revolution Perspective', *China Quarterly* 101 (1985): 1–31.

——, *Red Guard Factionalism and the Cultural Revolution in Guangzhou (Canton)*, Boulder, CO: Westview Press, 1982.

Rosenbach, William E. and Taylor, Robert L. (eds.), *Contemporary Issues in Leadership*, Boulder, CO: Westview Press, 1984.

Rude, George, *The Crowd in the French Revolution*, London: Oxford University Press, 1959.

——, *The Crowd in History, 1730–1848*, London: Lawrence & Wishart, 1981.

Schelling, Thomas C., *Micromotives and Macrobehavior*, New York: Norton, 1978.

Schramm, Wilbur (ed.), *The Process and Effects of Mass Communication*, Urbana: University of Illinois Press, 1965.

Scitovsky, Tibor, *The Joyless Economy*, New York: Oxford University Press, 1976.

Shue, Vivienne, *The Reach of the State: Stretches of the Chinese Body Politic*, Stanford, CA: Stanford University Press, 1988.

Smelser, Neil J., 'The Rational Choice Perspective: A Theoretical Assessment', *Rationality and Society*, 4, 4 (1992): 381–410.

Swanson, Guy E., Newcomb, Theodore, and Hartley, Eugene L. (eds.), *Readings in Social Psychology*, New York: Henry Holt, 1952.

Tarrow, Sidney, 'National Politics and Collective Action: Recent Theory and Research in Western Europe and the United States', *Annual Review of Sociology, 1988.*

Taylor, Michael, *Community, Anarchy and Liberty*, Cambridge: Cambridge University Press, 1982.

——, *The Possibility of Cooperation*, Cambridge: Cambridge University Press, 1987.

——, (ed.), *Rationality and Revolution*, Cambridge: Cambridge University Press, 1988.

Thurston, Anne F., *Enemies of the People: The Ordeal of the Intellectuals in China's Great Cultural Revolution*, New York: Alfred A. Knopf, 1987.

Tilly, Charles, *From Mobilization to Revolution*, Reading, MA: Addison-Wesley, 1978.

Tsebelis, George, *Nested Game: Rational Choice in Comparative Politics*, Berkeley: University of California Press, 1990.

Tsou Tang, *The Cultural Revolution and Post-Mao Reform: A Historical Perspective*, Chicago: University of Chicago Press, 1986.

Unger, Jonathan, *Education under Mao: Class and Competition in Canton Schools, 1960–1980*, Seattle: University of Washington Press, 1985.

Walder, Andrew G., *Communist Neo-Traditionalism: Work and Authority in Chinese Industry*, Berkeley: University of California Press, 1986.

Wang Xizhe, *Mao Zedong and the Cultural Revolution*, Hong Kong: Plough Publications, 1981.

Watson, James L. (ed.), *Class and Social Stratification in Post-Revolution China*, Cambridge: Cambridge University Press, 1984.

Weber, Max, *The Theory of Social and Economic Organization*, New York: Oxford University Press, 1949.

Welch, Claude E. Jun., *Anatomy of Rebellion*, Albany: State University of New York Press, 1980.

White, Gordon, *The Politics of Class and Class Origin: The Case of the Cultural Revolution*, Canberra: Australian National University Contemporary China Centre, 1976.

White, Lynn, III, *Policies of Chaos: The Organizational Causes of Violence in China's Cultural Revolution*, Princeton, NJ: Princeton University Press, 1989.

Willer, Ann Ruth, *Charismatic Political Leadership: A Theory*, Princeton, NJ: Princeton University Press, 1968.

Wood, Geof, ed., *Labelling in Development Policy: Essays in Honour of Bernard Schaffer*, London: Sage Publications, 1985.

Zald, Mayer N. and McCarchy, John D. (eds.), *The Dynamics of Social Movement: Resource Mobilization, Social Control and Tactics*, Cambridge, MA: Winthrop Publishers, 1979.

Zimmermann, Ekkart, 'Macro-Comparative Research on Political Protest', in Ted R. Gurr (ed.), *Handbook of Political Conflict: Theory and Research*, New York: Free Press, 1980.

Chinese-language Materials

Beijing Education Bureau, 'Guanyu Dui Chuzhong Biyesheng Jiating Qingkuang Jinxing Diaocha De Qingshi [Request to Start Family Background Investigation of Junior High Graduates]', 14 January 1964.

Beijing Garrison Command, *8341 Budai Zhizuo Xianjin Jingyan* [Advanced Experiences in Supporting Leftists by Unit 8341], 4 vols., Beijing: 1969.

Cao Zhi, *Zhonghua Renmin Gongheguo Renshi Zhidu Gaiyao* [The Personnel System of the People's Republic of China], Beijing: Beijing University Press, 1985.

Center for Chinese Research Materials, *Hongweibing Ziliao* [Red Guard Publications], 20 vols., Washington, DC, 1975.

—— *Hongweibing Ziliao Zengbian* [Red Guard Publications, Supplement I], 20 vols., Washington, DC, 1980.

The Central Administrative Bureau of Industry and Commerce, *Siying Gongshangye Shehui Zhuyi Gaizai Dashiji* [Chronicle of the Socialist Reform of Private Industry and Commerce], 1957.

The Central Committee of CCP, 'Guanyu Gaodeng Xuexiao Luqu Xinsheng De Zhengzhi Shencha Biaozhun [Political Criteria for Admitting New College Students]', 1962.

—— 'Dui 1962 Nian "Gaodeng Xuexiao Luqu Xinsheng De Zhengzhi Shengcha Biaozhun" De Jidian Jieshi Yijian [Interpretations of the 1962 Edition of "Political Criteria for Admitting New College Students"]', 1964.

—— 'Guanyu Jiangdi Guojia Jiguan 3 Ji Yishang Dangyuan Ganbu

Gongzi Biaozhun De Jueding [Resolution Concerning Cutting the Salaries of Party Cadres at Level Three and Above]', 7 February 1959.

The Central Group of Ten Persons, 'Guanyu Fangeming Fenzi He Qita Huaifenzi De Jieshi Ji Chuli De Zhengce Jiexian De Zanxing Guiding [How to Define Counter-revolutionary and Bad Elements, and How to Deal with Them]', 10 March 1956.

Central Party School, *Zhonggong Dangshi Cankao Ziliao* [Reference Materials of Party History], 8 vols., Beijing: People's Press, 1980.

Chen Zaidao, '720 Shijian Shimo [The Whole Story of the 20 July Incident]', in *Gemingshi Ziliao* [Materials on Revolutionary History], Beijing: Historical Material Publishing House, Vol. 12, 1981.

The Education Commission, *Zhongguo Jiaoyu Nianjian* [Yearbook of Chinese Education, 1949–1985], Beijing: People's Education Press, 1985.

——, *Zhongguo Jiaoyu Dashiji* [Chronicle of Chinese Education] Beijing: People's Education Press, 1986.

He Mengbi and Duan Haoran, *Zhongguo Gongchandang Liushinian* [The Sixty Years of the CCP], Beijing: People's Liberation Army Publishing House, 1984.

Hubei Labour Bureau, *Gongzi Biaozhun Xuanbian* [Selected Documents on Wage Policy], Wuhan: 1973.

Hubei Provincial Public Security Bureau, *Wenhua Dageming Xuexi Wenxuan* [Study Materials of the Cultural Revolution], 12 vols., 1967.

Hubei Provincial Revolutionary Committee, *Wuchan Jieji Wenhua Dageming Wenjian Huibian* [Selected Documents of the Great Proletarian Cultural Revolution], 3 vols., Wuhan: 1968–9.

Lin Biao, *Lin Biao Wenxuan* [Selected Works of Lin Biao], Wuhan: 1968.

Liu Feng, 'Liu Feng De Jianghua [Liu Feng's Speech]', 3 October 1969.

Mao Zedong, 'Maozhuxi De Jianghua [Chairman Mao's Speeches]', 1, 5, 11, 13, 14, 23, and 28 April 1969.

——, *Mao Zedong Sixiang Wansui* [Long Live Mao Zedong Thought], 3 versions, Wuhan: 1968–9.

Ministry of Labour, 'Guanyu 1963 Nian Gongzi Gongzuo Anpai [Wage Plan of 1963]', 21 July 1963.

The National Planning Commission and Ministry of Labour, 'Guanyu Dangqian Laodongli Anpai He Zhigong Gongzi Wenti De Baogao [Report Concerning the Arrangement of Labour Forces and the Distribution of Wages]', 18 December 1956.

Shanxi Provincial Editorial Board of Local Chronicles, *Shanxi Dashiji 1949–1983* [Chronicle of Shanxi, 1949–83], Taiyuan: 1985.

The State Council, 'Guanyu Jiangdi Guojia Jiguan 10 Ji Yishang Ganbu De Gongzi Biaozhun De Jueding [Resolution Concerning Cutting the Salaries of Party Cadres at Level Ten and Above]', 18 December 1956.

Suo Guoxin, *1967 Nian De 78 Tian: Eryue Niliu Jishi* [Seventy-eight Days in 1967: The February Adverse Current], Changsha: Hunan Literature Publishing House, 1986.

Wang Nianyi, *Dadongluan De Niandai* [The Chaotic Decade], Zhengzhou: Henan People's Press, 1988.

Wuhan Education Bureau, 'Gaodeng Xuexiao Nianchu Baobiao, 1964–5 [Early Report on the Situation of Higher Education Institutions, 1964–5]'.

——, 'Guanyu 1961 Nian Weiluqu Zhongxiaoxue Biyesheng De Anpai Qingkuang [Arrangements for Elementary and Middle School Graduates Who Were Not Accepted by Higher Education Institutions]'.

——, 'Guanyu Biyesheng Shixiang Qingkuang De Fanying [Report on the Thinking of High School Graduates]', May 1965.

——, 'Guanyu Shixing Zhongdian Zhongxue Xishou Baosongsheng Mianshi Ruxue Banfa De Tongzhi [Circular Concerning the Admission of Recommended Students to Key Schools]', 26 July 1964.

——, 'Guanyu Zhongdeng Xuexiao Zhaosheng Gongzuo De Baogao [Report on the Admission of New Students to Middle Schools]', 23 November 1965.

——, 'Guanyu Zhongdeng Xuexiao Zhaosheng Luqu Fenpei Gongzuo Ruoguan Wenti De Qingshi Baogao [Report on the Problems Resulting from the Admission of New Students to Key Middle Schools]', 26 July 1965.

——, 'Putong Zhongxue Zhonghe Baobiao 1965–6 [Wuhan Middle School Statistics, 1965–6]'.

——, 'Quanrizhi Jigong Zhiye Xuexiao Zhonghe Baobiao, 1965–6 [Wuhan Technical Training School Statistics, 1965–6]'.

——, 'Quanrizhi Xiaoxue Zhonghe Baobiao, 1965–6 [Wuhan Elementary School Statistics, 1965–6]'.

——, 'Wuhan Shi Zhongxiaoxue Xuesheng Jiating Chusheng Dianxing Diaocha, 1965–6 [Wuhan Elementary and Middle School Student Family Background Survey, 1965–6]'.

Wuhan Education Bureau and Wuhan Public Security Bureau, 'Guanyu Jiyibu Miqie Peihe Zuohao Gaodeng Zhongdeng Xuexiao Zhaosheng De Zhengzhi Shencha Gongzuo De Jidian Yijian [Suggestions on How to Implement the Political Criteria for Admitting New College Students and Senior High Students]', 27 April 1964.

Wuhan Intermediate People's Court, *Wuhan Fayuan Zhi* [The History of Wuhan Court], Unpublished draft, 1992.

Wuhan Party History Office, *Zhonggong Wuhan Dangshi Dashiji* [Chronicle of Wuhan Party History], Wuhan: Wuhan University Press, 1989.

——, *Zhonggong Wuhan Difang Dangshi* [The Local Party History of Wuhan], Wuhan: 1985.

Wuhan Senior High Admission Committee, 'Chuzhong Biyesheng Tuijian Gongzuo De Qingkuang Fanyin [Report on Recommendation of Junior High Graduates for Senior High]', September 1966.

Wuhan Statistics Bureau, *Wuhan: 1949–1984*, Wuhan: 1984.

——, *Wuhan Sishinian: 1949–1989* [Forty Years of Wuhan: 1949–89], Wuhan: Wuhan University Press, 1989.

Yan Jiaqi and Gao Gao, *Wenhua Dageming Shinianshi* [The Ten-year History of the Cultural Revolution], Tianjin: Tianjin People's Press, 1986.

Zeng Siyu, 'Zeng Siyu De Fayan [Zeng Siyu's Talk]', 27 October 1969.

——, 'Zeng Siyu De Jianghua [Zeng Siyu's Speech]', 27 March 1971.

Zhao Cong, *Wenge Yundong Licheng Shulue* [A Concise History of the Cultural Revolution], 4 vols., Hong Kong: Union Research Institute, 1971–8.

Zhao Yu, 'Li Shunda Zai Wenhua Geming Zhong [Li Shunda in the Cultural Revolution]', *Huanghe* [Yellow River], 4 (1986).

Zhejiang Provincial Party School, '*Wenhua Dageming*' *Shiqi Ziliao Xuanji* [Selected Materials on the Cultural Revolution], Hangzhou: 1984.

Cultural Revolution Mass Organization Publications from Wuhan

82 Zhanbao [2 August Battlefield Report].

715 Daxuean Diaocha Baogao [Report on the Massacre of 15 July].

913 Zhanbao [13 September Corps' Battlefield Report].

32111 Zhanbao [32111 Battlefield Report].

Bingtuan Zhanbao [Corps Battlefield Report].

Buwang 624 [Never Forget 24 June].

Chedi Jiekai Shengwei Zhuaban De Heimu [The Inside Story of the Provincial Office of Grasping Revolution and Promoting Production].

Chedi Maizang Wuhan Dichu Fangeming Xiuzhen Zhuyi Jituan [Bury the Counter-revolutionary Revisionist Group of Wuhan], 2 vols.

Chedi Pipan Hubei Shengwei Ziliao Huibian [Selected Materials on Thoroughly Criticizing the HPPC].

Chen Zaidao Yu Zhibao [Chen Zaidao and His Support to the Conservatives].

Chen Zaidao Zhibao Zuixinglu [Chen Zaidao's Crimes in Supporting the Conservatives].

Chen Zaidao Zhong Hanhua De Zuizheng [Evidence against Chen Zaidao and Zhong Hanhua].

Chen Zaidao Zhong Hanhua Zhiliu Fangeming Zuixing [Crimes Committed by Chen Zaidao, Zhong Hanhua, and the Like].

Chiweijun [Red Guard Army].

Dadao Chen Bohua [Down with Chen Bohua].

Dadao Fangeming Xiuzheng Zhuyi Fenzi Chen Zaidao [Down with Counter-revolutionary Revisionist Chen Zaidao].

Dadao Song Kanfu [Down with Song Kanfu], 11 vols.

Dadao Wuhan De Heluxiaofu [Down with the Khrushchev of Wuhan].

Dadao Wuhan Touhao Zouzipai Song Kanfu [Down with the Number One Capitalist Roader Song Kanfu], 3 vols.

Dapipan [Mass Criticism].

Daqiao Zhanbao [Bridge Battlefield Report].

Deng Ken Zai Wuhan Shi Zhongxue Biyesheng Daibiao Huiyi Shang De Jianghua [Deng Ken's Speech at the Meeting of Middle School Graduates].

Dongfanghong [The East is Red].

Duoquan Zhanbao [Power Seizure Battlefield Report].

Fangeming Fenzi Liu Zhen De Zibai [The Confession of Counter-revolutionary Liu Zhen].

Fangeming Xiuzheng Zhuyi Fenzi Cheng Yun Fandong Yanlun Huiban [Selected Reactionary Speeches of Counter-revolutionary Revisionist Cheng Yun], 3 vols.

Fangeming Xiuzheng Zhuyi Fenzi Li Pingqing Fandong Yanlun Huibian [Selected Reactionary Speeches of Counter-revolutionary Revisionist Li Pingqing].

Fangeming Xiuzheng Zhuyi Fenzi Liu Huilong Zuixing Dashiji [Major Crimes Committed by Counter-revolutionary Revisionist Liu Huilong].

Fangeming Xiuzheng Zhuyi Fenzi Song Kanfu Zuixinglu [Crimes Committed by Counter-revolutionary Revisionist Song Kanfu].

Fangeming Xiuzheng Zhuyi Fenzi Wang Renzhong Ducao Xuanbian

[Selected Harmful Writings of Counter-revolutionary Revisionist Wang Renzhong].

Fangeming Xiuzheng Zhuyi Fenzi Wang Renzhong Zuixinglu [Crimes Committed by Counter-revolutionary Revisionist Wang Renzhong].

Gangongzong [The Workers Headquarters].

Geganlian [The Federation of Revolutionary Cadres].

Gongjianfa Yixiaocuo Huai Toutou Fandong Zuixinglu [The Reactionary Crimes Committed by a Handful of Evil Leaders of the Wuhan Law Enforcement].

Gongyi Dalou Xue'an [Bloodshed at Gongyi Building].

Gongzao Zongshi [The Workers' Rebel Headquarters].

Guanyu Ganggongzong Wenti Diaocha Baogao [Report on the Case of the Workers' Headquarters].

Guanyu Xue Puruo Wenti De Cailiao [Materials on the Problems of Xue Puruo].

Guanyu Yang Chunting Tongzhi De Diaocha Baogao [Investigation Report on Comrade Yang Chunting].

Hongbayue Gansidui Tongxun [Newsletter of the Red August Dare-to-Die Corps].

Hongbayue Gongshe [Red August Commune].

Hongbayue Zaofanbao [Red August Rebels].

Hongse Baodong [Red Insurrection].

Hongweibing [The Red Guards].

Hongwuce [Red Wuhan Institute of Topography].

Hou Lianzheng Hezuizhiyou [Hou Liangzheng is Innocent].

Hubei Shengwei Shujichu Changwei Huiyi Jilu [The Minutes of Meetings of the Hubei Provincial Party Committee Secretariat]

Hubei Xinhua Yinshuachang Geweihui [The Revolutionary Committee of Hubei Xinhua Printing House].

Jiangcheng Fengbao [Wuhan Storm].

Jiangcheng Qianshao [Wuhan Outpost].

Jiangcheng Zhuangge [A Glorious Epic in Wuhan].

Jianzhu Geming [Revolutionary Construction Workers].

Jinggangshan [Jinggang Mountain].

Jinjunbao [March Daily].

Kangbao [Resisting Suppression].

Kuangwanshi [Madmen Corps].

Liangtiao Luxian De Dabodu [Struggle between Two Lines].

Liehuo [Raging Flames].

Liu Huilong Sanfan Yanxing [Liu Huilong's Anti-Mao Speeches].

Lun Ge Yu Bao [On Revolution and Conservatism].

Pitao Zhanbao [Battlefield Report on Criticizing Tao Zhu]
Qiandaowangua Chen Zaidao [Slash Chen Zaidao].
Qingli Jieji Duiwu Ziliao Zhuanji [Special Collection on the Campaign to Purify Class Ranks].
Qiyue Binbbian De Pochan [The Failure of the July Mutiny].
Qiyue Fengbao [July Storm].
Qiyue Jiangcheng Zhanqi Hong [Red Flag of July in Wuhan].
Shengshi Geming Sanjiehe Ganbu Jianjie [The Profiles of Cadre Candidates for the HPRC and the WMRC].
Song Kanfu Zuixinglu [Song Kanfu's Crimes].
Suqing Tan Lifu De Liudu [Eliminating the Pernicious Influence of Tan Lifu].
Wang Renzhong Fandong Yanlunji [Selected Reactionary Speeches of Wang Renzhong].
Wang Renzhong Fan Mao Zedong Shixiang Yanlunji [Wang Renzhong's Anti-Mao Thought Speeches].
Wang Renzhong Hexurenye [The Kind of Person Wang Renzhong Really Is].
Wang Renzhong Sanfan Yanlunlu [Wang Renzhong's Anti-Mao Speeches].
Wang Renzhong Shi Zhengya Wuchan Jieji Wenhua Dageming De Zuikui Huoshou [Wang Renzhong is the One Responsible for the Suppression of the Mass Movement during the Cultural Revolution].
Wang Renzhong Zuixinglu [Crimes Committed by Wang Renzhong].
Wenge Pinglun [The Cultural Revolution Review].
Wenge Tongxun [Newsletter on the Cultural Revolution].
Wuda Sanjiacun An [The Case of the Three-family Village at Wuhan University].
Wuhan 82 Zhengzhi Pohai Shijian Zhuanji [Special Issue on the 2 August Incident of Wuhan].
Wuhan Baiwanxiongshi 754 Bingtuan Zuixinglu [The Crimes of the 754 Corps of the Million Heroes].
Wuhan Dichu Wuchan Jieji Gemingpai Zaijing Douzheng Fangeming Xiuzheng Zhuyi Fenzi Chen Zaidao Dahui Jishi [Report on a Denouncement Season against Counter-revolutionary Revisionist Chen Zaidao in Beijing].
Wuhan Dichu Wuchan Jieji Wenhua Degeming Dashiji [Chronicle of the Great Proletarian Cultural Revolution in Wuhan].
Wuhan Gangershi [Wuhan Second Headquarters].
Wuhan Gongan Jianghan Fenbu Zuixing Cailiao [Materials on the Crimes Committed by the Jianghan Branch of the Wuhan Public

Security], 4 vols.

Wuhan Gongan Zhengya Geming Qunzhong Yundong De Taotian Zuixing [The Wuhan Public Security's Crime in Suppressing the Revolutionary Mass Movement].

Wuhan Gongjianfa Fujing Huibaotuan Zuie Zhixing [The Trip to Beijing by Wuhan's Law Enforcement's Delegation].

Wuhan Gongren [Wuhan Workers].

Wuhan Heluxiaofu [The Khrushchev of Wuhan].

Wuhan Hongbayue [Wuhan Red August].

Wuhan Hongdaihui [Wuhan Congress of Red Guards]

Wuhan Shijian [The Wuhan Incident].

Wuhanshi Geming Gongdaihui Choubei Xiaozhu Huitai Jiyao [Summary of Negotiations on the Formation of the Wuhan Revolutionary Workers' Congress].

Wuhanshi Sanjiehe Ganbu Jianjie [Profiles of Cadre Candidates for the WMRC].

Xindongzhong [New East Lake Middle School].

Xinhuagong [New Central China Institute of Technology].

Xin Huashi Fuzhong [New Middle School Attached to the Central China Normal College].

Xinhuda [New Hubei University].

Xinhuda Tongxun [Newsletter of New Hubei University].

Xinroulian [New Slaughterhouse].

Xin Shierzhong [New No. 12 Middle School].

Xinshuiyun [New Water Transport Institute].

Xinzhongyuan [New Zhongyuan Machine].

Yangzijiang Pinglun [Yangtze Review].

Zaixianfeng [On a Perilous Peak].

Zhanduan Chen Zaidao Zhiliu Shengxiang Jiedao Zhong De Mozhao [Cut off Chen Zaidao's Hands in Neighbourhood Committees].

Zhang Chunqiao Yao Wenyuan Tongzhi Zai Shanghai Shi Geming Weiyuanhui Baogaohui Shang De Jianghua [The Speeches of Zhang Chunqiao and Yao Wenyuan at a Meeting of the Shanghai Municipal Revolutionary Committee].

Zhang Tixue Tongzhi De Jianghua [Comrade Zhang Tixue's Speech].

Zhengdang Jiandang Jingyan [Experiences in the Reconstruction of Party Organization].

Zhengjing Quanguo De 720 Fangeming Baoluan [The 20 July Counter-revolutionary Revolt that Shocked the Whole Country].

Zhengzhi Pashou—Wang Renzhong [Political Thief—Wang Renzhong].

Zhongyang Fuzhe Tongzhi Jianghua Chaolu [Selected Speeches of

Central Leaders], 3 vols.

Zhongyang Shouzhang Jianghua [Speeches of Central Leaders].

Zhongyang Shouzhang Zuixin Zhongyao Jianghua Huiji [Latest Speeches of Central Leaders].

Zhouzongli Zhongyao Jianghua [Speeches of Premier Zhou].

Ziliao Zhuanji [A Special Issue of Study Materials].

Index